PSYCHOANALYSIS
The Science of Mental Conflict

Essays in Honor of
Charles Brenner

Charles Brenner

PSYCHOANALYSIS
The Science of Mental Conflict

Essays in Honor of
Charles Brenner

Editors

Arnold D. Richards & Martin S. Willick

THE ANALYTIC PRESS

The Analytic Press

Distributed solely by

Lawrence Erlbaum Associates, Inc., Publishers
365 Broadway
Hillsdale, New Jersey 07642

Library of Congress Cataloging-in-Publication Data

Psychoanalysis, the science of mental conflict.

  Includes bibliographies.
  1. Psychoanalysis—Addresses, essays, lectures.
I. Brenner, Charles, 1913–   . II. Richards,
Arnold D.   III. Willick, Martin S., 1933–   .
[DNLM: 1. Psychoanalysis.   WM 460 P97448]
RC509.P836   1986   616.89'17   86-3414
ISBN 0-88163-054-3

Printed in the United States of America
10 9 8 7 6 5 4 3 2 1

Contents

The Technique of Psychoanalysis

The Clinical Practice of Psychoanalysis

The Teaching of Psychoanalysis

The Application of Psychoanalysis

Contributors

Sander M. Abend, M.D., New York, NY
Jacob A. Arlow, M.D., New York, NY
Leon Balter, M.D., New York, NY
Lucy (Brenner) Biven, Ann Arbor, MI
Harold P. Blum, M.D., Roslyn Estates, NY
Dale Boesky, M.D., Troy, MI
Allan Compton, M.D., Los Angeles, CA
Lester H. Friedman, M.D., New York, NY
Paul Gray, M.D., Washington, DC
William I. Grossman, M.D., Tenafly, NJ
Irving B. Harrison, M.D., White Plains, NY
Theodore J. Jacobs, M.D., New York, NY
Edward D. Joseph, M.D., New York, NY
Yale Kramer, M.D., New York, NY
Leo Rangell, M.D., Los Angeles, CA
Theodore Shapiro, M.D., New York, NY
Martin Wangh, M.D., Jerusalem, Israel
Edward M. Weinshel, M.D., San Francisco, CA

Acknowledgments

We would like to express our appreciation to all the contributors to this volume, not only for their excellent papers, but also for their cooperation in each stage of the planning and production of the volume. We are especially pleased that we have been able to complete the project within two years of Dr. Brenner's 70th birthday (November 18, 1984), the occasion for this Festschrift. For us, editing this volume has been a labor of love and an expression of our profound gratitude to Dr. Brenner for his contribution to our development as psychoanalysts. In so acknowledging Dr. Brenner's very important influence on both the way we think about psychoanalysis and the way we practice psychoanalysis, we of course join company not only with numerous contemporaries, but with a great many older and younger colleagues as well.

The contributors to this volume have been selected from the large universe of psychoanalysts who have been influenced by, and are appreciative of, Dr. Brenner's contributions to the theory, technique, and clinical practice of psychoanalysis. We regret that, owing to space limitations, we could not include all the worthy papers submitted for consideration for the volume. We would like to thank four colleagues whose support and encouragement to both of us were very important in the planning and preparation of the book: Dr. Robert Kabcenell, Dr. Ernest Kafka, Dr. Michael Porder, and Dr. Sherwood Waldron. Dr. Richards acknowledges the editorial assistance of Dr. Paul Stepansky in preparing his summary and overview of Dr. Brenner's work, and thanks Dr. Henry Bachrach, Dr. Bernard Brodsky, Dr. Charles Fisher, Dr. Donald Kaplan, Dr. Arthur Lynch, Dr. Arlene Kramer Richards, and Dr. Roy Schafer for helpful critical commentary on preliminary versions of this essay. Dr. Richards also thanks Mrs. Barbara Frank for ably typing his portion of the manuscript.

Finally, both Dr. Willick and Dr. Richards would like to express their deep appreciation to Dr. Paul Stepansky, Editor-in-Chief of The Analytic Press, and Eleanor Starke Kobrin, manuscript editor and production co-ordinator for the volume. We believe that their sensitivity, competence, and efficiency set a standard that is rarely equaled in the publishing field.

ADR & MSW
May 14, 1986

Introduction

> What words one uses in constructing one's theories and what their deriva-
> tives were is less important, in most instances, than what meaning the
> words have in terms of the new data and new generalizations about those
> data that constitute psychoanalytic theory. Words for what is new necessa-
> rily derive from what is familiar. This means neither that the words that have
> been redefined in this way should be retained nor that they should be re-
> placed. Sometimes one course is followed, sometimes the other. Either can
> be defended or preferred, provided one realizes that it makes no great dif-
> ference. It is not language that is important. One can think or speak in one
> language as well as in another. What one says is the important thing, not
> how one says it [Brenner, 1980, p. 208].

This passage from "Metapsychology and Psychoanalytic Theory" is quint-
essentially Charles Brenner. Although he penned these remarks in the
context of his defense of the language of metapsychology, they stand as
eloquent testimony to the values that have guided him throughout a distinguished career as both theorist and practitioner.

This is the credo of a "classical" analyst, disinclined to supplant the language of Freud's discoveries with trendier words that offer no real gain to
conceptual understanding or explanatory power. It is at the same time the
credo of a classical analyst who understands full well that theory-building
is an evolving enterprise and that the words through which the analyst
frames his theories must themselves evolve if they are to do justice to the
ever growing data base generated by the psychoanalytic method. If for
three decades Brenner has been content to innovate by addressing the
meaning of traditional psychoanalytic concepts, drive, defense, superego, affect, it is because he has never been a revolutionary, intent on de-
molishing the psychoanalytic edifice bequeathed us by Freud. His appre-

ciation of the fundamental principles that are Freud's legacy has culti-
vated in him a great respect for the language in which these principles
were formulated. It is Brenner's signal strength to have retained the language of classical analysis, all the while showing how the meaning of psychoanalytic concepts must evolve if analysis is to remain a fully adequate
science of mind.

Brenner is no psychoanalytic maverick. He has no "school" and seeks
no "followers." Yet he has emerged as one of the preeminent theorists of
his generation, one whose substantive innovations are masked by the
classical terminology he retains and by his modest disclaimers that his
theoretical contributions are but clarifications or refinements of traditional thinking. As I hope to demonstrate, however, Brenner's contributions in a variety of areas are far from incremental; they culminate in significant reformulations and bear witness to the continuing ability of
classical psychoanalytic discourse to accommodate the growth of psychoanalytic knowledge. And this is perhaps Charles Brenner's greatest
contribution as both theoretician and educator, to have shown that the
concepts of classical analysis are not frozen in the past but rather are flexible instruments of conceptual and clinical advance. He is a conservative
who believes in process, and his work admirably bears out his cautionary
reminder that "what one says is the important thing, not how one says it."

PSYCHOANALYSIS AS SCIENCE

Brenner's *Elementary Textbook of Psychoanalysis,* first published in 1955
and revised in 1973, is the most notable explication of psychoanalytic
principles in the history of the discipline. It has probably been read by
more analysts, psychiatrists, psychologists, physicians, and students than
any other work in the field. In its elegance and lucidity, it is matched only
by Freud's own Introductory Lectures. It is in this early work that Brenner
outlined the principles that guide him in his estimation of psychoanalysis
as a natural science. For Brenner, it is Freud's discovery of the psychoanalytic method and his objective attitude toward the data generated by this
method that place analysis squarely within the domain of the natural sciences. This distinctive method of data gathering, along with the interrelated hypotheses of psychic determinism and unconscious mental processes, is one of three pillars of the psychoanalytic edifice. The language
of psychoanalytic theory is commensurate with the data obtained by
means of the psychoanalytic method. The heuristic test of this language is
its clinical explanatory value.

Corollary to this perspective is Brenner's belief that the mere fact that it is possible to reformulate analysis in language compatible with that of other disciplines says nothing about the desirability of such translation. In a contribution published in 1969, he discusss Gardner's attempt to make psychoanalytic terminology dovetail with the language of neurophysiology. Brenner (1969a) observes that Gardiner's integrated strategy is belied by the fact that Gardiner "thinks" in terms of neurophysiology and aims at a unified science in which the concepts of both disciplines become coterminous with those of chemistry and physics. Lost in this integrative shuffle, however, is the distinctive nature of psychoanalytic data, the complex thought processes issuing in wishes, fantasies, and anxieties. Until the precise relationship between mental representation and neuronal functions can be stipulated, which neither Gardner nor any of his successors has been able to do, it is idle to judge the admissibility of psychoanalytic concepts in terms of their compatibility with neurophysiology. Analogizing at the level of terminology, which is all Gardner really does, cannot establish conceptual compatibility and can provide no basis for jettisoning the mere metapsychological language commensurate with psychoanalytic data.

Brenner further observes that Gardner's attempt to place a notion of "organismic equilibration" at the heart of psychoanalytic theory is fraught with logical difficulties: "If one follows the line of reasoning which it embodies, one would expect that evolution has eliminated psychosis and severe neurosis altogether or that it will do so in the course of time" (p. 50). Brenner adds that an equilibration model does violence to the data of psychoanalytic observation by ignoring the fact that "the urge to achieve instinctual gratification and to avoid unpleasure dominates mental activity to an extraordinary degree" (p. 51). For Brenner, then, "the pleasure principle is not only central to the psychoanalytic theory of the drives; it is central to the whole of the psychoanalytic theory of mental conflict as well" (p. 51). In supplanting this principle with an organismic "need" to adapt to external stimuli or to achieve a table equilibrium among opposing tendencies of the mind, theorists ignore the facts of mental life as disclosed by the psychoanalytic method: "Such theories may explain very well what the experimenter observes in a psychological laboratory. But they do not explain nor do they fit what the clinician daily observes of the wellsprings of human behavior and the conflict in human life to which they give rise" (p. 51).

Such remarks are central to Brenner's work and highlight the radical disjunction between his approach and that of theorists like George Klein, Heinz Kohut, and John Gedo. The latter all evoke some notion of the "self" and its organization in order to supplant the pleasure principle with an updated version of Gardner's organismic equilibration hypothesis. In "Psychoanalysis and Science," a paper presented in 1968 and stimulated in part by the New York University Symposium on "Psychoanalysis and Scientific Method" in the fifties, Brenner amplified his response to Gardner. He argues that a science is defined not by the nature of the subject matter under investigation but rather by the approach it adopts toward that subject matter. It is by virtue of the analyst's investigative attitude that psychoanalysis qualifies as a natural science. In adopting this position, Brenner was disputing the claim, made most forcefully by Kohut in his influential paper of 1959, that analysis departs from the natural sciences by virtue of its reliance on "introspection" in its data gathering. Brenner maintains, contra Kohut, that introspection is a notoriously unreliable tool for obtaining information about mental phenomena: "An independent and outside observer with the help of the psychoanalytic method can gain a far more accurate and useful and informative view of the mental functioning of the patient's verbal communications, than anyone can from introspection" (p. 689). For Brenner, the introspective tendency to attribute our own thoughts and feelings to others is something "we must unlearn with experience." He agrees that we may reasonably assume that other people's minds are very similar to our own, but adds that "it is risky to go too far in this direction, that too great a reliance on what we call empathy and intuition leads to the undesirable type of activity that we call wild analysis" (p. 690).

In "Psychoanalysis: Philosophy or Science" (1970), a contribution to *Psychoanalysis and Philosophy,* he buttresses his argument by stressing that Freud did not "base his theories on introspective data but on observation—in particular on the close and extended observation of mentally ill (neurotic) patients who came to him for treatment" (p. 36). Freud's unparalleled achievements, he believes, derive not from his introspective powers but from his ability to evaluate with scientific objectivity "previously unknown and largely unsuspected data derived from the psychoanalytic method" (p. 37). In the guise of self psychology, Kohut's contrary position of 1959 would blossom into the point of view that Freud's greatness derived largely fom disciplined introspection, and that it is *only* through introspection and empathy that the analyst obtains important data about his patients' mental functioning. For Brenner, the pleasure principle and "extrospection" of the natural scientist would remain central.

Brenner's most recent contribution on the scientific status of psychoanalysis is the 1980 "Metapsychology and Psychoanalytic Theory." Here, in response to critics such as George Klein and Merton Gill and Roy

Schafer, who deem metapsychology an undesirable, pseudoscientific ac-
cretion to the "hermeneutic" core of analysis, Brenner undertakes a careful review of Freud's various uses of the term, beginning with a statement
in 1898 in which he construed metapsychology as the bridge connecting
the unconscious biological and the conscious psychological. At a later
stage in his career, Freud equated metapsychology with the psychology
of the unconscious, and still later in his 1915 paper "The Unconscious,"
he seemed to equate the metapsychological with the economic aspects
of mental functioning. But Brenner goes on to adduce fairly compelling
evidence that Freud ultimately came to equate metapsychology with psychoanalytic theory in general, rather than simply with the psychoanalytic
theory of unconscious mental processes; in Freud's footnote to the title of
"Metapsychological Supplement to the Theory of Dreams" (1915b), "metapsychology" and "psychological system" are used synonymously.

On the basis of this philological judgment, Brenner takes issue with the
attempt by Rapaport and Gill (1959) to dissect metapsychology into six
discrete assumptions and viewpoints. His argument is that each viewpoint invoked by Rapaport and Gill implicates all the others, so that "so-
called structural theory, for example, is not merely a structural point of
view. Its propositions are dynamic, genetic, adaptive, economic, and
structural propositions" (p. 198). In short, metapsychology as a notational
shorthand for psychoanalytic theory cannot be differentiated from the individual viewpoints that jointly comprise it: metapsychology itself *denote*
the fact of this mutual implication. Psychoanalytic understanding and the
theory that encapsulates it is the confluence of these several viewpoints.

In a related vein, Brenner takes issue with the attempt by Robert
Waelder (1962) to divide psychoanalysis into a hierarchy of "levels" based
on a putative proximity to the data of observation. Disputing Waelder's
judgment that metapsychology is less proximate to the data and hence
"far less necessary" to analysis than less abstract levels of explanation,
Brenner argues that Waelder's entire classificatory schema is based on a
fundamental misconception "of the nature of scientific observation and
theory formation":

> In every branch of science even the simplest observations involve ideas of
> the highest order of abstraction. In physics, for example, such high level ab-
> stractions as space and time are data of observation. In psychoanalysis, as in
> every other branch of science, both theories and observations involve
> greater numbers of abstractions. What makes a theory useful and dependa-
> ble has no relation whatever to its abstractedness. A theory is either well
> supported by a large amount of data that are relevant, or, it is poorly sup-
> ported by data. The correct basis for a hierarchy of theories of any science is
> not abstractness or concreteness. It is the degree to which a given theory is

supported by the relevant data or, conversely, how speculative it is. "Speculative" is not a synonym for "abstract," nor is "well supported by relevant
data" its antonym [p. 200].

Through his defense of metapsychology as a mode of discourse commensurate with psychoanalytic data, Brenner returns to his view that analysis
as a natural science takes up an observational stance no different from
that of other natural sciences. He disputes the hermeneutic claim that
analysis forfeits its claim to scientific status by virtue of its preoccupation
with "meaning." For Brenner, the analytic concern with meaning only
highlights the fact that analysis is a separate branch of science addressing
its particular subject in the manner of any other science:

> The data of psychoanalysis are principally wishes, fears, fantasies, dreams,
> neurotic symptoms, associative material, etc., expressed in language and
> gestures that have meaning. In other words, psychoanalysts do deal with
> meanings as data, which physicists and neurophysiologists, for example, do
> not. But what psychoanalysts *do* with their data is no different in principle
> from what any other scientists do with their data. What psychoanalysts do
> that is of particular importance . . . is that they make inferences with respect
> to the causes of the wishes, fears, fantasies, dreams, neurotic symptoms,
> and associative material that constitute their data of observation. They pos-
> tulate the same cause and effect relationships with respect to their data as
> physicists, for example, do with respect to theirs. That is to say, psychoana-
> lysts try to discover or, to be more precise, to infer what it is that causes the
> normal and pathological mental phenomena they observe. Their discover-
> ies or inferences are what constitute psychoanalytic theory, just as, for ex-
> ample, Newton's inferences, which are more usually called his laws of
> motion, constitute the theory of celestial and terrestial mechanics that bears
> his name [p. 205].

It is from this standpoint, and with the data of psychoanalytic observation
in mind, that Brenner proceeds to defend the much attacked notion of
psychic energy.

> Is it justified and useful as a concept and as a term? I believe so, but not be-
> cause the word, energy, was derived in the first instance from a term and
> concept of physics. I believe so because I think that drive theory is a valid
> and useful generalization (theory) about mental functioning and that in that
> theory there should be some term to designate the concept that drives have
> the capacity to impel the mind to activity—a capacity that varies in strength
> from time to time. What that concept is called *matters not at all, any more
> than it matters whether one speaks English, French, Spanish, or German in
> discussing it. Call it psychic energy, motivation, impetus, or "abc." The tag is
> unimportant. It is the concept that matters. If you drop the concept alto-
> gether, as many analysts would like to do, you have to discard drive theory as*

well and you have to substitute something else for it. Just changing the *name* from "drive" to, say, "motivation" changes nothing in the theory. It makes the theory no more "psychological," no less "mechanistic," no more "human," than it was before [pp. 210–211].

Here, as always, Brenner's concern is not with words but with the theoretical assumptions that underlie them and the implications of these assumptions for psychoanalytic theory-building. To jettison the notion of psychic energy is to abandon drive theory in its common form; it is to make a "real change" in psychoanalytic theory, which has held since Freud that mental life is composed of conscious and unconscious wishes that impinge on the mental apparatus with varying degrees of intensity. In drawing attention both to the assumptions that underlie the abandonment of individual psychoanalytic concepts and to the implications of such a move, Brenner highlights the magnitude of Freud's achievement: the promulgation of a theory of mental life that achieves cohesiveness and explanatory force through the conceptual interweaving of all its major concepts.

THE DRIVES, AGGRESSION, AND STRUCTURAL THEORY

In the second chapter of the *Elementary Textbook,* Brenner (1955) suggests a position on the drives that dovetails in most essentials with that of Freud. The drives, he tells his readers, are "abstractions from the data of experience. They are hypotheses—operational concepts, to use a term which is fashionable nowadays—which we believe enable us to understand and explain our data in as simple and as systematic a way as possible" (p. 20). His contention that there are two kinds of psychic energy, one associated with libido and one with the aggressive drive, implies a basically biological concept of the drives. He departs from Freud only in contesting the validity of the concept of repetition compulsion and the idea that the gratification associated with aggression is beyond the pleasure principle. With respect to the latter point, he is content to cite Hartmann and inform the reader that "the majority of psychoanalysts appear to have accepted this view" (p. 30).

In chapter 2 of *The Mind in Conflict,* written almost 30 years later in 1982, Brenner draws a clearer distinction between his views and those of Freud. At the onset, alluding to Freud's concept of the instinct as a "frontier concept" at the interface of mind and body, he disputes the contention that psychoanalytic data by themselves can never be an adequate basis for a satisfactory theory of the drives. Rather, Brenner argues that a satisfactory theory of drives can derive *only* from psychoanalytic data. In contesting the need to anchor psychoanalytic drive theory in nonanalytic data derived from biology, physiology, animal observation, and the like, Brenner also contests Freud's attempt to "biologize" libido by tracing its origins to particular regions of the body. For Brenner, as for Freud, the connections between libido and the erogenous zones are "indisputable and intimate," but Brenner adds that "this is not the same as saying that libido arises from mouth, anus, genitals, etc." (p. 14). He then cites certain facts that weigh against Freud's conceptualization, including the intensification of libidinal wishes at the time of menopause and the climacteric, and the efflorescense of sexual wishes during the oedipal period. Brenner continues:

> Everyday analytic experience demonstrates, for example, that events occurring in the context of a relationship between patient and analyst, such as impending separation or the commencement of analysis, can powerfully increase, i.e., stimulate, the urgency of libidinal wishes, but no one would conclude from such observation that the relationship between patient and analyst, i.e., the transference, is a source of libido, much less the source of it. In the same way, it is not truly convincing to conclude from the very intimate relationship between erogenous zones and libidinal derivatives that the zones are the *source* of the libidinal drive. That they are intimately linked is certain. That one is the source of the other is less so [pp. 14–15].

In the seemingly fine distinction that concludes this passage, we see Brenner's emancipation from certain mechanistic accoutrements of Freud's approach to motivation. It is tantamount to the espousal of an entirely psychological and "personalized" approach to drive behavior.

This attitude carries over to Brenner's discussion of aggression (1971b). Here he differentiates between the theory of the aggressive drive, which derives from "the accumulation of psychoanalytic evidence," and the theory of the death instinct, through which Freud sought to give the phenomenon of human aggressiveness a transcendent biological meaning. Brenner argues that just as Freud required a somatic source for libido, that is, the excitation of the nerve endings in the erogenous zones, so he required one for aggression. He believed he had located this in "the universal tendency of living matter to die," an idea Brenner finds invalid on grounds both empirical and logical. More important, it cannot be inferred from psychoanalytic data and so has no place in psychoanalytic explanation. Clinical explanations of aggression, including self-destructive behavior, implicate only those aspects of Freud's theory that derive from psychoanalytic data. Through such data we

> explain such behavior in terms of murderous childhood wishes, fears of retribution, fears of loss, and self-punitive trends. None of these depend on the assumption that a death drive is common to all living matter. It depends es-

sentially on the data furnished by the application of the psychoanalytic method [p. 21].

Brenner's critique of the death instinct as nonpsychological and nonpsychoanalytic paves the way for his redefinition of the drives as "generalizations" about two classes of "wishes" corresponding to two types of motivation. This definition, in turn, leads him to accord pride of place not to the drive itself, but to drive derivatives, the "wish for gratification" that is uniquely individual. It is in his attention to the variousness of drive derivatives as uniquely individual embodiments of the drives that Brenner approaches the position of hermeneuticists like George Klein and Roy Schafer. For Brenner, that is, it is insufficient simply to impute to analysands libidinal or aggressive conflicts stemming from their drives. And it is of little moment to go one step further and categorize the analysand's wishes as oral, anal, or phallic. Rather,

> What is important in respect to each patient is to learn as much as possible about the libidinal ad aggressive drive derivatives which are important at the moment, including their relationship to childhood derivatives and to subsequent experience and development. What is important, in other words, is to learn as much as possible about what a patient wishes, about who is involved in his wishes, about how and why he has just those particular wishes about those particular persons [p. 26].

It is ironic that Brenner, in his sensitivity to the experiential specificity of the analysand's conflicting wishes, adopts a position of nominal agreement with those analysts who, unlike him, seek to dispense entirely with psychoanalytic metapsychology. The essential difference, of course, is that Brenner arrives at his position using the language and conceptual framework of classical analysis. Indeed, his stance is a refinement of classical thinking; it is premised on an entirely psychoanalytic appreciation of the drives and generalizations about wishes. Klein (1976) and Schafer (1976), on the other hand, feel that they can articulate the singularity of the individual's conflicts and wishes and wishful impulses only by supplanting psychoanalytic drive theory, which includes the crucial notion of the drive derivative, with a new vocabulary and a new conceptual framework. Brenner finds such departures gratuitous:

> Critics of the psychoanalytic theory of the drives often charge that it is impersonal and mechanistic. The facts do not justify the charge. Such critics either ignore or misunderstand the distinction between drive annd drive derivative. The former is impersonal and general, the latter is general and specific. Drive theory includes both (p. 26).

It is to Brenner's lasting credit to have shown how clarifying emendations to the psychoanalytic theory of the drives, which amount to Freud's

own position refined and shorn of the extra-analytic presuppositions, culminate in a substantive revision of the structural theory. Rejecting Freud's
speculations about the biological origins of the drives, Brenner is led to
reassess the notion of the id, which Freud envisioned as the repository of
the drives. Freud, and most analysts since him, viewed the drives as con-
stitutionally determined and present from the very beginnning of postna-
tal life. The clear implication is that drives are more independent of experience than are those aspects of mental functioning subsumed under the
rubric of "ego." Brenner, however, drawing on all the available psychoanalytic evidence, suggests that drive-related activities, whether libidinal or
aggressive, are from birth influenced by experiential factors that gain expression in ego development. In short, clinical analysis does not sustain
the separation of ego development from issues of drive expression and
drive gratification. It follows that a sharp distinction between ego and id,
even a sharp *heuristic* distinction, must be brought into question.

Brenner makes the same point when he notes that what psychoanalytic
theory subsumes under ego functions are distinguishable from drives and
drive derivatives only in situations of conflict. Ego functions, he reminds
us, are executants of drives and hence come into opposition to drives
only when drive derivatives evoke unpleasure and defense. For Brenner,
then, conflict is a *sine qua non* of structural theory itself. In *The Mind in
Conflict* (1982a), he supports this point by appealing to Anna Freud's remark that "in the absence of conflict there is no division among the mental
agencies, or, in other words, no id, ego, or superego" (p. 73). In a similar
vein, he cites David Beres, who remarked that in order to be consistent,
repressed wishes and fantasies must be regarded as belonging properly in
the heading of the ego. In thus stressing the role of the ego in drive gratification from the very beginning of life, he implicitly departs from Freud,
who was content to situate repressed wishes first in "the unconscious" of
the topographical theory and ultimately in the "id" of structural theory.

Brenner's reformulation of structural theory culminates in the revised
estimation of the superego set forth in chapter 8 of *The Mind in Conflict*
(1982). In the *Elementary Textbook* (1955) Brenner accepted the traditional view of the superego as one agency in the psychic apparatus. In articles published over the next two decades (1959, 1982a), he significantly
enlarged our clinical appreciation of this mental agency by drawing attention to the role of both masochism and libidinal gratification in superego
formation. By contrast, in *The Mind in Conflict* Brenner offers an entirely
new perspective on the superego, construing it as a compromise formation functionally analogous to other compromise formations revealed by
psychoanalytic investigation: neurotic symptoms, dreams, delusions,
character traits, and so on. Brenner continues to stress that the superego

is a "structure" that enters into psychic conflict along with id and ego. But as id and ego are presumably *not* compromise formations, Brenner's recent formulations appear to forego the symmetry of the three intrapsychic agencies of traditional structural theory. This suggests that, implicitly at least, Brenner has arrived at a theoretical juncture where he questions the validity and clinical usefulness of conceptualizing mental life in terms of three structurally equivalent mental agencies. I will not venture to predict where Brenner's theorizing will lead him, beyond speculating that his forthcoming contributions will offer increasingly nuanced depictions of the interrelated constituents of psychic conflict while simultaneously incorporating certain features of the hermeneutic theorists like Klein and Schafer. Brenner seems to have understood well the aphorism of his friend and colleague, Jacob Arlow, that id, ego, and superego exist not in the patient but in psychoanalytic textbooks. It is conceivable that Brenner will eventually articulate a model of the mind in conflict in which the interpretation of the elements of conflict is such that the traditional concepts of id, ego, and superego become superfluous.

AFFECTS

For Brenner the problem of affect is coterminous with the problem of anxiety. His earliest publication on the topic, misleadingly entitled "An Addendum to Freud's Theory of Anxiety" (1953), is actually a seminal contribution to affect theory that paves the way for his recent formulations regarding depressive affect. Brenner begins by arguing against Freud's theories of actual and traumatic neuroses. Here again his point of departure is diametrically opposite that of Kohut, whose early acceptance of the concept of actual neurosis was crucial to his later theorizing (Ornstein, 1978).

With respect to actual neurosis, Brenner critically reviews the data suggesting that anxiety can arise automatically owing to a quantitative flooding of the psychic apparatus. His conclusion is that analysis has not generated any data suggesting that anxiety can emerge independently of a psychical source. Otherwise, he finds no evidence of Freud's claim that neurotic anxiety can arise from simple frustration or sexual strivings. Returning to the traumatic neuroses, Brenner finds that available analytic data contradict Freud: they suggest that the anxiety associated with traumatic states derives from the conflicts evoked by traumautic situations and not from a "rupture of the stimulus barrier, that is, from the sexually quantitative variations in psychic energy or citation" (1953, p. 21).

Brenner considers one final basis for Freud's views on the actual neurosis, a point central to the "addendum" he proceeds to formulate. This concerns the affective state of infants who are separated from their mothers. Brenner suggests that we cannot really know *what* an infant experiences under such circumstances and that it is therefore unwarrantedly adult-omorphic to equate the infant's emotion with "anxiety." For Brenner it makes more sense to characterize the emotion of the traumatically distressed infant as "extreme unpleasure rather than specifically as anxiety, although we may reasonably assume that as the infant matures it develops the capacity to be anxious in danger situations." Pursuing this line of reasoning, Brenner offers the following conceptualization:

> Anxiety is an emotion (affect) which the anticipation of danger evokes in the ego. It is not present, as such, from birth or very early infancy. In such very early periods, the infant is aware only of pleasure or unpleasure as far as emotions are concerned. As experience increases and other ego functions develop (e.g., memory and sensory perception), the child becomes able to predict or anticipate that a state of unpleasure (a "traumatic situation") will develop. This drawing ability of a child to react to danger in advance is the beginning of the specific emotion of anxiety, which in the course of further development we propose becomes sharply differentiated from other unpleasant emotions [p. 22].

Brenner's formulation, like Freud's, rests "on the assumption that there is a genetic relation between anxiety in later life and the emotion of the child in traumatic situations of infancy" (p. 23). But unlike Freud's theory of the actual neurosis, Brenner's alternative explanation "leaves open the possibility that the emotion experienced in the traumatic situation is also related genetically to other unpleasant emotions in later life" (p. 23). In a revealing passage that foreshadows his future theoretical concerns, Brenner adds that his formulation leaves open the possibility that this state of psychic helplessness that we associate with traumatic situations may be "the forebearer of depression as well as anxiety" (p. 23).

The addendum of 1953, an important revision of the psychoanalytic theory of affects, is revealing of how in general Brenner approaches the task of theory-building. He begins with a careful review of Freud's contributions on a topic, locates an aspect of Freud's theory that is not borne out by clinical data, and then offers a clinically based reformulation that serves as a point of departure for subsequent theorizing. In this instance, his differentiation of the infant's reaction to danger and the child's (and the adult's) experience of anxiety ties the latter to the maturation of ego functions and, hence, to psychological referents. As an added benefit, "it avoids the unwelcome necessity of assuming that there are two kinds of anxiety" (p. 22). Finally, in suggesting that affect theory must posit developmental linkages not only between infantile unpleasure and later anxi-

ety, but between such unpleasure and the crystallization of unpleasant affect, it opens an avenue for future theoretical work.

But it was not until twenty years later, in a presentation for the 28th International Psychoanalytic Congress, that Brenner took up the challenge
posed by his early paper. He begins "Depression, Anxiety, and Affect
Theory" (1974a) by reprising the basic premise of the 1953 "Addendum":
"that early in life, before any substantial degree of ego development has
taken place, all affects can be divided into pleasurable and unpleasurable" (p. 29). Now, however, he makes this point to highlight the fact that
the generic unpleasure associated with the traumatic insults of infancy
are the source not only of later experiences of anxiety but of experiences
of depression as well: "These emotions, too, no less than the emotions of
anxiety, are genetically related to the unpleasure of the traumatic state; in
some ways they develop out of it" (p. 30). Brenner next distinguishes between the unpleasurable affects of anxiety and grief by appealing to their
differing ideational content:

> Grief, for example, is unpleasure associated with ideas that in general have
> to do with instinctual frustration, i.e., disappointment, with ideas of inade-
> quacy, inferiority, with ideas of loneliness and often the idea that things will
> never be any better, that frustration, loneliness, and inferiority will persist,
> that they are inevitable (p. 30).

Thus Brenner invokes a temporal referent to differentiate the two principal categories of affect: anxiety concerns something bad that will happen
in the future, depression something bad that has already happened. The
nexus of Brenner's theory of affects, then, is "that psychologically, i.e.,
subjectively speaking, affects are distinguishable from one another on
only two grounds. First, whether they are pleasurable or unpleasurable,
and second, what thoughts are connected with them, what their ideational content is" (p. 30).

Brenner systematizes this idea in a companion paper, "On the Nature
and Development of Affects, A Unified Theory" (1974b). Here affects are
introduced as complex phenomena that include sensations of pleasure,
unpleasure, pleasure and unpleasure in varying combinations, and ideas.
A pleasurable or unpleasurable sensation together with an associated
idea constitutes the mental phenomenon known as an affect. Affects originate early in life, when ideas first become linked to sensations of pleasure
and unpleasure. The development of affects, and their differentiation
from one another, go hand in hand with subsequent ego and superego
development.

The advantages of Brenner's unified theory of affects are manifold.
Consistent with his innovations in other areas, this theory reformulates

what we can know about affects from the data of clinical analysis. In so doing, he dispenses with unwarranted biological inferences that cannot be verified by analysis and with more subjective inferences about the nature of the "emotions" experienced very early in life. At the clinical heuristic level it provides criteria for distinguishing different affects, along with a workable language for explaining these differences.

The clinical yield of Brenner's theory is perhaps more salient with respect to depression. By situating the anlagen of depression in the amorphous unpleasure of early life, he shows how adult depression, no less than adult anxiety, yields to analytic unraveling with respect to its essential structure and meaning. Like symptoms of anxiety, depressive symptoms are crystallizations of complex affect, that is, compromise formations issuing from the various wishes, fears, defenses, self-punitive trends, and environmental pressures brought to bear at a given point in time. Whether or not patients are consciously aware of being depressed, "the affect of a depressed patient has the same complex structure as does any other fantasy, thought, action, or symptom" (1974a, p. 32).

Brenner continues this line of thought in "Affects in Psychic Conflict" (1975), a rich presentation whose accessibility and pragmatic clinical importance belie the nuances of reasoning that inform it. Here Brenner shows how affect theory, in relation to both anxiety and depression, provides a crucial vehicle for discerning the unique constellation of conflicts presented by each analysand. This paper is especially noteworthy for its wealth of clinical examples highlighting the role of depressive affect in conflict formation. In addressing conflict through the vehicle of affect theory, Brenner adopts an approach that is entirely dynamic. Moving toward a position to be spelled out more fully in *The Mind in Conflict*, (1982) he shows how psychoanalytic affect theory can afford the clinician a detailed grasp of the elements of intrapsychic conflict that far surpasses the insights provided by the potentially reifying constructs of traditional structural theory.

In a "Depressive Affect, Anxiety, and Psychic Conflict in the Phallic-Oedipal Phase" (1979a), Brenner elaborates on the phenomenology and dynamic meaning of specifically depressive conflicts. This paper, one of very few in which Brenner advocates a terminological departure from the language of classical analysis, introduces the term "calamity" as a substitute for "danger." The former, it is argued, connotes bad experiences that are either impending or have already happened; it can therefore be linked equally well to anxiety or depressive affect. "Danger," by contrast, has primarily a future orientation and is therefore less suggestive of the past events or circumstances associated specifically with depressive affect. Brenner proceeds to recast the major danger situations of classical theory, loss of object, loss of the object's love, and castration anxiety as the three calamities of childhood. He takes pains to dispel the timeworn belief that each of these correlates neatly with a specific psychosexual stage. He argues, for example, that fear of loss of the object and of the object's love frequently plays an important role even in the phallic-oedipal phase. For Brenner, the calamities are interwoven into a tangible and analyzable whole, so that to segregate them along a time line is to compartmentalize the child's mental life artificially.

With this in mind, Brenner goes on to argue that both depressive affect and anxiety enter castration conflicts regardless of the individual's sex, though the former is predominant in girls and the latter in boys. As always, his theoretical formulations culminate in useful therapeutic precepts: (1) View the unpleasurable affect as a symptom masking unsatisfactory compromise formations; and (2) proceed with the work of analysis by looking for the cause of the particular genre of unpleasure that gains expression in the symptom. These and other clinical insights are eloquently put forth in the third chapter of *The Mind in Conflict,* a distillation of over three decades of thinking and writing about the role of affect in psychoanalytic theory and practice.

DEFENSES

In his presentation of structural theory in the *Elementary Textbook,* Brenner uses the term "ego" in a reified way far removed from the mode of discourse typifying his more recent work. This is particularly true of his explanation of signal anxiety, where he invokes an ego that "produces anxiety as a signal of unpleasure. With the help of the pleasure principle in this way, the ego is able to offer a successful opposition to the emergence of the dangerous impulses" (1955, p. 79). Not so his concept of defense, which even in 1955 has much the same character to be found in his writings of the 1970s and 1980s. To the question, "What defenses does the ego offer against the id?," the *Elementary Textbook* answers as follows:

> The ego can use anything which lies at hand that will serve the purpose. Any ego attitude, any real perception, a change in attention, furtherance of another id impulse which is safer than the dangerous one and will compete with it, a vigorous attempt to neutralize the energy of the dangerous drive, the formation of identifications, or the promotion of fantasy can be used alone or in any combination in a defensive way. In a word, the ego can and does use all of the processes of normal ego formation and ego function for defensive purposes at one time or another [p. 80].

In a series of papers following the *Elementary Textbook,* Brenner develops his view of defensive processes as content-neutral by focusing on repression. In 1957 he ended a scholarly review of Freud's concept of repression by underscoring the status of repression in Freud's final view of defense: Repression is but one of several defense mechanisms the ego may employ against drive derivatives, the latter being the source of anxiety. The target of repression is ordinarily a libidinal drive, but it may be an aggressive drive derivative or superego demand as well. Finally, the mechanism of repression is the establishment of a countercathexis of the ego; it follows that repression becomes possible only after significant ego development has occurred.

In a paper published ten years later, Brenner (1967) explicitly attempted to apply the principle of multiple function to the theory of repression. He was thereupon led to revise Freud's classical concept of repression which he contends has two aspects: (1) the belief that repression is tantamount to barring certain mental elements access to conscious mental life, and (2) the derivative notion that the intrusion of these elements into consciousness betokens the failure of repression or "return of the repressed." Against this, Brenner argues that repression results from an interplay of forces within the mind in which the balance is predominantly in favor of those forces seeking to bar one or several mental representations from consciousness. Since the repressing forces usually achieve but limited success, it follows that repressed mental elements routinely enter conscious mental life, quite apart from those instances in which their return signifies the outright failure of repression. In a similar vein, Brenner calls into question the belief that neurotic symptoms signal a failure of repression and are thus tantamount to the return of the repressed:

> Repression signifies a dynamic equilibrium between forces striving for discharge (e.g., an instinctual derivative) and other opposing forces (defenses, superego prohibition). If something happens to shift the balance among these forces in a direction which is unfavorable to the ego's defenses, the result will be an increased emergence into conscious mental life and action of the previously instinctual derivative. If the shift is long continued, and if the emergence of the instinctual derivative is felt to be dangerous (arousing signal anxiety), the compromise which results will be of the nature of a neurotic symptom or character trait. By the same token, a shift in the equilibrium which is favorable to the defensive forces, and which diminishes a patient's tendency to react with anxiety to an instinctual derivative which has given rise to a neurotic symptom, will result in the symptom disappearing or becoming less severe [pp. 398-399].

We might say that for Brenner the vicissitudes of symptomatic behavior and character pathology derive from the continually changing balance between opposing forces within the mind. In a paper of 1981, "Defense and Defense Mechanisms," he elaborates as implicit in this viewpoint a "major, even a radical revision of this part of conflict theory" (p. 558). He now states boldly that discrete defense "mechanisms" simply do not exist. Rather, "defense is an aspect of mental functioning that is definable only in terms of its consequences, reduction of unpleasure associated with the drive derivative, i.e., with the instinctual wish, or with superego functioning" (p. 559). It follows for Brenner that the very aspects of mental functioning which in certain contexts function as defenses against drive derivatives can in other contexts facilitate gratification of the same derivatives. Since the mental mechanisms traditionally equated with defenses serve nondefensive purposes as well, it is erroneous to characterize them as intrinsically defense related.

The argument that there are no ego functions exclusively subserving defense implies a radically broadened concept of ego. Brenner's revision here does not parallel that of Hartmann (1939), who assigned certain aspects of ego functioning to an entirely "conflict-free" sphere. Rather, in contending that no ego function can be assigned a priori to a particular sphere of functioning, Brenner adopts a viewpoint that is nonmechanistic and nonreductionistic, and, as such, "faithful to the facts of life" (p. 563). The language in which he casts his insights into the reversibility of defensive and drive-related purposes is action-oriented, dovetailing in certain respects with the "action language" proposed by Schafer (1976). Consider Brenner's characterization of a defense as a "say no to whatever is the target of defense" (p. 562). Consider as well how he describes the mind at work:

> When unpleasure is aroused or threatens to be aroused, one does whatever one can to avoid and reduce it. When one desires ratification and pleasure, one does whatever one can to achieve it . . . It is the function served by what one does that determines whether it is properly called defense (pp. 564–565).

The ready identifiability of a particular analysand's "repertory of defenses" is another traditional assumption called into question by Brenner's functional estimation of defensive processes. His contention that all aspects of ego functioning are all-purpose, capable of subserving, variously, drive gratification, ego defense, and superego prohibition, militates against the belief that analysands have limited defensive repertories. For Brenner, any repertory of defense necessarily draws on every aspect of ego functioning:

> Thus to speak of a characteristic repertory of defense is really to say only that prominent neurotic symptoms and/or character traits are apt to be persistent in any patient and to require repeated analysis and interpretation in

the course of treatment. . . . It is not patients who show a limited repertory of defensive methods; it is one or another symptom, or other compromise formation, which is characterized by a special method or methods of defense [pp. 567–568].

In chapter 5 of *The Mind in Conflict* (1982) Brenner offers additional insights drawn from his estimation of defense. Linking his reconceptualization of defensive processes to his unified theory of affect, he observes that defenses may be directed not only against drive derivatives or affect or superego functioning, but against the anxiety or depressive affect they mobilized. In the latter instance, defense may be directed at the sensation of unpleasure, the ideational correlate of the unpleasure, that is, the real or fantasied calamity, or both. Further, defenses neither disappear during the course of analysis nor become increasingly "normal." Rather, their character and preemptoriness alter as the balance among opposing mental forces changes in response to the analytic work (p. 92).

It is clear that Brenner's reformulation of the concept of defense and the status of defensive processes in mental functioning will not win easy acceptance. In particular, his proposal that we dispense entirely with the notion of defense mechanisms will likely encounter strong resistance in view of the longevity of this concept and its identification with both Freud and his daughter Anna. But here, as elsewhere, Brenner theorizes in a clinically relevant way that enhances our understanding of the analytic process. He is awed neither by traditional concepts nor by their traditional deployment. Rather, he is intent on doing full justice to the data that follow from the use of Freud's psychoanalytic method. Drawing on scientific sensibilities tempered by broad clinical experience, he subjects each psychoanalytic formulation he examines to the tests of clarity, consistency, logical validity, and clinical usefulness. His proposaal that we abandon the concept of defense mechanism is not offered lightly; though it may make case presentations more difficult or simply less facile, it augurs well for our day-to-day clinical work. It aids us in keeping the analysand "as a whole" in the foreground, relegating isolated drive derivatives and defenses to a subordinate role both conceptual and clinical.

TECHNIQUE

The psychoanalytic situation is organized according to the psychoanalytic theory of mental functioning and in keeping with the goals and aims of psychoanalysis as a therapy. Whatever is consonant with the dynamic principles of psychoanalysis and with the goals of psychoanalytic therapy is properly part of the analytic situation. Whatever is in conflict with those principles and goals is not legitimately part of the psychoanalytic situation and should be avoided and discarded [Arlow and Brenner, 1966, p. 43].

In this passage from "The Psychoanalytic Situation," we encounter again the leitmotif of Brenner's work. The "theory of mental functioning" that "organizes" the psychoanalytic part of the analyst's task is to understand the nature and origins of his patient's mental conflicts" (Brenner 1976, p. 33). Issues of technique can be addressed only from the standpoint of the analyst's comprehension of the analysand's psychic conflicts. Brenner's work in this area has a twofold intent: (1) to show how specific aspects of technique subserve psychoanalytic conflict theory, and (2) to see to it that no single element of technique, and no single explanation or justification of an element of technique, achieves a weight disproportionate to its status within this theory of mental functioning. Brenner repeatedly cautions his psychoanalytic colleages regarding the pitfalls, theoretical and clinical, of overvaluing specific aspects of technique, or specific rationales for technique, currently in vogue. In the Arlow–Brenner (1966) paper, the cautionary note centers on the view of the "psychoanalytic situation" popularized by Leo Stone, René Spitz, Elizabeth Zetzel, and others in the early 1960s. These authors invoke an "*a priori* assumption that the psychoanalytic situation re-creates the relationship between mother and infant during the earliest months of life" (1966, p. 23). They hold as a corollary that analytic termination is invariably an "experience that parallels that of weaning" (p. 24). Arlow and Brenner counter that "while this is doubtless true in many instances, it seems unlikely that it is invariably the case" (p. 23). They warn here against what Hartmann (1939) called a genetic fallacy: "The fact that the first situation is dependence in the life of every individual, his relationship with his mother," they write, "does not prove that every subsequent relationship of dependence produces the prototype" (Arlow and Brenner, 1966, p. 26). They offer case examples that run counter to the then current estimation of the analytic situation: a patient who did not react to termination with separation anxiety and another, for whom the "basis of the transference was not the patient's early tie to her mother, but her later relationship with her father" (p. 28). Arlow and Brenner's approach in this paper illustrates the empirical open mindedness, the receptivity to the yield of psychoanalytic inquiry that will guide Brenner through a succession of works on technique: "The meaning of the psychoanalytic situation is not the same for every patient . . . analytic data are the only basis on which one can validate the unconscious significance which the analytic situation holds for a particular patient" (p. 43).

Brenner's determination to examine and justify elements of technique with respect to the dynamic principles of analysis is expressed in his reconsideration of dream interpretation. In the chapter on dream psychology in *Psychoanalytic Concepts and the Structural Theory* (Arlow and Brenner, 1964), Brenner recasts the analytic understanding of dreaming from the standpoint of structural theory. Brenner goes beyond Freud's formulations in *The Interpretation of Dreams* (1900) by reconceptualizing dreams as the product of the interplay of id, ego, and superego; as such, they are compromise formations. The technical consequence of this structural reappraisal is, ironically, the dethroning of dream interpretation from its privileged position in clinical work. As but one example of compromise formation, the dream is hardly unique in affording the analyst a view of the analysand's unconscious conflicts. This position is articulated with great force in a paper, "Dreams in Clinical Psychoanalytic Practice" (1969b):

> It is not only the case with dreams that they are a compromise formation among instinctual id wishes, defenses motivated by anxiety or guilt and superego demands or prohibitions. The same is true of neurotic symptoms, parapraxes, slips, jokes, many character traits, one's choice of a profession, one's sexual practices and preferences, daydreams, conscious childhood memories, including screen memories, one's reaction to a play, film or book, one's social habits and activities in general, and above all, in every patient's so-called free associations [p. 336].

In his Brill Lecture of 1966, "Some Comments on Technical Precepts in Psychoanalysis" (1969c), Brenner uses his view of dreams as situated on a continuum of compromise formations to reconsider two standard technical precepts: (a) Never interpret a patient's first dream, and (2) dream interpretation is the "royal road to the unconscious." Brenner argues that technical precepts, these included, are not universal truths applicable to all analysands regardless of time and place; rather, technical strategies can be justified only in terms of the requirements of specific psychoanalytic situations, which subsume the cognitive style and interpretive orientation of a particular analyst. The first precept he appraises as follows: "A first dream may and should be used like any other analytic material: in a way that is appropriate to the circumstances of the analytic situation at the time. No single rule-of-thumb can suffice to cover all the various possibilities" (p. 342). As for the "royal road," here Brenner is equally pragmatic. Dreams are valuable grist for the analytic mill, to be sure, but they enjoy no privileged status. Certain analysts may be especially drawn to them in elucidating the analysand's conflicts, but other analysts, with different cognitive styles and interpretive orientations, may focus more profitably on other kinds of interpretable phenomena. In either case, analysis may proceed to a satisfactory conclusion:

Whether the one view and the practical consequences which appear to be associated with it has any substantial advantage over the others is not possible to decide at present. All that one can say at present with any degree of assurance is this: There is no convincing evidence that dream interpretation still offers the quickest and easiest road to knowledge of the hidden workings of the mind at the present time as it doubtless did 65 years ago [p. 345].

Brenner similarly demystifies some long-held assumptions regarding transference analysis. In the same paper, he judges anachronistic the traditional dictum that transference should be interpreted only when it constitutes a resistance. Rooted in Freud's initial belief that "the pervasive effect of a strongly positive transference" is central to the analytic treatment (p. 336), this dictum and its rationale are undercut by the theoretical reformulations undertaken by Freud conceptualized the therapeutic action of analysis in terms of overcoming resistances and observed that positive transference could as easily serve resistance as could the negative variety. This theoretical shift anticipated what we have learned in the decades following: *all* transference must be analyzed, as one simply cannot tell in advance whether a transference is in the service of defense.

As for the traditional belief that transference acting out necessarily impedes analysis, here again Brenner avoids categorical injunctions in favor of a more measured appreciation of the vicissitudes of different psychoanalytic situations:

In other words, acting out in the transference is sometimes readily analyzable, sometimes analyzable only slowly and with difficulty, and sometimes not at all, at least for the time being. It is not always especially accessible to analysis, as our precept would have it. It is not necessarily an impediment or danger to analysis which must be forestalled in some nonanalytic way [1969c, p. 31].

Finally, as for the dictum that every interpretation must be a transference interpretation if it is to be effective (p. 347), Brenner presents counterinstances demonstrating that this precept too yields to the requirements of specific transactions. Take, for example, the patient who comes to an analytic session upset because of the sudden death or illness of a close relative. The transferential aspects of his reaction are certainly important. But one is not thereby "justified in following the maxim to the extent of ignoring and failing to interpret to the patient other aspects of his reaction to the situation which are important to recognize and understand" (p. 348).

The prudent correctives are elaborated in Brenner's *Psychoanalytic Technique and Psychic Conflict* (1976). Here Brenner stresses that transference, understood as the valence of the past in the relationships of the present, is hardly unique to the analytic situation. On the contrary, it is ubiquitous in everyday life. It follows, then, that the distinguishing characteristic of the analytic relationship is not transference per se, but rather "its place in the relationship, i.e., the analyst's attitude toward the transference and the use he makes of it. It is the analytic attitude that is the hallmark of analysis, not the phenomenon subsumed under the heading of transference" (p. 112). Since it is the analytic attitude toward transference manifestations, not a preoccupation with transference analysis, that is constitutive of psychoanalysis, summary pronouncements about the latter's preeminence in analytic treatment are misleading. Rather, the requirements of specific analyses will determine the role of transference interpretation relative to other types. Consistent with his technical revisions (1969c), Brenner insists that "transference should be neither ignored nor focused on to the exclusion of all else; it should be neither excluded from analytic work nor dragged in by the heels" (1976, p. 128).

This attitude toward transference is central to the argument of the important 1979 paper, "Working Alliance, Therapeutic Alliance, and Transference." Here in the same questioning spirit in which he contested Stone's (1961) characterization of the analytic situation in 1966, Brenner confronts the widely accepted notion, first formulated by Zetzel (1965) and Ralph Greenson (1965), of a therapeutic or working alliance distinct from transference and exempt from interpretation. Examining the data invoked by Zetzel and Greenson in support of the concept's clinical usefulness, he concludes that the evidence does not justify a position of an extratransferential and uninterpretable dimension of the analytic relationship. He also questions whether the working alliance, however conceived, can be promoted by anything other than accurate and well-timed interpretations. For Brenner, the analyst's humanistic bearing toward the patient is neither constitutes an analytic relationship nor is sufficient to insure a successful analytic outcome. Implicit in the working alliance paper is the belief that the analyst's attitude toward the analysand, no less than that of the analysand toward the analyst, is a compromise formation. In a more recent publication, "Countertransference and Compromise Formation" (1985), Brenner expands on this formulation. Earlier (1979b), he asserted that all aspects of the analysand's relationship with the analyst, including the desire to cooperate, are interpretable. In 1985 he makes the same point with regard to the analyst, whose countertransferential attitude toward the analysand is invariably a compromise formation and consequently is understandable in terms of the components of conflict, affect states, defenses, self-punitive trends, drive derivatives, and the like.

The working alliance and countertransference papers are in a sense complementary. Jointly they offer a broad perspective on issues of technique. Adopting this perspective, we can no longer make easy correlations of specific affects or clinical syndromes with individual drive derivatives; for example, depression cannot be equated with problems in the oral phase. Similarly, particular therapeutic reactions are not easily associated with individual agencies within the psychic apparatus; negative therapeutic reactions cannot be equated with superego problems. In each case Brenner obliges us to look at both sides of the explanatory coin—at the issues of drive gratification and drive-related prohibitions that codetermine every symptom, behavior, and character trait. Like his theoretical contributions, his contributions to technique achieve their explanatory force through terminological clarification. In the paper on the "working alliance" (1979b), Brenner steers us away from a seductive terminological innovation simply by reminding us of the universality of transference. In the countertransference paper (1985), he offers new insights into the analyst's relation to the analysand by showing us the "explanatory reach of the concept of compromise formation" first used by Freud in the 1890s.

In his contributions to technique, as in all his work, Brenner is keenly aware of the interdependency of theory and practice. His illuminating commentaries on technical issues often have the serendipitous side effect of clarifying the theoretical status of the concept under review. For example, Brenner's cautionary remarks regarding transference analysis contribute to our understanding of the status of transference within analytic theory. Inn the chapter on defense analysis in *Psychoanalytic Technique and Psychic Conflict* (1976), his technical arguments against the dictum that defenses should invariably be analyzed before the instinctual derivatives they ward off add to our understanding of the concept of defense. In the course of arguing that drive, affect, defense, and the like should be interpreted as they appear in the patient's associations "and not according to some schematic formula" (p. 64), he observes that analysis cannot alleviate defensive operations, but can only alter the structure and adaptive adequacy of compromise formations: "Defenses are never abolished as such, not even the 'pathogenic' or 'infantile' ones" (p. 74). Likewise, his commentary on free association in relation to technique is theoretically enlightening as a critique of the suitability of this term to characterize what actually occurs in analysis:

> Free association is a bad term to apply to the psychoanalytic method. . . . It obscures the fact that an analytic patient is often asked to associate to a specific conscious stimulus. And second and more important, it obscures the fact that Freud's great discovery, the discovery that became the very cornerstone of psychoanalytic technique, was that associations are never free.

They are, on the contrary, always caused by some psychic stimuli or other [p. 190].

Similarly, Brenner's paper on the "working alliance" is not only a storehouse of information on the relative dosages of frustration and gratification that should typify the analytic situation, but a persuasive demonstration of the fact that such issues cannot be dissociated from understanding of the theoretical status of transference. Brenner's most recent contribution to technique, soon to be published in *The Psychoanalytic Quarterly*, also enriches theory. This reassessment of working through not only examines the clinical development we customarily associate with this concept but also questions whether the term is clinically useful as a characterization of such development.

The five foregoing synopses hardly constitute a comprehensive presentation of Brenner's contributions to psychoanalysis. At best they provide a helpful overview of certain broad areas to which he has given continuing attention over the course of his analytic career. Although synopses cannot capture the subtlety of Brenner's expositions, their usefulness exceeds the summary of "content" they provide. Taken together, they highlight the interrelationships between Brenner's contributions to the various topics and convey a clear sense of the unity of his psychoanalytic outlook. By this I mean that all of Brenner's contributions to theory and practice are grounded on a consistent and clear-sighted estimation of what psychoanalysis *is* and what it is that psychoanalysts *do*. His conception of analysis as a science of mental conflict based on data obtained in the analytic situation informs all his contributions to theory. Similarly, his belief in the interpretability of the myriad of symptomatic, behavioral, and characterological compromise formations through which psychic conflict is expressed informs all his contributions to the technique of psychoanalysis. His specific reappraisals of affect, defense, instinct theory, structural theory, and principles of technique follow from these essential principles of his psychoanalytic *Weltanschaung*.

In recent years Brenner has done much to keep the dialogue among analysts of different theoretical persuasions on track by explicating these topics in terms of the basic principles of the psychoanalytic view of mental life. Whether we consider his questioning of a technical assumption (e.g., the primacy of dream interpretation in analysis), his critique of recent terminological innovations (e.g., therapeutic alliance), or his reaffirmation and amplification of a basic theoretical precept (e.g., the role of compromise formation), it is these superordinate principles that are both the points of departure and the conceptual testing ground for his proposals.

Through his emphasis on the principles that guide theory and practice, Brenner has emerged as one of the outstanding teachers of his generation, a teacher whose pedagogical message transcends the specific content of his books and papers. One may say that Brenner is an analyst whose deep commitment to Freudian principles has sharpened his probing reevaluations of the concepts and explanatory perspectives that Freud himself developed. And this is perhaps Brenner's greatest contribution as a theorist and as a teacher—his work demonstrates that an analysis can retain both the vitality and the innovativeness that will take it beyond Freud's legacy only by adhering to the principles of mental functioning fundamental to Freud's science of the mind.

REFERENCES

Arlow, J. A. & Brenner, C. (1964), *Psychoanalytic Concepts and the Structural Theory.* New York: International Universities Press.

_____ _____ (1966), The psychoanalytic situation. In: *Psychoanalysis in the Americas,* ed. R. E. Litman. New York: International Universities Press, pp. 23–43.

Brenner, C. (1953), An addendum to Freud's theory of anxiety. *Internat. J. Psycho-Anal., 34*:18–24.

_____ (1955), *An Elementary Textbook of Psychoanalysis,* 2nd ed. New York: International Universities Press, 1973.

_____ (1957), The nature and development of the concept of repression in Freud's writings. *The Psychoanalytic Study of the Child, 12*:19–46. New York: International Universities Press.

_____ (1959), The masochistic character: Genesis and treatment. *J. Amer. Psychoanal. Assn., 7*:197–226.

_____ (1967), The mechanisms of repression. In: *Psychoanalysis—A General Psychology: Essays in Honor of Heinz Hartmann,* ed. R. M. Lowenstein, D. Newman, D. Schur, & D. Solnit. New York: International Universities Press, pp. 390–399.

_____ (1969a), Discussion of Gardner: Organismic equilibration and the energy-structure. Duality in psychoanalytic theory: An attempt at theoretical refinement. *J. Amer. Psychoanal. Assn., 17*:41–53.

_____ (1969b), Dreams in clinical psychoanalytic practice. *J. Nerv. Men. Dis., 149*:122–132.

_____ (1969c), Some comments on technical precepts in psychoanalysis. *J. Amer. Psychoanal. Assn., 17*:333–352.

_____ (1970), Psychoanalysis: Philosophy or science. In: *Psychoanalysis and Philosophy,* ed. C. Hanly & M. Lazerowitz. New York: International Universities Press, pp. 35–45.

_____ (1971a), Some problems in the psychoanalytic theory of the instinctual drives. In: *Currents in Psychoanalysis,* ed. M. Marcos. New York: International Universities Press, pp. 216–230.

_____ (1971b), The psychoanalytic concept of aggression. *Internat. J. Psycho-Anal.,* 52(2):137–144.

_____ (1974a), Depression, anxiety, and affect theory. *Internat. J. Psycho-Anal.,* 55:25–32.

_____ (1974b), On the nature and development of affect: A unified theory. *Psychoanal. Quart.,* 43:532–556.

_____ (1975), Affects and psychic conflict. *Psychoanal. Quart.,* 44:5–28.

_____ (1976), *Psychoanalytic Technique and Psychic Conflict.* New York: International Universities Press.

_____ (1979a), Depressive affect, anxiety, and psychic conflict in the phallic-oedipal phase. *Psychoanal. Quart.,* 48:177–197.

_____ (1979b), Working alliance, therapeutic alliance, and transference. *J. Amer. Psychoanal. Assn.,* 27:137–158.

_____ (1980), Metapsychology and psychoanalytic theory. *Psychoanal. Quart.,* 49:189–214.

_____ (1981), Defense and defense mechanisms. *Psychoannal. Quart.,* 50:557–569.

_____ (1982a), *The Mind in Conflict.* New York: International Universities Press.

_____ (1982b), The concept of the superego: A reformulation. *Psychoanal. Quart.,* 51:501–525.

_____ (1985), Countertransference as compromise formation. *Psychoanal. Quart.,* 54:155–163.

_____ (in press), On working through. *Psychoanal. Quart.*

Freud, S. (1887–1902), *The Origins of Psycho-Analysis. Letters to Wilhelm Fliess, Drafts and Notes: 1887–1902,* ed. M. Bonaparte, A. Freud, & E. Kris. New York: Basic Books, 1954.

_____ (1900), The interpretation of dreams. *Standard Edition,* 4 & 5. London: Hogarth Press, 1953.

_____ (1915a), The unconscious. *Standard Edition,* 14:161–215. London: Hogarth Press, 1957.

_____ (1915b), A metapsychological supplement to the theory of dreams. *Standard Edition,* 14:222–235. London: Hogarth Press, 1957.

_____ (1926), Inhibitions, symptoms and anxiety, *Standard Edition,* 29:87–172. London: Hogarth Press, 1959.

Greenson, R. R. (1965), The working alliance and the transference neurosis. *Psychoanal. Quart.,* 34:155–181.

Hartmann, H. (1939), *Ego Psychology and the Problem of Adaptation.* New York: International Universities Press, 1958.

Klein, G. S. (1976), *Psychoanalytic Theory: An Exploration of Essentials.* New York: International Universities Press.

Kohut, H. (1959), Introspection, empathy, and psychoanalysis. *J. Amer. Psychoanal. Assn.,* 7:459–483.

Ornstein, P. (1978), *The Search for the Self, Selected Writings of Heinz Kohut, 1959–1978, Vol. 1.* New York: International Universities Press.

Rapaport, D., & Gill, M. M. (1959), The point of view and assumptions of metapsychology. *Internat. J. Psycho-Anal.,* 40:153–162.

Schafer, R. (1976), *A New Language for Psychoanalysis.* New Haven: Yale University Press.

Stone, L. (1961), *The Psychoanalytic Situation: An Examination of its Development and Essential Nature.* New York: International Universities Press.

Waelder, R. (1962), Psychoanalysis, scientific method and philosophy. *J. Amer. Psychoanal. Assn.,* 10:617–637.

Zetzel, E. R. (1965), The theory of therapy in relation to a developmental model of the psychic apparatus. *Internat. J. Psycho-Anal.,* 46:39–52.

CARL W. BRAUN

The Neurological Career of Charles Brenner

NEUROLOGICAL INVESTIGATION

From 1938 to 1949 Charles Brenner devoted a major part of his professional life to neurology and neurological investigations. He collaborated and directed research with individuals who made major contributions to neurology, neurosurgery, and neurophysiology in the United States from 1940 to 1970. Their names are familiar to the current generation of neurologists: D. M. Rioch, H. Houston Merritt, Knox Finley, Derek Denny-Brown, Arnold Friedman, E. P. Spitz, Raymond Adams, Leo Davidoff, and Sidney Carter. That the association and attendant accomplishments occurred while Charles Brenner was developing the very tools and skills that would allow him to achieve his subsequent status as a psychiatrist would be unusual in any era. That it took place in the 1940s, when antipathy for psychiatry among neurologists was prevalent, makes the association all the more unique.

As a Harvard undergraduate Brenner majored in chemistry rather than biochemistry, a choice that was to be fortuitous in his future collaborations. In the summer of 1931, before entering medical school, he decided on a career in psychoanalysis and began a course of independent reading that would prepare him for that discipline. It is noteworthy that he used the three "free afternoons" a week allotted to medical students to study not psychoanalysis but neurophysiology. A recently arrived assistant professor, D. M. Rioch, allowed Brenner to work in his laboratory on the neurotoxicity of dichloro-difluoro-methane (Freon), a newly introduced refrigerant. This was to be Brenner's first published work.[1] Rioch subse-

Footnote numbers refer to Publication List of Dr. Brenner beginning on page 32.

quently supervised Brenner's honors thesis dealing with the anatomical connections of the corpus striatum and rhinencephalon. This work, published in 1938,[3] employed techniques of ablation and electrical stimulation in a variety of experimental animals to expand on previous studies by Bard and Rioch. It defined interactions of the corpus striatum with other, as yet undefined, structures. (It would be another 20 years before investigators, using neurochemical techniques, would delineate the Dopa-mediated connections of the substantia nigra with the corpus striatum and with it the biochemical basis for Parkinson's disease). This study also showed little or no role for the corpus striatum in behavior and refocused attention on the rhinencephalon.

In 1935, following graduation from Harvard Medical School, Brenner started a two-year internship at the Peter Brent Brigham Hospital, including a four-month rotation at a state psychiatric facility. From this period, further papers, one in psychiatry,[4] and two in general medicine[2,5] originated. In 1937 he became a psychiatry resident at the Boston Psychopathic Hospital (later Massachusetts Mental Health). The following year he began a neurology residency at the Boston City Hospital under Tracy Putnam. Putnam, the co-discoverer with Merritt of Dilantin, was to be named in 1940 Director of Neurological Institute of New York.

At Boston City Hospital, Brenner had a close association with two men who were to have a significant influence on American neurology: Derek Denny-Brown and H. Houston Merritt. It is remarkable that Charles Brenner was able simultaneously to maintain an amiable and productive relationship with these two individuals so different in background, temperament, and approach. Denny-Brown, a visiting investigator from the United Kingdom, was asked to remain in the United States to conduct neurological investigations for the Office of Scientific Research and Development. (The other branch of the OSRD was to become better known through the Manhattan Project.)

Concluding his neurology residency in 1939, Brenner was invited to join the staff of Boston City Hospital as an investigator and clinician. His collaborations with Denny-Brown were focused on peripheral nerve injury secondary to pressure, [11,12,16,17] and cold injury.[22] These investigations were characterized by a vigorous application of experimental techniques with detailed histological documentation. Thirty years later these papers continue to be cited in works dealing with peripheral nerve injury.

During this time Brenner was the senior author, with Arnold Friedman, Houston Merritt, and Denny-Brown, of a paper dealing with post-traumatic headaches.[15] At a time when posttraumatic headache was considered an expression of "compensation neurosis," Brenner et al. showed that posttraumatic headaches often persisted long after resumption of work and legal settlement. While stressing the importance of previous psychiatric history, the paper anticipated by twenty years the thesis that posttraumatic headaches had a significant organic component.

In the seventeen papers that Charles Brenner wrote between 1939 and 1945, his scope of interest was wide. With Arnold Friedman, who would become one of the country's authorities on headache, Brenner was to write seven papers [14,18,19,20,23,24,27] in addition to the earlier mentioned paper on posttraumatic headaches. A study carried out in 1941 with Knox Finley is of particular interest to neurologists for documenting histologic damage to the brain by insulin and metrazol.[7] It showed the importance of sequential bouts of injury. The cautionary stance towards the use of prolonged insulin coma as a form of therapy for psychosis was timely. In 1943 a short but important paper showed that sulfanilimide was the safest topical antibiotic for brain surgery, an important contribution for military surgery at the time.[10]

The most important medical relationship Brenner established was with H. Houston Merritt. Merritt's research in cerebrospinal fluid and syphilis had already established his neurological credentials, and in these areas Brenner collaborated for his third neurological paper in 1939 dealing with a comparison of the Davies-Hinton and Wassermann reactions in cerebral spinal fluid.[6] Merritt and Brenner were to write ten more papers together dealing with a variety of subjects including treatment with dilantin,[8] the role of the pneumoencephalogram in the diagnosis of brain tumor,[13] physiology of headaches,[20] reviews of cerebrospinal fluid,[25] anticonvulsants,[26] epilepsy,[28] and psychiatric symptoms in organic brain disease.[27]

In this collection one paper stands out for its anticipation by thirty years of important research in neurochemistry. Brenner, as senior author with Merritt, described the effects of choline derivatives on the electrical activity of the cerebral cortex.[9] Brenner's conclusions that acetylcholine has an effect on nerve cells and synapses, that it plays a role in epilepsy, and that acetylcholine esterase modulates acetylcholine were to be fully supported by subsequent investigators.

During World War II Brenner not only was an active investigator but also served as chief of the epilepsy clinic at the Boston City Hospital. With Denny-Brown he designed a syllabus for neurology residents that helped to train a generation of neurologists.

In 1945 Derek Denny-Brown was named chief of neurology at Boston City Hospital, and Houston Merritt was offered and accepted the directorship of a newly established neuropsychiatric unit at Montefiore Hospital in New York City. He assembled a group of physicians who were to have a lasting influence on New York neurology: Arnold Friedman would later establish one of the first centers for the study and treatment of head-ache; Sidney Carter became one of the founders of child neurology in the United States; Leo Davidoff was the newly named chief of neurosurgery; Joseph Ransohoff, a medical student and subsequently a resident in neurosurgery, was to go on to become chief of neurosurgery of New York University Hospital. Merritt asked Brenner to take charge of the proposed psychiatric division.

What had promised to be an outstanding new institute of neuropsychiatry floundered on the financial rocks encountered by so many hospitals after World War II. In 1949 Merritt succeeded Tracy Putnam at Neurological Institute. The Boston group went with Merritt, and Brenner was asked to join the move. But at this juncture Brenner prepared to devote himself soley to psychoanalysis.

The year 1949 marked the end of a decade of productive collaboration. There never was any question that Brenner would eventually devote his full energies to psychiatry. Between 1941 and 1945 he was the only psychiatrist at Boston City Hospital, and he continued to study and care for psychiatric patients while working with a group of neurologists who had little sympathy for psychoanalysis. That he was eagerly accepted by this group is testimony to the quality of his investigative skills and his ability to work easily with individuals of strikingly different temperaments. While the discipline of neurology benefited greatly from Charles Brenner's contributions, it also contributed to the development of his psychiatric career. From his earliest associations, Brenner recognized the primacy of mastering investigative technique. Only with confidence in how to approach a problem could he trust the data produced by that approach. Neurology was a stern taskmaster, for it insisted on a close methodical eliciting of history and physical findings followed by sequential analysis of localization, physiological interaction, and finally pathological possibilities. Neurology rewarded adherence to this approach with the satisfaction of reaching a scientific solution to a problem. It was a self-centered specialty with traditional contempt for less rigorous disciplines.

It must have puzzled many of his neurological colleagues that Brenner left an established academic career in neurology to pursue what they felt was barely a science. To his credit, Brenner saw in psychoanalysis a scientific discipline that required the same attention to approach and intellectual honesty that he had brought to neurology.

PUBLICATIONS OF CHARLES BRENNER, M.D.

1. Note on the action of dichloro-difluoro-methane on the nervous system of the cat. *J. Exper. Pharmacol. & Therapeut.*, 59:176–181, 1937.

2. Endemic amebic dysentery in New England. *New Eng. J. Med.,* 217:859–860, 1937.
3. Experiments on the corpus striatum and rhinencephalon (with D. M. Rioch). *J. Comp. Neurol.,* 491–507, 1938.
4. On the genesis of a case of paranoid dimentia precox. *J. Nerv. & Ment. Dis.,* 90:483–488, 1939.
5. Erythropoiesis in bleeding peptic ulcer (with R. H. Lyons). *Amer. J. Med. Sci.,* 198:492–501, 1939.
6. A comparison of the Davies-Hinton and Wassermann reactions in the cerebrospinal fluid (with H. H. Merritt). *New England J. Med.,* 221:891–894, 1939.
7. Histologic evidence of damage to the brain in monkeys treated with insulin and metrazol (with K. H. Finley). *Arch. Neurol. & Psychiat.,* 45:403–438, 1941.
8. Treatment of patients with epilepsy with sodium diphenyl hydantoinate, etc. (with H. H. Merritt). *J. Nerv. & Ment. Dis.,* 96:245–250, 1942.
9. The effect of certain choline derivatives on the electrical activity of the cerebral cortex (with H. H. Merritt). *Arch. Neurol. & Psychiat.,* 48:382–395, 1942.
10. The effect of certain sulfonamides on the electrical activity of the cerebral cortex (with S. Cohen). *J. Amer. Med. Assn.,* 123:948–950, 1943.
11. Paralysis of nerve induced by direct pressure and by tourniquet (with D. E. Denny-Brown). *Arch. Neurol. & Psychiat.,* 51:1–26, 1944.
12. Injuries to peripheral nerves. *War Med.,* 5:21–35, 1944.
13. Normal air encephalograms in patients with convulsive seizures and tumors of the brain (with H. H. Merritt). *New Engl. J. Med.,* 230:224–225, 1944.
14. Post-traumatic and histamine headache (with A. P. Friedman). *Arch. Neurol. & Psychiat.,* 52:126–130, 1944.
15. Post-traumatic headache (with A. P. Friedman, H. H. Merritt, and D. E. Denny-Brown). *J. Neurosurg.,* 1:379–392, 1944.
16. The effect of percussion on nerve (with D. E. Denny-Brown). *J. Neurol., Neurosurg., & Psychiat.,* 7:76–95, 1944.
17. Lesion in peripheral nerve resulting from compression by spring clip (with D. E. Denny-Brown). *Arch. Neurol. & Psychiat.,* 52:1–19, 1944.
18. Post-traumatic vertigo and dizziness (with A. P. Friedman and D. E. Denny-Brown). *J. Neurosurg.,* 1:36–46, 1945.
19. Principles in the treatment of chronic headache (with A. P. Friedman), *N. Y. State J. Med.,* 45:1969–1971, 1945.

20. Experimental evidence of the physiologic mechanism of certain types of headache (with A. P. Freidman and H. H. Merritt). *Arch. Neurol. & Psychiat.,* 54:385–388, 1945.

21. Experimental evidence of the physiologic mechanism of certain types of headache (with A. 22. A new absorbable material for use in neurological and general surgery (with E. B. Spitz et al.), *Science,* 102:621–622, 1945.

22. Pathology of injury to nerve induced by cold (with D. E. Denny-Brown et al.). *J. Neuropath. & Exp. Neurol.,* 4:305–323, 1945.

23. Management of patients with chronic headache (with A. P. Friedman and H. H. Merritt). *J. Amer. Med. Assn.,* 132:498–501, 1946.

24. Psychosomatic treatment of chronic headaches (with A. P. Friedman). *Bull. Los Angeles Neurol. Soc.,* 11:68–71, 1946.

25. Clinical examination of the cerebrospinal fluid (with H. H. Merritt). *Wisconsin Med. J.,* March:1–19, 1946.

26. Studies in new anticonvulsants (with H. H. Merritt). *Bull. New York Acad. Med.,* 23:292–301, 1947.

27. Psychiatric syndrome in patients with organic brain disease (with A. P. Friedman and H. H. Merritt). *Amer. J. Psychiat.,* 103:733–737, 1947.

28. Epilepsy (with H. H. Merritt). In: *Progress in Neurology and Psychiatry.* New York: Grune & Stratton, 1947.

29. Treatment of the migraine attack (with A. P. Friedman). *Am. Practitioner,* 2:467–470, 1948.

30. A new instrument for the performance of biofrontal lobotomy (with L. M. Davidoff). *Ass. Res. Nerv. & Ment. Dis.,* 27:638–641, 1948.

31. Psychologic factors in the etiology and treatment of chronic headache (with A. P. Friedman and S. Carter). *Psychosomat. Med.,* 11:43–45, 1949.

32. Mental reactions in patients with neurological disease (with D. Beres). *Psychoanal. Quart.,* 19:170–191, 1950.

33. Clinical examination of the cerebrospinal fluid. In: *Oxford System of Medicine,* 1950.

34. Psychological mechanisms in chronic headache (with A. P. Friedman). *Assn. Res. Nerve & Ment. Dis.,* 29:605–608, 1950.

35. A case of childhood hallucinosis. *The Psychoanalytic Study of the Child,* 6:235–243, 1951.

36. Defenses in symptom formation — a panel report: Problems of symptom formation. *Bull Amer. Psychoanal. Assn.,* 8:142–149, 1952.

36. An addendum to Freud's theory of anxiety. *Internat. J. Psycho-Anal.,* 34:18–24, 1953.

37. Psychoanalytic studies in psychiatry. *Annual Survey of Psychoanalysis,* 2:315–348, 1954.
38. *An elementary textbook of psychoanalysis.* New York: International Universities Press, 1955.
39. Re-evaluation of the libido theory (report of panel discussion). *J. Amer. Psychoanal. Assn.,* 4:162–169, 1956.
40. A reformulation of the Psychoanalytic theory of parapraxes. *Bull. Phila. Assn. Psychoanal.,* 5:110–113, 1955.
41. Facts, coincidence, and the psi hypothesis. *Internat. J. Psychoanal.,* 38:51–54, 1957.
42. The nature and development of the concept of repression in Freud's writings. *The Psychoanalytic Study of the Child,* 12:19–46, 1957.
43. Reformulation of the theory of anxiety. In: *A General Selection From The Works Of Sigmund Freud,* ed. J. Rickman. Garden City, NY: Doubleday, 1957.
44. Articles on psychoanalysis, psychology and psychiatry. *World Book Encyclopedia.* Chicago: Field Educational Enterprises, 1958, 1960.
45. The masochistic character: genesis and treatment. *J. Amer. Psychoanal. Assn.,* 7:197–226, 1959.
46. Various book reviews, appearing in the *Psychoanal. Quart.* e.g., review of Freud's Concept of repression and defense, in 31:562–563, 1962.
47. In memoriam Albert A. Rosner, *Psychoanal. Quart.,* 31:382–384, 1962.
48. Psychoanalytic concepts and the structural theory (with J. A. Arlow). New York: International Universities Press, 1964.
49. The psychoanalytic situation (with J. A. Arlow). In: *Psychoanalysis In The Americas,* ed. R. E. Litman. New York. International Universities Press, 1966, pp. 390–399.
50. In memoriam Charles Davison. *Psychoanal. Quart.,* 35:275–276, 1966.
51. The mechanism of repression. *Psychoanalysis—A General Psychology,* ed. R. M. Loewenstein. International Universities Press, New York: pp. 390–399, 1966.
52. Psychoanalysis: classical theory. *International Encyclopedia of the Social Sciences.* New York: Macmillan, 1968.
53. Archaic features of ego functioning. *Internat. J. Psycho-Anal.,* 49:426–430, 1968.
54. Psychoanalysis and science. *J. Amer. Psychoanalyt. Assn.,* 16:675–696, 1968.
55. The psychopathology of the psychoses: a proposed revision (with J. A. Arlow). *Internat. J. Psycho-Anal.,* 50:5–14, 1969.

56. Metapsychology and neurophysiology (discussion of paper by Gardner). *J. Amer. Psychoanal. Assn.*, 17:41–53, 1969.
57. Some comments on technical precepts in psychoanalysis. *J. Amer. Psychoanal. Assn.*, 17:333–352, 1969.
58. Dreams in clinical psychoanalytic practise. *J. Nerv. & Ment. Dis.*, 149:122–132, 1969.
59. Discussion of #55 at the Rome Congress of the Int. Psychoanalyt. Assn. (with J. A. Arlow). *Internat. J. Psychoanal.*, 51:159–166, 1970.
60. Psychoanalysis: Philosophy or science? In: *Psychoanalysis and Philosophy*, ed. C. Hanly & M. Lazerowitz. (pp. 35–45) New York: International Universities Press, 1970.
61. The psychoanalytic concept of aggression. *Internat. J. Psychoanal.*, 52:137–144, 1971.
62. Some problems in the psychoanalytic theory of the instinctual drives. chapter 15, in: *Currents in Psychoanalysis, ed. I. M. Marcus, pp. 216–230. New York. International Universities Press, 1971.*
63. *An Elementary Textbook Of Psychoanalysis.* 2nd ed. New York: International Universities Press, 1973.
64. Some observations on depression, on nosology, on affects, and on mourning. *J. Geriat. Psych.*, 7:6–20, 1974.
65. Depression, anxiety and affect theory. *Internat. J. Psychoanal.*, 55:25–32, 1974.
66. On the nature and development of affects: a unified theory. *Psychoanal. Quart.*, 43:532–556, 1974.
67. Affects and psychic conflict. *Psychoanal. Quart.*, 44:5–28, 1975.
68. Encyclopedia articles on repression, structural theory, aggression, role of id. in: *International Encyclopedia of Neurology, Psychiatry Psychoanalysis and Psychology.*
69. Depression, anxiety & affect theory: a reply to the discussion by Dr. Paula Heimann. *International J. Psycho-Anal.*, 56:229, 1975.
70. Alterations in defenses during psychoanalysis. In: No. 6 of the *Monograph Series of the Ernst Kris Study Group of the N.Y. Psychoanalytic Institute.* New York: International Universities Press, 1975.
71. *Psychoanalytic Technique and Psychic Conflict.* New York: International Universities Press, 1976.
72. Depressive anxiety affect, and psychic conflict in the phallic-oedipal phase. *Psychoanal. Quart.*, 48:177–197, 1979.
73. The components of psychic conflict and its consequences in mental life. *Psychoanal. Quart.*, 48:547–567, 1979.
74. Working alliance, therapeutic alliance, and transference. *J. Amer. Psychoanal. Assn.*, supplement to 27:137–157, 1979.

75. Metapsychology and psychoanalytic theory. *Psychoanal. Quart.*, 49:189–214, 1980.
76. *A Psychoanalytic Theory of Affects. Emotion: Theory, Research and Experience. vol. 1: Theories of Emotion.* NY: Academic Press, 1980.
77. Jacob A. Arlow. An appreciation. *Psychoanal. Quart.*, 50:475–478, 1981.
78. Defense and defense mechanisms. *Psychoanal. Quart.*, 50:557–569, 19
79. The concept of the superego: as reformulation. *Psychoanalyt. Quart.*, 51:501–525, 1982.
80. *The Mind in Conflict.* New York: International Universities Press, 1982.

Reflections

No one works without hope of reward, yet some rewards come un-hoped for because so unexpected. It never occurred to me that some day a group of colleagues, both friends and former students, would each con-tribute to a book of papers on psychoanalysis dedicated to me. Because it comes as a complete surprise, it is all the more thrilling. Because the many contributions are at such a high level scientifically and profession-ally, it is all the more gratifying. I treasure the book itself, I treasure the thought and effort that went into it, and I treasure the affection and es-teem of those who have contributed to it.

I am specially grateful to Drs. Arnold D. Richards and Martin S. Willick, the book's editors. To conceive such a book, to plan it, and to carry the plan to completion require a degree of devotion and an amount of hard work which go beyond what all but a very few are capable of. I thank them both most warmly.

They have gone further than that, however. As editors, they have of-fered me the opportunity to write for this volume something beyond an expression of my heartfelt pleasure and gratitude at having it dedicated to me. They have very kindly suggested that I might wish to put down some thoughts about the application of the views I have proposed during the past several years concerning the components of psychic conflict and its consequences for psychic development and functioning.

As I see it the most important thing to keep in mind is this. Everything in psychic life with which one has to deal as an analyst is a compromise for-mation. It is always a combination of the gratification of a drive derivative (an instinctual wish originating in chilhood), of unpleasure in the form of anxiety and depressive affect associated with the drive derivative, of de-fenses whose function is to minimize that unpleasure, and of associated

39

superego functioning (guilt, self-punishment, remorse, atonement, etc.). No thought, no action, no plan, no fantasy, dream or symptom is ever simply one or another of those. It is always multiply determined by all of them.

When presented in this way as a theoretical generalization, this is a statement with which I would expect most analysts to agree. More than that, I would expect them to greet it as, by now, so familiar as not to require special emphasis. After all, one of Freud's early analytic discoveries was that every psychoneurotic symptom is just such a compromise formation among wish fulfillment, defense, and self-punishment. "No one," I would expect most analysts to say, "needs to be reminded at this late date of the principle of multiple function or multiple determination in mental life." Yet my experience is that we all do need to be reminded of it, and repeatedly. What is accepted as theory is, as a rule, neglected in practice.

I say this on the basis of my experience as teacher, as consultant and supervisor, and as auditor and participant in psychoanalytic discussions. I know that I myself had to make a very conscious decision years ago to listen to whatever a patient said as a compromise formation. It required continuing effort to adhere to that decision until it eventually became the natural and easy, rather than the difficult and unnatural, thing to do. As analysts we are constantly concerned with understanding the meaning of analytic material, that is, with the meaning of what a patient says and does. In recent years that concern has customarily taken the form of our trying to decide whether we are confronted by a defense, or by a wish fulfillment, or by some form of self-directed aggression due to superego functioning. It has not been usual in everyday clinical work to take into account that id, ego, and superego functioning are always involved in every piece of analytic material. To learn to think that way as one works is like learning to think in a foreign language, as contrasted with being able to translate into it while thinking only in one's native tongue. It takes time and conscious effort to learn, but in the end the time and effort spent are amply repaid. One no longer listens to a patient with the purpose of answering the question, Is this wish fulfillment, defense, or superego? One knows in advance that the answer is yes to all three in every case. One learns to ask instead, What wishes of childhood origin are being gratified here? What unpleasure (anxiety and depressive affect) are they arousing? What is the defensive aspect of what I'm hearing and observing? What is its superego aspect? When one is fairly sure one has reliable answers to these questions, one is in the best position to answer the essential technical questions, What should I interpret to the patient? or, more generally, What intervention should I make? and When is the best time to make it?

In brief, then, the most important single thing to keep in mind is that all analytic material is a compromise formation and must be listened to and thought of as such. The better one understands the various determinants of any compromise formation, the better able one is to analyze the patient who has produced it.

An important corollary is this: To say everything is a compromise formation, means *everything*. Not just symptoms, not just neurotic character traits, not just the slips and errors of daily life, but everything, the normal as well as the pathological. Just as nothing is ever only defense or only wish fulfillment, so nothing is ever only "realistic" as opposed to "neurotic." One of the principal contributions of psychoanalysis to human psychology is precisely this. The various components of conflict over wishes of childhood origin play as important a part in normal psychic functioning as they do in pathological psychic functioning.

There is no doubt about the great practical importance of the difference between a normal compromise formation and a pathological one. Both, however—the normal as well as the pathological—are compromise formations in which drive derivatives of childhood origin, anxiety and depressive effect, defense, and superego functioning play determinative roles. It is not a greater concern for reality which distinguishes the normal from the pathological. Normal religious piety is no more realistic than are delusions of persecution. Defenses to mitigate anxiety and depressive affect are no more mature, no less primitive, in normal than in neurotic compromise.

What distinguishes a normal from a pathological compromise formation is far too subtle, far too complex to be recognized by any single, simple criterion. A compromise formation can be classified as normal or pathological only by taking into account all the components of the conflict which underlies it. If a compromise formation permits an adequate amount of drive gratification, without too much unpleasure in the form of anxiety and depressive affect, without too great interference with functional capacity as a result of defense, without too much in the way of self-destructive and self-punitive tendencies due to superego functioning, and without too much disturbance in a person's relations with his environment, then and only then does the compromise formation deserve to be classified as normal. Should it fail to meet any of these criteria, it must be classified as pathological.

In one's analytic work one should not analyze, that is, try to understand the conflictual determinants of only what is pathological in a patient's psychic life. One can often learn much of great value from analyzing what is normal, whether the normal one analyzes is a bit of behavior, a character trait, a sexual preference, or the choice of vocation. This is especially worthwhile to keep in mind in connection with manifestations of transfer-ence. It is beside the point whether a patient's fantasy about the analyst's life or behavior is accurate or not or even whether it is based in some part on reliable information. There is no "real relationship" between patient and analyst which is dynamically different from the "transference rela-tionship." The important distinction is not between "reality" and "transfer-ence." The distinction to be made is between what is analyzable and what is not. Every feature of a patient's psychic functioning is a compromise for-mation among the components of conflict of childhood origin. This is as true of the patient's relationship with the analyst as it is of every other fea-ture of his psychic functioning. Whatever can be analyzed is analytically valuable. What can be analyzed only imperfectly or unsatisfactorily is necessarily less valuable, at least for the time being.

The importance of analyzing transference has been recognized since the very early days of psychoanalysis. The need to analyze defense is also familiar to every analyst, even though the recognition of that need came two or three decades later than was the case with transference. Still more recent is the realization of the significance of superego analysis to suc-cessful analytic treatment. In fact, very little has been written on the sub-ject, compared with what is to be found on transference and defense analysis. I believe that a better understanding of the role of conflict in su-perego formation and functioning will improve our ability to analyze suc-cessfully those aspects of psychic functioning which fall under the head-ing of the superego.

What has not been fully appreciated till now is that the superego is itself a group of compromise formations which have in common their concern with morality: with what is right and good as opposed to wrong and bad, with guilt, with punishment, with atonement, and with forgiveness. These compromise formations derive in the main from conflicts of the oedipal period. As such, they embody the oedipal child's concept of morality: good/right—what will please/mollify one's parents, and the reverse for bad/wrong. It follows that the overriding consideration in superego func-tioning is to win the love and approval of one's parents as one sees one's parents when one is 2½–6 years old.

All of this has two corollaries which are particularly important to keep in mind in doing clinical work. One is that superego pathology is not a matter of lacunae or defects. Everyone, whether saint or sinner, has a functioning superego. One must judge superego pathology or normality as one does that of any compromise formation. The other is that libidinal as well as aggressive wishes play a role in superego formation and func-tioning. Thus, masochism is a normal part of the superego.

What I have written so far has had to do principally with the ubiquity and importance of compromise formation in psychic life. I turn now to the role of one of the components of the conflicts underlying compromise formations, namely, to the role of depressive affect in psychic conflict.

Defense and conflict arise in childhood whenever the gratification of a drive derivative arouses unpleasure. In some cases, the unpleasure in some variety of unhappiness or misery over life as it is. The child feels itself to be deserted and alone, or unloved, or castrated. In other cases, the unpleasure concerns what the child believes is about to happen: that it is in danger of being deserted, unloved, or castrated. The second of these two forms of unpleasure, anxiety, needs no special discussion here. Its role in conflict and compromise formation is well known to all. The first, which I shall discuss, is depressive affect. Its role in conflict and compromise formations is an important part of the views on those subjects I have proposed during the past several years.

Depressive affect plays a role in triggering every major conflict in psychic life. In every instance of conflict and compromise formation one must recognize the role of depressive affect if one is to understand one's patient as fully as possible. In some instances, moreover, the role of depressive affect is dominant. If one fails to take account of it, one cannot adequately understand one's patient's conflicts and the compromise formations resulting from them.

One such instance is afforded by patients in whose compromise formations depressive affect plays a major role in the sense that it is a significant or major part of their symptomatology. Such instances are often called cases of depressive illness or, for short, of depression. The psychodynamics found in these patients is analogous to the psychodynamics which characterize patients in whose symptomatology anxiety plays a prominent role. In both unpleasure persists to a major degree despite whatever defensive efforts are made to mitigate it. In the one case, the unpleasure which is part of the patient's compromise formation (neurotic syndrome) is anxiety; in the other, it is depressive affect. But the reason is the same in both: persistence of unpleasure despite defense. When depressive affect is part of a patient's symptomatology, it will invariably prove to be a persistence into adult life of childhood misery associated with childhood drive derivatives. As a child, the patient felt deserted, unloved, or castrated, or any combination of the three, because of its drive derivatives (instinctual wishes) and this conviction has persisted, however disguised and distorted, into adult life. Depressive affect in adult life is not always a consequence of trauma in the earliest, oral phase of psychosexual development; it is not necessarily a consequence of real or fantasied object loss; identification does not invariably play a crucial role in its genesis; and its relationship to aggression is far from the simple one implied by the formula that depression is the result of aggression turned against oneself. The belief that depressive affect in adult life is necessarily oral, that it is always caused by object loss, and that it results from aggression turned against oneself as a result of identification with an ambivalently loved object is erroneous. It is an error ingrained in the literature of psychoanalysis and psychopathology, but it is an error nonetheless. The role of depressive affect in psychic life is analogous to that of anxiety. Both are universally present forms of unpleasure which act as triggers for defense and conflict when they are intimately associated with a childhood drive derivative, something which invariably happens at times in the course of everyone's development. Mental illnesses in which conscious depressive affect plays a major role can be very severe, even fatal. Many are certainly inaccessible to analysis. But the same is true of mental illnesses in which anxiety plays a similarly major role. Like anxiety, depressive affect is a universal phenomenon in psychic life. Like anxiety, depressive affect triggers psychic conflict. Like anxiety, depressive affect plays its part in normal psychic life as well as in psychopathology. It is not a disease or even a syndrome. It is an affect whose role in psychic conflict it is important to understand in general and to analyze in each patient in particular.

Like anxiety, depressive affect can play a crucial role in a patient's psychopathology even when it is not prominent in the final compromise formation. Conflict is initiated to mitigate anxiety and depressive affect. When defense is successful in doing so, neither anxiety nor depressive affect is an obvious or conscious part of the resulting compromise formation. This is often, though by no means invariably, true of that aspect of feminine psychology which is often called penis envy, for example. Girls in their early years are often convinced that the fact, that, unlike boys, they are without a penis is both a reason for their not being loved and preferred as they wish to be and a consequence of it. The intense depressive affect consequent upon the conviction of many little girls that they are castrated, unloved, or both gives rise to a great variety of defensive reactions whose complex interaction and consequent compromise formations result in what is often called the psychology of women, by which is meant the psychological reactions seen in women but not in men. In fact, however, those young boys who either feel themselves to have been castrated, even if only symbolically, or who have a strong wish to be a girl and hence to be rid of their penis, show the same sorts of compromise formations. The "psychology of women" is not found exclusively among women by any means.

To return to my main point about depressive affect, it plays a major role in the conflicts and compromise formations of persons of either sex whose childhood fantasy is that they are or have been castrated. This is true whether or not depressive affect is a prominent, conscious part of the resulting compromise formation. When analyzing such patients, one must take this fact into account.

I hope that these remarks give some indication of how the major innovations contained in my views on psychic conflict and compromise formation are applicable in clinical work with analytic patients. Obviously there is much more to be said about the relevance to technique of what is known today about psychic conflict. I limited myself as I did for two reasons. One is that I have already written at some length on the subject. The other is that despite the generous hospitality of its editors, this book is for me to treasure and enjoy as a gift from my colleagues rather than to use as a vehicle for expressing ideas of my own. I shall therefore add but one further remark. Because of the place of conflict in psychic life, whatever I have been able to contribute to a better understanding of the nature of conflict and compromise formation has application not only to clinical work but to aspects of human psychic functioning and development outside the range of clinical work. Conflict and compromise formation are as significant a part of normal, human, psychic functioning and development as they are of psychopathology. Knowledge of the components of conflict and of the compromise formations which are a consequence of it is as essential to an understanding of normal people and their works as it is to an understanding of psychopathology. Conflict and compromise formation are the essence of both.

PART ONE

The Theory
of Psychoanalysis

Charles Brenner has made a number of major contributions to psychoanalytic theory. Perhaps the most outstanding contribution is his revision of the psychoanalytic theory of conflict. He has always insisted, however, that theories of psychoanalysis be derived from the psychoanalytic situation and the psychoanalytic method. In this section, four distinguished psychoanalysts discuss theory from a number of different perspectives.

Jacob A. Arlow demonstrates how different views of pathogenesis exert powerful effects on the theory of technique and the practice of analysis. He points out that when technical procedures based on specific concepts of pathogenesis breach or disregard the fundamental features of the psychoanalytic situation, the scientific validity of the findings is compromised.

William I. Grossman reviews the controversy between Horney and Freud over theories of female sexuality. His careful and critical examination demonstrates how the controversy can be used to increase our understanding of basic psychoanalytic models.

In a far-ranging discussion of what has endured in psychoanalytic theory and practice, Leo Rangell emphasizes the "fit" between practice and theory. While focusing on what has endured, he reviews current debate about such issues as transference, insight, structure, conflict, and deficit.

Theodore Shapiro discusses the use of sign and symbol in structural theory. He argues for a retention of aspects of the topographic theory to bring structural theory into relation with modern language theory.

JACOB A. ARLOW

The Relation of Theories of Pathogenesis to Therapy

As a rational form of psychotherapy, psychoanalysis derives its practical, technical procedures from theories of pathogenesis related to a general concept of mental functioning. Since the data of psychoanalysis are obtained primarily from observations made during the treatment of neurotic illness, it follows that a theory of pathogenesis should be part of a more general theory of mental functioning. Over the years, Freud found it necessary to elaborate and change his views on pathogenesis several times (Breuer and Freud, 1895; Freud, 1912b, 1916, 1926). His early collaborators, like Abraham (1924), Ferenczi (1916), Rank (1924), and Reich (1927), contributed perspectives of their own, usually by emphasizing one or another of the elements concerning pathogenesis that Freud had discussed.

Thus, theories of pathogenesis have a long and continuing history in the development of psychoanalysis. As the total sum of psychoanalytic experience grew larger and analysts "widened the scope" of conditions considered suitable for treatment by psychoanalysis (Stone, 1954), new etiological factors and comprehensive theories of pathogenesis were proposed. To this day, there is no general agreement among psychoanalysts as to precisely why people develop neurotic illness or character pathology. If anything, controversy on the subject has become more intense than ever. There are more theories in competition, and the division among their proponents is growing increasingly sharper.

What this chapter attempts to do is demonstrate how different views of pathogenesis exert a powerful effect on the theory of technique and on how treatment is conducted. The psychoanalytic situation is not only our

49

therapeutic instrument; it is our investigative tool. Freud (1912a, 1925) organized the psychoanalytic situation in keeping with certain essential principles of his theory of mental functioning, namely, the dynamic interplay of psychic tendencies in conflict. The psychoanalytic situation makes it possible to evoke and elucidate derivatives of dynamic conflicts and give the patient insight into his or her pathology. However, when technical procedures based on specific concepts of pathogenesis breach or disregard the fundamental features of the psychoanalytic situation, the scientific validity of the findings is compromised, whether or not there is an apparent amelioration of symptoms.

I have discussed elsewhere (Arlow, 1981) some of the elements that may account for why certain hypotheses concerning pathogenesis are quickly accepted and enthusiastically espoused. Foremost, I believe, is the promise of therapeutic effectiveness. Psychoanalysis was born in an atmosphere of healing the sick, and it has retained that essence to the present time. In spirit, as Stone (1961) pointed out, all analysts are doctors, whether or not they have a medical degree. The psychoanalytic community is essentially a community of practitioners dedicated to the relief of suffering. This factor reminds us of the well-known syncretism of psychoanalysis, that it is at one and the same time a method of investigation and a form of therapy. There is the ever-present danger that therapeutic zeal may override scientific objectivity.

Another reason that certain theories of pathogenesis seem particularly appealing resides in the element of specificity. This factor pertains to those theories of etiology that propose relatively simple, discrete, specific causes for psychopathology. Such theories seem to suggest that the task of treatment will be made easier, that technical procedures can be focused, and that ultimately a more successful outcome of treatment will be obtained. Under this heading may be included those theories that emphasize the effects of a single traumatic event or the outcome of a specific constellation of relationships, for example, the birth trauma, failure to individuate, the effects of unempathic mothering, the less than adequate mother, or the combination of a weak father and strong mother, and the like. Specificity of etiology makes for "easier" reading of the clinical data, a seemingly more direct approach to the patient's problem, which in turn leads to simplified technical procedures.

Finally, there is the appeal that relates to each individual practitioner's propensity to countertransference. These are subtle features, involving problems that touch on the unconscious motives and gratifications that may be stimulated in the exercise of psychoanalytic work. Theories of pathogenesis may generate a "psychological compliance" consonant with the individual's unconscious motives and fantasies, for example, supplying in the therapeutic relationship what the patient and the therapist both feel they missed as children: rescuing the patient by being a better, more empathic parent; undoing for the patient the humiliation the therapist feels he himself endured as a child; or using the psychoanalytic situation to fulfill some ideal of perfection or grandiosity—to be the perfectly reasonable and compassionate therapist, to bask in the reflected glory of the patient's achievements or in the warm glow of the patient's adulation. We will have occasion later in this essay to examine how certain theories of pathogenesis lead to technical procedures that are compatible precisely with the latent countertransference tendencies just mentioned.

A special pitfall in the path of psychoanalytic technique may result from the narcissistic investment in a particular theory of pathogenesis (Rothstein, 1983). As part of the polemical controversies being waged over new theories, partisans devoutly dedicated to a particular approach may fall into the practice of attending selectively, observing what conforms to their point of view and disregarding contravening evidence. This is by no means a problem peculiar to psychoanalysis. Investigators in every field have called attention to this phenomenon, but the conditions peculiar to psychoanalysis—the individual, private nature of our practice—make it important for us to take special notice of this possibility. In any case, the potential practical effect of such a mental set may have deep implications for the conduct of therapy.

Ordinarily, theories of pathogenesis and theories of technique are not in the forefront of the analyst's mind as he pursues his technical work, but one can recognize the influence of such theories in how the therapist conducts the analysis. What I have found most striking in my experience as a supervisor is that many analysts will follow technical procedures based on a view of pathogenesis that they no longer support and no longer consider valid. These theories of pathogenesis continue to constitute a guiding influence on the analyst's technique without his being aware of the fact. This may become especially evident in situations of therapeutic impasse or when the analyst is confronted with some particularly stubborn resistance. It can be said that he regresses technically, that is, he falls back upon procedures which by now he considers discarded nostrums.

Of all the theories of pathogenesis propounded in the course of the history of psychoanalysis, one of the earliest, the one that Breuer and Freud (1895) used to explain the symptoms of hysteria, seems in my observation to continue to exert the most profound effect on psychoanalytic technique. Freud's first model of the dynamics of pathogenesis of hysterical symptoms was based on a medical model, and the terminology appropriate to the concepts he used borrowed heavily from ideas that were then current in tissue pathology and neurophysiology (Arlow, 1956). Psycho-analytic conceptualization could not help but be influenced by the ambience in which it was spawned. In medical research at the turn of the century, the search for specific traumatic agents was pervasive. Freud began his career as a neuropathologist at a time when studies of tissue pathology were dominated by concepts of trauma and the noxious influence of specific microbes. Breuer and he decided that the noxious influence at the base of hysterical symptoms was a specific traumatic event. The memory of the event and the feelings connected with it, having been repressed, behaved like foreign bodies in the mind. These constituted the core of a secondary organization, which drew into its structure contiguous memories, events, and impulses until it began to sound very much like the pathology of the tubercle or, if acute, took on a form resembling a purulent abscess. Relief followed when the analogs of the toxic substances, the repressed memory and its associated affect, could be drained off through a process called catharsis. Thus, recollection and abreaction became the logical therapeutic consequences of this theory of pathogenesis. The purpose of technique was to bring the forgotten memory back into consciousness and to encourage the patient to discharge the pent-up emotion.

Whatever may be the official standing of this concept in our body of theory today, the technical precepts that followed from this theory of pathogenesis are still honored in psychoanalytic technique. Perhaps this is a reflection of how psychoanalysis is taught. The "Studies on Hysteria" appears at the very beginning of the student's experience in most psycho-analytic curricula and as a rule represents the first introduction to the mysterious art of psychotherapy. Somewhere it remains in the student's mind as a model of how to conduct treatment. What we learn early seems to stay with us longest. Perhaps this is the educational counterpart of the phenomenon of "imprinting." More than that, a theory of repressed trauma and pent-up affect is most appealing, because it is neat and simple and its technical implications are specific and direct. The guidelines it suggests for therapeutic intervention are clear and unmistakable.

Technical elaborations of this principle of pathogenesis are ubiquitous. One may recognize this in the primary position therapists accord the recollection of repressed memories, and in efforts to undo the childhood amnesia, to fill in the gaps in the individual's biography. With it goes the idea that the recovery of a forgotten memory necessarily leads to symptomatic improvement. This is not always the case. In addition, when a patient fails to improve after a significant interpretation, we often hear it said, "The patient has gotten intellectual insight but not emotional insight." This sounds indeed very much like a reverberation of the cathartic model of treatment, to wit, the patient has recollected the event but he has not discharged the appropriate concomitant affect.

When suggestion, hypnosis, and even physical pressure on the forehead failed to bring about recollection, Freud (1925) changed his technique and introduced the dynamic principle of free association. This technique laid bare the operation of resistance and defense. Nevertheless, it must be recognized that, at this period, resistance was understood as the barrier to recollection. At that time, Freud still expected to achieve his therapeutic goals by having the patient recall repressed memories. In perhaps the very last paper that Freud wrote on technique (1937), he made it clear the even long analyses using free association did not always bring about the desired revival of the memory of infantile experience. He said it was necessary to effect a reconstruction, a plausible hypothesis that corresponded as closely as possible to the available data.

In this connection, Kris (1956) said that the interpretive work in analysis would be a hopeless task if its aim were to reconstruct exactly "what had happened . . . Reconstructive work in analysis cannot aim at such a goal . . . . The material of actual occurrences, of things as they happen, is constantly subjected to the selective scrutiny of memory under the guide of the inner constellation . . . they are molded, as it were, into patterns and it is with these patterns rather than with the events that the analyst deals" (Pages 76–77). The recall of forgotten memories in treatment is primarily the result of progress in therapy and the instrument for further progress, but it is not the cause of cure. Nevertheless, I have observed on many occasions that therapists who had been doing very creditable interpretive work remained dissatisfied with what was happening in the analysis because the patient had failed to recall precisely the kind of memory that was expected. Sometimes therapists delay for a long time giving an interpretation, especially a reconstruction, because they wait for the material to emerge from the patient as a memory. Without being aware of it, they pursue the cathartic model of therapy.

What follows is a typical example of this *modus operandi*. After many months of very sensitive and accurate work, the analyst was able to make the patient see that her lifelong resentment of her younger brother had dimensions other than her anger at having been displaced in the affections and attentions of the mother. The associations revealed envy of the brother because he was a boy and resentment that she had not been given a penis. In this context there appeared hitherto unreported memories of trying to harm her brother while he was in her charge. When he was very young, she would pinch him when no one was looking. When she was older, she would twist his arm and threaten him if he reported these acts to their parents. Several dreams were reported, of which this one is typical. The patient is taking care of her brother at the seaside. They are walking near the surf. Suddenly a shark comes out and bites off his leg but also bites the patient's arm. Among her other symptoms, this patient complained of a fear of mice and of insects. She was afraid of being bitten by these creatures, whom she regarded as her enemies. The interpretation was offered that, among other things, the material indicated a hostile impulse towards her brother's genitals. The patient responded with a memory of reaching into her brother's diaper with the intention of feeling his genitals. But the therapist did not carry the interpretation of the material any further. The therapist did not point out the wish to grab the genitals and to eat them, although she was well aware that this was the nature of the unconscious wish. She explained that she was waiting for the patient to remember that she had such an impulse. It would be better if the patient recalled the impulse and reacted to it with appropriate feeling.

It would indeed have been better, but the fact that the patient felt guilty, feared retaliation, could not face what she considered the horrendous implications of her wish, is precisely what brought about the defense of repression in the first place. Had she been confronted with an appropriate interpretation of the repressed impulse to castrate, the patient could come to realize from her own reaction that in the present, as well as in the past, she found her destructive wish too horrible to tolerate. The conflictual wish has to be brought into consciousness, but so, too, do the defensive reactions of the ego. Both have to be recognized as part of the patient's conflict. Becoming aware of the means of warding off forbidden impulses is just as much a part of the process of gaining insight as is awareness of the repudiated impulse.

Having made his momentous discoveries concerning infantile sexuality, Freud (1912b) modified his views on pathogenesis. The untoward consequences of repressed memory and affect he now replaced with the ill effects of repressed libido. Pent-up, undischarged libido became the pathogenic element that brought about symptoms of anxiety. Such a theory gave a more solid biological base to Freud's findings and was in closer consonance with his observations of infantile sexual strivings. The case of Little Hans (Freud, 1909), most often recalled as the clinical documentation *in statu nascendi* of castration anxiety stemming from the Oedipus complex, actually was written to demonstrate that every attack of anxiety that this little boy experienced was a direct expression of an upsurge of undischarged libido. The implications for technique were obvious. Whenever the patient reported an experience of anxiety, the technical responsibility of the therapist became to demonstrate from the data how some upsurging libidinal impulse had been thwarted. Since libidinal cathexes of the system Ucs were barred by the intersystemic censor from discharge into the system Cs, it devolved upon the therapist to arrange for their discharge by bringing them into connection with verbal representations of the system Pcs. The words of the analyst's interpretations constituted the bridge over which these libidinal cathexes were transported from the system Ucs into consciousness (Freud, 1915). Apparently, repeated often enough, such interpretations could transport a sufficient quantum of libidinal cathexis, capable of rearranging the economic imbalance.

Essentially this theory of pathogenesis was a modification of the repressed memory and affect theory from the "Studies on Hysteria." Instead of repressed affects in general serving as the etiological agents, a specific set of affects, those representing derivatives of the sexual drive, were responsible. Not surprisingly, the technical goal of undoing repression was sometimes misunderstood in terms of encouraging sexual license.

It was in this conceptual setting that Wilhelm Reich (1927) saw the goal of analytic therapy to be the achievement of full genital orgasm, and in his theories of orgone therapy, he pursued this idea ad absurdum. Apart from Reich, it is possible, however, to detect lingering residues of the effects of this concept of pathogenesis on certain technical practices even today. This may be seen in the tendency to interpret quickly and directly, and sometimes almost exclusively, the derivative manifestations of unconscious sexual strivings. Often this is done early in the course of treatment, before the patient is aware of how his system of defenses and resistance operates, and before he has had an opportunity, from his own experience, to observe the persistent intrusion into everday thinking and experience of derivatives of his unconscious sexual wishes. In an effort to "empty out the contents of the unconscious," a correct interpretation is treated as if it were a dose of medicine, to be repeated often with increasing intensity, supposedly effective no matter what the conditions under which it is administered. The metaphor is a very real one. Our literature contains many references to "dosages of interpretation." So if the earlier model of pathogenesis, based on the concept of repressed memory and affect, leads some people to delay giving appropriate interpretations, the later model of liberating undischarged libido may work in the opposite direction.

There are several schools of thought in psychoanalysis that stand apart from the others in their views of pathogenesis. One of these centers on the ideas put forward by Melanie Klein (1940). One can see in her concepts the most consistent utilization of a theory of pathogenesis based on abnormal endowment of drive energy, specifically the energy of the aggressive instinct. In effect, she maintains that the normal, appropriate balance between eros and thanatos has not taken place in mental illness. As a result, the psychic apparatus struggles to redress the balance, primarily by processes of projection and introjection. The timing of this disturbance seems to be very early in life, and the symptomatology tends to be conceptualized as an expression of concrete fantasy formations, formations envisioned at a level of complexity unacceptable to more developmentally minded and conservative psychoanalysts. These issues remain a subject of continuing controversy, and while the critics of the Kleinian school have nonetheless borrowed many of their concepts, the debate seems no closer to resolution.

Despite disclaimers by partisans on both sides of the controversy, the implications for technique are enormous. Since it would be impossible here to give a full treatment of the subject, let me cite only three examples. The first relates to the interpretation of transference phenomena. By projecting the major causes of the individual's conflicts back into the first few months of life and by positing a very elaborate system of intricate mental contents, the Kleinians bypass the arduous task of correlating the data of the analysis in developmental terms in favor of a direct interpretation of the phenomena of the transference. They read the reaction of the patient to the analyst as a direct repetition of the fantasies of earliest childhood. As a result, the use of *symbolic interpretation* becomes a preeminent feature of Kleinian technique. The conscious presentations of the patient are interpreted not as defensively transformed derivatives of unconscious fantasies but as direct, that is, symbolic, representations.

Second, using Kleinian concepts, Strachey (1934) conceptualized the therapeutic process in terms of introjection of a good object and extrusion of a bad object. According to him, the essential, so-called mutative interpretations in the course of treatment are those that clarify the transference, interpretations that distinguish between the analyst and his objective, reasonable attitude of helpfulness and the harsh, destructive, archaic, introjected superego. According to Strachey, during treatment the patient, bit by bit, piece by piece, introjects the calm, nonjudgmental, understanding analyst and reconstitutes him as a good object within the superego. This new object, the good one, replaces the earlier, more primitive, bad object in the superego of the patient, the object that had been the pathogenic agent. By way of contrast, the introjected reasonable analyst, reconstituted within the superego, becomes the beneficent agent of cure. To begin with, this is a very narrow, very specific, concept of the psychoanalytic process and of the structure and functioning of the superego. The important observation concerning technique, however, is the sharp focus this approach places on the interpretation of the transference to the exclusion of all other elements that participate in the psychoanalytic process of cure. A similar attitude, although based on quite different grounds, pervades the approach of Gill (1982). For him, as for Strachey, interpretations of analytic data other than transference phenomena seem practically irrelevant.

The third illustration pertains to the technical implications of the concept of projective identification. According to this mechanism, which may read as a form of defensive maneuver, the patient rids himself of the ill effects of a bad object by projecting it into the analyst. This vicissitude of the object influences the analyst's therapeutic stance. When the analyst becomes aware that he is experiencing a certain kind of affect, he interprets this directly in terms of something that the patient was experiencing. Other possibilities are disregarded, such as the fact that the analyst's mood may reflect the patient's intent to please, seduce, provoke, frustrate, and beguile the analyst.

It has been suggested in recent years that theories of pathogenesis may be placed in one or another of two categories. Either the individual suffered some injurious experience during childhood or something needed was not supplied (Friedman, 1978). In a general way this underlies the conceptualizations of most of the so-called object relations school of theories.

Of course, no sharp line of distinction can be drawn between these two categories of untoward childhood relations with objects, but they lead to definite technical approaches, namely, either to correct what had gone wrong or to supply what had been missing. In this spirit, the treatment situation is seen in terms of the diadic mother-child relationship and is conceived of as a latter day extension or reinstitution of the appropriate nurturing developmental process. Nacht (1962) expects the analyst to fulfill the role of the ideally empathic mother. A very large body of recent psychoanalytic literature attests to the emergence of the earliest mother-child relationship as one of the dominant elements in psychoanalytic theories of pathogenesis and, accordingly, in matters of therapy as well. The temptation to play the role of the good mother in gratifying transference wishes is very appealing. In addition, I have observed an unmistakable tendency to retranslate developments from later stages in life back into the terms of the earliest diadic interaction (Arlow, 1981). It is more than likely that some of the current emphasis on the analyst being "humane" and revealing himself as a "real" person derives from the aforementioned theories of pathogenesis.

There are some theories of pathogenesis that center on the idea that neurotic illness is traceable to a specific early injurious relationship with one or another of the important objects of childhood. Consequently, proponents of such views have introduced technical procedures directed towards correcting the effects of such injurious relationships. One can observe this in the contributions of Alexander (1950) and Zetzel (1956). Although their contributions represent conceptualizations of very different approaches and degrees of sophistication, the ideas nonetheless belong together. Alexander proposed that during therapy the analyst should aim to bring about a "corrective emotional experience," one that would dramatize the difference between the bad relationship with the original object and the realistic, adaptive, helpful relationship with the analyst. One can recognize in this formulation an idea very similar to the one put forward by Strachey. Zetzel suggested that a working therapeutic alliance could not be effected in some patients unless a certain amount of preliminary work, aimed at interpreting and undoing the distorted early relationship to the mother, was first accomplished. All of these approaches imply, however subtly, some departure from the neutral, technical stance of the analyst, and may lead one to neglect interpreting certain aspects of the transference (see, for example, Kanzer, 1975; Arlow, 1975; Brenner, 1979). Whether rationalized as "humane" or "real" or "empathic," such approaches introduce the element of role playing into the transference. These issues arise in an even more significant context as psychoanalysts engage psychopathological entities beyond those of the classic transference neuroses.

There is a certain appeal of specificity to some of the theories of pathogenesis based on narrow conceptualizations of object relations theory. Not only does it become possible, according to these theories, to read surface phenomena in terms of recapitulation of early abnormal or injurious object relationships, but the use of one dominating, specific pathological mechanism, for example, the idea of splitting the object representation, may offer intriguing possibilities of simplifying treatment. I have observed one of the consequences of this point of view. I heard that, in a course on technique, a colleague had proposed that, to undo the injurious effects of splitting, one should keep pointing out to the patient during treatment that the analyst has both a good side and a bad side, that he is the same person when he makes an unpleasant observation as when he makes a pleasant one. Further in the course of treatment, according to this view, one should keep reminding the patient that the parents had a good side as well as a bad side.

The most consistent and comprehensive theory of pathogenesis and concomitant technical innovation appears in the work of Kohut (1971, 1977). In his view, the process of narcissistic pathology, and a good deal of other pathology, begins with specific forms of inadequate parenting, with a failure of empathic caring and responsiveness. The normal development of healthy narcissism has not taken place because of inadequate mirroring and insufficient experiencing of the grandiose self. The treatment situation becomes the setting where the untoward effects of thwarted narcissism are overcome, and the patient may grow and develop according to his true "core self." This is the result of the benign, empathic attitude of the therapist. It is the therapist who supplies what was lacking in the past and who thus places the patient back on the course of correct development. In this theory, pathogenesis and therapy are very specific. They focus on the principle of empathy and the technical innovations that Kohut proposes flow directly from these concepts. In keeping with these principles, he proposes radical changes in the therapeutic stance of the therapist and in the nature of his technical innovations. Tracing out patterns in the patient's communications and determining the unconscious drives presenting derivatives to consciousness play a minor role.

This is possible because Kohut depends on empathy as a direct form of observation. The empathic therapist *perceives* immediately and directly the nature of the patient's experiences. He reads them from the manifest content. The validity of the therapist's empathic perception is seldom brought into question. Kohut seems to give little weight to the possibility that countertransference may distort clinical perception. He regards indirect introspection as a universal form of scientific observation, and in contrast to other observers (e.g., Beres & Arlow, 1974), he dispenses with the need for cognitive disciplining of insights made possible through empathy and available through introspection. Kohut's views on pathogenesis have, in fact, given rise to a set of technical procedures that depart radically from the practices of the past.

Self-psychology and object relations theory as well are two manifestations of a very powerful trend in modern day psychoanalysis, namely, the emphasis on the role of the nurturing mother and on preoedipal oral, as contrasted to anal, factors in pathogenesis. The technical implications of this approach have been clearly and succinctly criticized by Neubauer (1979):

> Those who emphasize the reexperiencing of early needs and wishes in the analytic relationship often assign a secondary role to interpretation, reconstruction and insight. They rely upon object relations and identification with the therapist rather than transference interpretation. Sometimes the analyst will keep non-interpretive interventions within the bounds of psychoanalytic technique, but at other times these types of interventions appear to be beyond the psychoanalysis proper and may interfere with the development of an analytic process [pp. 34–35].

Friedman (1978) characterizes the techniques of these new schools as a replacement form of therapy, that is, an attempt to recreate and improve during the analytic treatment the mother-child relationship of the first years of life. Treatment represents a recapitulation of development under more favorable conditions with an appropriate mother surrogate. In this process, there is supposed to be a restructuring of the psychic apparatus, a developmental advance under the aegis of an appropriate, empathic, affective relationship with the therapist. One of the ideas implicit in this approach is that growth is a nonstructured phenomenon that happens automatically, if it is not interfered with by the noxious intrusions of the less than adequate, unempathic mother. I have stated, "Theories of pathogenesis based on the malignant effects of experience during the early months of life hark back to the time when the individual had only needs and no responsibilites. The least culpable, the completely innocent victim is, of course, the very young infant." (Arlow, 1981, page 503). Against this background, the burden of therapy is made much lighter. The patient learns the far from unpleasant truth that he was the passive victim of inadequate (and therefore unfair) treatment, and the therapist can feel unambivalently benign in the pursuit of his work.

The implications of replacement types of therapy for technique are clear; their impact is unavoidable. Some degree of role playing beyond the usual position of benevolent neutrality must follow in the wake of such concepts of pathogenesis. In consequence, the analysis of the transference must be compromised. Furthermore, as the significance of intrapsychic conflict is diminished, less attention is paid to the endogenously determined pressures emanating from the individual's drives and wishes. It is no accident that so many of the recent theories of pathogenesis originate with colleagues who are uncomfortable with drive theory. Technically, the net effect of these trends is to favor supplying a specific type of interpersonal experience over helping the patient attain insight.

It may be useful to sharpen the issues by referring to the fundamental aspect of psychoanalytic technique: the structure and the use of the psychoanalytic situation. Devising the psychoanalytic situation as the investigative and therapeutic instrument of psychoanalysis ranks among the most important and revolutionary of Freud's contributions. The technique of free association in a standard setting, with the analyst playing a neutral role, derives from the concept of pathogenesis as a result of the dynamic thrust of unconscious conflict over persistent, unacceptable impulses. This conflict remains unresolved because of vicissitudes at different stages of development. Accordingly, the rationale of treatment is to seek by interpretation an insight to bring about a restructuring of psychic functioning, so that the ego can master the previously uncontrolled and automatic response to the danger of unpleasure. The analyst observes and records the unstable equilibrium of the analysand's conflicts and influences this equilibrium in one way or another so that the analysand can gain insight and control over the way he handles his conflicts. If the analysis of intrapsychic conflict ceases to be of significance, there is little point in studying the evolution of the interaction between wish and defense in the psychoanalytic situation. If one disregards the vicissitudes of the dynamic unconscious conflict, then the logical question becomes: Why use the psychoanalytic situation as the setting for therapy?

SUMMARY

In this presentation, I have attempted to correlate theories of pathogenesis with certain therapeutic techniques. Different theories of pathogenesis tend to influence the practitioner in different ways, which he may or may not be aware of. Currently many competing theories of pathogenesis are being put forward, and many of them have deep implications for how one conducts an analysis. It is not unusual for practitioners to pursue techniques based on contradictory theories of pathogenesis without being aware that they are doing so. These factors play their role beyond the ever-present important influence of countertransference intrusions into the therapeutic relationship.

Given the nature and depth of the controversies in the field at the present time, it is more important than ever to clarify one's theory of pathogenesis and to be self-conscious about the methodology of interpretation that one uses. The attraction of a simple theory of pathogenesis, one that suggests a specific form of therapy and seems to hold out the promise of greater therapeutic effectiveness, is very powerful. It opens the way to what I call the phenomenological error, that is, interpreting isolated data out of context on the basis of manifest surface elements. If one entertains a strong bias for a particular theory, one can wait patiently for the data that seem to fit, disregarding the dynamic flow of the material until what appears seems to be proof of the basic premise. Specificity of pathogenesis, accordingly, may be appealing since it enables one to bypass the arduous work of interpreting defense and resistance by delineating a precise reconstruction of unconscious conflicts. Now more than ever, then, issues of psychoanalytic methodology should be preeminent as we approach the study of issues of pathogenesis and technique.

REFERENCES

Abraham, K. (1924), A short study of the development of the libido viewed in the light of mental disorders. In: *Selected Papers*. London: Hogarth Press, pp. 418–479.

Alexander, F. (1950), Analysis of the therapeutic factors in psychoanalytic treatment. *Psychoanal. Quart.,* 19:482–500.

Arlow, J. A. (1956), *The Legacy of Sigmund Freud.* New York: International Universities Press.

_____ (1975), Discussion of Dr. Kanzer's paper. *Internat. J. Psychoanal. Psychother.,* 4:469–473.

_____ (1981), Theories of pathogenesis. *Psychoanal. Quart.,* 50:488–514.

Beres, D. & Arlow, J. A. (1974), Fantasy and identification in empathy. *Psychoanal. Quart.,* 43:26–50.

Brenner, C. (1979), The working and therapeutic alliance. *J. Amer. Psychoanal. Assn.,* 27:137–157.

Breuer, J. & Freud, S. (1895), Studies on hysteria. *Standard Edition,* 2:1–252. London: Hogarth Press.

Ferenczi, S. (1916), Stages in development of the sense of reality. In: *Contributions of Psychoanalysis.* Boston: Richard C. Badger.

Freud, S. (1909), Analysis of a phobia in a 5-year-old boy. *Standard Edition,* 10:5–149. London: Hogarth Press, 1955.

_____ (1912a), Recommendations to physicians practicing psychoanalysis. *Standard Edition,* 12:109–120. London: Hogarth Press, 1958.

_____ (1912b), Types of onset of neurosis. *Standard Edition,* 12:231–238. London: Hogarth Press, 1958.

_____ (1915), The unconscious. *Standard Edition,* 14:166–204. London: Hogarth Press, 1957.

_____ (1916), Introductory lectures on psycho-analysis. *Standard Edition,* 16. London: Hogarth Press, 1963.

_____ (1925), An autobiographical study. *Standard Edition,* 20:3–74. London: Hogarth Press, 1957.

_____ (1926), Inhibition, symptoms and anxiety. *Standard Edition,* 20:87–172. London: Hogarth Press, 1959.

_____ (1937), Constructions in psychoanalysis. *Standard Edition,* 23:255–269. London: Hogarth Press, 1964.

Friedman, L. (1978), Trends in the psychoanalytic theory of treatment. *Psychoanal. Quart.,* 47:524–567.

Gill, M. (1982), *Analysis of Transference, Volume I.* New York: International Universities Press.

Kanzer, M. (1975), The therapeutic and working alliances. *Internat. J. Psychoanal. Psychother.,* 4:48–68.

Klein, M. (1940), Mourning and its relation to manic-depressive states. In: *Contributions to Psychoanalysis.* London: Hogarth Press, 1948, pp. 311–338.

Kohut, H. (1971), *The Analysis of the Self.* New York: International Universities Press.

_____ (1977), *The Restoration of the Self.* New York: International Universities Press.

Kris, E. (1956), Recovery of childhood memories in psychoanalysis. *The Psychoanalytic Study of the Child,* 11:54–88.

Nacht, S. (1962), The curative factors in psychoanalysis. *Internatl. J. Psycho-Anal.*, 43:206–211.

Neubauer, P. (1979), The role of insight in psychoanalysis. *J. Amer. Psychoanal. Assn.*, 27, suppl.:29–40.

Rank, O. (1924), The trauma of birth and its importance for psychoanalytic therapy. *Psychoanal. Rev.*, 11:241–245.

Reich, W. (1927), The function of the orgasm. *Internationale Psychoanalytischer Verlag.* Vienna.

Rothstein, A. (1983), *The Structural Hypothesis—An Evolutionary Prospectus.* New York: International Universities Press, pp. 9–30.

Stone, L. (1954), The widening scope of indications for psychoanalysis. *J. Amer. Psychoanal. Assn.*, 2:567–594.

———— (1961), *The Psychoanalytic Situation.* New York: International Universities Press.

Strachey, J. (1934), The nature of the therapeutic action of psychoanalysis. *Internat. J. Psycho-Anal.*, 15:127–159.

Zetzel, E. (1956), The concept of transference. In: *The Capacity for Emotional Growth.* New York: International Universities Press, 1970, pp. 168–181.

WILLIAM I. GROSSMAN

Freud and Horney: A Study of Psychoanalytic Models via the Analysis of a Controversy[1]

I t has been said (Kris, 1947) that the subject matter of psychoanalysis is "human behavior viewed as conflict." The conflicts are mental conflicts, and the theories of psychoanalysis deal with their nature, origins, and resolutions.

Although controversies about psychoanalytic theory differ in important respects from the intrapsychic conflicts that are its subject, there are close links between the two types of "conflict," as well as some significant similarities. The unconscious conflicts of individual theorists and the latent psychological content of their theories may be the subject of applied analysis, and in some cases, of clinical analysis as well (Abend, 1979; Arlow, 1981). However, the conflicts between theoreticians promote the development of theories and are useful for exploring that development and the properties of the theories.

Contradictions, inconsistencies, vagueness, blatant errors, and prejudice are indicators of unconscious conflict in individuals. The same phenomena in theoretical discourse may also point to unresolved but fundamental problems in the theory (see also Freud, 1971). However, as in any disagreement between people, the acknowledged points of disagreement may not be the only, or most important, conceptual basis of the

---

[1]Earlier versions of this paper were presented to the Philadelphia Association For Psychoanalysis, 14 April 1978; The New Jersey Psychoanalytic Society, 12 June 1980; The Cleveland Psychoanalytic Society, 18 February 1983.

controversy. In such cases, it is useful to distinguish between manifest and latent *theoretical* issues, instead of considering the clinically interesting *psychological* issues. In the controversy between between Horney and Freud, female sexuality was the manifest issue through which more fundamental but latent differences of broad theoretical outlook were argued.

Latent theoretical content can vary in its scope and complexity. In a broad sense, there are philosophical conceptions of human beings — assumptions about biological and social aspects of human functioning, about what the theory is supposed to explain, about psychoanalytic treatment as a method of observation, to mention only a few latent issues. In this paper, the "latent contents" under consideration include aspects of those issues and are conveniently discussed as basic models underlying the clinical and developmental theories of psychoanalysis.

The same point may be put in a somewhat different way. If there is a controversy about an aspect of psychoanalytic theory, as there was concerning female sexuality over fifty years ago and again recently, the disagreements can be looked at in a number of different ways. We may ask whether different observations have been made that contradict one theory or are more consistent with another. We may try to discover whether something that was missing before has been added. Sometimes we find that over a period of years, perspectives begin to change, some new ideas emerge, observations are formulated differently. This happened recently in relation to ego psychology and clinical problems of narcissism. The question then arises whether major revision of theory is required, or merely some reorganization and reformulation.

One assumption here is that in Freud's own work there were different kinds of changes: new observations, new ideas, and more elaborate changes from one theory of anxiety to another, one theory of drives to another, and one theory of structure to another. However, given the importance of these changes in both structure and content, there were more fundamental models — that is, the frameworks or formats for explanation — that did not change.

On the other hand, where major controversies led to schisms, as they did between Freud and Adler, Jung, Horney, and W. Reich, mere modification of content was not the issue. Instead, the basic explanatory structure of the theory was changed. Where this is not the case, the *theory* can accommodate modification, even when individuals cannot.

This way of looking at theory and at controversy opens the way to a method for examining controversies in psychoanalysis, while clarifying problems in formulating theory. The exploration of the explanatory models in alternative theoretical formulations helps us to see whether the issues involve data or minor modifications in conceptualization, or whether essential assumptions are being altered and matters of fundamental principle discarded. At the same time, the careful exploration of the controversy helps to clarify what is essential to psychoanalytic explanation. In this way, conflicts about psychoanalytic theory during its development reveal how the theory is constructed, just as mental conflict reveals the structure of mind.

The disagreement between Freud and Horney about female sexuality provides a case study in which the topic of female sexuality was the manifest issue. A blend of theoretical, methodological, and emotional differences (Fliegel, 1973), the disagreements appeared to concern matters of fact and interpretation at the clinical and developmental level. However, fundamental principles and explanatory models were the real theoretical issues, initially obscured and "latent." Horney (1939) was eventually explicitly aware of this. She wrote that she had her "first active doubts" about Freud's concepts of psychoanalysis in relation to female sexuality, came to recognize the debatable premises on which this system was built, and arrived at the conviction "that psychoanalysis should outgrow the limitations set by its being an instinctivistic and a genetic psychology" (p. 8). We cannot discard the possibility that an emotional issue about female sexuality *initiated* a revision of the underlying concepts. That interesting possibility awaits careful historical investigation.

The following discussion concerns, first, a description of some of Freud's models; second, Horney's ideas on female sexuality, and third, the significance of the modifications introduced by Horney, with some aspects of Freud's concepts highlighted.

FREUD'S MODELS

The word "model" has been used with varying degrees of precision and concreteness in formulating theories about observable phenomena. I shall use "model" rather loosely to indicate the form or framework of theoretical explanation, a conceptual analogue. In this sense, models indicate possible relationships between observations or elements of a theory. "Models" are here distinguished from "theories," which are bodies of explanation (see Wilson, 1973, for an excellent discussion). On the other hand, models are usefully distinguished from imagery and metaphor, which may be made to serve as models. As Langer (1967) says, "The use of a model belongs to a higher level of conception [than imagery], the level of discursive thought and deliberate analogical reasoning" (p. 63). Langer adds that in illustrating "a principle of construction or functions, quite apart from any semblance" (p. 68), models provide scientific concepts such as psychological research requires.

Looking at psychoanalytic theory construction in terms of how models are used brings us very close to Freud's comments about his own theory-building. He described (1915, p. 117) how one needed to use concepts and abstractions taken from outside the field of observation and apply them to the data. (See also Maguire, 1983, on metatheoretical assumptions.) Later Freud said his theories consisted of "analogies, correlations and connections" (1920, p. 60). Analogies are models, often of a simple and concrete kind. For example, Freud used the mystic writing pad to illustrate with a concrete model the problems of consciousness and memory.

Psychoanalysis is a complex theory, which is probably why it has never received an adequate systematic statement. It contains, in fact, a number of models of different range and complexity, some explicit and some implicit. Freud may not have been aware that the models I discuss later, and others, were used at many different levels of theory.

A number of very basic psychoanalytic models were discussed by Rapaport (1951). In keeping with his interest in having psychoanalysis solve the problems of psychology in general, he specified the psychoanalytic models of thinking, motivation, and affects. He showed how a drive-discharge model encompassed both primary and secondary models of all three functions. To these models he added models of psychic structure, hierarchies of motivation, of action, and of relative functional autonomy.

These abstract models of mental functions appear to have held little interest for clinicians. The clinical usefulness of the models, like the usefulness of other abstract metapsychological generalizations, has been widely regarded as doubtful.

In search of a general, clinically applicable model, Gedo and Goldberg (1973) offered an examination of the models for representing psychic structure at different stages of individual development. They presented a hierarchical, epigenetic model of their own. The clinical application of the new formulation was demonstrated by using it to discuss Freud's published cases.

My interest in Freud's models is not to find an abstract model from which predictions may be made, that is, Rapaport's interest. Nor is it to construct a new model for psychoanalysis, the aim of Gedo and Goldberg. I hope to show that Freud took his models of mental organization from biology and applied the same models both to his more abstract and general theories and to discussions of clinical problems. This contrasts with the usual assumption that Freud used biology only in a reducetionistic way.

The Adaptation Model

The most general model that Freud borrowed from biology was an epigenetic-adaptation model (Hartmann, 1939). "Epigenesis," an embryological term, refers to stepwise development and progressive organization, such that the sequence and timing of one stage determines the way the next stage of the embryo develops (see Erikson, 1945; Gedo & Goldberg, 1973; and Maguire, 1983, for discussion). The adaptational aspect of the model was derived from the theory of natural selection in evolution. Its sources were Darwin, Spencer and Jackson (see Ritvo, 1974). The power of this model derives from its being an organismic model of interaction and progressive change in response to inner developments and external forces. Such a model is readily extended to meaningful and purposeful human interaction, as well as to components of mental function. This concept of "interaction" is complex since in it the organism both acts on and is acted on by its environment. Different emphases in the use of the model are possible, depending on whether the organism, mind, ego, or drive is considered to be active or passive in relation to the environment.

This biologically derived framework was the basis for Freud's organizing theoretical principles. He applied it to both phylogenetic and individual development (Rapaport, 1960; Schur & Ritvo, 1970). The importance of conflict in psychoanalytic theory probably stems from this basic model, on which are built the explanations of normal and pathological development, dream formation, and the onset of neurosis. Thus, the idea of interaction, perceived as a "struggle for survival," is reborn as a struggle between repressed and repressing forces when transposed to the mind.

For both physical and mental characteristics, the basic model is of a developing organism with its hereditary traits and its impulses, changing as a result of interaction with its environment. The outcome is a change in constitution, so that the organism and environment interact with one another in a new way, leading to further change. The essential schema is: internal constitution interacts with external stimulus to produce a new constitution.

For Freud's work, this schema is characteristic of the "vital processes" of civilization and of individual development, as well as of evolution. On the phylogenetic level, the origin of species, including the human species, was the result of such interactions and changes. On the level of civilization, the resolution of primal conflicts led to the origin of the sense of guilt and the superego (Freud, 1930). These two processes in the biological and cultural evolution of mankind constitute the "primaeval period which is comprised in the life of the individual's ancestors" (Freud, 1905,

p. 173). They provide the hereditary background for what Freud called "the other primaeval period," childhood. Individual development thus provides another example of this model, in which innate constitution and maturational factors interact with experience. New organizations result, producing new interactions.

An example on the level of intrapsychic processes is dream formation. Schematically simplified, the dream is the product of an unconscious wish interacting with a day residue, an unsolved problem of the dream day. In this example, we can begin to see how the dynamic organism-environment conflict — Darwin's struggle for survival — becomes a conflict between the Unconscious and the Preconscious. The former is the repository of the archaic inheritance, the latter the inner representative of the claims of the environment. The dream content is a compromise formed from the interaction between an infantile wish ("constitution") and the day residue ("environment").

These examples show that for Freud the same dynamic model of progressive organizations operated from phylogenesis to the mental life. In keeping with the evolutionary views he held, there is an implication that the repetitive resolution of such conflicts led to a successive development and complexity in organization.

These broad applications of the basic interaction model to phylogeny and ontogeny are found, in another version, in Freud's views on the etiology of neurosis. Throughout the early writings on hysteria and neurasthenia, Freud was preoccupied with the relative importance of trauma and disposition, accidental factors and heredity, precipitating factors and constitution. For both of the paired polarities of heredity — accidental factors — and disposition — precipitating factors — a "complemental series" could be set up. With a greater internal tendency to neurosis, a less significant trauma would produce illness. With a severe trauma, stronger constitutions with lesser predispositions would succumb. When the hereditary factors were seen as playing the part of disposition to childhood experience, and childhood experience the disposition to neurosis (Freud, 1916–1917), the general models for development in phylogenesis, ontogenesis, and psychopathology became identical. As a further consequence of Freud's repeated use of the same model, he could insist that the processes in the "normal" and the "neurotic" were similar, rather than absolutely different in kind. He rejected in principle a false antithesis between heredity and environment. With the interaction model, constitution can be expressed only through response to environmental factors and through selecting aspects of environment for response. Environmental factors can operate only through a responsive constitution, selecting the aspects of constitution to be called into play. In this view, behavior, in

the broadest sense, is a phenotype generated by the interaction of geno-
type and environment.

The preceding examples indicate in outline the use of the adaptive interaction model in providing the broad developmental framework of psychoanalysis. In the following discussion, specific developmental concepts illustrate Freud's application of the same model, the same format of
explanation, to more restricted aspects of the theory having differing degrees of abstractness, and specificity.

In the *libido theory,* the component instinctual drives were conceptualized as special kinds of impetus of somatic origin, based on special chemistry and special bodily sensitivities to environmental objects and satisfactions. Interaction with the caretakers modified the intensity and
course of drive satisfaction and frustration, leaving alterations in the drive
system in the form of fixations and mental elaborations of infantile experience. The drives were one force, the environment another. The outcome
of their conflict in childhood was an altered direction of drive development and a disposition to some version of "normality," to neurosis, or to
perversion.

Freud's views on the *latency period* illustrate the wide latitude he allowed for variations and overlapping of phases in an innately organized
program of maturation responding to environmental forces. Characteristically, Freud's remarks on latency sometimes emphasized the innate program and sometimes the environmentally produced alterations. Simply
stated, latency was a programmed tendency, subject to culture and
seduction. It might be partially or totally omitted, with sexual activity
continuing until puberty (1916–1917). In this context, seduction meant
early stimulation of a drive, interfering with repression and latency.

The development of the *seduction concept* in Freud's work illustrates
the conservation of a basic model with changes in the role played by a
single concept in the explanation of neurosis. At first, the idea of seduction referred to concrete sexual acts. Freud believed that hysterics invariably had been seduced. Later, he realized that children often had fantasies of being seduced without acts of seduction taking place. Finally,
realizing that a mother inevitably stimulated her child in the ordinary
course of child care, he recognized the mother as every child's first
seducer. The fantasies of seduction were based on universal experiences.
The idea of seduction had thus become, in a sense, a general principle of
development, as well as referring to concrete acts of molestation.

Even the awakening of the "spontaneous" and "universal" Oedipus
complex could be determined by the attraction of the parent to the child
(Freud, 1916–1917). It is biological in a special sense: it depends on the
early awakening of sexual impulses and the long period of dependence

on the parents. Thus, it is biosocial—the social structure meets the biological need; the biological need is awakened by the social structure. The "universality" depends on the "universal" conjunction of the two sets of factors. It then follows naturally, for Freud, that the Oedipus complex is the form given by the human family to the conflict between Eros and Thanatos (Freud, 1930, p. 132).

The examples presented—the drive concept, latency, seduction and the Oedipus complex—show that the balanced, interactive, adaptive model entered into psychoanalytic theory in a variety of ways, and at a number of levels, at least in principle. This last qualification is necessary because Freud, at times, would emphasize one side of the constitution-environment pair, and underplay the other. At other times, he might not mention the adapting agent (ego or person) either. In any case, the four preceding illustrations are also components of Freud's account of a conflict-theory of psychosexual development. A brief discussion of a model, as applied to psychosexual development, will serve as a background against which Horney's ideas may be considered.

Psychosexual development, according to Freud, proceeds as a series of interactions between dispositions and environment, mediated by a developing "ego," the meaning of this term varying during the course of Freud's work. Maturation, physical and mental, contributes to the changing dispositions, but its place in the model was somewhat ambiguous. Since maturation, although influenced by environmental factors, is not determined by them, Hartmann and Kris (1945) introduced the clarifying distinction between maturation and development. In any case, mental conflict was at various times a regulator of the organism-environment conflict, and also its consequence. In other words, within the larger organism/environment-adaptation/conflict model, mental development also proceeds via conflict resolution. The processes of conflict resolution, both interactive and intrapsychic, are for Freud the motor of mental development. Intrapsychic conflict as a broad principle is thus a manifestation of adaptation internalized, and the normal progression from one psychosexual stage to the next is promoted by conflict.

Freud's conception of heterosexual development was built on these ideas. In deriving femininity and female sexuality from a prior series of conflict-determined steps, he was merely following his model, as he did for masculinity. The derivation of vaginal cathexis from the oral and the anal was one part of this process. In the development of the male, there was a parallel in the derivation of the cathexis of the penis from the cathexis of the stool. The clitoral-vaginal transfer concept was another expression of the same developmental conflict model.

Since both masculine and feminine heterosexuality were the outcome of developmental processes, Freud rejected ideas of innate or "primary" masculinity and femininity. The ubiquitous, variegated, polymorphous disposition had been one of the first cornerstones of his sexual theories. He believed, therefore, that both male and female sexuality started with an undifferentiated, bisexual stage and developed out of transformations of orality and anality. Because of Freud's unfortunate manner of expressing himself (as when speaking of the libido as masculine), it often sounds as though he believed in what is often called primary masculinity and secondary femininity. In principle, however, both male and female genital sexuality are endpoints in complex development, based on intrapsychic conflict. The fact that normal psychosexual development takes place in this way in Freud's model accounts, on one hand for the ease with which disorders may occur, and on the other hand, for the close affiliation between normal and pathological phenomena. This basic model of Freud's was unacceptable to Karen Horney, who objected to the idea that normal femininity arose from conflict. Her approach to this problem is the subject of the next section.

HORNEY'S CONTRIBUTION

Karen Horney's (1967) contributions to the psychoanalytic study of feminine psychology have gained increasing favor in psychoanalytic circles. While certainly not neglected by so-called neo-Freudian schools, her elaboration of a culturally oriented viewpoint and her break with the New York Psychoanalytic Society in the early 1940s led many analysts subsequently to ignore her work. At the present time, her work is often either exploited or rejected (Blum, 1976) as culturalist. At the same time, some psychoanalytic authors (Barnett, 1968; Kestenberg, 1968; Chasseguet-Smirgel, 1976) are returning to her ideas about the discovery and denial of the vagina in childhood, the boy's feeling of inferiority with his mother, and her critique of Freud's phallocentric bias.

Even a casual review of Horney's papers on *Feminine Psychology* reveals her gifts as a clinician and theoretican. Her feminist critique of psychoanalysis and of the influence of male-oriented culture on feminine mental life is the source, often unacknowledged, of some of today's most cogent feminist writings. Her early papers are especially impressive in this respect, since Horney knew, as well, how to defend psychoanalysis against trivial and ill-informed criticism. It is important, therefore, to be precise about the real theoretical differences between Freud and Horney, and whether accepting her observations necessitates accepting her theory.

A number of Horney's clinical ideas fit comfortably into our current perspective. She emphasized the need for a careful analysis of the patient's current conflicts and their context, as we expect in an ego-psychological clinical approach. Avoiding reductionism of the clinical data to primitive impulses, she emphasized the object-related aspects of instinctual conflict. It was this orientation to penis envy and the castration complex that produced her derivation of clinically observed penis envy from Oedipal disappointment. She believed that the penis envy observed in analysis arose from the disappointment of the girl's intense attachment to her father. Freud, however, had suggested a preoedipal beginning in the girl's first genital comparison. Horney recognized, as well, that the mother's attitude toward femininity would act as a bridge between social views of women and the young girl's "wounded womanhood." Realizing that reconstructions of normal childhood from psychoanalytic data might be uncertain, she advocated the psychoanalytically oriented observation of normal children and the children of other cultures. Horney's clinical and theoretical analysis of masochism, as well as of other phenomena, stressed the crucial role of self-esteem and narcissism. Her views on "the self" and the vicissitudes of self-esteem and grandiosity are echoed, unacknowledged, in some current theories.

Horney's essay on the castration complex in women (1967[1922]) noted the prevalent axiom that females feel at a disadvantage because of their genitals. This fact, she suggested, had not seemed to require an explanation because, to masculine narcissism, the reason is self-evident. She found questionable the idea that one half of the human race can overcome its discontent with its assigned sex only in favorable circumstances. This was "unsatisfying" to female narcissism and to biological science, she said.

Horney went on to explain why penis envy seemed to be a typical occurrence. She stated that the little girl's sense of inferiority is not "primary"—a term that seems to mean something like "spontaneous," "innate," or "without a cause." The girl is suffering from a *real* disadvantage in the gratification of her pregenital impulses. The little boy can handle, look at, and exhibit his penis. Owing to the high narcissistic value placed on urination, penis envy is an "almost inevitable phenomenon" in the life of girls and "one that cannot but complicate female development (1967, p. 42)." She added that the prospect of motherhood could be no real consolation at the time of such pregenital issues.

The next question was whether penis envy was the "ultimate force" behind the castration complex. To be considered were the factors determining whether penis envy was "more or less successfully overcome or whether it becomes regressively reinforced so that fixation occurs (1967, p. 42)." This led Horney to examine the girl's object relations, particularly her Oedipus complex, more closely. She concluded that the girl could overcome penis envy without detriment by passing from the autoerotic desire for a penis to the desire for a man, her father, via identification with her mother. She referred to these as spontaneously occurring "womanly and maternal" developments. On the basis of either a hostile or a loving identification with her mother, the girl's fantasy of sexual possession by the father emerged. The inevitable disappointment of this wishful fantasy gave rise to the clinical manifestations of the castration complex. The intense love relationship with the father would give way to an identification with him and to a rejection of femininity. The girl's earlier envy of her mother's possession of children now reinforced with its own intensity the reactivated wish for a penis.

Whereas feelings of guilt were aroused by the incestuous attachment, angry and vengeful fantasies resulted from the disappointment. Rape fantasies and fantasies of damage and castration then represented the love relationship with the father. In short, according to Horney, the castration complex and the clinically observed penis envy were the product of "wounded womanhood." Penis envy is more easily exposed, she believed, because it is without the guilt that is attached to the more deeply repressed fantasy of castration in a sexual act with the father.

Horney's formulations had a number of virtues. Based on clinical evidence, her explanation undercut the temptation to explain the adult symptom as simply the persistence or reactivation of its earliest infantile counterpart. That is, the clinical evidence of the castration complex was to be understood instead as a reaction to the failure of feminine strivings. In keeping with the best psychoanalytic tradition, she said that the reactivated infantile representation bore the marks of the stages from which regression had occurred. Second, this formulation took cognizance of the role of the preoedipal relation to the mother, albeit in rudimentary form. Moreover, it provided an explanation for the girl's change of objects from mother to father. One further virtue of Horney's approach did much to enhance its appeal without adding to its clinical or theoretical value: it offered a "naturally" feminine line of development, in contrast to those views that seemed to regard feminine development principally as failed masculinity. This seemed like a desirable way to correct a male bias in developmental theory. Later, basing her thoughts on the work of the philosopher Georg Simmel, Horney elaborated the thesis that the male view of women permeates our theories of development and that social devaluation of women leads to the rejection of womanhood. As a further consequence, she said, we tend to regard the boy's development as straight-forward and the girl's as a divergent one. *The contrast of straightforward and divergent developments is a distortion in the interpretation of theory, although a frequent one.*

Horney's illuminating and provocative work was influential in forming the background for Jones' (1927, 1933, 1935) later criticism of the theory of the phallic phase. The idea of a "phallic phase" in girls had been tied to the problem of penis envy and the castration complex. The sense of these concepts seemed contaminated by bias. Although Horney's first paper on the castration complex had been presented prior to Deutsch's (1925) contribution and Freud's "Infantile Genital Organization" (1923) and "Some Psychical Consequences of the Anatomical Distinction Between the Sexes" (1925), Horney's work was not directly discussed by either Deutsch or Freud. As Fliegel (1973) suggests, Freud's (1925) paper seems so closely related that it may well have been an answer to Horney.

For instance, Horney (1967, p. 43) insisted that a girl's intense attachment to her father precedes penis envy. Freud begins his discussions with the observation that in women with strong attachments to their fathers there is a long prehistory to the Oedipus complex (Freud, 1925) and an earlier intense attachment to their mothers (Freud, 1931). Where Horney derived penis envy from the Oedipus complex, Freud derived the Oedipus complex from penis envy. Where Horney emphasized the girl's early *identification* with her mother, Freud stressed the early *object libidinal* impulses. A case might be made as well for the idea that Freud's paper on the phallic phase in 1923 was prompted by Horney's paper on the castration complex, too.

In respect to its descriptive content, Horney's paper on the castration complex is no longer remarkable. Penis envy, elaborately described Oedipal fantasies, regressive derivatives, such as rape fantasies, inhibition of masturbation, wish for a child based on identification with the mother, all are long familiar to any clinician. However, her formulations of specific clinical propositions, or the findings of particular fantasies, or even developmental sequences are not the concern of my presentation. In themselves, these ideas were never seriously challenged. They can be fitted into a variety of frameworks and models. Even the developmental sequence that Horney suggested was not contested. As Fliegel (1973) said, both Freud and Horney agreed on the sequence penis envy/Oedipus complex/regression to castration complex. The critical difference, the fulcrum of the disagreement between Freud and Horney, and subsequently between Freud and Jones, was the relative importance of the *first* observation of the genital difference as a causal factor in later developments.

The outline and criticisms of Freud's schema of feminine development are so well known that I shall not repeat them. The essential point was that for Freud the discovery of the genital difference initiated the *psychological* differentiation into masculinity and femininity. The reaction of children to this discovery had a special significance. Penis *envy* and penis *wish* were motivating forces in development that could *promote* femininity by turning the girl away from her libidinal attachments to her mother. This would initiate her Oedipus complex. As Freud was to say later, the castration complex promotes femininity in both males and females. It was an economical explanation and retained a certain consistency in its formulation of masculine and feminine development.

For Horney, the essential elements of Freud's formulations that were biased and unacceptable were bisexuality, "primary penis envy" as a motive, the "secondary" derivation of the Oedipus complex, that is, of heterosexuality, and the idea that the vagina was unknown to both sexes. An associated disagreement seemed to be the weight given to narcissistic injury in feminine development. In her subsequent papers on women, Horney also described some aspects of male development. She offered a different viewpoint, owing to her recognition that the feminine wishes of boys had been examined in relation to their fathers, but not as an expression of their attitudes towards women.

Although it would be useful to examine the details of various formulations in her papers on female sexuality, I shall discuss only what Horney modified, her methods of analysis, and some of her assumptions. By doing so, we can see how an apparent difference of emphasis contains the seeds of a different theory. Although the modifications themselves need not necessarily have produced new theory, historically they did so.

In Horney's formulations, bisexuality was replaced by a concept of "primary heterosexuality" leading to the girl's oedipal orientation. Horney could still say, in 1967 (p. 43) that one origin of this "womanly and maternal development" was narcissistic in character, the goal being possession of the father or a child from him. This formulation retained the elements of Freud's (1917) account of these events, but decisively subordinated them to the maternal identification.

Discarding the concept of bisexuality was a most important step for Horney. It had two effects: It introduced a concept of primary biological femininity, and it initiated her rejection of the genetic point of view. Bisexuality, as Freud and others wrote of it, was often treated as though it really meant "primary masculinity." Those associated with Freud's formulations wrote that the girl gives up her "masculinity" and acquires passive aims.

The idea that acquiring passive aims is to be equated with giving up "masculinity" reflects the tendency to regard clitoral masturbation and the active aims of the early phallic phase as "masculine." Freud did not consistently avoid this pitfall, despite his recognition that activity and passivity could not simply be equated with masculinity and femininity, respectively, nor could passive aims be equated with passivity. However, these confusions are a part of *childhood* fantasy. The confusions of childhood became the problems of theory. Since "bisexuality" was the conceptual means for treating the girl's early development as masculine, it was contaminated for Horney, who discarded it.

In place of bisexuality, Horney suggested that the attraction between the sexes was an "elementary principle of nature" and a "primal, biological principle" (1967, p. 68). She also spoke of an "innate instinctual wish to receive from the man" (p. 111, also p. 142). This biological perspective was expressed, as well, in the belief that the boy "instinctively divines the existence" of the vagina, while "the girl's incestuous wishes are referred to the vagina with the unerring accuracy of the unconscious" (pp. 65–66).

Having argued for the primal nature of heterosexual attraction, Horney proceeded to base penis envy on this attraction. It is the attraction to the opposite sex that draws attention to the penis, she said. The interest is libidinal, autoerotic, and narcissistic, and is the first manifestation of the "mysterious attraction." She spoke of it as "partial love" and added that the libidinal desire for the penis and the narcissistic wish to possess it are often difficult to distinguish clinically in the associations of women. In this way, both primary penis envy and the castration complex were derived from primary feminine heterosexuality. The other side of this biological determinism of feminine impulses is the social determinism of male society as the antogonistic generator of neurosis. Freud (1937) was to say, "The repudiation of femininity can be nothing else than a biological fact" (p. 252). Horney might have said instead, "The repudiation of natural femininity is a masculine social fact."

Following Freud's implied rebuttal to her first paper, Horney offered a more deliberate critique and reversal of Freud's views. Throughout, she used Freud's own phrases, ironically reversing their application. Where he attributed an attitude to one sex, Horney attributed it to the other. Examples of this technique will be recognized in the following discussion.

Since primary heterosexuality, not penis envy, turned the girl to her father, the castration complex was a "secondary formation" – the same expression Freud (1925) had used in describing the Oedipus complex. Although Horney later argued that the Oedipus complex was a culturally determined phenomenon, she accepted as instinctive (based on tensions and organ sensations) the boy's knowledge that "his penis is much too small for his mother's genital" (1967, p. 142).

The postulation of heterosexual impulses, and of the unconscious knowledge of both the vagina and of sexual relations, now led Horney to two other reversals of the Freudian position. The first was that neither the sight of the father's penis and of the mother's genitals nor the intellectual knowledge of their existence is necessary for the "psychological consequences of the anatomical distinction between the sexes" to take effect. *In this respect, the environmentalist discounts the importance of experience for the acquisition of knowledge.* For her next reversal of Freud, however, the *actuality* of the small genitals of the boy and the girl is the essence. The girl's knowledge that "her genital is too small for her father's penis . . . makes her react to her own genital wishes with direct anxiety . . . [The boy, knowing that] . . . his penis is much too small for his mother's genital . . . reacts with the dread of his own inadequacy . . ." (Horney, 1967, p. 142). In consequence, genital anxiety is primary in the girl and genital inadequacy is primary in the boy, the reverse of Freud's view. The "wound to his self-regard" may lead to the boy's disgust with the male role. The boy withdraws his libido from his mother and "concentrates it on himself and his genital." This is, then, Horney's derivation of the phallic phase, an intensification of phallic narcissism. The boy is left with a "narcissistic scar" and a denial of the vagina. For Horney, the fact that this phase is narcissistic implies an *earlier* object orientation (p. 139) and an anxious retreat from it. (p. 144)

Two other reversals follow from this. First, the feelings of inferiority in the girl are secondary to her escape into the "fiction of maleness" (p. 67) and her castration fantasies derive from this defensive position, as well. The second reversal is that the castration anxiety of the boy is secondary to his anger at being frustrated, the wound to his self-regard, and his compensatory wish to be a woman. Horney remarked that analysis with a woman analyst brings out the man's fear of being rejected and derided. "The specific basis of this attitude is hard to detect, because in analysis it is generally concealed by a (unconscious) feminine orientation . . ." (1967, p. 144).

Horney's reevaluation of female sexuality had led her to the view that Freud's and Abraham's formulations—and later those of Deutsch and others—had created a male-biased theory, specifically, that it was a male view of women and that it was defensive. She therefore reversed the point of view and treated as defensive those attitudes that had been considered primary by Freud, and the reverse. In doing so, she called attention to features of both masculine and feminine conflicts that *had* been neglected.

Her interpretations point to a wider range of variations in the development, fantasies, and conflicts of both women and men. Unfortunately, her ideas were presented as a reversed theoretical alternative rather than as a supplement. Her point of view and Freud's both became fixed as they polarized.

Horney freely admitted a number of times that some of her reconstructions were conjecture. However, she had made the point and demonstrated that initial assumptions different from Freud's could alter the reconstruction of childhood from clinical data. She saw, as well, that the reconstruction of *normal* childhood from analyses of neurotics had problems of its own. She thought that the way to solve these problems was to observe normal children and other cultures. However, having correctly perceived that the basic Freudian conception of psychobiology and developmental conflict had been misused, she tried to overcome the difficulty by a misapprehension of her own. She went on to set up the dichotomy of culture on the one side, and anatomical, physiological, personal, and psychic development on the other. Her explanations tended to take a form that pitted natural impulses against culture. Where Freud and others had tried, at times, to make intrapsychic development a simple rationalization of biologic necessity, Horney made personal development an expression of natural growth blocked by culture. The same current can be shown to be a subsidiary one in Freud's work. It is also present in the work of others, notably Wilhelm Reich. Both Reich and Horney emphasized the "blockage" of naturally healthy impulses by the culture, although their conceptions of "natural" impulses were different from one another's and from Freud's. For Horney, the biological premises I have noted led her to minimize the importance of sexuality as a motive and to see aggression as a response only to frustration. As in a variety of post-Freudian schools, the rejections of biological factors, of infantile sexuality and the genetic approach go together—as a matter, not of theoretical necessity, but of history.

DISCUSSION

The models and formulations of Freud and Horney deserve a far more detailed comparison and analysis than is possible here. The outstanding aspect is their radically different conceptions of development. For Freud, normality needed to be explained because it was guaranteed neither by nature nor culture. Heterosexuality was not guaranteed by phylogenesis, but had to be achieved by each individual in the course of development via intrapsychic conflict. Both normal and pathological development were possible outcomes of typical developmental conflicts. Drives, ego factors, and environmental events contributed to the instigation and resolution of mental conflict. The genetic approach documents the unfolding and resolution of conflicts throughout development. For Freud (1930), a psychoanalytic explanation is genetic.

The genetic approach in psychoanalysis is easily, and often unwittingly, evaded by developmental approaches in which child behavior, the events of childhood, or biological and social forces are substituted for mental conflict and its resolution as the generator of mental development. Freud easily slipped, for instance, from speaking about sexual fantasies to speaking of the biological forces propelling them, as though they were identical or otherwise interchangeable. In his best moments, he could be very clear about the distinction.

Only a part of Horney's criticisms offered a challenge to the basic Freudian model presented earlier. Where she reversed the formulations for males and females, the model itself is unchanged. All that has taken place is a kind of role reversal. That is, the males have narcissistic injury before castration anxiety, and the women, anxiety before narcissistic injury, instead of the reverse, as Freud had said. The decision between the two formulations must rest on observation, provided that there is agreement on the conceptual framework and on the observations to be considered relevant.

On the other hand, Horney's insistence on primary feminine impulses as the main motivating force was the beginning of her abandonment of the epigenetic model and the genetic point of view. Primary femininity and the unconscious, inborn knowledge of the genital difference and function made heterosexuality a matter of phylogenetic inheritance. In this way, she could bypass the psychological mechanisms that, for Freud, constituted a kind of recapitulation of phylogenetic sexual differentiation ("the great riddle of sex") in the life of each individual.

Although an epigenetic model could be constructed including some kind of "primary" masculinity and femininity, Horney had other objectives. In the first place, she wanted to refute the designation of the earlier phases as "masculine." Second, she began to develop a new perspective based on Simmel's ideas. This led her to emphasize the influence of ideology permeating society, affecting psychological development from birth.

In Freud's conceptualization of his developmental model, phallic narcissism played an important part and provided motivational force in normal development. At the same time, narcissistic injury could play a role in both normal and pathological development, providing for the closeness of the normal and abnormal. Both Horney (1967) and Jones (1927, 1933), however, argued that the phallic phase was not a developmental phase, because they considered narcissistic defenses and conflict to be evidence of pathology. Horney went still further, attacking Freud's idea that the normal and the pathological were not sharply distinguished. To both Horney and Jones, it seemed implausible that nature would accomplish its purpose of creating femininity by means of penis envy. The idea that femininity should depend on the sight of a penis, or that nature would entrust the development of femininity to a "chance occurrence" seemed absurd. Jones appears to have mistaken some conventional idea of femininity based on behavior, anatomy and physiology for a psychosexual concept. From a psychosexual, psychoanalytic perspective on gender, a person's ideas about femininity necessarily include an idea of some masculine counterpart, and the reverse. That is, mental representations of gender depend on comparisons between the sexes.

To Horney, the difficulty women had with being feminine needed an explanation. That is, being satisfied with feminininity would seem "natural" and being dissatisfied "unnatural"—and therefore in need of explanation. The answer, provided by her sociopolitical critique, was that culture could interfere with natural and spontaneous heterosexuality by the devaluation of women. However, the idea that the cultural devaluation of women contributes to women's conflicts with their femininity fits easily into the Freudian model. Horney's reasons for changing the entire model must go unexplored here, but they seem to be related to her ideas about health and pathology. Possibly her reasons were of a more personal nature as well.

As we have seen, Freud, Horney, and Jones differed on the role of narcissism as a normal factor in the sexual development of boys and girls. Horney added that the important role assigned to penis envy in the psychoanalytic formulations of female sexuality was itself an affront to feminine narcissism, an opinion widely echoed in recent feminist critiques of psychoanalysis. This aspect of the controversy draws our attention to the role of narcissism in both theory formation and in gender development.

Both Horney and Jones pointed to biology to support the idea that both masculinity and femininity develop along independent, "natural" lines, rather than one differentiating from the other. Today too the contributions of various factors to the development of gender differences, beginning early in infancy, are taken to support the idea of "primary" masculinity and femininity.

Much of what is called "primary femininity" (Stoller, 1976) today involves the narcissistically invested aspects of biological, social, and psychological makeup that are readily observable outwardly and are conventionally recognized. The psychoanalytic contribution to the study of gender, however, has been the exploration of fantasies revealing the meaning of these differences throughout development. From this point of view, the narcissistic value of these characteristics distinguishing the sexes is of particular interest to a psychoanalytic understanding of gender.

Freud considered the narcissistic investment of the genitals the cornerstone of gender development beginning with the recognition of the anatomical distinction. However, the infantile mental life already recognizes other differences between people before the difference of the genitals attains significance. The narcissistic value placed on masculinity and femininity would therefore seem to be a stage in the transformation of the narcissism attached to all kinds of differences throughout development. In this case, it is a "narcissism of not-so-small differences," to paraphrase Freud.

This important step elaborates the meanings attached to differences recognized earlier in development in association with the differentiation of self and object. We have here a counterpart to the transformations of anal fantasies into those of "the infantile genital organization" (Freud, 1916–17, 1971, 1933). The "anatomical distinction between the sexes," once recognized, derives some of its significance from the conflicts that have marked the child's other struggles with the differences between itself and others. Freud noted a kind of re-editing process in development when he wrote that the classification "active" and "passive" in the anal stage *looks, from the viewpoint of the genital stage, like masculinity and femininity.* In a similar way, we may suppose that the values attaching to differences between self and other, such as big and small, clean and dirty, are assimilated to the meaning of the genital difference. Children's traits that the observing adults conventionally regard as masculine and feminine take on that meaning and an associated narcissistic value for the child and seem to play a role, as well, in adult antagonisms between the sexes.

In practice, we know that the transformations of pregenital into genital fantasies are achieved slowly and usually incompletely. Instead of this transformation that accompanies optimal oedipal resolution, we often see displacements of pregenital fantasies onto manifestly genital and heterosexual behavior. Similarly, the transformation of narcissism attaching to all kinds of differences is generally incomplete and is reflected in gender stereotypes and other social stereotypes. It is not the process of generalization that points to the persistence of the more primitive attitude towards differences, but rather the stereotyping of the values attached to differences. The fact that masculinity and femininity are generally discussed in terms of paired opposite traits similarly betrays the origin of such classification schemes. Freud's triads of subject-active-masculine and object-passive-feminine is an example of dichotomous grouping that has psychological reality for many people. However, examination of the biology of sex and the psychology and behavior of gender reveals *differences* rather than *opposites*.

Our patients' conflicts concerning gender often take the form of treating sexual differences as opposition or of denying differences of their significance. The denial of differences is intended to ward off the potential narcissistic injury of "classification by opposites," which so easily becomes pride or stigma, good or bad, superior or inferior and so on. These dichotomies are important, of course, in the establishment of identity. Their importance for the security of gender identity probably contributes to the persistence of the narcissism attached to sexual differences in our patients, our theories, and in society at large.

CONCLUSION

Horney's earliest papers on female sexuality were offered as elaborations and corrections of particular ideas on female sexuality and retained, or at least did not openly challenge, the basic model. Soon, however, her criticism became much more extensive. In the end, she systematically rejected a number of basic principles, along with the model discussed, and formulated the theories for which she became famous.

Just as female sexuality is a special case of broader problems of psychoanalytic theory, the controversy between Freud and Horney illustrates how the examination of controversy can increase understanding of basic models. By the choice of a critical moment in the development of psychoanalysis, a point of conflict and divergence in the history of psychoanalytic thought, aspects of the theory are revealed that might not be evident otherwise. Thus, while the subject of the paper has been female sexuality as seen by Horney and Freud, the central issue is: What is essential to psychoanalytic theory? The method of examining a critical moment of controversy, or change, as a prototype has more general applicability and can be used to examine the development of Freud's thought as well. The important point is that the outcome of controversies, and the integration of new ideas and observations into a theory, may depend on how well basic concepts and models are understood. Often controversies and, therefore, the history of psychoanalysis are a blend of theoretical, methodological, and emotional differences. Differences of opinion that appear to involve matters of fact or interpretation may instead be based on entirely different fundamental principles and explanatory models. Such, I believe, was the case of Freud and Horney.

If this controversy led Horney to the formulation of a new theory, what did it do for Freudian theory? One answer is that it revealed a tendency among Horney's contemporaries to be inconsistent in their application of psychological principles in preference to biological explanations, to take too simplified a view of masculine developmennt, and to take for granted that the dissatisfaction of women with their lot was inevitable. Her recourse to sociocultural explanation pointed to the need for a more comprehensive formulation of the way sociocultural factors are involved in intrapsychic conflict. In this way, Horney's critique has led to the enlargement and enrichment of Freudian theory and the fuller realization of the potential embodied in its basic models.

REFERENCES

Abend, S. M. (1979), Unconscious fantasy and theories of cure. *J. Amer. Psychoanal. Assn.,* 27:579–596.

Arlow, J. A. (1981), Theories of pathogenesis. *Psychoanal. Quart.,* 50:488–514.

Barnett, M. C. (1968), "I can't" versus "he won't": Further considerations of the psychical consequences of the anatomical and physiological differences between the sexes. *J. Amer. Psychoanal. Assn.,* 16:588–600.

Blum, H. P. (1976), Masochism, the ego ideal, and the psychology of women. *J. Amer. Psychoanal. Assn.,* 24:157–192.

Chasseguet-Smirgel, J. (1975), Freud and female sexuality: The consideration of some blind spots in the exploration of the dark continent. *Internat. J. Psycho-Anal.,* 57:275–286.

Deutsch, H. (1925), The psychology of women in relation to the functions of reproduction. In: *The Psychoanalytic Reader,* ed. R. Fliess. New York: International Universities Press, 1969, pp. 165–179.

Erikson, E. H. (1945), Problems of infancy and early childhood. In: An Outline of Abnormal Psychology, ed., G. Murphy & A. J. Bachrach. New York: Modern Library, 1954, pp. 3–36.

Fliegel, Z. O. (1973), Feminine psychosexual development in Freudian theory: A historical reconstruction. *Psychoanal. Quart.,* 42:385–408.

Freud, S. (1905), Three essays on the theory of sexuality. *Standard Edition,* 7:135–243. London: Hogarth Press, 1953.

_____ (1915), Instincts and their vicissitudes. *Standard Edition,* 14:117–140. London: Hogarth Press, 1957.

_____ (1916–17), *Introductory lectures on psycho-analysis. Standard Edition,* 15 & 16. London: Hogarth Press, 1963.

_____ (1917), On transformations of instinct as exemplified in anal erotism. *Standard Edition,* 17:125–133, 1955.

_____ (1920), Beyond the pleasure principle. *Standard Edition,* 18:7–64. London: Hogarth Press, 1955.

_____ (1923), The infantile genital organization: An interpolation into the theory of sexuality. *Standard Edition,* 19:139–145. London: Hogarth Press, 1961.

_____ (1925), Some psychical consequences of the anatomical distinction between the sexes. *Standard Edition,* 19:248–258. London: Hogarth Press, 1961.

_____ (1930), Civilization and its discontents. *Standard Edition,* 21:64–145. London: Hogarth Press, 1961.

_____ (1933), New introductory lectures on psycho-analysis. *Standard Edition,* 22:5–182. London: Hogarth Press, 1964.

_____ (1937), Analysis terminable and interminable. *Standard Edition,* 23:216–253. London: Hogarth Press, 1964.

_____ (1971), Freud and female sexuality: A previously unpublished letter. *Psychiatry,* 34:328–329.

Gedo, J. E., & Goldberg, A. (1973), *Models of the Mind.* Chicago: University of Chicago Press.

Hartmann, H. (1939), *Ego Psychology and the Problem of Adaptation.* New York: International Universities Press, 1958.

Hartmann, H., & Kris, E. (1945), The genetic approach in psychoanalysis. *The Psychoanalytic Study of the Child,* 1:11–30.

Horney, K. (1939), *New Ways in Psychoanalysis.* New York: Norton.

_____ (1967). *Feminine Psychology,* ed. H. Kelman. New York: Norton.

Jones, E. (1927), The early development of female sexuality. In: *Papers on Psychoanalysis.* Boston: Beacon, 1961.

_____ (1933), The phallic phase. In: *Papers on Psychoanalysis.* Boston: Beacon, 1961.

_____ (1935), Early female sexuality. In: *Papers on Psychoanalysis.* Boston: Beacon, 1961.

Kestenberg, J. S. (1968), Outside and inside, male and female. *J. Amer. Psychoanal. Assn.,* 16:457–520.

Kris, E. (1947), The nature of psychoanalytic propositions and their validation. In: *The Selected Papers of Ernst Kris.* New Haven: Yale University Press, 1975, pp. 3–23.

Langer, S. (1967), *Mind: An Essay On Human Feeling.* Vol. 1. Baltimore: Johns Hopkins University Press.

Maguire, J. G. (1983), Epigenesis and psychoanalysis. *Psychoanal. & Contemp. Thought,* 6:3–27.

Rapaport, D. (1951), The conceptual model of psychoanalysis. In: *Psychoanalytic Psychiatry and Psychology: Clinical and Theoretical Papers. Austen Riggs Center, Volume 1,* ed. C. R. Friedman & R. P. Knight. New York: International Universities Press, 1954.

_____ (1960), Psychoanalysis as a developmental psychology. In: *Perspectives in Psychological Theory,* ed. B. Kaplan & S. Wapner. New York: International Universities Press, pp. 209–255.

Ritvo, L. B. (1974), Darwin's Influence on Freud. A dissertation presented to the Faculty of the Graduate School of Yale University. Ann Arbor: University Microfilms.

Schur, M., & Ritvo, L. B. (1970), The concept of development and evolution in psychoanalysis. In: *Development and Evolution of Behavior,* ed. L. R. Aronson, E. Tobach, D. S. Lehrman, & J. S. Rosenblatt. San Francisco: Freeman, pp. 600–619.

Stoller, R. J. (1976), Primary femininity. *J. Amer. Psychoanal. Assn.,* 24:59–78.

Wilson, E. (1973), The structural hypothesis and psychoanalytic metatheory: An essay on psychoanalysis and contemporary philosophy of science. *Psychoanal. & Contemp. Sci.,* 2:304–328.

LEO RANGELL

The Enduring Armature of Psychoanalytic Theory and Method[1]

My aim here is to present what I consider to have endured as the guiding principles for the conduct of an analysis. While these views reflect the opinions of a significant number of analysts who adhere to certain central tenets of psychoanalysis, what any one person regards as enduring can only be subjective and relative. I will attempt to acquaint you in the briefest way with the working "credo" of *this* psychoanalyst. What I hope to do is impart to those embarking upon their psychoanalytic careers a distillate of the convictions that have emerged in a practicing theoretician-clinician who has been immersed in every aspect of psychoanalytic activity for four decades.

Of course, to capture the enduring does not mean to be impervious or resistant to change. In attending to lasting critical issues, I am moved to add that disclaimer in view of the widespread espousal of change as a desirable trend in itself, even in matters of scientific understanding. Moreover, the psychoanalytic body, like audiences in general, is not above reacting to any stance or contribution by assuming, erroneously, that another, perhaps opposite, constellation has been neglected or opposed.

---

[1]An earlier version of this paper was presented at The Psychoanalytic Forum, American Psychoanalytic Association, Philadelphia, April 28, 1983. This annual lecture at the spring meeting of the American Psychoanalytic Association is especially directed to candidates and recent graduates. The purpose of the format is to provide an opportunity for nascent and young analysts to share the thoughts and experiences of a more senior analyst.

This is reminiscent of the anecdote—I call it an anecdote rather than a joke—in which a mother brings a gift of two ties to her son. He tries on one of them, at which the mother bursts into tears, stating, "I knew you would not like the other one."

This chapter will present what I consider to have endured, at least for me, for this contemporary period of time. Obviously, because of space limitations, this presentation can be only a running commentary of selected highlights that strike me as most important to include. (While many opinions will appear to be summary statements, I usually have elaborated upon them elsewhere and will indicate these sources where more detailed argument and related bibliography can be found) What has also endured is a constant openness to modifications that can advance understanding. For one who is regarded as the epitome of the classical analyst, Dr. Brenner has himself suggested a surprising number of changes in psychoanalytic theory—giving the lie to the myth that traditional means final or stagnant in thought.

I too have, at various times, added and suggested amendments to theoretical concepts. However, additions or amendments to theory or therapy do not automatically qualify as valid or accepted. Whether small and discrete propositions, more global suggested revisions, or entirely new systems of explanation and understanding, all have to pass the test of time, through the filter and crucible of clinical discourse. For all suggested changes, not rhetoric or repetition or intense group behavior, but continuing clinical observations will be the base for future validation (Rangell, 1985). In the long run, the criterion determining the value of the theory will be the "fit" between clinic and theory, or, as Arlow (1981) put it, its "ability to comprehend in the most parsimonious fashion the data of observation."

Not all suggested changes are confluent or compatible, and each has to be considered on its own. Change, popular interest in which has carried over from societal issues to scientific theory, has been a center of ferment and the subject in recent years of innumerable psychiatric and psychoanalytic conferences on both general theory and a variety of subtopics in both fields, at all developmental levels, and in all geographic ares. I have participated in many of these, and, throughout, my incentive and mode (in polarities in general and on this issue in particular) has been to balance the popular, and invariably temporary, swings.

My focus on what I believe endures can be profitable as a backdrop against which to judge changes as well. Changes can be rational, constructive, and helpful, or change can be an end in itself—change for change's sake, or it can be based on deep psychological reasons that demand that it be studied and understood, rather than automatically accepted and acted on. There is also the question whether suggested new directions are indeed changes or whether they merely lift out a part that has always been integrated into the whole.

Psychoanalytic technique brings about the psychoanalytic situation, which permits the unfolding of the psychoanalytic process toward the achievement of psychoanalytic goals (Rangell, 1968). Together these comprise the psychoanalytic method. In applying the technique to institute the sequence that constitutes the method of psychoanalysis, theory is as essential as it is in understanding neurosogenesis. Fenichel (1941) has shown how the metapsychological points of view of psychoanalytic theory apply to the theory of therapy as well. These are as closely integrated into the process of therapy as the "clinical theory" which G. Klein (1973) and his school would substitute for them.

Waelder (1962) pointed to a hierarchy of levels of abstraction according to the distance of theoretical concepts from clinical observation. Brenner (1980), discussing the metapsychology of psychoanalytic theory, differentiates abstract from speculative and points out that theoretical psychoanalytic generalizations are always closely bound to direct observations by the psychoanalytic method. I have stated (1985) that the abstract and the observable are interwined at all levels. Clinical inferences are also based on theory. The theoretical is involved in the immediate interpretation of every clinical observation, and what is considered the most abstract of theoretical formulations derives its strength ultimately from a clinical base. Transference for example, a central clinical phenomenon, is based on theory and concept, while the dynamic and genetic metapsychological points of view, like all the others, are built squarely into the clinical therapeutic process.

A central and permanent fulcrum of the technical procedure is the "analytic attitude" with which the analyst enters the analytic process and which he maintains throughout its course. To acquire the ability to achieve this stance, certain basic criteria for becoming an analyst need to be met. One's basic character before training needs to contain at least the potential for the relentless incorruptibility, resistance to seduction, and tolerance for frustration necessary to maintain the life of an analyst. The high priority of the value of truth had best bring with it ego satisfactions as well as superego peace if it is to last.

The analytic stance is the conduit for the analysis and the futherance of analytic therapy. The most difficult skill to impart by the training process, it requires a combination of preparedness and analytic experience to be achieved and maintained. To advance the analytic aims, the "attitude" of the analyst is to be able to encourage without seducing, to be neutral without being cold, to invite the undoing of repression while giving the patient reason to feel reassured against the threat involved. These requirements do not make for "an impossible profession." They can be, and indeed are performed every day. The capacity of the analyst to represent subtly and consistently a fusion of opposites becomes for the patient, unconsciously if not overtly, a model for the resolution of conflict. No two analysts do this in the same way, perhaps not even similarly. Each has his or her individual style, and there is room for differences. But these characteristics in a broad way, are held in common.

The analytic attitude is a necessary condition if the analyst is to be able to apply both the science and the art of psychoanalysis. Not all analysts have it or can maintain it consistently. A significant number of psychoanalysts, after training and even in practice, slowly or abruptly give it up. To the patient, the attitude of the analyst constitutes simultaneously a threat and an opportunity, a new experience welcomed to a greater or lesser degree.

Embedded in the question of analyzability is the prospective patient's unconscious affinity for the knowledge, the insight, that analysis will provide. I venture to say from experience that the patient's choice of analyst is not a random one, that the status and nature of the patient's deep desire to know may exert an influence on that initial decision. One patient told the analyst, many years into a productive analysis—a prolonged experience akin to an expansion of the "good hour" described by Kris (1956)—"You were direct from the start, you talked plain and simple, there was no bullshit." He had rejected other analysts he had interviewed, analysts more charismatic but unreliable. Other patients enter into an analytic situation on the basis of, I believe, some existing char acterologic affinity to a relationship that will combine acting out and countertransference. The choice of analyst can be of analytic interest. The die need not be cast in the first hour. Trial analysis is as much for the patient to test the analyst as for the analyst is to assess the patient's analyzability.

The positive effects of the new opportunity made available to the patient by the analytic environment, at the center of which is the person and mental attitude of the analyst, fosters the development of a therapeutic alliance between the analytic function of the analyst and the analyzing ego of the patient. This has been variously described, in historical sequence, as the effective positive transference (Freud, 1912); an ego alliance following a therapeutic split in the ego (Sterba, 1934); rational transference (Fenichel, 1941); basic trust (Erikson, 1950); primary transference, the primal matrix of transference, based on the early mother-child relationship (Greenacre, 1954); basic transference (Bibring, 1954), the diatrophic relationship (Spitz, 1956); anaclitic dyad (Gitelson, 1962); therapeutic alliance (Zetzel, 1956); mature transference (Stone, 1961), and the working alliance, or real relationship (Greenson, 1972; Greenson & Wexler, 1969).

The meaning of this relationship, and individual efforts to utilize it in action, have been the center of confusion and debate. Although each author gave to this alliance a different shade of meaning and origin, this aspect of the relationship, the working bond between the two participants, even with its vicissitudes and variations, is a necessary platform to sustain the rigors of the course of the analytic procedure. The analytic attitude has changed considerably since Freud's time – from the original hypnosis; through the laying on of hands; to Freud's evolving attitudes in the succession of his classical cases as he came increasingly to understand the transference; to the major step forward with Anna Freud's (1936) recommended equidistant stance; since then to a tendency to become rigid and less human; and now, it is hoped, to an effective combination of the scientific and humanistic.

A variety of behavior, however, results from attempts in practice to achieve a proper blend. This ranges from a too assiduous application of neutrality to an excessive closeness and intimacy from misapplication of the technical concept of empathy. The results at either end, from stiffness and artificiality on the one hand to supportive reassurance rather than the optimum necessary abstinence on the other, can stifle rather than encourage the emergence of unacceptable impulses or other repressed psychic elements.

In a carefully reasoned argument, Brenner (1979c) feels that the therapeutic alliance is no different from any other aspect of the relationship to the analyst and should be absorbed into the transference and treated as such. Although neurotic elements do encroach on this aspect of the relationship and are to be constantly assessed and accounted for, my own position is consonant with the prevailing view that the therapeutic alliance is a useful, even necessary, platform to sustain the patient's motivation to overcome the internal obstacles to the introspective process of analysis. It is on the basis of this strength that the ego of the patient can be confronted and its analyzing function enlisted toward the aim of overcoming the resistances that oppose it. While these are characteristically to the repressed libidinal and aggressive drives, the alliance is also especially valuable in permitting insight into the negative transference or into the more subtle area of openness to interpretations of the bribing of the superego in everyday life (Rangell, 1974).

The therapeutic alliance is not achieved by urging, anymore than it was originally achieved by the laying on of hands (Breuer & Freud, 1893–5), nor by holding (Winnicott, 1958, 1965) or by a diatrophic (Spitz, 1956) or anaclitic (Gitelson, 1962) or maternal (Zetzel, 1956) attitude on the part of the analyst. What stimulates trust in the patient for the analyst are the nonmoralizing and nonintrusive aspects of the analyst's neutral, uninvolved stance (Blum, 1983) and interpretations from this position that promise a diminution of anxiety and an increase of mastery. It is these events and developments that enlist the inquiring and testing ego to develop a trust that permits the analytic process to unfold.

Nonconflictual clinical material, of which the therapeutic alliance is one variety, does not present the urgency or the affects to require analysis. In the same way, not every transference reaction is equally subject to interpretation at each moment of the analytic hour. A too automatic approach in this respect, with a fixed and obsessive attention to every minute detail of the "here and now," can lead to a caricature of the analytic process. In the current analytic milieu, this tendency, especially in the inexperienced analyst, is as prevalent as exaggeration and misapplication of the aim of neutrality was in the past.

A fine line separates the appropriate from the strange in conceptualizing the therapeutic alliance and analyzing the transference. Experiences, too often seen in clinical presentations, can result that are easily categorized as absurd by those inclined to ridicule psychoanalysis. While transference elements can and do invade the therapeutic alliance, it is these intrusions rather than the alliance itself that require interpretation. The therapeutic alliance in its normal functioning is the vehicle for the analysis of the transference neurosis.

The analytic evolution of a therapeutic alliance is to be distinguished from the fostering or failure to interpret the defense mechanism of idealization. A common misunderstanding by followers of Kohut's (1971) recommendation, this practice, of maintaining idealization, is utilized by mutual consent of patient and analyst to preserve distortion rather than analyze it. Idealization, like other defenses, is to be analyzed when indicated in accordance with the dynamic rules of interpretation, such as from the surface down or resistances before content (Fenichel, 1941). The criterion in all instances is the readiness of the ego to deal with the emergence of the repressed content. The rule to refrain from interpretative analysis when the dynamic state does not indicate such interpretation applies to idealization as much as but no more than to any other repressed clinical content. These guideposts apply similarly and equally across the diagnostic spectrum, in neurotic as much as in narcissistic patients.

The "real relationship" (Greenson, 1972) of the analyst to the patient is the analytic relationship between the two, designed to further the analytic work to uncover and understand. It includes being human and natural and is vitiated if the opposite is the case. Anna Freud (1980) said , 'It is natural for human beings to be human. But if their analysts and teachers turn them into something wooden, and then try to turn them back into human beings, it becomes difficult" (p. 10). But humanness is not the essence, or indeed the contribution, of psychoanalysis. Psychoanalysis shares characteristics with other relationships and disciplines. Its uniqueness is not that the analyst "cares for" the patient, or loves him, or admires him in order to build his self-esteem, nor conversely that he deprecates him, as some patients or others might come to think.

The analyst cares for and respects the patient as a human being. Respect occurs to me as a concept not sufficiently explored in depth in psychoanalytic discourse or writings. To like the patient is desirable but is not a sine qua non. The analyst will, or should, admire him if he is admirable. Sometimes this is arrived at with the success of their goal. To "love" the patient becomes an interference and introduces a problem. Analytic empathy is embedded in a proper amalgam and integration of these positive cognitive–affective attitudes.

To accomplish the goals of the psychoanalytic process, the analyst's observing and regulating stance is equidistant between the psychic structures within the patient, between the internal and external world, between past, present and future. Surveying the interstructural relationships, treatment, encompassing the cognitive and affective, is not directed to the id alone, to effect discharge or sublimation; nor to the ego in isolation, toward mastery and control; nor to superego values specifically, for change or amelioration. All of these and their inter-relationships are addressed simultaneously. It is not only, as Freud (1933) said, "Where id was, there ego shall be," but also, as Loewald (1978) was moved to add, "Where ego is, there id shall come into being again to renew the life of the ego and of reason." (p. 16). Integration (Hartmann, 1950), or synthesis (Nunberg, 1931), are as close as we have been able to come to a definition of "normal," or of "mental health."

The analyst roams over the entire field, impinging upon the patient from within and without. "Free" associations that indicate that a patient has become stuck at any one point are like a needle on an instrument that has become stuck – it may need a tap to get it moving freely again. If the material consists only of dreams, or if the associations are all of one kind – all sexual or all deep, none recent and everyday or even trivial – the instrument may need a tap. The analyst's instrument (Isa kower, 1957) consists of both primary and secondary process receptors. Its overall scanning function is aimed toward the id and the ego, the conscious and the unconscious, the superego and the external world. As Arlow (1979) pointed out about the interpretive work of the analyst, "The aesthetic and cognitive components . . . proceed side by side." (p. 203).

Every analysis is a training analysis (Rangell, 1968). It is also a supervised analysis to the patient's ego, if the patient is to experience, savor, learn, and eventually be able to take over the analytic process. The "transmuting internalizations" described by Kohut (1971) take place not through an identification with the analyst's high regard for the patient, but by an introjection of the analyst's analytic function. This – not the analyst's style, preferences, or even his theories – is what is, or should be, identified with. Too many training analyses betray their nature in just such a way: transference, both positive and negative, is displaced from the candidate's analyst to his theories (Rangell, 1982b), usually with a permanent stultification of the subsequent scientific life and creativity of the new analyst.

A central focus and sine qua non in the psychoanalytic material uncovered and analyzed is conflict – internal-external conflicts internalized into the intrapsychic and progressing in their content through all developmental phases. Here Brenner has been a steadfast adherent and contributor. From the standpoint of drives, ego characteristics, superego values, or object-relations, one cannot overestimate the ubiquity and clinical necessity for the analysis of ambivalence, at all levels and in all its ramifications. Brenner (1982), following Freud, has amplified and clarified the mechanisms and vicissitudes of id-ego conflicts; I have at various times elaborated other aspects of intrapsychic conflict, which I consider have been insufficiently dealt with theoretically and paid inadequate attention in clinical analyses and in writings on the theory of therapy. I am referring to two specific aspects of intrapsychic conflict; one, the ubiquitous and significant conflicts between ego and superego (Rangell, 1974, 1976, 1980); the other, the introduction of a class of conflicts seldom written about, which I have called "choice" or "dilemma" conflicts (1963a, 1963b, 1969, 1971).

The ego, beset by conflicting pressures from internal psychic structures, and between these and the external environment, needs to "decide" and "choose" the path of discharge among the avenues open to it for resolution. Just as interpersonal conflicts become intrapsychic ones, intersystemic conflicts become intrasystemic choice conflicts within the ego, where their resolution is called for and routinely operative. Unconscious intention, will, decision, and choice enter the intrapsychic sequential pictures. Forerunners to action, these need to play as much a part in the therapeutic procedure as in theory. I cannot elaborate upon this subject further here; the reader is referred to my earlier work. In the complex fabric of a human life, the concept of intrasystemic conflicts introduced by Hartmann (1950) plays a useful, necessary, and constant role.

While I agree with Hartmann (1939) on the conflict-free, and with the concept of psychoanalysis as a general theory, I also concur with Anna Freud (1936), Kris (1947), and Brenner (1979a) that the psychoanalytic method is a treatment of conflict. A major theoretical division appears at this point: the need to assess the prominent place given in recent writings and movements to patients who suffer mainly from deficits, or at least purportedly more from deficits than conflict. Due to the need to be selective, many of the subjects I have been focusing upon are those that are either unclear or controversial. In all cases considered within the purview of psychoanalytic treatment both elements combine. Not only does conflict play a part in all cases with developmental arrests, but the reverse is also true — deficits and developmental limitations have preexisted conflict and been admixed with it. Blum (1983) has pointed out that antecedent factors result in arrests, and succeeding conflicts follow them. Deficits, deficiencies, insufficiencies of structure — somatic and psychic — play a part in all final psychic outcomes. These are also not limited to one diagnostic category — borderline, narcissistic, psychotic, or "the more disturbed" — but occur across the diagnostic spectrum. Moreover, many developmental arrests are due to fixations, which are themselves based on conflicts. By attracting future regressions, these can have the same effects as deficits in blocking subsequent development (Rangell, 1982a, 1984).

The treatment of so called deficit states without conflict — putting aside the philosophic question of "tragic man" (Kohut, 1977) as a prototype of modern neuroses — is not by psychoanalysis; the treatment of lacks or deficiencies is by replenishment, such as by education, training, or other rehabilitative modalities. Anna Freud (1976) put it subtly and well when she pointed out that analysis can help the ego correct what it did but not what was done to it.

The content of intrapsychic conflict scanned, uncovered and analyzed by the psychoanalytic method ranges from pregenital to oedipal and postoedipal. With increasing clinical and theoretical knowledge over the years, all levels are seen to be present and operative in all cases. Pathology of the self-representation within the ego is also variously involved in all cases. Self-pathology is not pathognomonic for borderline or narcissistic states and should not be automatically connected with them (Rangell, 1982a). The fallacy is the same and requires the same correction as when conversion historically was automatically associated with hysteria (Rangell, 1959).

There is no borderline case without oedipal conflicts, although these have been distorted by preoedipal determinants. Kernberg (1979), after years of exploring the pregenital backgrounds of borderline patients, came to this conclusion. It had been pointed out earlier by Arlow and Brenner (1964) about psychotics, while Boyer (1966) had made the same point about the relationship between deficits and preoedipal and oedipal conflicts in schizophrenia.

The goal is to resolve inter- and intrastructural conflicts. I have seen a generation of analysts trained to bypass structural conflicts in favor of issues of the self. In former years similar movement was toward the concept of ego identity (Erikson, 1956). In common with object-relations theory and some aspects of Kleinian analyses, such theoretical movements converge toward interpersonal analysis, focusing on conflicts between internal and external, or intrapsychically between introjections of the self and objects as undifferentiated wholes. What is regressively lost is an awareness of internal psychic divisions and explanations that can stem only from them. And, as always, theory is reflected in treatment. The transference then becomes a dyadic exchange rather than a more complex interchange between conflicting parts within each participant.

Turning away from structural conflicts not only alters the treatment of neuroses, but sacrifices the power to explain and understand them. Neurosogenesis and neurosolysis are reciprocal and complementary. Joining the patient in his defense against conflict gratifies resistances, which stem in part from an unconscious fear of fragmentation of the self. This contrasts with the analytic aim to restore a healthy self-representation by healing this and other splits within the ego caused by neurotic conflict and division.

Psychoanalytic activity revolves around the operations of the ego against anxiety. Freud (1926) saw anxiety as "the fundamental problem of neurosis," a view he never saw fit to change. Anxiety, in my opinion, is the motive for defense, even in the presence of other pathological affects (Rangell, 1978). Hence, anxiety is not the equivalent of depression, guilt, or shame, but occupies a special place in neurosogenesis even in the pathological presence of any of the latter. While Brenner (1979b) sees depression as operative at the same level as anxiety, other major affects, such as guilt or shame (Wurmser, 1981), can play an equally prominent role as depression without any of them reducing the role of anxiety. Anxiety results from loss of control of any other affect, just as of any impulse or other drive derivative or stimulus that threatens to overrun the stimulus-barrier.

The goal of analysis is not existential but analytic. The psychoanalytic process is conducted at the edge of the defense against anxiety. Analysis is not directed toward what a person is, but what he suffers. This is frequently misunderstood by analysts and the public alike. In fact, it is confluent with and should be reassuring to many patients who worry that analysis will change what they are, rather than what they suffer and wish to change. This distinction holds true even though the analysis of character comes to take precedence and to be the definitive analytic goal over the presenting symptoms. It is the latent and unconscious operations around anxiety that determine the motives and directions for the analytic path.

The basic anxieties still are those related to separation and castration, not anxiety over madness and death, as claimed in recent revisions (Green, 1975) purportedly based on new clinical experience. Infantile anxieties, which remain potent in the unconscious, do not change with changing styles. That "neuroses are, so to say, the negative of perversions," another of Freud's (1905, p. 165) seminal and early insights, in my opinion, still holds true (Rangell, 1975). Although this is not a formulation heard much today, my psychoanalytic practice attests to its continuing operation; phobia is a model of the neurosis which, in my experience, bears this out. The presence of perverse elements in phobia — without a pejorative connotation but referring to partial sexual impulses repressed by the patient — and of phobic anxiety, with or without a discrete phobic object, in cases of perversion, such as homosexuality, are clinical findings that confirm these ideas.

I would add the following explanatory note. From my cumulative clinical experience, castration anxiety is the most overlooked of the insights to come from analysis (Rangell, 1982c, 1983). This is partly because the psychoanalytic process is designed more for the exposure of separation conflicts than for castration conflicts. Mostly, however, it is the nature and strength of the specific resistances against castration conflicts that bring this about. This is also a subject I can but touch and leave.

Of the many other areas of almost permanent debate within the psychoanalytic process and method, I will briefly allude to my views on two. Transference versus reconstruction is one subject prominently pushed into a false polarity (Rangell, 1979). In a definition of psychoanalysis in 1954, I described the goal of analysis as the resolution of both the transference neurosis and the infantile neurosis, a formulation I have found to be sturdy and have no reason to change. The transference neurosis is an iatrogenic product en route to the patient's infantile neurosis.

Since Strachey's innovative paper of 1934 on the mutative effects of transference interpretation, the familiar fallacy of exclusivity has focused on this aspect of the therapeutic process. Following Strachey's opinion that "conflicts of the remote past [concern] dead circumstances and mummified personalities" (1969, p. 277), only what is "immediate" (Heimann, 1956, p. 307) or in the "here and now" (Gill, 1979, p. 265) has come to be thought of as having conviction or therapeutic effect.

Waelder (1967) has pointed out that history is an alternation of excesses. Not every association of a patient during an analytic hour refers to the analyst, even though one would gain that impression formerly from Kleinian or object-relations analyses, and, more recently, in the hands of some, even from ego analyses in structural terms. The automatic interpretation of every moment in the transference has become almost a moral imperative. Analysis should never abandon "common sense," an orientation in the conscious from which the unconscious is viewed. I concur with the objections to analysis by "transference only" expressed by Leites (1977), Anna Freud (1968), Stone (1981), and others. Freud (1900) stated that every dream in analysis stands on three legs, the past, the transference, and the extraanalytic present. I believe the same is true during analysis for any symptom and for the contents and free associations of every analytic hour. An analyst who is bound excessively to any one of the three overlooks the other two.

Another point I wish to comment on is that with the elevation of transference has come a denigration of insight, as it refers to the patient's past. Reconstructive connections have come to be regarded with suspicion, often leading to an attitude on the part of the analyst that paradoxically reinforces the defenses of the patient. Basch (1980), for example, discourages history taking as likely to lead to connections that "are either trivial or wrong." While this is partially true, it is a matter of degree. Writing from the Kohutian view, Basch (1980) states, "Only in the crucible of transference and in the glow of reawakened affect can the participants in the therapy become aware of how the past informs the present" (p. 179). I can partially agree, if the past is equally warmed in the process.

I am heartened by the reemphasis on insight (Blum, 1979; Anna Freud, 1979; Kennedy, 1979; Neubauer, 1979) and would have us pause to consider the meaning of insight's having to be reinforced. From my clinical experience, I would not only reestablish the relevance of insight, but also would speak for its central importance, however rarely some feel this may be achieved. Blum (1977) speaks for the value of reconstruction even of the early preoedipal period. Strachey's (1934) "mummified" personalities of the past exert very living effects in the present, as is known clinically even in average analyses. Psychoanalysis often acquires its deepest insights from the most defended directions, which dynamically are also the most subject to rerepression.

Consider the following few sentences spoken by a patient, chosen almost at random: (I would compare the metaphor employed by the patient with one I used in a case I reported (1952) of a doll phobia, in which I described the symptom of the doll as at the hub of a wheel). The patient said, "At the center of it all is my obsession about penis size. Everything radiates out from that, like when a bullet hits a windshield which cracks in all directions. My whole life stems from that." The patient was speaking of his homosexual perversion, his phobic anxieties, his pan-neurosis. He was also referring to his success in life. Everything he did and was had to be the biggest. One need not apologize for genetic reconstruction, as is commonly the case today, but one had better look to reconstruction of the past by way of the extraanalytic present and the transference to get it all, including castration and aggression in the center of other unconscious conflicts.

Transference is a special phenomenon of the psychoanalytic method. To maintain proper balance, the caution I am expressing against its excess is not to be taken as a reason to turn in the opposite direction. Brenner (1982) stated that the difference between transference that occurs in life and transference in analysis is that it is analyzed there. It is also, however, seen in sharper focus in analysis than anywhere else, because of the analytic attitude of the analyst, an attitude not encountered by the patient anywhere else in life. This instrument of analysis needs to be guarded and maintained, if the analyst is to remain eligible for a transference neurosis, which will reveal the patient's aggressive as well as libidinal drives, and castration as well as separation anxieties in the necessary transference aspects of their occurrence.

The psychoanalytic process is not a dialogue, as Leavy (1980) writes. Nor is it the monologue it is so often caricatured to be. It is a controlled relationship for a specific purpose. An ultimate paradoxical distortion of the meaning and method of this alliance is a description by Stolorow, Brandchaft, and Atwood (1983) of intersubjectivity between patient and analyst, on the basis of which the authors, having built a system of self-psychology upon borderline and narcissistic states, now state that there are no difficult patients, only ill-fitted therapeutic pairs.

I wish to draw attention now to what happens after insight, and the role of the patient between insight and change during the course of the psychoanalytic process (Rangell, 1981). As the first of a final two-step increment in analysis, the experimental intrapsychic scanning process, which before analysis had resulted to an excessive degree in the signal of anxiety, now responds preponderantly with the signal of safety. But decision and action are now the patient's to effect. Regression to oral dependency, not uncommon at this stage, requires the same neutrality and relentless analysis as at any other point in the analysis. As Freud pointed out and warned in his last communication (1940), the analyst is particularly called upon at this juncture to resist the temptation "to create men in his own image" by lending direction to the patient's final choices.

Here I stress the "responsibility of insight." If ego autonomy is the goal, one cannot have it both ways. Previous interdictions against acting out need to be superseded now by a realistic analysis of the role of action, defended against until now in the patient's life under the pressures of anxiety and conflict.

This brings up a subject of much interest to me, the question of the agent of decision and action. While a growing literature, including the work of G. Klein (1973), Schafer (1976), Kohut (1977), and Gedo (1979), indicates a preference for the whole as agent, whether the person, the self, or a self-schema, I had described (1969, 1971) the unconscious decision-making function of the ego within and entirely consonant with the structural and metapsychological points of view. I cannot elaborate on this further here, except to say that this important and insufficiently explored subject needs to be more generally absorbed and integrated. Kohut (1977), for example, stated that he found no place for intention, choice, decision, and action within classical structural metapsychology, a view I find singularly incomplete.

Does the point of view I have expressed make psychoanalytic theory a monolithic structure, as some see it or fear it to be? I see total psychoanalytic theory, as it has evolved with its additions and modifications from the beginning, in spirit and aim as the most complete theory of mental understanding, although it remains an unfinished one. The current state of total psychoanalytic theory, as I see it, encompasses "diversity in unity." That is why there are multiple, not one but five or six, points of view within metapsychology, and why the principles of multiple function (Waelder, 1930) and overdetermination (Freud, 1900) play central orienting roles in assessing all psychic phenomena. I believe that such a totally unified view, with a multiplicity of elements encompassed within its contents, is more logical, coherent, consistent than and preferable in theory and principle to the view that there is a different theory for different nosological entities, or to the suggestion of one modern theorist that "a cafeteria of paradigms" could be an advance, perhaps even a different theory for each patient.

REFERENCES

Arlow, J. A. (1979), The genesis of interpretation. *J. Amer. Psychoanal. Assn.*, 27 (Suppl.):193–206.

_____ (1981), Theories of pathogenesis. *Psychoanal. Quart.*, 50: 488–514.

_____ & Brenner, C. (1964), *Psychoanalytic Concepts and the Structural Theory.* New York: International Universities Press.

Basch, M. F. (1980), *Doing Psychotherapy.* New York: Basic Books.

Bibring, E. (1954), Psychoanalysis and the dynamic psychotherapies. *J. Amer. Psychoanal. Assn.*, 2:745–770.

Blum, H. P. (1977), The prototype of preoedipal reconstruction. *J. Amer. Psychoanal. Assn.*, 25:757–785.

_____ (1979), The curative and creative aspects of insight. *J. Amer. Psychoanal. Assn.*, 27(Suppl.):41–69.

_____ (1983), The psychoanalytic process and analytic inference: A clinical study of a lie and loss. *Internat. J. Psycho-Anal.*, 64:17–33.

Boyer, L. B. (1966), Office treatment of schizophrenic patients by psychoanalysis. *Psychoanal. Forum*, 1:337–346.

Brenner, C. (1979a), The components of psychic conflict and its consequences in mental life. *Psychoanal. Quart.*, 48:547–567.

_____ (1979b), Depressive affect, anxiety, and psychic conflict in the phallic-oedipal phase. *Psychoanal. Quart.*, 48:177–197.

_____ (1979c), Working alliance, therapeutic alliance, and transference. *J. Amer. Psychoanal. Assn.*, 27:137–157.

_____ (1980), Metapsychology and psychoanalytic theory. *Psychoanal. Quart.*, 49:189–214.

_____ (1982), *The Mind in Conflict*. New York: International Universities Press.

Breuer, J. & Freud, S. (1893–1895), Studies on hysteria. *Standard Edition*, 2. London: Hogarth Press, 1955.

Erikson, E. H. (1950), *Childhood and Society*. New York: Norton.

_____ (1956), The problem of ego identity. *J. Amer. Psychoanal. Assn.*, 4:56–121.

Fenichel, O. (1941), *Problems of Psychoanalytic Technique*. New York: Psychoanal. Quart.

Freud, A. (1936), The ego and the mechanisms of defense. In: *The Writings of Anna Freud*, vol. II. New York: International Universities Press, 1966.

_____ (1968), Difficulties in the path of psychoanalysis: a confrontation of the past with present viewpoints. *Writings*. Vol. VII, pp. 124–156, 1971.

_____ (1976), Changes in psychoanalytic practice and experience. *Internat. J. Psycho-Anal.*, 57:257–260.

_____ (1979), The role of insight in psychoanalysis and psychotherapy: Introduction. *J. Amer. Psychoanal. Assn.*, 27(Suppl.):3–7.

_____ (1980), Quoted in Tyson, R. L. Anna Freud—In Memoriam. Presented to Anna Freud Memorial Meeting, San Diego Psychoanalytic Institute and Society, and the Department of Psychiatry, University of California, San Diego, February 18, 1983.

Freud, S. (1900), The interpretation of dreams. *Standard Edition*, 4 & 5. London: Hogarth Press, 1953.

_____ (1905), Three essays on the theory of sexuality. *Standard Edition*, 7:135–243. London: Hogarth Press, 1953.

_____ (1912), The dynamics of transference. *Standard Edition*, 12:99–108. London: Hogarth Press, 1958.

_____ (1926), Inhibitions, symptoms and anxiety. *Standard Edition*, 20:87–172. London: Hogarth Press, 1959.

———— (1933), New introductory lectures on psychoanalysis. *Standard Edition,* 22:5–182. London: Hogarth Press, 1964.

———— (1940). An outline of psycho-analysis. *Standard Edition,* 23:144–207. London: Hogarth Press, 1964.

Gedo, J. E. (1979), *Beyond Interpretation: Toward a Revised Theory for Psychoanalysis.* New York: International Universities Press.

Gill, M. M. (1979), The analysis of the transference. *J. Amer. Psychoanal. Assn.,* 27:263–288.

Gitelson, M. (1962), On the curative factors in the first phase in analysis. In *Psychoanalysis: Science and Profession.* New York: International Universities Press, 1973, pp. 311–341.

Green, A. (1975), The analyst, symbolization and absence in the analytic setting (on changes in analytic practice and analytic experience). *Internat. J. Psycho-Anal.,* 56:1–22.

Greenacre, P. (1954), The role of transference: Practical considerations in relation to psychoanalytic therapy. In: *Emotional Growth.* New York: International Universities Press, 1971, pp. 627–640.

Greenson, R. R. (1972), Beyond transference and interpretation. In: *Explorations in Psychoanalysis.* New York: International Universities Press, 1978, pp. 441–450.

———— & Wexler, M. (1969), The nontransference relationship in the psychoanalytic situation. In: *Explorations in Psychoanalysis.* New York: International Universities Press, 1978, pp. 359–386.

Hartmann, H. (1939), *Ego Psychology and the Problem of Adaptation.* New York: International Universities Press, 1958.

———— (1950). Comments on the psychoanalytic theory of the ego. In: *Essays on Ego Psychology: Selected Problems in Psychoanalytic Theory.* New York: International Universities Press, 1964, pp. 113–141.

Heimann, P. (1956). Dynamics of transferences. *Int. J. Psycho-Anal.,* 37:303–310.

Isakower, O. (1957), Problems of supervision. Report to the Curriculum Committee of the New York Psychoanalytic Institute. (Unpublished).

Kennedy, H. (1979), The role of insight in child analysis: A developmental viewpoint. *J. Amer. Psychoanal. Assn.,* 27(Suppl.):9–28.

Kernberg, O. F. (1979), Some implications of object relations theory for psychoanalytic technique. *J. Amer. Psychoanal. Assn.,* 27:207–239.

Klein, G. S. (1973), Two theories or one? *Bull. Menninger Clin.,* 37:102–132.

Kohut, H. (1971), *The Analysis of the Self.* New York: International Universities Press.

———— (1977), *The Restoration of the Self.* New York: International Universities Press.

Kris, E. (1947), The nature of psychoanalytic propositions and their validation. In: *Selected Papers of Ernst Kris.* New Haven: Yale University Press, 1975, pp. 3–23.

———— (1950), On preconscious mental processes. *Psychoanal. Quart.,* 19:540–560.

———— (1956), On some vicissitudes of insight in psychoanalysis. *Internat. J. Psycho-Anal.,* 37:445–455.

ARMATURE OF PSYCHOANALYTIC THEORY AND METHOD   105

Leavy, S. A. (1980), *The Psychoanalytic Dialogue.* New Haven: Yale Univ. Press.
Leites, N. (1977), Transference interpretations only? *Internat. J. Psycho-Anal.* 58: 275–287.
Loewald, H. W. (1978), *Psychoanalysis and the History of the Individual.* New Haven: Yale University Press.
Neubauer, P. B. (1979), The role of insight in psychoanalysis. *J. Amer. Psychoanal. Assn.,* 27(Suppl.):29–40.
Nunberg, H. (1931), The synthetic function of the ego. In *Practice and Theory of Psychoanalysis,* Vol. 1. New York: International Universities Press, 1948, pp. 120–136.
Rangell, L. (1952), The analysis of a doll phobia. *Internat. J. Psycho-Anal.,* 33:43–53.
_____ (1954), Similarities and differences between psychoanalysis and dynamic psychotherapy. *J. Amer. Psychoanal. Assn.,* 2:734–744.
_____ (1959), The nature of conversion. *J. Amer. Psychoanal. Assn.,* 7:632–662.
_____ (1963a), The scope of intrapsychic conflict – microscopic and macroscopic considerations. *The Psychoanalytic Study of the Child,* 18:75–102.
_____ (1963b), Structural problems in intrapsychic conflict. *The Psychoanalytic Study of the Child,* 18:103–138.
_____ (1968), The psychoanalytic process. *Internat. J. Psycho-Anal.,* 49:19–26.
_____ (1969), Choice-conflict and the decision-making function of the ego – a psychoanalytic contribution to decision theory. *Internat. J. Psycho-Anal.,* 50:599–602.
_____ (1971). The decision-making process. A contribution from psychoanalysis. *The Psychoanalytic Study of the Child,* 26:425–452.
_____ (1974). A psychoanalytic perspective leading currently to the syndrome of the compromise of integrity. *Internat. J. Psycho-Anal.,* 55:3–12.
_____ (1975), Psychoanalysis and the process of change. An essay on the past, present and future. *Internat. J. Psycho-Anal.,* 56:87–98.
_____ (1976), Lessons from Watergate. A derivative for psychoanalysis. *Psychoanal. Quart.,* 45:37–61.
_____ (1978), On understanding and treating anxiety and its derivatives. *Internat. J. Psycho-Anal.,* 59:229–236.
_____ (1979), Contemporary issues in the theory of therapy. *J. Amer. Psychoanal. Assn.,* 27:81–112.
_____ (1980), *The Mind of Watergate. An Exploration of the Compromise of Integrity.* New York: Norton.
_____ (1981), From insight to change. *J. Amer. Psychoanal. Assn.,* 29:119–141.
_____ (1982a), The self in psychoanalytic theory. *J. Amer. Psychoanal. Assn.,* 30:863–891.
_____ (1982b), Transference to theory: the relationship of psychoanalytic education to the analyst's relationship to psychoanalysis. *The Annual of Psychoanalysis,* 10:29–56.
_____ (1982c), Some thoughts on termination. *Psychoanal. Inquiry,* 2:367–392.
_____ (1983), Some thoughts on Barry Siegel's thoughts on "Thoughts on Termination." *Psychoanal. Inq.* 3(4):705–714.

_____ (1984), Structure, Somatic, and Psychic. The Biopsychological Base of Infancy. In: _Frontiers of Infant Psychiatry,_ eds. E. Galenson, J. D. Call, & R. L. Tyson. New York: Basic Books, pp. 70–81.

_____ (1985), On the theory of theory in psychoanalysis. The relationship of theory to psychoanalytic therapy. _J. Amer. Psychoanal. Assn._ 33:59–92.

Schafer, R. (1976), _A New Language for Psychoanalysis._ New Haven: Yale University Press.

Spitz, R. (1956), Transference: The analytic setting and its prototype. _Internat. J. Psycho-Anal.,_ 37:380–385.

Sterba, R. (1934), The fate of the ego in analytic therapy. _Internat. J. Psycho-Anal.,_ 15:117–125.

Stolorow, R. D., Brandchaft, B., & Atwood, G. E. (1983), Intersubjectivity in psychoanalytic treatment: with special reference to archaic states. _Bull. Menninger Clin.,_ 47:117–128.

Stone, L. (1961), _The Psychoanalytic Situation. An Examination of Its Development and Essential Nature._ New York: International Universities Press.

_____ (1981), Some thoughts on the "here and now" in psychoanalytic technique and process. _Psychoanal. Quart.,_ 50:709–733.

Strachey, J. (1969), The nature of the therapeutic action of psychoanalysis. _Internat. J. Psycho-Anal.,_ 50:275–292, 1969. Orig. published in _Internat. J. Psycho-Anal.,_ 15:127–159, 1934.

Waelder, R. (1930), The principle of multiple function. In _Psychoanalysis: Observation, Theory, Application,_ ed. S. A. Guttman. New York: International Universities Press, 1976, pp. 68–83.

_____ (1962), Psychoanalysis, scientific method and philosophy. _J. Amer. Psychoanal. Assn.,_ 10:617–637.

_____ (1967), _Progress and Revolution._ New York: International Universities Press.

Winnicott (1958), _Collected Papers. Through Pediatrics to Psychoanalysis._ New York: Basic Books.

_____ (1965), _The Maturational Processes and the Facilitating Environment._ New York: International Universities Press.

Wurmser, L. (1981), _The Mask of Shame._ Baltimore: Johns Hopkins University Press.

Zetzel, E. R. (1956), Current concepts of transference. _Internat. J. Psycho-Anal.,_ 37:369–378.

Sign, Symbol, and Structural Theory

There is a remarkable conservatism of mind as well as of social form. Once a language, or a way of thinking—or more frequently a code of values—has been learned, it is difficult for individuals within a community or in a discipline to shift easily to new models or to make new interpretations of perceived nature into new categories. The Freudian (1923) shift from topographic to structural theory that became more well established with the publication of "Inhibitions, Symptoms and Anxiety" (Freud, 1926) may seem like ancient history to us in the 1980s; nonetheless, the practicing psychoanalyst during the early 1900s had become habituated to the topographic model. During my own analytic training, I remember Berta Bornstein remarking on the excitement of some analysts when topographic theory was replaced, because dynamic structural theory seemed so much easier to apply to clinical data. I also recall that during the 60s and early 70s Charles Brenner and his colleague (Arlow & Brenner, 1964) struggled to convince members of our analytic society that certain formulations of topographic theory were no longer necessary and could be dispensed with now that we had the structural theory and ego psychology as a theoretical base. Moreover, it would be a significant accomplishment to make our theory more parsimonious by full exploitation and exploration of the range and limits of the explanatory value of structural theory.

It seems like only yesterday that rhetoric and careful exposition were necessary to convince us of such formulations. Now we find ourselves in a time when Brenner's interpretation of Freud's psychoanalytic stance that the human being should be viewed as conflicted and one's mind as

107

structurally organized has come under new scrutiny. Even structural theory is now questioned by some who attempt to change the pace and direction of the march of history of ideas in our science. There is a long line of thinkers from Klein (1976) to Kohut (1984) to Schafer (1976) to Slap and Saykin (1983), who would have us rethink the role of structural theory and deny its clinical, heuristic value to practice. They argue that it is person-distant, remote from experience, and too mechanistic. Despite those claims, Brenner (1974, 1976, 1978, 1982) and many of his colleagues have tenaciously sought to reveal that psychoanalysis, at its best, is embedded in structural theory and that the irreducible minimum that enables us to understand patients and their minds comes from an analysis of conflict revealed in the phenomena of compromise, such as dreams, symptoms and actions. These behaviors take on meaning insofar as they are translated by analysis into the varying elements that make up psychic structure.

In this essay, I will address only one area of Brenner's work, that pertaining to sign and symbol in structural theory. It is a natural area for me to write about, since a large part of my intellectual activity within analysis has been in the study of the interplay of language and psychoanalysis (Shapiro, 1970, 1979, 1983; Shapiro & Perry, 1976). Brenner indicates in his seminal work, *Psychoanalytic Technique and Psychic Conflict* (1976), that after the introduction of the structural theory and the reappraisal of the role of anxiety in psychological conflict, the interpretation of symptoms and dream analysis were enlarged so that even dreams not amenable to approaches described in the Dream Book (Freud, 1900) could be brought under the same umbrella of understanding common to all other psychological phenomena and symptoms. That is, symptom, dream, and behavior all represented some form of psychic compromise to be analyzed into the contributing elements of the agencies of mind and the developmental calamities that gave rise to the attendant affects. Arlow and Brenner wrote in 1964 that the essence of dreams or any other psychological manifestation is that they are compromise formations. They also showed how what had been called dream work could be understood in terms of regression to childhood mentation. Brenner went on (1976): "....a dream is from the very start, a compromise among the three systems of the mind like any waking thought, fantasy or action." Moreover any dream that is unintelligible, is a consequence of defense. From here on Brenner's argument becomes more relevant to my central theme: "What is usually referred to as the text of the dream or its manifest content is never the dream itself. It is only *what the dreamer* – in our context, the patient – *tells us.* In fact, one can never know the manifest content of another person's dream... After all, what is important in analysis is not a dream, it is *what the dream means*" (pp. 137–138; italics added).

In order to direct our attention to the telling of the dream and away from the dream as an event during sleep and then imperfectly remembered, we must embark on a tour into the language of the patient and his idiosyncratic capacity to refer to aspects of his psychic life as yet untapped, except as a future event of the analysis. Indeed, even while a dream or symptom expresses, it also seeks to hide and lead us astray because of the conflict about exposing or even knowing. The inability easily to understand the dream on presentation is a sign of censorship or defense. Moreover, there is a further gap between the pictorial representation and the verbal narration, which of necessity involves secondary elaboration. As Weber (1982) stated, "The distance that separates narration from narrated, like that which separates spectator from spectacle is not an empty interval" (p. 20). Writing about the naming function of interpretation from the standpoint of the analyst, I (1970, 1979) indicated that the analyst expresses in words what the patient represents in other forms. Thus, to this point my ideas are consonant with Brenner's.

To contrast this viewpoint with others currently popular in psychoanalysis, let me digress for a moment. It could be said that some current theories that postulate developmental fault, whether in the separation-individuation process or in the failure of parental empathy, sometimes provide analysts with easy descriptions of patients' symptoms that are paraphrases of experience. Such paraphrases are closely related to angogic explanations of dreams (see Stein, 1984). They can become pseudo-explanations that further serve defense and are nonanalytic — not because they are not relevant to what was described, but because they do not break the manifest verbalizations and descriptions into simpler elements that point to the reorganization and signifying function of the symptom or dream as a surface experience or phenomenon that refers to something more remote and less apparent to consciousness. Indeed, Arlow (1981) argues that our theories of pathogenesis are themselves referential to and signifiers of our current theories. For example, he notes that if a pathogenetic agent is equated with a poisonous fecal substance, then the treatment mode, of course rests on the concept of catharsis; or that if neurosis reflects the consequences of traumatic event or relationship early in life, then a corrective emotional experience might be appropriate, and so forth.

However, nowhere within these modificaions of psychoanalysis is the need for analysis of the symptom into basic structural elements more elemental than in the structural theory as interpreted in the work of Brenner

(1982). He insists that the structural theory is the only one that requires us to view the contribution of id, ego and superego to symptom and dream alike and does not permit us to escape the necessity for looking at these varying phenomena as synthetic representations composed of contributions from these postulated part structures of mind. However, Brenner (1976) notes Lewin's (1952) view that the structural theory is most useful for understanding neurotic symptoms and character traits, whereas topographic theory is probably more useful for dealing with dreams. Lewin thus seems to indicate that theories be applied to data in a complementary way.[1] In this paper, I extend this view, which Brenner discounts, in order to bring structural theory into relation with modern language theory. I will first present some evidence of the merit of reconsidering Freud's own views, expressed at the very beginnings of psychoanalysis.

Freud's earliest models were embedded in a topographic vision because of the focus on repression and sequestered memory as the pathoplastic elements in neuroses. I believe that the psychoanalytic view of man in conflict emphasized by structural theory would suffer no harm if it also included some room for linguistic analysis in our clinical thinking; much of what goes on in structural theory must have something to do with the analysis of language and the varied signs used to represent something that is less apparent and more experience distant, known, as unconscious wishes in psychoanalysis and deep structures in linguistics. This point was taken up by Rosen (1966), who emphasized that what distinguishes Freud's work from others is that he considered and studied the apparently meaningless experiences of life and discovered that they are meaningful when reviewed under the light of psychoanalytic scrutiny. Freud wrote to Fliess on December 6, 1896: "As you know, I am working on the assumption that our psychical mechanism has come about by a process of stratification: the material present in the shape of memory traces from time to time is subjected to a rearrangement in accordance with fresh circumstances—to a retranscription. Thus, what is essentially new in my theory is the thesis that *memory is present not once but several times over, that it is registered in various species of signs*" (E, Kris, 1954, p. 173, italics added). We thus have from the originator of psychoanalysis himself an early indication of his interest in signs, symbols, signifiers, and representation.

---

[1]Actually Lewin (1952) wrote: "Nowadays most writers use both terminologies, the older when discussing dreams, the newer when writing about the neuroses. This cleavage is not deep-seated. It is due in the main to convenience and tradition" (pp. 295–296).

Later, in the Dream Book, he wrote: "If we attempted to read these characters according to their pictorial value instead of according to their symbolic relation we should dearly be led into error...A dream is a picture puzzle! (Freud, 1900, p. 277).

This point of view, reiterated throughout Freud's text, contains all the elements necessary to satisfy the definition of a structuralist model. I refer to structuralist now, not in the sense of structural theory, but from the standpoint of the philosophical concept of structure introduced by the linguist de Sausure (1911). For an elaboration of this idea, I refer the reader to Piaget's (1970) notion that structural theory must contain three elements: (a) wholeness, (b) the capacity for transformation, and (c) generative activity and self regulation. Freud's structural theory contains these three elements insofar as it permits variation in wholeness without preformism; that is, we are not simply what we were as children or homunculi in sperm, but elements of the past hold on as we become unique individuals later in life. The self-psychology school may be addressing the apparent wholeness of human experience while ignoring the structural elements out of which this wholeness develops, (for example, see concepts of cohesive self, self defect, selfobject) Things are not merely as they appear to be on the surface but are made up of other more elementary structures. The second element of structural theory— concerns the capacity for transformation that permits changes to occur, not only over time, but synchronically in concrete representations reported in a person's psychological life. They occur even within manifest experiences, so that any representation, such as a behavior or a dream, may stand for a whole group of ideas, a synscytium, or network of wishes and prohibitions. This is not only multiple function (Waelder, 1930), or the participation of conflict in each representation that Brenner (1982) describes, but the representation at different times in life of varying forms by species of defense[2] acting upon wishful elements that constitutes conflict.

Finally, the factor of generativity and self-regulation implies the homeostatic elements of any internalized symbolic structure functions in a manner that permits organismic or psychological adaptation. Adaptation takes place so that persons fit into a social environment while they are in-

---

[2]Species of defense refers to defense mechanisms. If I understand Brenner correctly he would not mind the notion of an abstractly inferred series of mechanisms that permits the ego to enlist many sorts of thought and behavior in service of defense. But he thinks it misleading to segregate a single area of ego functioning as exclusively defensive. More to the point, any ego function can be in service of both drive expression and defense.

ternally regulating their psychic life with regard to the meanings that dictate their behaviors and permit adaptation to the environment. Thus, a structuralist vantage point is one that not only coincides with a structural theory, but is compatible with aspects of linguistic theory. Moreover, there are elements in the topographic theory pertaining to dreams specifically that have relevance for clinical work which could be updated in linguistic terms and made consonant with Brenner's proposition that when we deal with patients analytically we deal with their talking about their symptoms and their talking about their dreams. I am in agreement, then, that the inner experience of the dream as it is represented may be less relevant than formerly thought. More important is the idea that what is said not only should be taken at face value (surface structure) but should be considered to signify deeper meaning, perhaps of universal fantasies and a compromise of wish and defense. There are examples in the idiom of our culture that are instructive: Patients say about themselves that they feel empty or suffer from anomie. Such expressions must be analyzed and should not be accepted as final; they are paraphrases of experience.

In 1917, Freud wrote "A Metapsychological Supplement to the Theory of Dreams" and commented on the various forms of regression that are possible in dreams. He included topographical, temporal, and formal alterations to describe the idea that there are immature methods of expression that take the place of the usual methods of presentation and can help us to understand patients' productions. Indeed they may be indispensable in alerting us to where we should carry our analysis. For example, if a past time is indicated by a setting in a dream, then the current situation may be layered on that former experience. Formal aspects of the dream that are inconsistent with current mental abilities may be referential to some disintegration of usual alert mental structures; they may lead us to other states of mind or altered ego states associated with experiences registered in such states. If the representation is pictorial or imagistic, then topographic considerations must be applied to analysis based on rebus thinking or plastic imagery – so that the inciting thought can eventually be uncovered.

Any theory that helps us to understand our clinical work and to grasp the rules of transformation of language is complementary to structural theory and permits the inclusiveness that Hartmann (1939) espoused in his wish that psychoanalysis be a general psychology. Several language theorists have written extensively about symbol formation and are relevant to our quest for understanding. They are Jakobson and Halle, Rosen, and Werner and Kaplan.

Jakobson and Halle (1956) alerted us to the role of metaphor and metonomy in language use. Rosen (1966) used metaphor and metonomy to discuss aspects of clinical practice to show how patients with varying diagnoses reference their world. Metaphor uses the sign function of similarity as a referential shorthand. (The Homeric reference to rosy fingered dawn is metaphoric insofar as we can understand the similarity in shape between the rising sun and a pointing finger; the smiling face represents yes, or permission to pass to the left of a car where such markers are used). Metonomy uses the contiguity of images or events as a means of reference. For example "the Crown" refers to the Queen; the "White House" refers to the President. Such continuities also play a major role in the formation of screen memories and in fetishism. For us to understand the relationship between signifiers and what is signified, signs must undergo a series of psychological transformations. When we break the whole, (i.e. the symptom) into its elements of wish, defense, and adaptation to reality, we analyze it into the components of conflict. However, all these systems suggest the centrality of language as well as conflict and compromise.

I suggest that we tacitly use early Freudian concepts such as dream work, primary and secondary process, and thing and word presentation to do our work and that we can now replace those with extra analytic concepts derived from language theory.

Werner and Kaplan (1963) explored symbol formation from an academic standpoint. Every symbol derives from at least a dual building process. The classical psychoanalytic concept of word and thing presentation and the transformations of dream work are Freud's version of a similar idea. "One arm of the building process is directed towards the establishment of a referent, the other directed toward articulation of a symbolic vehicle (sound pattern)" (Werner & Kaplan, 1963) p. 123. They make a distinction between the vehicle and the referent (i.e. that which is signified), the vehicle being the acoustic, visual, or other means of expressing a concept (I shall return to this when I discuss clinical material). The relationships between vehicle and referent are at least twofold; a vehicle may have multiple meanings, that is, it may be plurisignificant. For example, a single vocable may be used to refer to several referents (ideas or things). This involves *homonymy*. The second mode involves multiformity of referential expression, in which several words may be used to designate but one referent. This is the common notion of *synonymy*. The development of these double modes of expression within a diachronic framework is relevant to psychoanalytic developmental theory; it is also relevant to how patients act in regressed states on the couch. In such states they invariably use the inferred linguistic tools of transformation that correspond to Freud's concepts of condensation, displacement, symbolization, turning into the opposite — all associated with dream work and topographic theory. These concepts, derived from both linguistic analysis and psychoanalysis, do not permit us simply to paraphrase a patient's behavior in anagogic form but do require that we use the central tenet of free association (see A. Kris, 1982) to uncover what Freud thought was the basic referential system to which all behaviors ultimately could be reduced if we knew the coding devices used to represent the compromises made necessary by conflict.

Thus, the core of this proposal is that the structural theory that has become psychoanalysis could benefit from some complementary model that is clinically useful to alert both patients and analysts to the methods by which man symbolizes. These methods, the "symbol work," can be borrowed from linguistic sciences. Such an interpretation of theory would give us some idea of how minds organize experiences and how persons live in accord with these meaning organizations. Perhaps this exploration would also provide some understanding of why hermeneutic and Lacanian approaches to analysis have become so popular. They fill a perceived gap in structural theory, but they also ignore what remains essential to a psychodynamic point of view in the structural hypothesis and sometimes yield to ambiguity and opacity rather than greater clarity and rationality.

Brenner (1976) provides a clinical example to show the process of psychoanalytic understanding. In brief: A woman has an anxiety attack while flying on an airplane. The nub of her problem concerns competition with her youngest sibling, a boy. The idea is offered that the configuration of the joystick (i.e. the controls of the airplane) is a sign of control, which then could be referentially related to the penis as a signifier of her earlier conflict concerning her wish for equal status, represented in the current anxiety. Further on in the discussion, Brenner asked the patient what it was that had precipitated her relapse. The associations to her memories became relevant as they led to the unique line of thinking concerning her symptom, that is, how the anxiety was experienced. She described it as an empty feeling in her stomach. Moreover, "she could not remember the last time she had been sick to her stomach"; then she admitted reluctantly that the last time she had felt that way followed an episode of fellatio. The flow of her thoughts again led to the plane where she had not eaten, but she had had a large lunch earlier. She had dined on boiled sausages, which she had loved as a child. This complex flow of ideas and similarities may strike the reader as having significant categorical overlap because of our training as psychoanalysts, or because for human beings the double entry bookkeeping in the symbolic system permits metaphor, ambiguity, double meanings, and varying symbolic transformations to register in consciousness in rapid succession. However, our surmises take on further certainty when we hear of the context of the trip and its significance to her. She had been promoted and had been chosen by her boss, an older man, above her colleagues, many of whom were men. The easy reference to that sequence in relation to her earlier childhood conflict with her brother closes the circle of our anticipated conclusion.

In Brenner's example we are made privy to the symbolic transformations and to the multiple means of representing ideas that force us to satisfactory closure. They do not come to us with difficulty because the narrative is written in a way that makes it evident (see Spence, 1983). They are also apparent to us because as human beings we share language and a symbolic system that permits categorical overlap and use of the vehicle of language to refer to many things, some of them logical and necessary, others less logical and more peripheral or personally experiential. Multiple function, polysemy and structural elements are all working mechanisms that add up to the whole as a representation of something other than its simple designative referent. The syntax of the story is compelling. A boiled sausage may be only a boiled sausage under certain circumstances, but it certainly shares a configurational relationship to the penis, and a joystick as well. The word itself—joystick—gives the concept increased metaphoric thrust. It is the redundancy of form in this model that alerts one to the elements of conflict which make up the symptom. Those elements lead us to the current advancement in job position, the past hopes for equal treatment and the regeneration of anxiety as if the past were anachronistically active in the present. We could not have followed that route of reasoning had we not understood that things do not simply stand for themselves; they stand for referents out of sight, out of mind. To elaborate the need for not only assuming symbolic thinking, but also displaying the variant forms of symbolic transformations that go into structural analysis, I shall present a number of clinical vignettes from my own practice and experience. They demonstrate how such knowledge (which some claim as passive) is structured and indispensible as a tool for understanding how patients represent conflicts and how analysts reconstitute what is represented.

Let me begin with an example of a *homophonic* transformation that occurred in my own life. Early in my career I had a dream while in analysis. It was a pleasant enough dream in which I was led to a dock on Martha's Vineyard that I had visited the summer before. I was told that the boat at the mooring was mine. It was a large motorcraft—I was impressed, but surprised, that it was mine and protested with some ambivalence that I did not like motor boats, that I really had been fond of sail boats. How was I to accept this boat as mine, impressive as it was? Even in the dream it was not a part of my understood wishes. I had not longed for a yacht.

It would be all too easy to carry out an anagogic interpretation of this dream, making reference to a multiplicity of simplistic yacht to body part transformations and infer that we understand its meaning. However, its significance became known to me only through an understanding of its current derivative function in the context of my life at that time regarding career opportunities and career choice. Sailing had indeed been a new excitement, and I had generated some enthusiasm for the newly learned sport during the previous summer. I also had just began a new job and my practice, both of which occupied a great deal of time; I also was going to classes at the psychoanalytic institute, and had a young child. Then, I was offered a highly prized position that involved close association with Marianne Kris, among others, on a psychoanalytic research project. I was sorely tempted to add yet another job to my already full work load. However, it was clear to me that it would be most difficult in terms of time and distribution of psychic energy were I to take this job. And yet, how could I turn down a position where I would be an intimate in such distinguished company? I did not understand the relationship of this dream to my life, however.

As I began to try to put the dream images into words, I described the distinctions between a motor boat and sail boat, and I described the joy I had from my new skill at sailing. I seemed to feel some pressure to help the analyst understand what kind of boat it was that I had been offered and could not be satisfied that I had conveyed the image, although the distinction between motor and sail was simple. It was only when I uttered the name of a commercial motor boat, Chris Craft, that I realized that the fulfillment of owning a boat of this sort was related to the prestige and importance that it woud give me rather than what I had passionately enjoyed doing that summer. I will not belabor the homophonic relation to Kris, but it should be apparent that the elegant and prestigious new acquisition I had created in my dream stood for the ambivalent wish to take the position that would have compromised my coping in reality. The element of superego contribution to this difficulty is important in regard to how forbidden the prize might have been. To take a position (or for that matter a possession) so coveted by others so early in my career must be opposed from within. However, the referential notion of the two unlike boats' referring to the same homophone (Kris; Chris) was represented in the tension of my attempt to feel satisfied as I tried to relate the dream text. The discomfort in not being able to link the experience in life with the experience of the dream was expressed in a sense of verbal discontent in the communicative setting of the analysis itself—a kind of tip of the tongue phenomenon.

My own tension that I had not adequately represented my inner experience was parallelled by the feeling that whatever was unconscious in my ambitious strivings in my past was also forbidden. Such feelings were also signifiers of more elemental constellations in the arena of the transference. What would my analyst have thought had I appeared too arrogant so early? This had been a theme of early complaints about supervision and the relationship to the analyst himself. However, the rules of homophonic transformation somehow became the vehicle around which the symbol had been formed. Had I not been familiar with the commercial names of powerboats, I perhaps would not have been able to employ such a verbal image to represent the current derivative of an existing conflict. However, other vehicles would have been available as they always are.

In his book *Free Associations,* A. Kris (1983) indicates his conflict about becoming an analyst by recalling his intellectualized musing one day about how words could effect change in patients. Later that day he found himself daydreaming some lines from a romantic poem by Wordsworth. He vainly searched for the significance in the content of the poem until he spoke Wordsworth as words' worth—and decided to become a psychoanalyst.

The next image comes from a similar linguistic arrangement in which a patient reported a dream image of somebody with a mustache. It was a visual referent, and he described it simply. He seemed also to experience some tension in expression and began to use a more careful set of descriptors. However, one would have to know the context of his life to understand his conflict. This man was beset by anxiety concerning bodily ills, and he had focused on a minor congenital defect that marred his sense of perfect wholeness. These anxieties were used in various ways to justify passive withdrawal from sexual and other human experiences for which he said he had longed. He returned to the dream repeatedly, describing the mustache until he had made assorted circumlocutious, paraphrases of the image indicating the mustache involved hair on a lip—on the upper lip—not a beard. It was only when he uttered the word "harelip" that he remembered that he had met a friend who had a harelip, which he had thought unsightly. It marred the friend's physical beauty, and he marveled at this man's accomplishments despite his visible defect.

Again, the referential system that links cleft palate to harelip to mustache brought the imagery together in homophonic unity. What was to be signified referred to his central conflict about achievement and damage. However, the reference was not clear until the words were uttered, just as verbalizing had aided my understanding of the dream from my own experience. The analytic observer who takes the view that man is in conflict within himself may be comforted that the conflictual underpinnings gain access to consciousness through a referential system that has to be deciphered, and there is a code. Indeed, the analyst and patient must find the elements of the conflict by referencing the words in unaccustomed ways. The referencing system by which words point in the direction of understanding the conflict are firmly embedded in the concept of signifiers and the rules of transformation shared by other representational systems. Knowledge of such systems is useful in clinical practice and incompletely described in structural theory.

A more difficult reference system was used by another patient, who described a dream in which she found herself in company wearing layers of skirts. The outer skirt had a slit on the side, the under skirt had a slit in front. She felt quite comfortable in company, but also repeatedly attended to her skirt as though she were afraid that too much would be revealed. She remarked, "It should not be a problem, since the slit skirt under the outer layer of skirt was positioned differently. The top skirt, though slit also, covered the underlying slit very well." The verbal description led to a new discovery in the analytic situation not evident in prior meetings and less convincingly represented up to that time about the body ego concerns that were incorporated in both character and symptom. The referential use of the slit skirt that both reveals and covers the underlying slit permitted her to recognize the conflict about revealing and hiding her genitals. The slang expression "slit" became a paraphrase for her anxieties about what would be or would not be revealed in her current usage as well as in her conflicts about her sexual nature.

The examples used stem from dream imagery, but there are symptoms that are also importantly represented in other formal configurations and then verbally analyzed. A patient in his mid-30s was very ingratiating and obsequious toward the analyst. This character trait was in apparent conflict with his overall sense of competence in his work. Yet he always seemed to be yielding and deferential and more than aptly respectful. One sometimes felt that it was almost too good to be true, that behind some of these characterological and symptomatic manners lay an unsaid conviction that he was perhaps better than others. Although the feeling of superiority was not easily apparent in the analysis, it did become problematic in his life work. Given his obsequeousness it was not easy to decipher that in his relation to the analyst, he had taken a collegial view of himself, as if both of us were observing the patient in him, but he wasn't the patient.

He told me one day that he had a fantasy that I had an impending trip that would break his usual sequence of hours. I was to visit a medical convention, and he was asked to go too in order to present his views alongside me. He left the fantasy rather quickly only to return to it later, this time to tell of a memory from the past, although he did not realize the linkage until the thought was verbalized. He had been a sickly child, frequently in the hospital and sometimes taken to rounds in front of physicians. He also had used the intellectual defense of learning a great deal about his illness as a way of coping with his anxiety about whether he would survive. He then remembered being on a pediatric ward where a little girl repeatedly asked him to look at her burns, but exposed her genitals in so doing. One conflict in his current life concerned problems in performing intercourse. He had anxieties about impotence that were related to castration anxiety represented in bodily ills. The threat of my going on vacation became another context in which his anxiety about being left behind was heightened—his dependency and his illness and his sense of body infirmity might take hold during these times of abandonment. To undo his plight and deny his problem, he invited himself to the convention. He was with me as he had been as a child among the doctors who took care of him. Moreover, his deferential attitude toward the analyst was an important trait by which he covered both his anger at my leaving and his longing for our continued relationship at all costs.

In that vignette, it was clear that the fantasy had referential value. Its connection to his character trait was not easy to see unless we can accept that there was a form of regression to a representation in fantasy of a wish that held the elements of his conflict and also a concrete reference to his personal past. The image, not immediately obvious, was related by synonymy to my contextual understanding of the references in the past and the symptom that appeared as a character trait. I had first to assume that these elements were part of the whole, but I dared not view them as simply standing only for themselves. We had to dissect the image into levels of organization, which permitted a transformation of a wish and a conflict into thought, which could then be analyzed. The image was related to a thought, which had a referent from the past of a scene that stood for an idea, which derived from his interpretation of damage in the visualized concatination of burn, personal infirmity, and penislessness. Both topograhpic transformation and temporal transformation were operative and symbolically stated. There was a time, when he was with his doctor, that he was the center of attention. If he felt threatened by his infirmity, he could deny it within the context of the pairing. The analyst became a paradigmatic phobic companion. In order to make the leaps necessary to do the analysis, the analyst had to have some knowledge of the representability of ideas — the change in medium and vehicle of representation had to be apprehended. The focus of this idea is that memories are recorded and then represented in a variety of forms. The capacity for condensation in a single fantasy that signifies broader representation is likely at the heart of why free association is a useful technique for understanding. Although these ideas are crucial to analytic thinking and the structural theory allows for such possibilities, they offer little that is explicit to explicate the mechanisms of transformation.

Another patient struggled to discuss her sense of distress when she cheated on her husband. At those times she became even more dependent on him and increasingly solicitous. She wanted to indicate that she used being held, snuggling, as an important mode of covering up her aggressive unfaithfulness. She used the word "smuggle" to describe what she did but was uneasy because it did not sound right. Parapraxes, of course, are commonplace to the analyst. However, to alert oneself to their use as a means of representation, one should also understand the representational parameters that are involved in the formation of a new word. The word that was joined to snuggle to form "smuggle" could be inferred only if one knew that this patient also viewed her husband as somewhat overwhelming in his attentions to her. There were times when she wanted to be more distant. She struggled to find the other word that merged with snuggle and came upon it only by discussing her relationship to her mother, who intruded as she comforted. The patient experienced fear of being smothered even as she was warmed and held. Such condensations in the formation of parapractic neologisms are available only to the analyst who understands the mechanisms of symbol formation. (Of course, it could be said that the patient did manage to "smuggle" her love from one forbidden territory to another.)

Bodily sensations also have representational value for an idea as well as for a feeling state. A young woman who had been on a self-destructive binge, taking various drugs, was beginning to emerge from her difficulties by exercising greater control over her life. She dreamed that she had a stomach ache and went into the bathroom for an antacid. She confused the bottle on the shelf with an antiarthritic liniment named "Heat", and after she took some, her mouth became numb. She had an immediate thought within the dream that she had done something "self destructive."

The day before she had been with her sister, whom she felt received more affection from her father than she. In a fit of rage that she did not anticipate, she began to hit her sister violently and immediately after she felt that she was bad, that she didn't fit well into the family. Nursing her psychic wounds that evening, she returned to drugs, sniffing a line of cocaine. When the drug effect wore off, she felt guilty and went to sleep. Associating to the dream and bodily sensation, she noted similarities of the word heat to "taking the heat," leading the analyst on a merry chase of seeming references that led to no satisfying understanding at all. Finally, the patient realized that the sensation of numbness in her mouth that she had associated with something self-destructive was the same sensation she felt when she took cocaine. She began to understand that the dream and the bodily sensation within the dream were overlapping references to her symptom of self-medicating to alleviate the pain of her experience. The pain invariably began with a stomach-sickening anxiety either when she realized how angry and conflicted she was about taking from her parents or when she was in a setting where she felt "bad." The self-destructive behavior itself was represented by the bodily sensation, which was the metanymic reference for a variety of guilty representations and masochistic behaviors that revolved around her disappointment at not being fully accepted by her parents.

I have introduced in the last example the problem of the merry chase of the symbol. There can be many blind alleys that seem to be plausible. They only emphasize the need for the analyst to pay close attention to the affective excitement and sincerity with which the patient receives the new information provided by symbolic analysis.

Werner and Kaplan's (1963) work shows that polysemanticity and synonymy of words are equally likely ways of manipulating a vehicle as is homophony. The previous example, and the next, can be understood using that concept. Another patient referred to a recurrent image of a water pistol that he had seen a child use. As he focused and lingered over-long on the water pistol, the context of his associations permitted the analyst to raise the possibility that multiformity of referential expression was to be considered. A water pistol could be broken down (analyzed) not only as a holder of water, but also, from its configurational formal characteristics, as a reference that obeyed the *pars pro toto* rule of logic in primary process. Moreover, the equivalent genital referred to was also most frequently manipulated and played with in a place where water flow was prevalent, a bathroom. The patient's conflict concerning masturbatory activity was understood only by dissecting the obsessional imagery into its component conflictual parts.

Yet another patient in analysis, a slender black woman, was struggling in order to achieve a more prominent role in life. She presented a dream in which she exhibited herself dancing most comfortably and with pleasure. She visualized herself as plump and light skinned; and, as if this were not enough, there was the representational overkill of possessing a prominent penis. Some symbols bludgeon the observer with their clarity! But, here again, the significance of the image could be grasped only if one knew her idiosyncratic history. She provided a layered vision simultaneously and synchronically of what was valued at each stage of development. She came from poverty in an area where hunger was pervasive; being plump was important when she was three to five. Her dark skin had been a handicap when she was at college and became an asset only when the "black is beautiful" movement began. The addendum of a penis was explicable as an unconscious derivative of early wishes only in light of her competitive experiences with her brothers.

In the transference, it was clear that she presumed I would her love best if she could show me that penis envy was alive and well, just as she wished that her parents hade loved her as they did her brothers. Thus, the elements of popular translation may also creep into the analytic situation and structural theory has to be applied with full knowledge of the current value of symbols within the community. A symbol that may be universal to human experience is not always part of the idiocyncratic referential system of a particular person. Moreover, the most common universal meaning may not be the most temporally salutary when other meanings are preconscious. Freud warned against the interpretation of dreams by using a universal imagery key. Instead he referred us to the idiosyncratic aspects of more immediate and personally related associations. We may yield at times to universal symbolism, such as water's standing for birth. However, these are to be used only when we find ourselves in difficult situations. On the other hand, for a presidential candidate of the 1840's to have asked, "Where's the beef?" would have made no sense at all, but it did make sense in 1983.

We can carry out our work as psychoanalysts by using structural theory as a theoretical outline to understand how the ideas that patients present are related to inner struggles and to how they use experiences defensively and as moral restraints. To do the job well, we must also be alert to the mechanisms that patients use to represent their conflicts. Sometimes the ways in which they present their problems are habitual modes of expression characteristic of personal thought patterns or are common locutions used in a personal way. Some people are given to frequent use of metaphors. Others have more convoluted methods of dreaming. Many of us have noted that although one can catch on to styles of representation (Rosen, 1961), sometimes style gives way under the analysis, as though the patient's habitual defensive mode has been uncovered. We can wonder, for example, why, in the broader psychiatric arena, hysteria and catatonia have become in recent years less frequent as modes of representation. They seem to have fallen into disrepute, or maybe we found the key to such representations with the advent of Freudian analysis. Psychoanalysis may not permit patients to use representational forms that no longer seem to hold the attention which permitted secondary gains and adequate disguised expression of conflicted wishes as in former years.

The mechanisms of representation are not self-evident. I think perhaps topographic theory did provide us with some of the means to help us along, especially in regard to dream representation. Although analysts may no longer use topographic theory as it was written, they remember the rules of transformation Freud described in dream work and defense analyses. We ought at least give due respect to the significance of Freud's intention that the productions of patients should be viewed as symbolic transformations in various species of signs. This is an easy complement to the structural vantage point and one I believe most analysts use anyway. This discussion merely makes conscious a dimension of work that is part of practice, but is not talked about as much these days. It also introduces a terminology from language theory that may be useful in analyzing the symbols and signs that patients invariably bring to the consulting room.

As my argument suggests, I believe that psychoanalysts cannot escape their education in topography. However, topographic models are problematic because of their linkage to reified psychic levels full of contents and the controversial energic concepts. This presentation is a reminder to analysts that modern linguistic models cannot explain psychic compromises as structural theory does, but they do have relevance to fill in the gap made by abandoning topography. Moreover, all recent theorists seem to agree that verbal texts of patients are the *stuff* of the analysis. Verbal texts are linguistic and not random. We twist and turn and alter initial language forms in various symbolic ways that obey laws of recoding and also have referential specificity. It is time we learned to absorb some of the rich knowledge derived from linguistics and bring psychoanalysis into closer relationship with its origins. After all, Freud used his knowledge of philology and aphasia to inaugurate his own early theories.

REFERENCES

Arlow, J. A. (1979), Metaphor and the psychoanalytic situation. *Psychoanal. Quart.,* 48:363–385.
_____ (1981), Theories of pathogenesis. *Psychoanal. Quart.,* 50:488–513.
_____ (1964), *Psychoanalytic Concepts and the Structural Theory.* New York: International Universities Press.
Brenner, C. (1974), Depression, anxiety and affect theory. *Internat. J. Psycho-Anal.,* 55:25–32.

———— (1976), *Psychoanalytic Technique and Psychic Conflict.* New York: International Universities Press.

———— (1979), Depressive affect, anxiety, and psychic conflict in the phallic-oedipal phase. *Psychoanal. Quart.,* 48:177–197.

———— (1982), *The Mind in Conflict.* New York: International Universities Press.

Freud, S. (1900), Interpretation of dreams. *Standard Edition,* 4 & 5. London: Hogarth Press, 1953.

———— (1917), A metapsychological supplement to the theory of dreams. *Standard Edition,* London: Hogarth Press, 1957.

———— (1923), The ego and the id. *Standard Edition,* 19:1–59. London: Hogarth Press, 1962.

———— (1926), Inhibitions, symptoms and anxiety. *Standard Edition,* 20:75–172. London: Hogarth Press, 1959.

Hartmann, H. (1939), *Ego Psychology and the Problem of Adaptation.* New York: International Universities Press, 1964.

Jakobson, R., & Halle, M. (1956), *Fundamentals of language.* The Hague: Mouton.

Klein, G. (1976), *Psychoanalytic Theory: An Exploration of Essentials.* New York: International Universities Press.

Kohut, H. (1984), *How Does Analysis Cure?* ed. A. Goldberg & P. Stepansky. Chicago: University of Chicago Press.

Kris, A. (1982), *Free association.* New Haven: Yale University Press.

Kris, E., ed. (1954), *Origins of Psychoanalysis. Freud's Letters to Wilhelm Fliess.* London: Imago.

Lewin, B. D. (1952), Phobic symptoms and dream interpretation. *Psychoanal. Quart., 21,* 295–322.

Piaget, J. (1970), *Structuralism.* New York: Harper & Row.

Rosen, V. H. (1961), Relevance of "style" to certain aspects of defense and the synthetic function of the ego. *Internat. J. Psycho-Anal.,* 42:447–457.

———— (1966). Disturbances of representation and reference in ego deviations: In: *Psychoanalysis: A General Psychology: Essays in Honor of Heinz Hartmann,* ed., R. M. Loewenstein, L. M. Newman, M. Schur & A. J. Solnit. New York: International Universities Press, pp. 634–654.

———— (1977), *Style, Character and Language.* New York: Aronson.

Sausure, de, F. (1911), *A Course in General Linguistics.* New York: Philosophical Library, 1959.

Schafer, R. (1976), *A New Language for Psychoanalysis.* New Haven: Yale University Press.

Shapiro, T. (1970), Interpretation and naming. *J. Amer. Psychoanal. Assn.,* 18:399–421.

———— (1979), *Clinical Psycholinguistics.* New York: Plenum.

———— (1983), The unconscious still occupies us. *The Psychoanalytic Study of the Child,* 38:547–567.

———— & Perry, R. (1976), Latency revisited: The significance of age 7 ± 1. *Psychoanalytic Study of the Child, 31,* 79–105.

Slap, J. W., & Saykin, A. J. (1983), The schema: Basic concept in a non-metapsychological model of the mind. *Psychoanal. Contemp. Thought,* 6:305–325.

Spence, D. (1983), *Narrative Truth and Historical Truth: Meaning and Interpretation in Psychoanalysis.* New York: W. W. Norton.

Stein, M. (1984), Rational versus anagogic interpretation: Xenophon's dream and others. *J. Amer. Psychoanal. Assn.,* 32:529–556.

Waelder, R. (1930), The principle of multiple function. Observations and overdetermination. In: *Psycholanalysis: Observation, Theory, Application,* ed. S. A. Guttman. New York: International Universities Press, pp. 68–83.

Weber, S. (1982), *The Legend of Freud.* Minneapolis: University of Minnesota Press.

Werner, H., & Kaplan, B. (1963), *Symbol Formation.* New York: Wiley.

PART TWO

The Concepts
of Psychoanalysis

Among the many talents of Charles Brenner, perhaps none is appreciated more by students of psychoanalysis than his ability to clarify and explain complex psychoanalytic concepts. He has also reformulated a number of concepts, the most recent being the concept of depressive affect. Each of the four papers comprising this section deals with a specific psychoanalytic concept: perception, sublimation, the object, and affect.

Lucy Biven reviews the concept of perception. Combining theory and clinical data, she argues for the central role of conflict and compromise formation in every aspect of perception ranging from the normal to the pathological.

The concept of sublimation has undergone many changes since it was first introduced with emphasis on its instinctual roots. In a thorough and scholarly paper, Dale Boesky demonstrates that the confusion over definition of the term is caused by fundamental conceptual ambiguities.

Very few concepts have been used in so many ways and in so many diverse theories as the concept of the object. Allan Compton traces the beginnings of the object concept in psychoanalysis in the first of a series of papers that will review the many meanings of the term and their place in relation to psychoanalytic theory.

Irving B. Harrison offers a comprehensive review of the concept of affect. He emphasizes the presence of early affect in infancy, derived not only from interaction with the mother, but from the infant's unique, biologically based, and independent early ego.

LUCY BIVEN

Compromise Formation and Cognition: A Revision of the Psychoanalytic Theory of Perception[1]

I happened upon the topics of perception and cognition while puzzling over a problem in the chapter on transference and countertransference in Brenner's book *The Mind in Conflict* (1982). Before stating this problem, I should first acquaint the reader with the book's major premise, which is that conflict and compromise formation pervade mental life. Brenner writes, "The compromise formations that result from conflict are the chief stuff of all psychic life, the normal no less than the pathological" (p. 213). He explains that the determinants of compromise formation are id and superego derivatives, defense, and affect, in the form of anxiety and depressive affect.

Regarding transference and countertransference, Brenner writes that the compromise formations of transference are "characteristic of every object relation" (p. 195) and adds, "Transference and countertransference are indistinguishable dynamically and genetically" (p. 209). The problem that occurred to me is this: If the analyst's transference to the patient is no different from the patient's transference to the analyst, on what basis do we analyze? Obviously, some of our ideas about our patients must lie outside our transference reactions, or else we would always be speaking

[1]A version of this paper, presented to the Michigan Psychoanalytic Society on April 20, 1985, was granted the Society's Ira Miller, M.D. Clinical Essay Award.

about ourselves and never about the patient. Clearly, it is our cognitive capacity that enables us to understand the patient's conflicts. But herein lies another problem. If cognition plays an essential part in the analytic process, how can Brenner maintain that the compromise formations of transference are pervasive in object relationships? Stated more broadly, the problem is this: How far can one extend the domain of compromise formation in mental life, since compromise formation cannot account for one's knowledge of reality in general, anymore than it can account for the analyst's understanding of his patient in particular? In the early days of psychoanalysis this question did not exist because compromise formations were thought to be limited to neurotic symptoms. Insofar as one was neurotic, one's thoughts were dominated by fantasy. Insofar as one was healthy, one was capable of realistic knowledge about the world. This sharp division between fantasy and rational thinking has its roots in Freud's and Hartmann's ideas about psychic energy and in their notions of ego autonomy.

FREUD'S ENERGIC THEORIES

Freud's Views on Psychic Energy

In "The Interpretation of Dreams" (1900), Freud explained that instinctual energy was bent upon "free," or "unbound" (p. 599), discharge in the fulfillment of a wish. Allowed to strive blindly for gratification, the id (which he then called the "first system" (p. 566) would hallucinate the conditions of satisfaction, just as one does in dreams. Since this cannot provide real gratification, the ego (second system) inhibits the id's hallucination and in so doing diverts the id's psychic energy in the direction of the ego. So diverted, the psychic energy also changes in quality from a freely mobile state with the immediate aim of gratifying libidinal wishes, to a "quiescent" state (p. 599). In this quiescent, or bound, state, the energy no longer has the direct aim of libidinal gratification. Thus, Freud (1913) said that the energy was desexualized or "sublimated" (p. 209). Freud maintained that this sublimated energy is suited to the purposes of realistic rather than wishful thinking. He wrote that the ego uses the sublimated energy to assess the environment realistically and make alterations in it that insure instinctual gratification in the end.

In summary, Freud's views on psychic energy are as follows. The ego does not act until it has first inhibited the id, then has diverted the flow of id energy in the direction of the ego, and, finally, has transformed the energy from a libidinal to a sublimated state. One sees that Freud's notion of psychic energy involves a temporal separation between id and ego activities. This means that the ego temporarily operates in pure culture, free from the demands for instinctual pleasure, because the id is inactive. To this extent, Freud implied that the ego functions autonomously.

Freud's Implications of Ego Autonomy

Eleven years later, Freud described more fully this implied ego autonomy. In "Formulations of the Two Principles of Mental Functioning" (1911), he explained that although th ego acts with the ultimate goal of gratifying the instincts, these ego functions do not, in the short run, obey the pleasure principle. Instead, the ego acts in accordance with "the Reality Principle": Following the dictates of the Reality Principle "what was presented in the mind was no longer what was agreeable but what was real, even if it happened to be disagreeable" (p. 291).

Freud points to four ego functions involved in the reality principle. The first is the perception of external reality. The second is reality testing, whereby one distinguishes external reality from internal fantasy. The third step is trial action in secondary thinking. The fourth is judgment, leading to intentional action that will gratify the instinctual wish. Clearly, these four ego functions are cognitive ones that enable a person to make sense of the environment. Freud again implies that these cognitive ego functions of the reality principle operate in pure culture because the id is temporarily inactive (p. 219). He adds that operating in pure culture, the ego was allowed to follow its own "ego instincts" (p. 222), which are geared to adaptation to external reality.

HARTMANN'S ENERGIC THEORIES

Hartmann's Theory of Psychic Energy

Hartmann amended Freud's energic theory in two ways. First, while Freud believed that the id was the source of all psychic energy, Hartmann (1955) speculated that some energy "belongs from the very first to the ego" (p. 236). Second, since Freud had by then proposed the dual instinct theory, Hartmann (1950) wrote that aggressive as well as libidinal energy is rendered quiescent by the ego. He used the term "neutralized energy" (p. 128) to refer to all instinctual energy that the ego has taken over for its own use.

Hartmann's Theory of Ego Autonomy

Hartmann (1950) argued that since the ego has its own source of energy, it can develop on its own rather than as an offshoot of the id. He wrote of the ego's "primary autonomy" (p. 105), which in his view consists of various ego functions that develop outside the conflictual sphere. Hartmann added that while some primary autonomous ego functions later become involved in conflict, others do not. In addition to those ego functions that are primarily conflict free, others, such as defenses, which are originally involved in conflict, may become conflict free as well. Hartmann (1950) wrote of the "secondary autonomy" (p. 105) of the ego to refer to those functions which cross over from conflictual to nonconflictual spheres.

Hartmann (1937) described the conflict-free sphere as "that ensemble of functions which at any given time exert their effects outside the range of mental conflicts" (p. 8). As mentioned earlier, he included many ego functions in the conflict-free sphere, among them the cognitive functions of the reality principle. Like Freud, Hartmann emphasized that these ego functions allow one to adapt to the environment. Hartmann went beyond Freud, however, in severing the link between these autonomous ego functions and instinctual gratification. Freud wrote that the ego functions of the reality principle are only temporarily autonomous, that is to say, free from domination by the pleasure principle, and that these ego functions still have the ultimate aim of gratifying the instincts. Hartmann (1956) severed this tie to instinctual pleasure by postulating that "the activities of the [ego] functions that constitute the Reality Principle can be pleasurable in themselves" (p. 244). Hartmann believed that the ego functions of the conflict-free sphere can be permanently autonomous because they are a source of pleasure in themselves and do not necessarily have the ultimate aim of providinig instinctual pleasure.

In summary, Hartmann believed that the ego has a primary autonomy—that certain aspects of its development are unconflicted and that its psychic status is independent of the id. He also believed that many other ego functions are secondarily autonomous and conflict free. Hartmann maintained that these primary and secondary autonomous ego functions pursue adaptive aims, that they do not necessarily have the ultimate goal of instinctual gratification, and that they are a source of pleasure that derives from the ego rather than from the id.

COMMENT ON FREUD'S AND HARTMANN'S ENERGIC THEORIES

Both Freud and Hartmann professed to use the concept of psychic energy purely as a metaphor to explain the clinical situation. Insofar as they used this concept as a theoretical rationale for their clinical findings, the rationale is unsound. There is no reason to believe that any real energy in the brain is transferred from id to ego or that it is transformed in quality from an instinctual to a neutralized state. Freud could not credibly argue that there is a temporal separation between id and ego functions because the energy is transferred from one to the other. Instead he would have had to illustrate clinically that the two structures function separately; then he could use an energic metaphor to emphasize his clinical findings. Similarly, Hartmann's notion that conflict-free ego functions operate outside the range of the instincts cannot be justified by his theories of neutralized psychic energy. These notions of ego autonomy must be validated clinically, before any theories of psychic energy can be formulated.

Freud's and Hartmann's traditional views of the separation between cognitive and emotional capacities are at odds with Brenner's views that conflict and compromise formation pervade the human psyche. Both views cannot be correct. One cannot both say, as Freud and Hartmann do, that cognition operates in pure culture and maintain, as Brenner does, that compromise formation is ubiquitous. Since the theories of psychic energy cannot be the theoretical basis for Freud's or Hartmann's views, I looked to see if they are clinically valid. If they are, then Brenner is wrong. If not, this adds weight to Brenner's view that compromise formation is ubiquitous.

A partial resolution of the differences between Brenner's views and those of Freud and Hartmann is to be found in a closer examination of Freud's theory of the reality principle. In fact, it was an unforseen central problem in the reality principle that pointed the way to this partial resolution, and more important, provided a first step in revising our psychoanalytic understanding of perception.

THE PROBLEM IN THE REALITY PRINCIPLE

Mentioned earlier, there are four ego functions involved in the reality principle (perception, reality testing, trial action in secondary thinking, and judgment leading to intentional action). Only the first two, perception and reality testing, are of interest here. Freud (1925) defined perception as a simple sensory impression, a definition that allowed him to assume that all perceptions are accurate if one's sensory apparatus is intact. "We must recollect that all presentations originate from perceptions and are recollections of them. Thus, originally, the mere existence of a presentation was guarantee of the reality of what was presented" (p. 237). For example, if one sees a red object, the perception of its color depends on the senses, and the perception will be accurate unless one is color blind.

According to Freud, reality testing has two aims. The first is to distinguish fantasy from reality. He suggested that if by the use of an appropriate muscular action such as shutting one's eyes, the image disappears, one knows it is real. If the image remains, then it is a fantasy, which does not owe its existence to the senses. We see from this that the first aim of reality testing—to distinguish fantasy from the external world—depends on Freud's definition of perception as a sensory experience. The second aim of reality testing is to see if one's memory is distorted. In "Negation" (1925), Freud wrote, "The reproduction of a perception as a presentation [memory] is not always a faithful one.... In that case, reality testing has to ascertain how far such distortions go" (p. 128). The ego tests the extent of these distortions by rediscovering the object in the environment and comparing the accurate perception of it with the distorted memory. Thus, the second aim of reality testing—to correct any distortion in memory—depends on Freud's assumption that perceptions are always accurate.

Cognitive psychologists agree with Freud that we do accurately perceive unambiguous sensory stimuli. They do not, however, limit their inquiry to such simple perceptions. They are also interested in more complicated perceptions, where stimuli must be understood in relation to each other. One must not only perceive these stimuli through the senses, one must make inferences about the relationships between them. There is broad agreement among cognitive psychologists that cognitive capacities allow one to make such inferences (Neisser, 1976, p. 54) and that cognitive process involves, first, the selection and emphasis of certain stimuli in favor of others (Atkinson, Atkinson and Hilgard, 1983), and, second, the organization of these stimuli in a way that infers meaningful knowledge about the world. This meaningful knowledge is the end result of cognitive inference. "Most perceptible objects and events are *meaningful*. They afford various possibilities for action, carry implications about what has happened or what will happen, belong coherently to a larger context, possess an identity that transcends their simple physical properties. These meanings can be and are perceived" (Neisser, 1976, p. 71).

The meaning of a more complicated perception, then, relies on cognitive inference as well as on sensory capacity. For this reason complicated perception can be inaccurate, since one might draw incorrect inferences about the stimuli involved. We see from this that Freud's theory of reality testing, which defines perception as an accurate sensory impression of the environment, does not apply to complicated perceptions, where cognitive inference is involved.

Consider a child mixing red and blue paint together. He will register the sensory qualities of the color, smell, consistency, and flow of the paints. Beyond these sensory impressions, he may understand that blue and red blend to make purple. This understanding of the causal effect of mixing two colors to form a third is a cognitive inference that extends beyond the sensory impressions involved. When the child closes his eyes he still knows that blue and red make purple. Since this knowledge persists regardless of any muscular action, he cannot test the reality of his perception about the causal effect of mixing colors through his senses.

Consider now an unintelligent child mixing the same colors. He may think that purple appears by magic, or he may have no notion of causality but simply see the colors and perhaps attend to the consistency or smell of the paints. This child's cognitive abilities are unequal to the task of selecting and organizing relevant stimuli and inferring their meaning in a way that results in an accurate perception of the events before him. Since the child's perceptions are inaccurate, they cannot correct his memory of events. In fact, both the memory and the inaccurate perception are apt to be identical for the same reason, namely, the child's lack of intelligence.

Cognitive psychology teaches us that complicated perception involves the ability to infer the meaning of stimuli as well as the ability to register their sensory qualities. Because these inferences may be inaccurate, complicated perceptions may be inaccurate as well. Clearly, then, the two aims of Freud's theory of reality testing—first, to distinguish fantasy from reality using the senses as a guideline and, second, to correct distortion in memory by using accurate perception as a guideline—have no application to complicated perceptions. Complicated perceptions are not wholly dependent on the senses and are not always accurate.

Arlow illustrates another way that perception relies on inference and, hence, another way that perception may be inaccurate. In the paper "Fantasy, Memory and Reality Testing" (1969), Arlow discusses the distorting effect of fantasy on complicated perceptions. In the following extract, Arlow uses the term "perception" to refer to accurate impressions and ideas about the environment.

> When memory and perception offer material which is in consonance with fantasy thinking, the data are selectively perceived and used as material to serve as a vehicle for unconscious fantasy. This is not the objective reality which can be observed by outsiders and validated consensually. This is almost impossible to recollect because what the child experiences [his complicated perception] is, at the very moment of experience, a complex intermingling of [accurate] perception and fantasy. This complex intermingling has "really" happened as far as the individual is concerned [p. 39].

We have seen that cognitive capacities can select and organize sensory impressions in a way that infers meaning above and beyond sensory qualities. Here, Arlow explains that fantasy thinking can select and organize sensory impressions in a way that infers meaning above and beyond sensory qualities. Of course, fantasies are compromise formations, so one can restate Arlow's views in the following way: the determinants of compromise formation, namely, instinctual wish, defense, affect, and superego derivative, can select and organize sensory stimuli and infer meanings in ways compatible with their own ends.

A clinical example of a complicated perception organized by compromise formation is provided by Judy, a girl in late adolescence. Judy believed that all men were selfish, insensitive, and aloof. No matter how exuberant or kindly the man, she believed that the core of his character was uncaring. Sooner or later he would make a comment or gesture that would reveal the "truth" about him. Not surprisingly, this was also Judy's view of her father. Despite many indications to the contrary, including her own offhand observation that he beamed when he looked at her, she rationalized that he was an egocentric hypocrite who pretended to love her only to make a good impression on others.

The compromise formation that organized the meaning of Judy's perception of men had the following determinants. From the side of the instincts, she satisfied her aggression by condemning men. Her libidinal wishes were gratified because she felt that she alone understood "what makes men tick." From the side of affect and defense, she kept at bay her depressing sense of inferiority as a woman by maintaining that men are worse. She satisfied superego demands by externalizing all hostile intentions onto men and by steering clear of any enjoyable sexual relations with them. Judy's compromise formation selected and emphasized negative aspects of a man's behavior and rationalized that apparently positive aspects were insincere. In this way, she inferred that all men are bad.

The aims of Freud's theory of reality testing (to distinguish fantasy from reality and to correct distortion in memory) do not apply to Judy's perception of men anymore than they apply to the child's perception of mixing paints. When Judy closed her eyes and ears, her internal ideas about men were identical to her perceptions of them. She could not distinguish fantasy from reality by means of muscular action. In addition, her perceptions of men were inaccurate; therefore, she could not correct distorted memories of men by perceiving them.

Arlow's view of the effect of fantasy thinking (compromise formation) on complicated perception is clinically significant since he suggests that there is an important similarity between memory and perception. Both can be distorted by emotional factors in the same ways. Looking again at Judy, one would not say that her inferences about men had resulted from an accurate perception that she later distorted in memory. These inferences were operative in the act of perception; consequently, she never had an accurate perception of men. An analyst could not expect to recover a realistic knowledge of men hidden beneath a wall of defenses. When I suggested that her view of men was too extreme, pointing out that many women feel differently, Judy sighed in exasperation. She replied that men are nice to these women because they satisfy the selfish male ego. The only reason these women like men is because they are too stupid to know better. Not until she began to recover from her neurosis did I see any sign of a realistically benign attitude toward men.

To summarize this line of thought, complicated perceptions rely on inference rather than upon sensory perception alone; complicated perception is not entirely dependent on the senses. Both cognitive incapacity and compromise formaton can cause one to make incorrect inferences about sensory impressions; complicated perceptions are not necessarily accurate. For these reasons, the two aims of Freud's theory of reality testing—to distinguish fantasy from reality and to correct distorted memories—do not apply to complicated perceptions.

If one looks at steps three and four of the reality principle, namely, trial action in thought, whereby one infers the meaning of relationships between various stimuli, and judgment, whereby one infers which course of action is the best, one sees that in his 1911 paper Freud was writing about complicated perceptions. As we have seen, Freud's notion of reality testing does not apply to complicated perceptions, so one has no way of knowing if one's thinking or one's judgment is realistic or accurate. This inability to test the reality of accuracy of complicated perceptions is the problem in the reality principle.

The problem in the reality principle is not of central interest here, but a reason for the problem is central. The reason is this: both compromise formation and cognition can be involved in making inferences. This is Arlow's point, and it provides the basis for the discussion that follows. This discussion will resolve the differences between Freud and Hartmann on one hand, and Brenner on the other, insofar as complicated perception is concerned. The discussion will also offer a revised psychoanalytic theory of perception.

To review once more the positions of Freud, Hartmann, and Brenner, Freud believed that secondary thinking and judgment are cognitive processes that occur when the drives are inactive. He implied to this extent that complicated perceptions could be autonomous ego functions. Hartmann also believed that these cognitive activities could be conflict free and take place outside the realm of the instincts. He too believed that complicated perceptions could be autonomous ego functions. Brenner, however, sees all thoughts and judgments as compromise formations. He rejects theories of ego autonomy and places complicated perception squarely within the sphere of instinct and conflict.

REVISION OF THE PSYCHOANALYTIC THEORY OF PERCEPTION

I now propose to revise all three of these views of complicated perception. In what follows I offer a number of examples of complicated perceptions, that is, perceptions whose meaning is inferred. This clinical material allows the revision of Freud's and Hartmann's traditional views on two points. The examples illustrate, first, that cognitive activity does not operate in pure culture but functions simultaneously with compromise formation. This finding shows that insofar as complicated perception is concerned, Brenner is correct in maintaining that compromise formation pervades the human psyche and that, again, insofar as complicated perception is concerned, Freud was incorrect in holding that cognition operates when the drives are temporarily quiescent. Second the clinical material revises the traditional views of perception by showing not only that cognition and compromise formation operate simultaneously, but that one or the other can dominate perception. Compromise formation can dominate by influencing or distorting cognitive knowledge, and cognition can dominate perception by influencing the kind of compromise formations one has: cognitive activity directly influences emotional life. One, therefore, cannot maintain, as Freud did, that cognitive activity is designed only to gratify the instincts. One must say instead that the instincts, which are part of every compromise formation, sometimes bend to the dictates of cognition in ways that thwart instinctual gratification. One cannot maintain either, as Hartmann did, that cognition exerts its effects outside the range of mental conflicts. One must instead allow that cognition influences the kind of compromise formations one has and therefore exerts its effects on the instincts, which are part of every compromise formation.

This clinical material, which so strongly upholds Brenner's views about the ubiquity of compromise formation, also illustrates that his theory cannot by itself explain complicated perception. The clinical examples show, rather, that cognitive ideas as well as compromise formations are an essential part of every complicated perception.

In addition to refuting Freud and Hartmann's views on ego autonomy in complicated perception, the clinical material also opposes two other traditional views. First, it opposes Hartmann's idea that cognition involves pleasure emanating from the ego rather than from the id. Instead the vignettes illustrate that any pleasure involved in perception derives from compromise formation rather than from cognitive activity. Second, the clinical material opposes Freud and Hartmann's idea that cognitive functions are "ego instincts" intended for adaptation to the environment. While there is no question that cognition allows us to adapt in many cases, the material shows that cognition can also be maladaptive. The clinical material indicates that cognitive functioning, like compromise formation, is basic to perception and that it occurs regardless, for better or for worse.

The Simultaneous Occurrence of Cognition and Compromise Formation

The clinical material offered in this section shows that perception has two functions. The first function is a cognitive one, providing an idea of the world. The second function of perception is to provide "a vehicle for unconscious fantasy" (Arlow, 1969, p. 39), which means that perception conforms to the determinants of a compromise formation. In describing the determinants of compromise formation, I make no effort to offer a complete list but offer only enough information to convince the reader that the phenomenon in question is a compromise formation.

Consider again Judy's perception of men. She was highly tuned to any sign of boredom or irritation in men, and she could spot a genuinely unpleasant man with great ease. She also knew that her father seemed happy when he saw her, because she accurately selected and organized the relevant stimuli that led her to draw this inference. We know that the compromise formation outlined earlier organized the overall meaning of this cognitive activity – admitting to the truth of a man's unpleasant qualities and inferring that father's affection was hypocritical. Hence, Judy's cognitive idea about men was a vehicle for unconscious fantasy because it conformed to the determinants of her compromise formation.

The reader might argue that of course one sees this sort of picture when perceptions are inaccurate and that this is precisely the kind of muddle that occurs when emotion contaminates cognitive capacities (Anna Freud, 1965, p. 104). It is in answer to this argument that Brenner's view of the ubiquity of compromise formation is of critical importance. If Brenner's views are correct, compromise formation must play a part in all perceptions, accurate as well as inaccurate. The clinical material that follows illustrates that this is indeed the case.

A clinical example that illustrates this point concerns a nine-year-old boy. Alex was small for his age. He ardently wished to excel at sports but held an embittered conviction that he was destined to fail as an athlete.

With grim determination, he would join a competitive event—only to perform poorly. Every defeat fired his wish for revenge. So unbridled was this wish that it clouded his judgment and led him to attempt unrealistic feats that ended in yet other failures.

Alex was clearly self-defeating. He felt that his small stature was a "dirty trick" fate had played upon him. He lamented that he was too small ever to be good at sports. Alex's size did prevent him from excelling at some sports, but not at all of them. When I pointed this out to him, he paused with a look of disgust. "Can't you see I'm a shrimp?" he shouted, "Stop trying to make me feel better!"

Alex's perceptions of his size and of his poor athletic performance were accurate, but his conviction that he could never succeed as an athlete was an inaccurate perception. Both perceptions were fueled by the same compromise formation with the following determinants. On the aggressive side of the id, the wish to castrate father was directed against himself in the form of repeated defeats. On the side of the sexual instincts, he won mother's consoling affection. He defended against anxiety by becoming a harmless little failure. He defended against depressive affect by keeping alive the wish for revenge and the hope of victory over his rivals. He quelled superego condemnation by continually punishing himself with defeat.

As Alex's compromise formations changed in the course of analysis, he was able to perceive first his potential and then his real athletic success. He had recently developed a passion for baseball, partly because of his natural talent as a pitcher. He practiced with great industry and became quite skillful. He arrived at one session flushed with triumph. He had been among the first chosen to be on the school team. "At last," he said, "it's like a dream come true." The compromise formation that allowed for this new self-perception had the following determinants. On the instinctual side, the wish to castrate father found symbolic expression in striking out the batters, rendering their phallic bats ineffective. The libidinal wish for mother also found symbolic expression when he stepped on the pitcher's mound, which he called "the sweetest spot on mother earth." From side of defense and affect, he felt cushioned by his teammates against retaliation for his aggression. They also eased depressive affect aroused by defeat because they shared it with him. Alex's superego was satisfied since he felt he played well only to help his friends rather than for selfish reasons.

This change in Alex's view of himself is the kind analysts see all the time as patients get better. I bring it up now to show that the same compromise formation can accompany accurate as well as inaccurate cognitive ideas, as it did at the start of treatment, and also to show that as compromise formations change, cognitive knowledge changes too. At the end of analysis, Alex's new compromise formations were accompanied by a different view of himself.

Examples where perceptions have emotional as well as cognitive meanings, abound in educational settings. Susan, an 11-year-old, studied ancient Egyptian civilization. She was especially interested in burial rituals and became proficient at reading hieroglyphics. These studies gratified an oedipal compromise formation with the following determinants. Her curiosity about her parents' sexual activities found gratification in knowing about a sophisticated society and, especially, in decoding the mysterious hieroglyphics. On the aggressive side, her matricidal wishes were gratified by studying about the embalmed "mummies." From the side of affect and defense, she kept her anxiety and guilt at bay by rationalizing that she was studying a culture that was foreign to her own and had no connection with her own life. Her superego was gratified because she was such a conscientious student.

So far we have considered perceptions that are pleasant, or, as in Judy's malevolent perception of men and Alex's pessimistic view of himself, ones that provide as much pleasure as possible. Even when a perception is actively painful, however, it still has the same two functions. It provides a cognitive idea about the world and also conforms to the determinants of a compromise formation. The difference between painful perceptions and pleasurable ones is that when a perception is painful, compromise formations that oppose the cognitive meaning of the perception are present along with compromise formations that conform to it. Another example illustrates this point.

A number of years ago, Mr. G and his second wife came to see me about the man's 14-year-old daughter, who was reacting adversely to his recent marriage. After a few consultations, the couple concluded that the daughter suffered from a loyalty conflict between her natural mother and Mrs. G, of whom she was fond. With this understanding father and stepmother were able to restore family harmony.

I heard from the Gs from time to time. Mr. G's daughter progressed well, and the marriage was very happy. Seven years after their initial visit, Mr. G phoned and asked for an appointment. He explained that six months earlier, following a brief illness, his wife had died.

When he came to see me, Mr. G was the picture of distracted grief. He explained that since his wife's death his emotional condition had steadily worsened. He was having a recurring dream in which she was alive and well. They were together on holiday, idyllically happy in their mutual love. Toward morning he felt her beside him in bed, holding him as she had always done when she was alive. On waking, he found himself entwined in the bedclothes, clinging to her pillow. For a moment he did not know what was real, and then the horrible knowledge of her death visited him. Throughout the day this realization intensified, tormenting his thoughts. Everything reminded him that she was gone, that he was alone. Exhausted by his misery, he would eventually fall asleep. Again transported by his blissful dream, he experienced his few hours of relief only to awaken to the dreadful reality. So debilitating was this daily cycle that Mr. G began to fear for his sanity.

Viewed traditionally, one would say that Mr. G's wishes were at odds with his accurate perception of reality. At night he was able to deny his wife's death in happy dreams, but during the day the disparity between wish and knowledge clashed painfully. In fact, however, both the dream and the intense knowledge of reality were compromise formations in which denial was a prominent feature.

During the sessions that followed, Mr. G spoke incessantly of his suffering. When he reminisced about his wife, he seemed to do so only to aggravate his sense of loss. With obvious annoyance, he rejected any note of hope or relief that I offered. I asked about his childhood. He said that his mother had had little time for him. As a small boy, he had developed the habit of complaining in order to punish her as well as to arouse her pity and love. Only then did I understand there was a method in his misery.

The dreams and daily grief were different compromise formations with the same goal of bringing Mrs. G back to life. The dream was an obvious compromise formation. The libidinal element is clear. The denial of Mrs. G's death defended also against depressive affect. Superego factors included reaction formations against his anger with his wife for leaving him. The tormented sense of loss during the day was also a compromise formation emphasizing denial. On the libidinal side, Mr. G, by being as miserable as possible, tried to force his wife to take pity on him and return to life. He also aggressively punished her by reproaching her with his unhappiness. He defended against depression and rage in the unconscious magical belief that she would come back to him. His superego was satisfied because his rage was contained. Here was the paradoxical situation where Mr. G intensified the knowledge of his wife's death in order to deny it.

These were the compromise formations that opposed Mr. G's cognitive knowledge that his wife was dead. Yet this knowledge, painful as it was, also fulfilled the conditions of another compromise formation. Mr. G said that since his wife's death he had experienced a distressing sense of shame and subservience in the company of other men, even his oldest and best friends. He recalled similar feelings in childhood with his father.

Subsequent associations revealed that these feelings were part of a homosexual compromise formation that originally came about in response to mother's rejection as well as to Mr. G's childhood fear of oedipal retaliation. In the compromise formation, he wished to be father's wife and also expressed hostility to mother by rejecting her. The homosexual stance allowed him to escape the depressing effects of mother's rejection as well as his fears of father's wrath. His superego was satisfied because the obedient love for father replaced the murderous rivalry of the positive oedipal phase. This was the compromise formation whose conditions were fulfilled by the knowledge of Mrs. G's death.

I am unable to provide here the exhaustive clinical evidence necessary to convince the reader that every idea is accompanied by a consonant compromise formation. If the reader would like to be convinced that this is the case, I ask him to try to discover a cognitive idea that has no emotional meaning. The futility of this search would convince him that cognitive ideas are always accompanied by consonant compromise formations.

If one accepts that complicated perceptions have two meanings, one a cognitive idea about the world and the other a consonant compromise formation, one takes a step forward in appreciating Brenner's view that compromise formations pervade mental life, because they pervade complicated perceptions. One can take a similar step in refuting Freud's formulation that cognition occurs in pure culture when instinctual life is temporarily inactive.

If we think of the analyst making an interpretation, we see that his perception of the patient will have two meanings. One will be a compromise formation, which is the analyst's transference to the patient. The other is the analyst's cognitive understanding of the patient's conflicts. It is on the basis of his cognitive understanding that the analyst makes his interpretations.

The Causal Connection Between Compromise Formation
and Cognition

The fact that cognition and compromise formation operate simultaneously does not, however, invalidate Freud's and Hartmann's views that cognition occurs outside the realm of instinctual life and psychic conflict. One might argue that cognition and compromise formation occur simultaneously but independently of each other and that the cognitive capacities of the ego are still autonomous and conflict free.

The clinical vignettes just offered oppose this argument and point instead to a causal connection between cognition and compromise formation. The causal connection is this: either the pleasure principle or cognition dominates perception. If the pleasure principle dominates, then a compromise formation that is pleasant, or at least more pleasant than other compromise formations, influences and often distorts our cognitive ideas about the world. When cognition dominates a perception, our ideas about the world are not influenced or distorted by compromise formations, pleasant or otherwise. Instead, the cognitive idea mobilizes a compromise formation whose determinants conform to the idea.

To illustrate these points, the clinical vignettes are divided into three categories: (1) perception dominated by the pleasure principle; (2) perception where domination by either the pleasure principle or cognition is ambiguous; and (3) perception dominated by cognition.

Perception Dominated by the Pleasure Principle.   It is easy to see how the pleasure principle dominates perception when the compromise formations involved are generally pleasant ones. These compromise formations can distort one's cognitive capacities or else influence the kind of accurate knowledge one has. Judy's compromise formation distorted her ideas about men; the compromise formation Alex had by the end of analysis guided him toward the knowledge that he was a good athlete.

Though it is less obvious, the pleasure principle can also dominate painful perceptions. At the beginning of treatment, Alex's knowledge of his poor athletic performance was accompanied by a compromise formation characterized by frustrated rage and a hopeless sense of failure. Though this compromise formation, like all others, provided some measure of gratification, it aroused more pain than pleasure. Yet analytic work demonstrated that it was this compromise formation that caused Alex to see himself as a pitiful "shrimp." Painful as it was, the compromise formation offered Alex the most pleasure and the least pain possible.

Examples such as these, illustrate that there is no absolute link between the pleasure principle and compromise formation. All a compromise formation can do is to provide the most pleasure and the least pain for a given set of determinants. If the determinants are not felicitous, then the compromise formation will be a painful one. Painful as it might be, the compromise formation may be the most pleasurable one the patient can manage. As analysts, we see this kind of situation daily in our consulting rooms. In fact, patients usually seek our help because their compromise formations are painful.

Perceptions Where Domination by Either the Pleasure Principle or by Cognition is Ambiguous.   In Susan's case, it is impossible to determine whether the pleasure principle or cognition dominate perceptions involved in learning about Egypt. Perhaps her cognitive ability activated the oedipal compromise formation, or perhaps the compromise formation facilitated her learning. It is always difficult to determine the dominance of the pleasure principle of cognition in these kinds of perceptions, where an accurate cognitive idea about the world is accompanied by a pleasurable compromise formation.

Perception Dominated by Cognition.   In this section I will try to illustrate that cognition can dominate perception in two ways. First, a cognitive idea can resist distortion by compromise formation. Second, the cognitive idea can influence the kind of compromise formations one has.

To prove that cognition can resist distortion by compromise formation, one must find an example where an unwelcome idea about the world is opposed by a pleasurable compromise formation. One would also have to show that despite this opposition, the unpleasant idea is not distorted.

To begin the discussion, I ask the reader to consider the opposite situation, where unpleasant ideas are distorted by compromise formation. Returning again to Judy, we may recall that she accurately perceived her father's apparent happiness at seeing her. Later in treatment, Judy realized that father's affection was sincere, even though early on she had thought he was a hypocrite. Here we see a familiar picture. Judy's compromise formation caused her to infer that father's show of love was not real. In this way she avoided the painful idea that her father cared for her. Subsequent analysis revealed that this idea was indeed distressing because it aroused conflicted sexual feelings and because she could no longer project her hostile, castrating impulses onto her father. One sees with Judy that her negative view of her father was dominated by a compromise formation that afforded the most pleasure possible. In other words, her cognitive idea about father was dominated by the pleasure principle.

Consider now Mr. G's case. He had three different cognitive ideas, only one of which was accompanied by a pleasurable compromise formation. The first idea, in his dreams, was that his wife was alive. This idea was accompanied by a blissful compromise formation. The second idea, which occupied his waking hours, was an admixture of distortion and reality. It was as if he said "I know my wife is dead and gone forever, but I cannot bear it so if I plead and suffer enough she will surely take pity and return to me." The compromise formation accompanying this idea was a very painful one. Mr. G's third cognitive idea completely accepted that his wife was dead and would never return. This idea was accompanied by the homosexual compromise formation that caused him discomfort with his male friends.

If the pleasure principle had dominated Mr. G's perception, his most pleasurable compromise formation would have distorted his cognitive ideas. Had this been the case, he would never have known that his wife was dead, but would have remained happily deluded in waking life as he was in dreams. This did not happen. He remained aware, or partially aware, of his wife's death even though he would have been happier in total ignorance. Mr. G's cognitive knowledge of his wife's death resisted distortion by the most pleasurable compromise formation available to him. Cognition that resists such distortion dominates perception to the extent that the idea remains intact.

A second, more decisive way that cognition can dominate perception is by influencing the kind of compromise formation that accompanies the cognitive idea. The clinical material that follows focuses on the way a cognitive idea influences the determinants of its accompanying compromise formation. I do not mean to imply that an idea actually produces a particular set of determinants, but that given the range of determinants available, cognitive ideas will influence which determinants come to the fore in a compromise formation.

Mr. G's dream tells us nothing about the influence of cognition on the emotions, since the idea that his wife was alive was itself clearly distorted by compromise formation. In this compromise formation, his libidinal attachment to her far outweighed all other considerations. He and his wife were on holiday and, later, in bed together. Throughout the dream he was joyfully aware of their love for each other. So overwhelming was this sense of mutual love that it served the defensive function of warding off depressive affect. It also obliterated any anger he felt for her leaving him. It thus quelled superego condemnation for his anger.

The second idea, which was a combination of fact and distortion, was accompanied by a different set of determinants in a painful compromise formation. Here the libidinal side of the instincts found gratification only in magical expectation. On the aggressive side, Mr. G tried to punish his wife with his wretchedness and his incessant pleading. He satisfied consequent superego condemnation by punishing himself with his misery. He defended against depressive affect and anxiety involved in accepting his loss and starting a new life, in the unconscious belief that he could reverse fate.

Mr. G's third cognitive idea totally accepted his wife's death. This idea was accompanied by the unconscious homosexual compromise formation where his libidinal attachment to his wife was all but absent. It was replaced by his sexual longing for his male friends, who stood for his father. The hostility to wife/mother was also a prominent feature of this compromise formation. As we saw, his homosexual stance defended against depressive affect aroused by oedipal rejection by mother and against anxiety associated with oedipal retaliation by father. Superego dictates were satisfied when Mr. G relinquished hostility toward father and replaced it with love.

What we see in the latter two cases is that the cognitive idea in question activates libidinal and aggressive drive derivatives as well as defenses, affect, and superego manifestations. In other words, the cognitive idea affects the kind of compromise formations that accompany the idea.

If one were to view the situation the other way around and maintain that the compromise formations in question mobilize the cognitive ideas, one would have to ask why such compromise formations came to the fore all of a sudden. They made no appearance when Mrs. G was alive and well but erupted only after she had died. It would be too drastic a coincidence to suppose that for other reasons these compromise formations became active, giving rise to thoughts about his wife's death just at the time when she happened to die. One must conclude that Mrs. G's death was a fact Mr. G knew. This knowledge not only resisted distortion by compromise formation, but also had a direct impact on the determinants of his compromise formations.

Analysts have always known that compromise formation can distort and influence cognitive capacities. As Mr. G's case illustrates, however, the reverse can also be true. Sometimes cognitive capacities influence our compromise formations. On the basis of this evidence, we can refute Freud's notion that cognition exists for the ultimate aim of gratifyng the instincts. We have seen that unwelcome knowledge can evoke painful compromise formations that afford little instinctual gratification. We can also refute Hartmann's notion that cognitive capacities exert their influence outside the instinctual realm. The clinical material shows instead that cognition exerts its influence on compromise formation, of which the instincts are a part.

Although all the clinical material supports Brenner's view that compromise formation pervades mental life, it also illustrates that complicated perception is not simply compromise formation. Complicated perception also consists of a cognitive idea. When we found that these two factors occur simultaneously, we could still suppose that compromise formation was more important than cognition, if we assumed that compromise formation always had the power to direct and distort cognitive ideas. The fact that some cognitive ideas can resist distortion by compromise formation and can influence the kind of compromise formation one has puts cognition on a par with compromise formation in terms of its importance. Thus, we can say that Brenner's theories are correct but do not give us a full explanation of complicated perception.

Applying this understanding to the analytic situation, we see that the purpose of an interpretation is to introduce to the patient a cognitive idea that will change his existing ideas and their accompanying compromise formations. If compromise formations were not subject to such change, interpretations would always fall on deaf ears.

TWO MORE POINTS OF OPPOSITION TO TRADITIONAL VIEWS

The Pleasure Involved in Perception Does Not Emanate From the Ego

We have seen that cognition is always accompanied by a compromise formation. It is therefore not possible to assert, as Hartmann did, that the pleasure involved in perception results from the cognitive activities of the ego rather than from the instinctual gratifications of the compromise formation. In fact, the clinical material opposes Hartmann's view. Clinical material indicates that the more pleasurable the compromise formation involved, the more pleasurable the sensation that accompanies cognitive knowledge. Thus Alex's self-perceptions at the end of treatment and Susan's studies of Egypt were pleasurable because the compromise formations involved afforded much instinctual pleasure.

Of course, one can argue that since compromise formations have determinants from the ego and the superego as well as from the id, the ego and superego, along with instinctual gratification, can account for pleasurable perceptions. The only point I wish to underline is that the pleasure emanating from compromise formation, rather than from cognitive activity, appears to render a perception pleasurable or unpleasurable.

Cognition is a Basic Psychic Function Rather Than a Necessarily Adaptive One

We have seen in the clinical vignettes that cognitive activity takes place, but that it is not necessarily adaptive. Judy's cognitive capacities were ultimately distorted by her compromise formation in ways that led to maladaptive relationships with men. Alex's accurate perceptions of his small size did not encourage him to seek out ways to make the best of the situation. Mr. G's knowledge of his wife's death caused him to decompensate rather than adapt to a new way of life. On the other hand, Alex's knowledge that he had talent as a pitcher inspired him to become skilled. Susan's knowledge about Egypt was adaptive to educational pursuits.

Here we see situations where cognition occurs as part of all perception but does not necessarily lead one to adapt to the environment. Rather, it appears that as far as perception is concerned, cognitive functioning is basic. Like compromise formation, it occurs regardless.

To summarize these four lines of thought, the clinical material illustrates, first, that all perceptions have two meanings: one is a cognitive idea; the other is a compromise formation. We can thus understand that compromise formations accompany cognition, and we can abandon the traditional view that realistic thinking begins where irrational thought ends. Second, cognition and compromise formation have a mutually causal relationship. When the pleasure principle dominates perception, compromise formation distorts or influences what we know, or what we think we know. When cognition dominates perception, it affects the kind of compromise formations we have. Third, because cognition and compromise formation are always present in perception, one cannot support Hartmann's view that the cognitive capacities of the ego are always a source of pleasure, even when cognition dominates perception. Rather, the clinical material indicates that the amount of pleasure involved in the perception is commensurate with the pleasure afforded by the accompanying compromise formation. Fourth, cognition does not necessarily have an adaptive function.

SPECULATIVE REMARKS

Even if the reader accepts all these points, one critical question still remains: Why does some cognitive knowledge resist influence and distortion by compromise formation? Looking at the clinical vignettes about Judy and Alex, we see that complicated perceptions whose meaning is inferred are prone to such distortion. On the other hand, cognitive psychology teaches us that straightforward sensory perceptions are not prone to distortion by compromise formations. For example, red may be my favorite color, but when presented with a green object I will see green all the same. How are we to understand Mr. G's knowledge of his wife's death? It was not a simple sensory perception, but a complicated one because it included the inferred knowledge that his wife would never return. Why did this cognitive inference resist distortion by compromise formation? To this question, I offer some speculative thoughts.

The reliability of sensory perception allows us to make cognitive inferences that are also reliable. In other words, these inferences resist distortion by compromise formation. For example, we infer that the sun will rise each morning even before it does so. If I do not want the sun to rise, and if I incorrectly infer that it will not, the sun will rise anyway and my sense of sight will force me to know that it did. Having had this experience, I would be less likely to draw the same incorrect inference a second time. The repeated and consistent experience of seeing the sun rise each morning appears to militate against inferences distorted by compromise formation.

We also make inferences on the basis of information that is not gleaned directly from the senses. If this information, like sensation, is consistent, then our inferences based on it will also be resistant to distortion by compromise formation. Mr. G had learned that the dead never return to life on earth. This information was a repeated and consistent aspect of his social education. He could not help knowing that his wife was gone forever anymore than he could help knowing the sun will rise. The reader might note that in fact the sun does not rise, the earth turns. Nevertheless, the example is still valid because it emphasizes the *consistency* of what we learn rather than its accuracy. This consistency of experience appears to account, at least in part, for the stability of cognitive knowledge.

Considering once more the analyst's role, we realize that as we become experienced clinicians, we not only learn more about psychopathology, we become by repeated experience increasingly convinced of the truth of psychoanalytic theory. The more convinced we are, the less liable we are to fall prey to countertransference. This consistency of experience appears to enhance not simply the amount of what we know, but the stability of what we know.

CONCLUSION

This paper began with the intention of discovering whether Brenner is correct in asserting that compromise formation is ubiquitous in mental life or whether Freud and Hartmann were correct in maintaining the traditional view that cognition and emotion are mutually exclusive. This question was resolved insofar as complicated perception is concerned. One sees that complicated perceptions consist of a cognitive idea and a compromise formation that operate simultaneously and that exert mutual influence upon each other. These findings allow us to refute Freud's and Hartmann's positions and to agree with Brenner that compromise formation is ubiquitous in complicated perception.

Paradoxically, the very arguments that support Brenner's views point to the fact that one cannot entirely explain complicated perception in terms of compromise formation. Instead we see that cognition also pervades perception. While compromise formation often dominates perception and directs or distorts knowledge, cognition can also dominate perception and influence the accompanying compromise formations. So we see that while Brenner's theory of compromise formation is correct, it is not complete; to understand perception we must include cognitive capacity as an essential component.

The ease with which one can apply Brenner's theories to the clinical setting is the key ingredient in this paper. Once one had read *The Mind in Conflict* (Brenner, 1982), one sees compromise formation in all aspects of mental life. Without this understanding, there would be no reason to question Freud's and Hartmann's views, nor could one understand the clinical material well enough to refute them. Brenner's theories not only enhance our clinical skills and understanding, they enable us to formulate and even answer new questions.

REFERENCES

Atkinson, R. L., Atkinson, R. C., & Hilgard, E. R. (1983), *Introduction to Psychology.* New York: Harcourt Brace Jovanovich.

Arlow, J. A. (1969), Fantasy, memory, and reality testing. *Psychoanal. Quart.,* 38:28–51.

Brenner, C. (1982), *The Mind in Conflict.* New York: International Universities Press.

Freud, A. (1965), *The Writings of Anna Freud Vol. VI.* New York: International Universities Press.

Freud, S. (1900), The interpretation of dreams, *Standard Edition,* 5:509–623. London: Hogarth Press, 1968.

_____ (1911), Formulations on the two principles of mental functioning, *Standard Edition,* 12:218–226. London: Hogarth Press, 1968.

_____ (1913), On psychoanalysis, *Standard Edition,* 12:207–211. London: Hogarth Press, 1968.

_____ (1925), Negation, *Standard Edition,* 19:235–239. London: Hogarth Press, 1968.

Hartmann, H. (1939), *Ego Psychology and the Problem of Adaptation.* New York: International Universities Press, 1958.

_____ (1950), Comments on the psychoanalytic theory of the ego. In: *Essays on Ego Psychology: Selected Problems in Psychoanalytic Theory.* New York: International Universities Press, 1964.

_____ (1951). Technical implications of ego psychology. *Psychoanal. Quart.,* 20:31–43.

_____ (1955), Notes on the theory of sublimation. In: *Essays on Ego Psychology. New York: International Universities Press, 1964.*

_____ (1956), Notes on the reality principle. In: *Essays on Ego Psychology.* New York: International Universities Press, 1964.

Neisser, U. (1976), *Cognition and Reality.* San Francisco: Freeman.

DALE BOESKY

Questions About Sublimation

In this paper I attempt to demonstrate that those who have said that there is no satisfactory definition of sublimation are correct. It is not my primary purpose to clarify terms or to suggest that we discard the term sublimation, which is deeply entrenched in our literature and which is considered to be an essential concept by some of our leading theoreticians. Instead, I will demonstrate that this definitional confusion is caused by fundamental conceptual ambiguities. Further, I assert that those conceptual problems are directly related to the fact that sublimation has played a pivotal conceptual role in the evolution of the quantitative-energic (economic) dimension of metapsychology.

PROBLEMS WITH THE DEFINITION

The current definition of sublimation in *The Glossary of Psychoanalytic Concepts* (Moore & Fine, 1968) reads as follows:

> Sublimation: The deflection of the energies of instinctual drives to aims that are more acceptable to the ego and superego. Especially involved are those energies related to the satisfaction of oral and anal wishes (the pre-oedipal libido). Transformations of the energy itself, effected largely through the mechanism of identification, are emphasized in the related concept of neutralization . . . . The pleasures and achievements of artistic and intellectual creativity have provided traditional illustrations of sublimation, though in a larger sense all conflict-free activities that promote the synthesis of the total personality may be regarded in this category. Inadequacies or failures of sublimation, whether constitutional or developmental, may contribute to perversions, psychopathic behavior, and other adaptive disorders [p. 90].

It would be useful to question most of the key elements in this prevailing definition of sublimation. The following is a schematic list of the conceptual ambiguities contained in the definition:

1. If the definition is limited to artistic and intellectual activities, the definition depends on value judgments. But if any conflict-free activity that promotes the synthesis of the personality is included, the definition of sublimation fails to distinguish sublimation from other developmental processes or from the totality of normal mental functioning. Therefore the descriptive domain of the definition is unclear.
2. The participation of the ego and superego is limited to literally channeling psychic energy rather than interactive participation of drive derivatives with ideational content.
3. The principle energies involved are related to oral and anal wishes, that is, to pregenital drives.
4. The energy transformation is implicitly effected predominantly via the mechanism of identification.
5. The definition is contingent on the transformation of psychic energy by means of neutralization.
6. Sublimation is considered to be a manifestation only of health.

FREUD'S VIEWS OF SUBLIMATION

It is difficult to summarize Freud's views of sublimation because he never wrote a separate paper about the topic itself but discussed it only in relation to other issues; his views are scattered through some forty of his papers. More important, his views about sublimation changed substantially as he revised his theories of the drives and defenses and also when he introduced the structural theory; these refinements were complex and can only be indicated here without discussion. One can gain a better view of recent controversies about psychic energy (Applegarth, 1971; Wallerstein, 1977) by a careful reconsideration of Freud's evolving ideas about sublimation.

Descriptive Definition

Freud used the term sublimation in several ways. His most familiar use of the term in his early writings indicated a change in the aim of an instinct or drive toward a higher cultural activity. For example, he said (1905a, p. 156; 1908b) that a child's sexual curiosity about the human body can "be diverted ('sublimated') in the direction of art." This illustrates what I will call his descriptive definition and it is the definition which is most familiar. It is indicative of Freud's wish to call attention to his metaphorical use of the term sublimation (borrowed from chemistry) that he often enclosed the term in quotation marks. Three years later (1908a) he introduced the idea that sublimation is an important aspect of the formation of psychic structure.

First Metapsychologic Theory of Sublimation

This neither was a merely descriptive definition nor the loose usage of a metaphor. Rather, this was an inchoate metapsychological usage of the term sublimation, as is illustrated in Freud's remarks about character formation (1908a): "...the permanent character traits are either unchanged prolongations of the original instincts or sublimations of those instincts or reaction formations against them" (p. 175). It is not sufficiently recognized in the literature that Freud used the term sublimation in both a descriptive and a metapsychologic sense *and that he did so even in his early writings.* In fact, he continued throughout his writings to use the term sublimation in both senses: first, descriptively to indicate rather loosely the alteration of an instinctual aim in the direction of some higher cultural activity; and second, in a metapsychological sense to describe the role of sublimation in the formation of psychic structure and as a guardian of mental health — the sexual instincts were not only easily diverted but also could become fixated as a result of repression and then predispose that person to neurosis (1908b; 1909a, p. 138n; 1910a, p. 54).

The forces employed for cultural activities were "to a great extent obtained thru the suppression of what are known as the perverse elements of sexual excitation" (1908b, p. 189). This, together with his prior remarks in "Character and Anal Erotism" (1908a), seems to be one of the reasons for the assertion of many later authors (e.g. Deri, 1939; Fenichel, 1945) that only the component instincts — the pregenital, especially the scopophilic, oral, and anal instincts — could be sublimated (see also Freud, 1910a, p. 54). There were said to be constitutional limits on the capacity of any person to sublimate (see also Freud, 1909b, p. 203), and these limits could seriously alter the outcome of psychoanalytic treatment. The consequent view of the importance of sublimation for mental health has survived most of the numerous criticisms of the concept of sublimation and is widely accepted at the present time. Freud's use of the term in the descriptive sense never changed when he used the term only descriptively (1908b, 1910b, 1923a, 1930, 1933, 1939). But his metapsychologic usage of the term changed significantly in 1914 and again in 1923.

Complicating matters further, Freud used the term sublimation in a third way in two of his famous case studies. In the Dora case (1905a, 1917, p. 442) and in his report on the Wolf Man (1918), he used the term sublimation almost synonomously with our present usage of the term compromise formation. Freud also used the term very loosely in a fourth category of such diversity that one might call it a miscellaneous usage. For example, in a letter to E. Jones about the objections raised by Havelock Ellis to Freud's sexual theories, Freud said this was merely an example of sublimated resistance (Jones, 1957, p. 493).

In summary, the vicissitudes of instincts in 1910 were gratification, repression, or sublimation. Essentially, these were the only visicissitudes of instincts in the first dual instinct theory. (See also Freud, 1915b, ed. note, pp. 143–145). Instincts sublimated into character traits constituted the first metapsychologic theory of sublimation.

Second Metapsychologic Theory of Sublimation

The announcement of the ego ideal and the distinction between object libido and ego libido (1914) foreshadowed Freud's next metapsychologic view of the role of sublimation and deepened his views of the relations between sublimation and repression. Repression proceeded from the self-respect of the ego, and therefore the formation of an ideal would be the conditioning factor for repression (Freud, 1914, p. 94; 1921, p. 131n). Sublimation was still an instinctual vicissitude (1915a). Freud made a sharp distinction in 1914 between idealization, which entailed a change in the object, and sublimation, which required a change in the aim of an instinct, but he reversed this view later (1923a) and announced that both object and aim were altered in sublimation. He also distinguished between mere aim inhibition due to fear, and true sublimations, which entailed that the original sexual aims be abandoned (1923a, p. 258; 1933, p. 97).

"The Ego and the Id" (1923b) provides Freud's most systematic attempt at a metapsychologic definition rather than a merely descriptive definition of sublimation. Sublimation was now essential to him as a mechanism to provide the ego with a supply of desexualized psychic energy:

> [the] transformation of an erotic object choice into an alteration of the ego is also a method by which the ego can gain control over the id and deepen its relations with it . . . the ego forces itself upon the id as a love object...the transformation of object libido into narcissistic libido which thus takes place obviously implies an abandonment of sexual aims, a desexualization — a kind of sublimation, therefore. Indeed, the question arises, and deserves careful consideration, whether all sublimation does not take place

through the mediation of the ego, which begins by changing sexual object libido into narcissistic libido and then, perhaps, goes on to give it another aim [p. 30].

On theoretic grounds Freud (1923b) felt compelled by economic considerations to postulate the existence of a displaceable, neutral energy that could be added to a qualitatively differentiated erotic or destructive cathexis. For example, he felt this to be a way he could account for the shift from love into hate in paranoia. "Without assuming the existence of a displaceable energy of this kind we can make no headway. The only question is where it comes from, what it belongs to, and what it signifies" (p. 44). *With those very words, Freud specified his view of the inseparable link between psychic energy and sublimation.* He continued:

> . . . this displaceable libido is employed in the service of the pleasure principle to obviate blockages and to facilitate discharge [p. 45]. If this displaceable energy is desexualized libido, it may also be described as sublimated energy; for it would still retain the main purpose of Eros-that of uniting and binding.... If thought processes . . . are to be included among these displacements, then the activity of thinking is also supplied from the sublimation of erotic motive forces . . .[p. 45].

Then, in the following passage, Freud linked his idea of sublimation regularly occurring through the transformation of libido to his emerging view of identification: "The ego deals with the first object-cathexes of the id (and certainly later ones too) by taking over the libido from them into itself and binding it to the alteration of the ego, produced by means of identification. The transformation (of erotic libido) into ego-libido . . . involves an abandonment of sexual aims, a desexualization" (p. 45–46).

These passages are perhaps the clearest examples in Freud's writings of his proposal to account for all mental processes, including thinking, as energized by transformation of object libido into ego libido by means of sublimation. It is essential to keep in mind that Freud had always considered accounting for the energy that activated the mind and fueled the functioning of the mind to be of paramount importance (1895). Freud stated categorically in the 1915 edition of the "Three Essays": (1950b) "It should be the task of a libido theory of neurotic and psychotic disorders to express all the observed phenomena and inferred processes in terms of the economics of the libido" (p. 218). This theoretic ambition made sublimation a key conceptual tool; sublimation was comparable to a fuel refinery for the production of this essential desexualized psychic energy, and Freud's theoretic commitments required a basis for supplying continuing amounts of desexualized psychic energy. It is an example of referring to psychic energy as both mental and physical, since the raw fuel for the mental, desexualized, sublimated psychic energy arose from the body sources of libido.

Freud believed also that one category of neurosis, the actual neuroses, could develop without conflict because of the damming up of libido as a consequence of unhealthy sexual practices. The relevant point here is that to the end of his life Freud adhered to the view that these actual neuroses were examples of the damming up of psychic energy in which ideational content was irrelevant. These were neuroses without motivational considerations. *This meant that a form of psychic energy was convertible directly into an affect without ideation.* The concept of psychic energy that Freud used in his views of the actual neuroses was thus "officially" to be taken only as a metaphor, but nonetheless Freud seemed to use it conceptually to mean literal and physical energy as well. This is precisely the problem also with his energic views of sublimation. These problems with the concept of psychic energy are well known, but it is not so widely understood that this ambiguity is also a major problem with the term sublimation.

It will be recalled that Freud believed that in the course of development, the Oedipus complex is literally smashed, a result, in part, of identifications that replaced the oedipal object cathexes. "The libidinal trends belonging to the Oedipus complex are in part desexualized and sublimated (a thing which probably happens with every transformation into an identification) and in part inhibited in their aim and changed into impulses of affection" (1924, p. 177). The preceding passage is one of the most extreme proposals Freud made about the role of sublimation in the formation of psychic structure. Modern views of these issues would question: the "smashing" of the libidinal and aggressive drive derivatives of the Oedipus complex; the restriction of the mechanism of sublimation to identification secondary to decathexis of the oedipal objects; and the requirement that such a decathexis precede identification since identifications can occur during continuing object relationships.

When Freud later (1925) spoke of the smashing of the Oedipus complex, he allowed for partial sublimation only of its libidinal cathexis. It was not until Freud wrote "Civilization and Its Discontents" (1930) that he considered work to be an example of sublimation and at the same time first mentioned the possibility of sublimating aggressive drives. He did not develop either idea and cautioned against premature efforts to reconcile his earlier views of sublimation with his later views of aggression (Jones, 1957, pp. 464–465). While it is well known that Freud believed that the superego is weaker in women, it is less widely recognized that he said that women also can not sublimate as well as men. This, he said, is because women have little sense of justice, which is related to the preponderance of envy in their mental life. He felt that because their social interests are therefore weaker, they have less capacity for sublimating their instincts (1933).

CRITICISMS AND CONTRIBUTIONS AFTER FREUD

Glover's (1931) critique of the contradictions and ambiguities in the concept of sublimation stands as one of the major contributions to the literature on this topic. He concluded that sublimation was not a single mechanism but was instead a group of functions. (see also Brierly, 1947). He said that if we could not distinguish the displacement of instinctual aims in sublimation from the substitution of instinctual aims in neurotic symptom formation and indeed from the entire process of symbolism as the classic example of substitution, we could not then arrive at a coherent metapsychologic definition, nor even at a descriptive definition of sublimation. He and many other authors (Hartmann, 1964; LaPlanche & Pontalis, 1973; Loewald, 1983) questioned the demarcation of any merely descriptive definition. Should all work be included in the definition of sublimation? What about the hobbies and avocations of adults or the games and play of children?

The confusion attendant upon mixing value judgments with scientific definitions has been widely recognized (Sterba, 1930; Bernfeld, cited in Glover, 1931; Fenichel, 1945; Hartmann, 1964; Kris, 1955; Lampl de Groot, 1965; LaPlanche & Pontalis, 1973), characteristically by Freud himself (Jones, 1957; letter 33, pp. 464–465). And, of course, certain creative activities occur in states of psychosis and intoxication. Can only the pregenital instincts be sublimated? Freud seemed to favor that view (1908a, 1908b) and was followed on that point more concretely by Deri (1939) and Fenichel (1945). According to Fenichel, sublimation of genital impulses is theoretically excluded because the genital allows full orgastic discharge, and therefore the deflection of aim required for a true sublimation is impossible. Alpert (1949) was the first to demonstrate the neglect of the phallic phase of psychosexual development in the literature on sublimation prior to 1949. It also is curious that the literature on sublimation rarely includes consideration of athletic activity. As psychoanalytic experience with the structural model deepened, it became apparent that investment of human activity with "energy" derived from the instincts was a fundamental aspect of most human activity, so that it would be arbitrary to isolate any one aspect of human behavior solely on the criterion that this given piece of behavior expressed drive wishes.

The absence of Freud's (1920) integration of his views of sublimation and aggression has also been widely noted (e.g., Sterba, 1930; Glover, 1931; Hartmann, Kris, & Loewenstein, 1949; Lampl deGroot, 1965; Hacker, 1972; LaPlanche & Pontalis, 1973). This is even more striking when we consider that Freud made numerous updated notes for inclusion in the 1920 and 1924 editions of the "Three Essays." Inasmuch as he introduced his final dual drive theory in 1920 and announced the structural model in 1923, we are left to wonder about his silence on how to integrate his views of sublimation and aggression. There are some suggestive clues. Waelder (1960) reported Freud's comments at a small scientific meeting in the late 1920s after the presentation of a paper devoted to the topic of sublimation. "In his discussion, Freud took the view that 'sublimation' was not a well defined psychic mechanism like repression or reaction formation but rather a loose characterization of various processes that lead to socially more valuable activities" (p. 124). Waelder (see also Hartmann et al., 1955, and Sandler & A. Freud, 1981a, 1981b) noted that it was a property of all defenses to allow substitute gratification (p. 184).

Anna Freud

Anna Freud also wrote so extensively about sublimation that I cannot here even adequately summarize her contributions. I can only select those aspects of her work that are relevant to my topic. She said that "sublimation means the displacement of an instinctual aim from its original, forbidden aim to another, socially approved one" (1951a, p. 124). She included sublimation, together with the unconscious and repression, among the most important terms and concepts of psychoanalysis (1930, p. 110). Most revealing of her commitment to the importance of sublimation conceptually was her 1936 pronouncement in "The Ego and the Mechanisms of Defense": "To these nine methods of defense...we must add a tenth, which pertains rather to the study of the normal than to that of neurosis: sublimation, or displacement of instinctual aims" (p. 44). Although she adhered to the view that sublimation was a defense mechanism until the end of her life (1978, pp. 247, 275; 1979, p. 325), she did state (1965a) that one must assess the context of the existing sublimation as only a part of the total clinical picture. Still she always (Sandler & A. Freud, 1981a, 1981b) felt that sublimation is exceptional in that it is always normal or leads to what is normal. As Blum (1983) noted, Anna Freud established a bridge between the defensive and developmental aspects of sublimation. She was among those who insisted that sublimation is a relatively late developmental achievement (see also Nunberg, 1955) because sublimations presuppose the existence of the superego (A.

Freud, 1936, p. 52; 1951b, p. 156; 1972, p. 26; 1979, p. 124). She raised
other questions (Sandler & A. Freud, 1981): We should ask not only how
early in life sublimations are formed but also how late? Can one make
new sublimations or must all sublimations date to pregenital times?
    In 1949, Anna Freud added the aggressive drives to her definition of
sublimation (see also A. Freud, 1979, p. 325). She agreed that the pregenital drives were more important in sublimation (1951a, p. 123–124).
Her complex views of sublimation were repeatedly illuminated by her
awareness of the highly important contribution to sublimation of the ego
(1965c, p. 124), and of developing object relations (e.g. 1952, p.
232–234; 1965; 1966; 1979). She repeatedly relied on the capacity for
sublimation as an indicator of mental health (1958, p. 124; 1965b, p. 62;
1965c, p. 135; 1966a, p. 219; 1969, p. 141; 1972, p. 33). She warned of
the difficulty in making a clinical distinction between true sublimation in
children and transient sexualizations (1965c, p. 125). She (1966b), Hartmann (1955), and Peller (1956) were to my knowledge the only authors
who mentioned the link between sublimation and the developmental
transition from primary to secondary process thinking (1966a, p. 91). Her
contribution of the concept of developmental lines sheds light on the relation of sublimation in the child's transition from body to toy and from
play to work (1965a, p. 80–82; 1979, p. 126).

Fenichel: Sublimation and the Therapeutic Task

Fenichel (1945) used Freud's early views of the relation of sublimation
character traits, and mental health as the basis for his own tehcnical strategies. He wrote that since sublimated character traits allow free, albeit
deflected, drive discharge, and reactive character traits check the drives
with countercathexis, then "the transformation of reactive traits into
genuine ones of the 'sublimation type' is the main task in character analysis" (p. 471). The opinion is still prevalent that sublimatory potential is an
important prognostic indicator as well as a useful clinical basis to monitor
treatment progress. The definition of sublimation offered in the glossary
of the Manual of Psychiatric Peer Review (Peer Review Committee, 1981)
is as follows: "Sublimation refers to the process of replacing behavior that
expresses primitive impulses by adaptive, age appropriate, socially acceptable, and satisfying activities" (p. 48). That definition fails to distinguish adequately sublimation from other aspects of normal mental functioning. The question may be raised whether the "sublimation" potential,
which has achieved prevalent acceptance as a prognostic indicator,
might be more advantageously viewed as consisting of a number of component processes.

Hartmann: Sublimation and Neutralization

Hartmann more than anyone before him saw the error of viewing sublimation too narrowly as only an aspect of the drives (Panel, 1955). His bril-
liant essay "Notes on the Theory of Sublimation" (1964) convincingly illustrated the problems arising from efforts to synchronize Freud's early and
later views of sublimation. Freud's shift from a merely descriptive to a
metapsychologic definition had important advantages in Hartmann's
view because it avoided the contradictions of the prior descriptive definition. Hartmann confronted the concept of sublimation also with the
sexualization or resexualization of numerous ego functions. Hartmann
devised his concept of neutralization in part to avoid the inevitable errors
inherent in any known clinical-descriptive definition of sublimation. He
agreed with Glover (1931) that only a qualitative change in energy might
prove to be a distinguishing criterion of sublimation. But in disagreement
with Glover, who insisted on both displacement of aim as well as change
in the mode of energy, Hartmann wanted only the latter because he correctly saw that we were still not sufficiently clear about the relations between our views of displacement, identification, and substitutions of
other kinds (e.g., symbolism). I think it important to emphasize that when
Hartmann welded his views about sublimation and neutralization to a literal transformation of psychic energy, he was following at least the spirit
of Freud's later model of sublimation as the means by which the mind was
fueled with desexualized libido. Hartmann said it was essential that the
nature and relevance of this energy transformation be clearly conceptualized so that we can understand the role of sublimation and neutralization
in the buildup of psychic structure. He defined neutralization as "the
change of both libidinal and aggressive energy away from the instinctual
and toward a non-instinctual mode. The process of neutralization is essential in what we usually call sublimation..." (1955, p. 227).

Hartmann evidently accepted the following proposal of Kris (1955) to
clarify the relation between the two concepts: sublimation would refer to
the change of aims of the instincts, and neutralization would refer to the
necessary underlying energy transformation. Hartmann and Kris seemed
here to agree on preserving the deeply entrenched term sublimation as a
loosely defined descriptive term and using neutralization as a carefully
defined metapsychologic concept. Neutralization — the transformation of
energy into a mode more appropriate to functions of the ego, together
with a delay in energy discharge — also played a decisive role in the mastery of reality, the formation of constant and independent objects, thinking, and intentionality. But this is one of the questions about Hartmann's
proposal. If neutralization was assigned all those critical developmental

tasks, we now had no way of distinguishing it from other processes of normal psychological development.

Hartmann's reminder of the hereditary core of neutral energy available to the ego was the basis for his concept of primary autonomy, and neutralization was the concept he proposed to account for the stability of ego functions that had been ignored in prior views on sublimation. The resistance of these functions to regressive sexualization, which reversed neutralization, was designated secondary autonomy (Panel, 1955) and constituted one definition of ego strength. Hartmann (1964) also pointed out that the developmental aspects of sublimation were poorly understood. Certainly neutralization contributed to superego formation. Almost all prior authors had emphasized the reverse aspect and spoke mostly of the contributions of the superego *to* sublimation. Further, the knowledge of an artist's conflicts and fantasies often does not sufficiently explain why their working out takes the form of art. This of course was the genetic fallacy wherein adult functions were reduced to their childhood precursors.

Hartmann urged better understanding of what factors enhance or retard sublimation in children. He agreed with Anna Freud and others that sublimation could function as a defense but showed that it had highly important nondefensive functions as well. He warned against the misleading equation of sublimation with normality. He showed that changes in the degree of neutralization do not always change the instinctual *aims*. He observed that defenses themselves, including reaction formation, also draw on neutralized energy.

There are some questions about Hartmann's views of sublimation. He, like Freud, was keenly aware of the danger of reifying energic concepts, and if asked about it he would probably have said that we were expected to understand that he spoke of psychic energy only in a metaphorical manner. But also like Freud, Hartmann nevertheless often seemed to write about physical rather than mental psychic energy: "Once the ego has accumulated a reservoir of neutralized energy of its own, it will . . . develop aims and functions whose cathexes can be derived from this reservoir, which means that they have not always to depend on ad hoc neutralizations" (1964, p. 229). He agreed with the proposal of Kris (1965; Panel, 1965) to distinguish an "energy flux" from this resevoir. The totality of the reservoir of neutralized energy formed the basis for the secondary autonomy of the ego, but the energy flux represented transitory redistributions of drive energy. Was this merely a metaphor? The notion of the ego's operating better with more neutralized psychic energy also implies energy isolated from ideational content. Mindless drives are drives devoid of integrated relatedness to other mental processes because they cross conceptual frames of reference without explicit acknowledgement

(Kaywin, 1966). This is also, of course, the criticism often mounted in the antimetapsychology controversy of recent years (e.g., Klein, 1976; Gill, 1976; Schafer, 1976). I believe that Hartmann confused our understanding of his proposals about neutralization by writing about neutralization in a manner that obviously isolated the drives from ideational content. He did that partly because of another of his theoretic goals: to account for the energic basis of ego functions.

In the Panel (1955) discussion of sublimation, Hartmann noted that we should distinguish between the ideational content of sublimated activity, including the altered aims and the ego functions that mediated the sublimated activity. He thus urged us to distinguish the cathexis of objects from the cathexis of ego functions. This raises highly complex issues (which cannot be pursued here) and illustrates why sublimation has seemed an essential concept in the developmental theories of Freud, Hartmann, and, as we shall see, Loewald. Hartmann (1964) was trying to do the same thing Freud wanted to do. He was trying to define an economic (psychic energy) basis for the processes that we call ego functions as well as for the drive-determined conflicts and symptoms of patients. He wanted to do that by using a unitary theory of psychic energy for both the development of psychic structure and the analysis of ideational content, a goal directly in agreement with Freud's own theoretic ambition to account for mental processes by his libido theory. This point, I believe, has been insufficiently noted in the literature on sublimation. The critical assumption here is that we can speak of the same "energy" as cathecting an activity of the mind and as cathecting a mental idea.

There was a dissenting voice at the 1955 Panel. Loewenstein said that certain forms of sublimation are highly stable and fruitful but operate with instinctualized rather than neutralized qualities. Moreover, he said, many of these views of neutralization are impressionistic, because we lack any definite clinical criteria for distinguishing the degree of neutralization of the energy involved in any specific activity or sublimation. One could add that in the thirty ensuing years of accumulated psychoanalytic experience we have had no additional evidence to indicate that Loewenstein was incorrect.

Hartmann's (1964) proposal to link primary process mental activity with the instinctual mode of discharge and the secondary process with the neutralized mode (p. 228–229) seems to simplify the developmental and maturational aspects of the primary process (McLaughlin, 1978). Finally, Hartmann never integrated his views of sublimation with the modulation of affects in the sense of ideationally linked affects. He chose instead to emphasize the vicissitudes of psychic energy. Indeed, the literature on sublimation is curiously silent on the question of the taming of af-

fects, the achievement of tolerance for unpleasure, and the interrelated-
ness of affects and drives.

LATER CONTRIBUTIONS

Kaywin (1966) came closer than any other author to the views I have
proposed concerning sublimation. He too pointed out that tension, ideational, and affective variables were confusingly imposed on energy concepts in the existing literature on drives. He noted that from a developmental angle it was difficult to distinguish sublimation from those processes we designate as progressive, for example, learning, maturation, and
change of function. Kaywin's major contribution was to use the distinction introduced by Rapaport and Gill (1959) between general and special
levels of psychoanalytic theory as the primary basis for his criticism of
prior views of sublimation, which depend on transformation of psychic
energy. Although I believe he was correct, I think he did not go far
enough in examining the concept of psychic energy itself as inherently
ambiguous. In fact, he explicitly accepted psychic energy as a concept at
the *general* level of theory and challenged the *differentiated* libidinal and
aggressive drive energies at the special level of theory because at that
level, energy itself cannot have aims.

Sandler and Joffe (1966) also challenged Hartmann's views of neutralization. They proposed that skills be distinguished from sublimations,
which do not create the skills but can advantageously utilize the existing
skills. (A similar point was made by Odier, 1953.) They also distinguished
between more stable and enduring sublimations and those that were less
stable by using the analogy of anaclitic object relationships and true object constancy. This was quite similar to Heimann's (1942) and Kernberg's
(1975) view of sublimation. It was not merely the alteration of the aim of a
drive that made a sublimation stable, but the person's total relationship to
the activity.

Sandler and Anna Freud (1981a, 1981b) were among the few to consider the role of fantasy: ". . . behind every sublimation there is, at some
level, an unconscious fantasy gratification of the instinctual wish. The unconscious fantasy which might be unconsciously gratified would be
much closer to the original activity than the overt sublimation appears to
be" (1981a, p. 1981; see also Heimann, 1942). Recognition of the key role
of fantasy in sublimation paves the way to a better understanding of the
motivation for sublimation. (See also Sandler, 1985, p. 231.)

They also observed that there is no clinical correlation or quantitative
relationship between sublimation and the amount of sexual gratification.

This raises an issue that is central to my discussion. It was in the context of addressing the relatively glaring contradictions that emerge from a close examination of the concept of sublimation that Sandler and Anna Freud reminded us that the idea of sublimation was put forward to understand relatively gross phenomena, such as the case of someone who is unable to obtain sexual gratification and finds a more socially aceeptable alternative form of expression. When we look microscopically at the concept, then, our theory, like many others, may break down. Anna Freud said that this applies to all the defense mechanisms. Under close examination, they all merge together.

However, one should not look at them microscopically but *macroscopically*, as large and separate mechanisms, structures, events. Then they will stand out from each other, and the problems of separating them theoretically will become negligible. This raises the problem that terms such as sublimation when carried over from the topographic model to the structural model tend to lose their conceptual boundaries. Gross and Rubin (1972) also questioned the narrowness of Hartmann's (1964) energic views. Kernberg (1975) attempted a definition of sublimation in terms of object relations theory. The transformation according to Kernberg, is not an energic one but rather is a progression from a crude, self-centered level of object relations capacity to an advanced and fully developed totality in the capacity for truly object related interactions with those who are important to the person and a fully differentiated awareness of the self.

Loewald

The foundation for Loewald's current views on sublimation was evident in his paper, "On Motivation and Instinct Theory" (1971), in which he stated that instincts have a legitimate use in psychoanalytic theory only as a psychologic, not as a biologic, concept. This is the point of greatest relevance to my later comparison of Brenner and Loewald about their views of drives. Where Freud's drives arise in the body and are later influenced by development, Loewald's drives are *formed* by interaction with the object and are influenced by the body.

Loewald (1983) stated that Freud's introduction in 1914 of the contrast between object and narcissistic libido was the true beginning of Freud's structural theory. Precisely because Loewald views the developmental dialectic between object and narcissistic libido as central to the formation of psychic structure, he has found the developmental implications of sublimation to be of considerable importance. Loewald reasons thus: Object cathexis and identification are the parallel investments of object libido and ego libido. Therefore, ego libido as a theoretic proposal is crucial because it opens the way to *internalization* as the path for the formation of psychic structure and ego development.

Loewald prefers also to speak of an undifferentiated phase in the infantile psyche when identification and object cathexes are indistinguishable. Thus, for him the detachment of libido from the object in *later* development—the transformation of object libido into ego libido—is a reenactment of what he considers to be the primordial unity of the infantile psyche and its object. The very fabric of the ego itself, according to Loewald, is thus built up from the original primary differentiations of self and object, which in turn depend on the shift from object libido to narcissistic libido. Loewald reinstates Freud's 1923 proposal that all sublimation may arise through the desexualization of the object and the consequent cathexis of the ego. According to Loewald, Freud was saying that the self literally is formed and integrated by a series of transforming internalizations. Sublimation therefore comes about by a profound change of object libido, not merely a displacement of the aim nor merely a refinement of its aims. Sublimation, for Loewald, is the reactivation of the primordial unity of the mother-child dyad into intrapsychic transactions. This is what Loewald says neutralization should mean. He agrees with Greenacre's (1957) criticism of Hartmann's idea about neutralization and proposes that we consider not the Hartmann change in the energy itself but a shift to more complex levels of organization of the entire psyche. If internalization is the universal road to sublimation, then the fundamental element in sublimation is ego development itself. Loewald thus frees us of the one-sided energic definition of sublimation, which is untenable. His views are also more in keeping with the clinical observation that stable sublimations can function with relatively instinctual, that is, nonneutralized qualities. Also, Loewald's psychic energy is not physical and mental at the same time.

But there are some other questions to consider about this formulation. Rapaport (1957) observed that Freud's view of object libido transformed into ego libido was also the simplified 1923 mechanism for superego and ego-ideal formation; The ego was said to offer itself to the id as an object. If so, when does secondary narcissism become pathological and when does it build healthy psychic structure? Why would we observe clinically grandiose ego ideals *without* sublimated cathexis? Rapaport said this contradiction had been neglected in the literature, and that is still true. Loewald does acknowledge that repression allows some gratification, but he says that in sublimation discharge is toward higher values. He implies that the unreliability of value judgements as a definitional criterion for sublimation is not too important. Yet repression is also an essential component in stable and highly valuable compromise formations leading to religious, scientific, and artisitic creativity. There is also a question to consider regarding those identifications that occur with a continuing object cathexis if one wishes to propose decathexis of the object as the basis for the transformation of object libido into ego libido. He does not adequately resolve the question he raised concerning how we are to distinguish sublimation from all other processes of development and progression in the ordinary course of the formation of psychic structure. If there is a longitudinal problem in distinguishing sublimation from progression in general, then in cross section there is also the problem of distinguishing sublimation from other processes of conflict resolution, both normal and abnormal. Certainly Loewald is correct to insist that we respect the conceptual frontier between body and mind, but he seems to assume that we can cross the equally important conceptual boundary between the data of psychoanalysis and the conjectures concerning intrapsychic events in the preverbal phase of mental development. There seems to be no clarification yet from Loewald (1983) about his use of the term libido in his proposals concerning the origin of the libido as being not in the mind of the baby but in the crucible of the of the mother-infant dyad. Freud's libido was a form of psychic energy originating in the soma of the infant and in the psychic apparatus of the infant, without consideration for inchoate object representations; and this was the basis for Loewald's criticisms in his 1971 paper. It therefore is unclear at this point which kind of libido Loewald is discussing in his views of sublimation (1983). Loewald has chosen so far to speak of sublimation solely in terms of libido disconnected from ideational content, which leaves the issue of motivation unexplained. Possibly we will learn more from him about these questions in his future work on the topic.

Brenner

Brenner (1982) has introduced several ideas that can clarify the concept of sublimation. He has advocated that we view drives as exclusively psychological rather than as a frontier concept with both mental *and* physical referents. This allows us to preserve drives as an essential cornerstone in the foundation of psychoanalytic theory, while at the same time freeing us of the insoluble contradictions we must face if our theoretic commitments force us to adhere to a physical, nonmetaphoric form of psychic energy. Brenner has reminded us that thinking is just as somato-psychic as sexuality, that all psychology is ultimately an aspect of underlying brain processes, and that the ultimate validity of drive theory can and should depend solely on psychoanalytic data. He showed that as long as libido was considered to be the only drive, the frontier concept, or the somato-psychic view of drives seemed tenable; but this was far less valid within the framework of the final dual-drive theory.

Brenner (1982) further proposed a useful distinction between drives and drive derivatives: A drive derivative is the specific wish of an individual for gratification observable by means of the psychoanalytic method; it is specific, personal, and unique. The concept of drives, or libido, is a generalization about drive derivatives based on many individual observations and inferences. It applies to all persons (p. 26). Psychic energy was originally hypothesized at this higher level of generalization in part to describe the capacity of the drives to impel the mind to work; It is not actual energy. Hypothetical changes in it can not correspond to alterations in brain energy or any other kind of physical energy. Since the drives fluctuate in intensity, it is useful to make gross clinical estimates of increasing or decreasing magnitudes, but even such seemingly simple clinical estimates can be very difficult to judge. Existing definitions of sublimation, which are linked to energy transformation isolated from ideational content, have defied clinical validation for more than fifty years, and it seems unlikely that such hypotheses can ever be clinically validated.

Brenner's (1982) views about defense mechanisms also clarify the concept of sublimation as a defense. He pointed out that there are no aspects of ego functioning deployed for defense that can not also function for nondefensive purposes and that any aspect of ego functioning can be used for defensive purposes. His views of repression are also illuminating (p. 110). It will be recalled that Freud said that sublimation spared the need for repression, an idea he espoused partly because his early concept of repression indicated a static rather than a mobile view of the balance between defense and drive gratification. Freud did not conceive then of defenses shifting normally. Access to the system Cs. of a repressed idea in the system Ucs. was a failure of repression with a consequent "return of the repressed." The repression had to fail in order for defensively altered discharge to occur. But the modern view of defense is that repressed drive derivatives normally gain access to conscious awareness and also influence behavior *while still repressed*. Further, this holds true of mental life in general, not just of pathology, because compromise formation is a usual tendency of the mind, not an exceptional one. It appears, then, that the question of mutual exclusivity between sublimation and repression resolves into one of frames of reference.

The last of Brenner's ideas I wish to discuss has to do with his proposed revision in our theory of the formation of the superego. He has suggested that there is more to superego formation than is generally recognized.

Identification with parental prohibitions against incest and parricide are only part of the mechanism of superego formation. Any aspect of ego functioning that evokes parental approval or avoids disapproval can play a part in superego formation. Libidinal gratification has been relatively neglected in the literature about superego formation. This is relevant to the question of what phase in development must be achieved for sublimation to occur, as well as to the question of whether the drives can be modified by experience. The fact is that the drives can be extensively influenced, especially as to aims and object. Nowhere is this more clear than in the formation of the superego itself. It is the descriptive definition of sublimation that makes it seem plausible to say that sublimation can be only a late achievement. In the metapsychologic sense it is difficult to see how the alterations in the drives that occur in normal development are supposed to differ from the alteration of drives in sublimation.

Brenner's principal contribution here is to demonstrate that the superego is not only an instigator of conflict but is itself the consequence of conflict. Clearly, then, sublimation, in its metapsychologic sense, would not begin with latency, after superego formation is consolidated. Instead, "sublimation" must be viewed as participating in the very processes by which the superego is formed and as being subsequently dependent on the superego. The consequence of this theoretic alteration is an enriched and deeper view of the reciprocal developmental relationship between sublimation and superego.

CONCLUSION

My purpose in this discussion has not been to advocate that we stop using the term sublimation, but rather to examine the reasons why the term has been able to survive such buffeting. Despite good arguments against its confusing and elusive meaning, it is still alive (Kubie, 1962). Loewald (1983) captured the appeal of the term when he said: "...the concept points to something of exceeding importance: without this function of transformation from lower to higher levels of mentation, man would not be man" (p. 319). A leading cause of confusion has been Freud's use of sublimation as integral to his views of psychic energy. Sublimation was introduced as a concept at the very beginning of Freud's discoveries and was never integrated or synchronized with his later (1926) views concerning the drives, intrapsychic conflict, the structural hypothesis, repression and anxiety, the developmental aspects of psychic structure, and compromise formation.

One might compare the concept of sublimation to a constellation of stars used by navigators in ancient times. The Big Dipper seemed to represent a visual configuration of stars in closer proximity to each other than they actually were. Indeed, one of the stars might even have belonged to a different stellar system or galaxy, and yet it appeared to be a part of a unified visual gestalt. That mattered little when the purpose was navigation rather than astronomic study since it was no small achievement for the navigator to know that he could find true North by locating the Big Dipper. Many clinical observations show that sublimation is often a compromise formation involving not only the drives, or even the drives and an ego, but the superego as well. (Glover, 1931; Alpert, 1949; Nunberg, 1955; Waelder, 1960). This is not to say that all sublimations are compromise formations. Rather, when a given instance of 'sublimation' does represent a compromise formation, Brenner has helped us to see that defenses contributed to the sublimation and that sublimation as a compromise formation is not itself a defense.

The literature on sublimation refers to vicissitudes of libido but not to modulation of affects and only rarely to fantasy or to the importance of fantasy for the clinical observation of sublimation. Even the most simplistic early view of identification as an important mechanism for sublimation implied the role of unconscious fantasy since identification itself is the expression of a fantasy wish to be like someone else. We have placed too heavy a burden on this solitary concept of sublimation if we credit it with the transcendence from lower to higher forms of behavior, and as the basis for creativity, the central mechanism for the formation of psychic structure, and the guarantor of mental health—let alone with distinguishing human beings as the highest species. It is also insufficient merely to say that sublimation is a group of processes. It seems advantageous to view sublimation as an achievement of humanity that expresses the fact that the mind is enriched as well as burdened by the drives. It does not seem useful to view sublimation as an isolated process or mechanism. When we say "sublimated," we really mean that the drives have made a contribution to behavior or that valuable or adaptive behavior has developmental precursors and current components related to the drives. It is a general tendency of the human mind to be capable of numerous drive-propelled substitution processes, including symbolism, metaphor, displacement, symptom formation, and "sublimation." The human being, of course, is the sublime animal.

SUMMARY

Freud's view of sublimation as an aspect of the instincts was importantly influenced and confused by his views of psychic energy as both physical and mental. It has not been sufficiently appreciated that sublimation has occupied a pivotal conceptual position in the history of psychoanalysis because of its integral linkage to Freud's quantitative-economic theories and psychic energy. Sublimation has not been coherently defined either descriptively or clinically. Efforts to define sublimation from a meta-psychologic viewpoint rather than descriptively have so far been problematic because they have depended on notions of drives isolated from ideational content and on a dualistic psychic energy that is both mental and physical. The human mind is capable of numerous substitution processes in normal and pathological functioning and development. There is reason to question whether it is useful to designate sublimation as a special and separate example of such substitutions.

REFERENCES

Alpert, A. (1949), Sublimation and sexualization. *The Psychoanalytic Study of the Child,* 3/4:271–278. New York: International Universities Press.

Applegarth, A. (1971), Comments on aspects of the theory of psychic energy. *J. Amer. Psychoanal. Assn.,* 19:379–416.

Blum, H. (1983), Foreward: Defense and resistance, historical perspectives and current concepts. *J. Amer. Psychoan. Assn.,* 31:5–18.

Brenner, C. (1982), *The Mind in Conflict.* New York: International Universities Press.

Brierly, M. (1947), Notes on psychoanalysis and integrative living. *Internat. J. Psycho-Anal.,* 28:57–105.

Deri, F. (1939), On sublimation. *Psychoanal. Quart.,* 8:325–334.

Fenichel, O. (1945), *The Psychoanalytic Theory of Neurosis.* New York: Norton.

Freud, A. (1930), Four lectures on psychoanalysis for teachers and parents. In: *The Writings of Anna Freud. Vol. 1,* 1922–1935. New York: International Universities Press, pp. 73–133, 1974.

_____ (1936), The ego and the mechanisms of defense. *Writings,* Vol. II, 1966.

_____ (1949), Notes on aggression. *Writings,* Vol. IV., pp. 60–74, 1968.

_____ (1951), Psychoanalysis and genetic psychology. *Writings.* Vol. IV, pp. 107–142, 1968.

_____ (1951b), Observations of child development. *Writings,* Vol. IV, pp. 143–162, 1968.

_____ (1952), The mutual influences in the development of the ego and the id. *Writings,* Vol. IV, pp. 230–244, 1968.

_____ (1958), Child observation and prediction of development. *Writings,* Vol. V, 1956–1965, pp. 102–135, 1969.

_____ (1965a), Metapsychologic assessment of the adult personality: The adult profile. *Writings,* Vol. V, pp. 60–75, 1969.

_____ (1965b), The assessment of normality in childhood. *Writings,* Vol. VI, pp. 54–107, 1965.

_____ (1965c), Assessment of pathology Part I. Some general considerations. *Writings,* Vol. VI, pp. 108–147, 1965.

_____ (1966a), Links between Hartmann's ego psychology and the child analyst's thinking. *Writings,* Vol. V, pp. 204–220, 1969.

_____ (1966b), The ideal psychoanalytic institute. *Writings,* Vol. VII, 1966–1970, pp. 73–93, 1971.

_____ (1969), Difficulties in the path of psychoan-alysis. *Writings,* Vol. VII, pp. 124–156, 1971.

_____ (1972), The widening scope of child psychology, normal and abnormal. *Writings,* Vol. VIII, 1981. also in: *The Psychoanalytic Study of the Child,* 26:79–90.

_____ (1978), Inaugural lecture for the Sigmund Freud chair at the Hebrew University. *Writings,* Vol. VIII, 1981, pp. 334–343.

_____ (1979), Child analysis as the study of mental growth, normal and abnormal. *Writings,* Vol. VIII, pp. 119–136, 1981.

Freud, S. (1895), Project for a scientific psychology. *Standard Edition,* 1:283–397. London: Hogarth Press, 1966.

_____ (1905a), Fragment of an analysis of a case of hysteria. *Standard Edition,* 7:3–122. London: Hogarth Press, 1953.

_____ (1905b), Three essays on the theory of sexuality. *Standard Edition,* 7:125–243. London: Hogarth Press, 1953.

_____ (1908a), Character and anal erotism. *Standard Edition,* 9:167–175. London: Hogarth Press, 1959.

_____ (1908b), "Civilized" sexual morality and modern nervous illness. *Standard Edition,* 9:177–204. London: Hogarth Press, 1959.

_____ (1909a), Analysis of a phobia in a five-year-old boy. *Standard Edition,* 10:3–149. London: Hogarth Press, 1955.

_____ (1909b), Notes upon a case of obsessonal neurosis. *Standard Edition,* 10:153–318. London: Hogarth Press, 1955.

_____ (1910a), Five lectures on psychoanalysis. *Standard Edition,* 11:3–55. London: Hogarth Press, 1957.

_____ (1910b), Leonardo daVinci and a memory of his childhood. *Standard Edition,* 11:59–137. London: Hogarth Press, 1957.

_____ (1914), On narcissism: An introduction. *Standard Edition,* 14:67–102. London: Hogarth Press, 1957.

_____ (1915a), Instincts and their vicissitudes. *Standard Edition,* 14:109–140. London: Hogarth Press, 1957.

_____ (1915b), Repression. *Standard Edition,* 14:141–158. London: Hogarth Press, 1957.

_____ (1917), Introductory lectures on psychoanalysis. *Standard Edition,* 16:243–463. London: Hogarth Press, 1963.

_____ (1918), From the history of an infantile neurosis. *Standard Edition,* 17:3–122. London: Hogarth Press, 1955.

_____ (1920), Beyond the pleasure principle. *Standard Edition,* 18:3–64. London: Hogarth Press, 1955.

_____ (1921), Group psychology and the analysis of the ego. *Standard Edition,* 18:67–143. London: Hogarth Press, 1955.

_____ (1923a), Two encyclopedia articles. *Standard Edition,* 18:235–259. London: Hogarth press, 1955.

_____ (1923b), The ego and the id. *Standard Edition,* 19:3–66. London: Hogarth Press, 1961.

_____ (1924), The dissolution of the Oedipus complex. *Standard Edition,* 19:173–179. London: Hogarth Press, 1961.

_____ (1925), Some psychical consequences of the anatomical distinction between the sexes. *Standard Edition,* 19:243–258. London: Hogarth Press, 1961.

_____ (1926), Inhibitions, symptoms, and anxiety. *Standard Edition,* 20:77–174. London: Hogarth Press, 1959.

_____ (1930), Civilization and its discontents. *Standard Edition,* 21:59–145. London: Hogarth Press, 1961.

_____ (1933), New introductory lectures on psychoanalysis. *Standard Edition,* 22:3–182. London: Hogarth Press, 1964.

_____ (1939), Moses and monotheism. *Standard Edition,* 23:3–137. London: Hogarth Press, 1964.

Gill, M. (1976), Metapsychology is not psychology. In: *Psychology Versus Metapsychology.* ed. M. Gill & P. Holzman. New York: International Universities Press, pp. 71–105.

Glover, E. (1931), Sublimation, substitution, and social anxiety. In: *On the Early Development of the Mind.* Vol. I, New York: International Universities Press, pp. 130–159, 1956. Also in: *Internat. J. Psycho-Anal.* (1931), 12:part 3, 263–297, 1931.

Greenacre, P. (1957), The childhood of the artist. *The Psychoanalytic Study of the Child,* 12:47–72. New York: International Universities Press.

Gross, G., & Rubin, I., (1972). Sublimation. The study of an instinctual vicissitude. *The Psychoanalytic Study of the Child,* 27:334–359.

Hacker, F. (1972), Sublimation revisited. *Internat. J. Psycho-Anal.* 53:219–224.

Hartmann, H. (1964), Notes on the theory of sublimation. In *Essays on Ego Psychology.* New York: International Universities Press, pp. 215–240. Also in: *The Psychoanalytic Study of the Child* (1955) 10:9–29. New York: International Universities Press.

_____ Kris, E., & Loewenstein, R. (1949), Notes on the theory of aggression. *The Psychoanalytic Study of the Child,* 3/4:9–36. New York: International Universities Press.

Heimann, P. (1942), A contribution to the problem of sublimation and its relation to processes of internalization. *Internat. J. Psycho-Anal.,* 23:8–17.

Jones, E. (1957), *The Life and Work of Sigmund Freud.* Vol. 3. New York: Basic Books.

Kaywin, L. (1966), Problems of sublimation. *J. Amer. Psychoanal. Assn.,* 14:313–333.

Kernberg, O. (1975), *Borderline Conditions and Pathological Narcissism.* New York: Aronson.

Klein, G. (1976). *Psychoanalytic Theory: An Explanation of Essentials.* New York: International Universities Press.

Kris, E. (1955), Neutralization and sublimation. *The Psychoanalytic Study of the Child,* 10:30–46.

Kubie, L. (1962), The fallacious misuse of the concept of sublimation. *Psychoanal. Quart.,* 31:73–79.

Lampl-de Groot, J. (1965), *The Development of the Mind.* New York: International Universities Press.

LaPlanche, J., & Pontalis, J. B. (1973), *The Language of Psychoanalysis.* New York: Norton.

Loewald, H. (1971), On motivation and instinct theory. *The Psychoanalytic Study of the Child,* 26:91–128.

_____ (1983), Sublimation: An inquiry. Freud Lecture, New York Psychoanalytic Society. (Reporter: D. Berger). *Psychoanal. Quart.,* 52:319–321.

McLaughlin, J. (1978), Primary and secondary process in the context of cerebral hemisphere specialization. *Psychoanal. Quart.,* 47:237–266.

Moore, B, & Fine, B. (1968), *A Glossary of Psychoanalytic Terms and Concepts.* Second Edition. New York: American Psychoanalytic Association.

Nunberg, H. (1955), *Principles of Psychoanalysis.* New York: International Universities Press.

Odier, C. (1953), Essay on sublimation. In *Drives, Affects, and Behavior, Vol. I.* ed. R. Loewenstein. New York: International Universities Press, pp. 104–119.

Panel (1955), Sublimation. (Reporter: J. Arlow). *J. Amer. Psychoanal. Assn.,* 3:515–527.

Peer Review Committee, American Psychoanalytic Association (1981). Peer Review Manual for Psychoanalysis. In: *Manual of Psychiatric Peer Review.* 2nd edition. New York: American Psychoanalytic Association.

Peller, L. (1956). The school's role in promoting sublimation. *The Psychoanalytic Study of the Child,* 11:437–449. New York: International Universities Press.

Rapaport, D. (1957), A theoretic analysis of the superego concept. In: *The Collected Papers of David Rapaport.* ed. M. Gill. New York: Basic Books, 1967.

_____ & Gill, M. (1959), The points of view and assumptions of metapsychology. *Internat. J. Psycho-Anal.,* 40:153–162.

Sandler, J. (1985), Towards a reconsideration of the psychoanalytic theory of motivation. *Bull. Anna Freud Centre,* 8:223–244.

_____ Joffe, W. (1966). On skill and sublimation. *J. Amer. Psychoanal. Asn.,* 14:335–355.

_____ & Freud, A. (1981), Discussions in the Hampstead Index on "The ego and the mechanisms of defense": IV. The mechanisms of defense, part 1. *Bull. Hampstead Clin.,* 4:151–200.

_____ & _____ (1981), Discussions in the Hampstead Index on "The ego and the mechanisms of defense": V. The mechanisms of defense, part 2. *Bull. Hampstead Clin.,* 4:231–278.

Schafer, R. (1976). *A New Language for Psychoanalysis.* New Haven: Yale University Press.

Sterba, R. (1930). A contribution to the theory of sublimation. Unpublished English translation of: Zur Problematik der Sublimierungslehre. *Internat. J. Psychoanal. 16.*

Waelder, R. (1960), *Basic Theory of Psychoanalysis.* New York: International Universities Press.

Wallerstein, R. (1977), Psychic energy reconsidered: Introduction. *J. Amer. Psychoanal. Assn.,* 25:529–537.

ALLAN COMPTON

The Beginnings of the Object Concept in Psychoanalysis

This paper is the first of an extended series that traces the development of the object concept in Freud's work and then in the work of other analytic authors. It is intended to demonstrate the beginning of Freud's object concepts in the context in which they arose. Freud's early writings are the data of observation. The purpose here is to provide a basis for clarification of subsequent psychoanalytic concepts in the work of Freud and other analysts.

In the last forty years, the term object has appeared with increasing frequency in the psychoanalytic literature and, at times, has seemed to dominate the field of psychology. It is apparent, however, even from a scrutiny of only Freud's early work—essentially, through 1900—that the term object can hardly stand alone to represent a concept with any clarity. The question, "Object of what?', is always appropriate and even necessary whenever the term appears in unmodified or unsupported form. We have to deal presently with a multitude of object concepts: object choice (of at least two types), object finding, object loss, object image, object concept (of a child, for example), object cathexis, object love, ambivalence, object relations, object representation, libidinal object, constant object, permanent object, transference object, imago, archaic imago, need satisfying object, part object, whole object, ideal object, transitional object, self-object differentiation.

Because the relations between what is and what is not mental are housed in the object concept, we also must deal with "processes of internalization" and their ostensible results—internal objects, internalized objects, units of internalized object relations, introjects, the structures that result from "transmuting internalizatons," self objects, good objects, bad objects. Some clarification of these many and divergent usages might help to bring order to the current debates about object relations and object relations theories. The pursuit of clarification of the object concept, including the establishment of a basis for it, has significance beyond that debate, however. At least one of the multiple ambiguities has given rise to a very obvious difficulty: Does the term object in psychoanalysis refer to a tangible physical presence or to something mental, or to both? Brenner (1973) says, "In the psychoanlaytic literature the term 'object' is used to designate persons or things of the external environment which are psychologically significant to one's psychic life, whether such things be animate or lifeless . . . Likewise the phrase 'object relations' refers to the individual's attitude and behavior toward such objects" (p. 98). Dorpat (1976), in contrast, says, "Psychoanalytic object relations theory concerns the processes involved in the formation of self and object representations (p. 856)." Arlow (1980, p. 112) says that the object is the mental representation of something that is the source of intense libidinal gratification.

Although very few psychoanalytic authors define their object concept, examples of divergent usage can be readily cited. The discrepancies may appear to be easily explained and relatively innocuous, but that is not, in fact, the case. What is buried in the ambiguous usage is one of the most fundamental problems of psychology: How does anything become mental? It has seemed to me, therefore, worthwhile to return to origins in an effort to dissect the component concepts of "object."

Many psychoanalytic authors have indicated the necessity to study Freud's theoretical propositions in their original clinical and theoretical context. However, despite some excellent models for careful scrutiny of the historical evolution of concepts (for example, Brenner, 1957; Stewart, 1967), such studies remain relatively uncommon.

"Object" is one of the more complex words in Western languages, and accordingly it is subject to ambiguity and misunderstanding. It also appears to be one of the commonest technical, or formal, words in the psychoanalytic literature.

The German word *Objekt* is identical in form and in meaning with the English "object." The words in both languages are derived from the Latin preposition "ob," which means to or towards, combined with the Latin verb "jacio" (to throw, cast or hurl), joined in the Latin word "objicio" (objeci, objectum), which means to throw in the way of or to expose. The 1971 edition of the Oxford English Dictionary lists three primary meanings with 19 subsidiary meanings and 28 derivatives of the word object. Webster's New International Dictionary, 1924 edition, perhaps best cap-

tures the derivation and meaning of the noun form with brevity in the
following:

> object-[Latin objectus, past participle neuter, objectum-a thing thrown or
> put before] That which is put, or may be regarded as put, in the way of some
> of the senses; something visible or tangible.

Freud used the term object to indicate a number of different concepts.
Several of these object concepts appeared in his early work and have persisted in psychoanalysis ever since, largely unrecognized as differentiable
concepts. I shall now turn to establishing the context of clinical work and
theory construction in which Freud's object concept or concepts arose.

Freud was a neuroscientist pushed by practical necessity into clinical
practice. His patients' complaints turned his interest to psychopathology.
When he began to try to understand and treat the hysterical and "neuras-
thenic" symptoms presented to him, the theories he elaborated at first remained respectably neurophysiological (1888, 1892a, 1892b, 1893).

Ideas relating mental functioning to excitation in the nervous system
were part of the scientific culture of the 1880s. These ideas antedated
clear concepts of structural relations in the nervous system and had, in
fact, been present in European medicine for several centuries. (See
Breuer & Freud, 1895; López-Piñero, 1983). Freud seems to have picked
one of these ideas around which to organize his theoretical propositions.
That idea, which later became known as "the principle of constancy," first
appeared in Freud's private correspondence as a "theorem" in 1892:

> The nervous system endeavors to keep constant something in its functional
> relations that we may describe as a "sum of excitation." It puts this precondi-
> tion of health into effect by disposing associatively of every sensible accre-
> tion of excitation or by discharging it by an appropriate motor reaction
> [1892b, pp. 153–154].

"Accretions of excitation" must come from somewhere, that is, they
must have sources. The differentiation of exogenous and endogenous
sources of excitation first appeared in Breuer's chapter, "Theory", in "Studies on Hysteria" (1895, p. 199), as did the idea of sexuality as an important
endogenous source. The theoretical interest of both Breuer and Freud at
that time was, however, focused largely on exogenous sources of excitation—traumas (1892a, p. 137).

By 1894 Freud was aware of the importance of sexuality in the neuroses
generally (1894a, p. 52; see also Breuer & Freud, 1895, p. 257). His theory
that certain neuroses stemmed from current sexual practices (1895a,
1895b), while others, the psychoneuroses, arose from actual genital experiences during childhood (1896, p. 149) was presented over the next

two years. The pivotal concept in his explanatory hypotheses remained neurophysiological excitation. Despite continuing occasional use of the notion of endogenous excitation, there was as yet no theory of instinctual drives.

Freud's view of sexuality in the 1890s is most clearly presented in the Fliess correspondence. In "Draft E. How Anxiety Originates" (1894b), Freud's understanding of the *Aktual neuroses* can be seen to depend on distinctions not only between exogenous and endogenous sources of excitation but also between somatic and mental sexual excitation (see Stewart, 1967; Compton, 1972).

> Things are simpler [for exogenous excitation]...the source of excitation is outside and sends into the psyche an accretion of excitation which is dealt with according to its quantity. For that purpose, any reaction suffices which diminishes the psychical excitation by the same quantum...But it is otherwise with endogenous tension, the source of which lies in one's own body (hunger, thirst, the sexual drive). In this case, only *specific* reactions are of use – reactions which prevent the further occurrence of the excitation in the end organs concerned, . . . [Freud, 1894b, p. 192].

These concepts are expanded in the "Schematic Picture of Sexuality"sent to Fliess in 1895 (Freud, 1895c, p. 202). In this diagram, the term "object" appears for the first time that I can discover in Freud's work. In the diagram and the accompanying discussion of the reasons for sexual anesthesia in women (p. 204), the *sexual object* is both an external source of excitation and the means for relieving excitation stemming from endogenous and exogenous sources. The "specific action" necessary to relieve somatic tension in the "endorgan" is that the sexual object must be brought into a "favorable position." The excitatory properties of the sexual object depend, however, on the prior existence, in any given instance, of sexual excitation in both somatic and psychic forms. This is a cybernetic – that is, nonlinear – model, in which feedback processes modulate oscillations towards a goal: buildup of tension tends towards relief of tension. The term sexual object has meaning within this context as both a source and a goal (or target), or, in more abstract terms, as a dynamic element in an interacting system of feedback loops.

This theory of sexuality was stated for private consumption; while complex and sophisticated in many respects, it is undeveloped in certain other respects. For our present purposes the dual referents of the term object should be noted: (1) a theoretical construct in a set of related constructs, essentially, excitation source and target, (2) represented by a person other than the subject whose sexual excitation is being considered.

Freud's interest at this point was in sexual excitation, somatic and mental, and the object concept introduced is, although complex, only adjunctive and not elaborated. In the "Project for a Scientific Psychology" (1895d), where his interest was much broader in scope, the pivotal concept remained the handling of excitation by the nervous system, but the term object acquired further meaning and complexity in contexts other than that of genital sexuality. A role for an "object" is first required, ontogenetically, Freud said, because of the peculiar conditions imposed upon the nervous system by the combination of endogenous excitation and helplessness. Infants are incapable of bringing about the "specific actions" necessary to discharge the excitation resulting from endogenous sources. Nonspecific discharges of excitation occur and have the result of drawing "extraneous help . . . [and] establishing a secondary function . . . of communication." The specific action is performed for the infant, and the resulting "experience of satisfaction" — relief of tension in the organ which is the source of excitation — has the additional effect of establishing a "cathexis" of the "neurones which correspond to the perception of an object . . . (Freud, 1895d, p. 318)."

Decrease of excitation, the experience of satisfaction, and feelings of pleasure are axiomatically linked in this theory. The term neurones means just that, physical neurones, and cathexis is a physical process. The problem for which explanation is being sought here is: How does an "object" acquire a role in the subject discharge system at all? The first step in an answer is the establishment via neuronal cathexis of the object-perception as a lasting element. This step introduces two additional object concepts, mental in their nature: first, the object perception, which Freud later called a "percept"; second, some form of storage for the percept, later to be called a "mnemic image."

Freud's (1895d) next step in explaining the role of an "object" in the subject discharge system depends upon an axiomatic definition of a wish. A "wishful state" is a longing for the particular perceptual image associated with the prior experience of satisfaction (p. 330). If a perceptual image arises, the neural processes tend to produce a "sensation of identity," (p. 329), possible only if the new perceptual image matches the cathected one. The construct used to exemplify these theoretical neurophysiological propositions is the infant at the mother's breast. In this step an evocation of the stored object image by the "wishful state" is implied. This does not, however, appear to require recognition of another type of object concept.

Nonmatching of the perceptual object with the wished for mnemic image leads to other processes, among them, mental interest, which develops into cognition. Freud (1895d) adds, "An object *like this* was simultaneously the first satisfying object and further his first hostile object (p. 331)."

The idea of the hostile object appears somewhat surprisingly and is less extensively developed. Besides experiences of satisfaction being linked with object images, Freud (1895d) said, so are experiences of pain. If the image of "the (hostile) object is freshly cathected in some way—for instance, by a fresh perception—a state arises which . . . includes unpleasure and an inclination to discharge (p. 320)." There is, however, a significant problem here: since unpleasure signifies an increase in excitation, where, in this instance, does the increase come from? It must be that ". . . unpleasure is *released* from the interior of the body and freshly conveyed up . . .," generated by secretory "key neurones." This idea of key neurones generating unpleasure in response to a percept resembling a mnemic image associated with pain never reappeared in Freud's work. (See Compton, 1972.) Yet without this mechanism there is no explanation for the effects of the reappearance of the hostile object percept, nor any explanation for statements later on concerning the temporal precedence of "hostile objects."

Another problem comes into focus when the idea of a "hostile object" is added to that of a 'satisfying object'. An experience of satisfaction, an enteroceptive perception, is linked, coincidentally but irrevocably, with another perceptual experience of an exteroceptive nature. The experience of pain, exteroceptive or enteroceptive, apparently may also be linked with percepts of what else is simultaneously present in other sensory fields. All of this is proposed by Freud to occur at an experiential level. Freud emerges with a qualitatively differentiated pair of "objects," satisfying and hostile. This seems to imply that an infant experientially develops an object concept or concepts of this kind. Does this represent an additional meaning of "object" at this stage of psychoanalytic (really prepsychoanalytic) theory, an "experiential object," as it were, which occurs in both satisfying and hostile form? Object of what? The infant has learned to associate a certain percept with a memory consisting of satisfacton + percept or pain + percept. Reappearance of the percept evokes the memory, and an affective response occurs: pleasure or pleasurable anticipation, pain or fearful anticipation (anxiety). The linking of the percept with the anticipatory affect thus apparently creates an affective-experiential learned concept of the stimulus provided by another person. In the case of the "satisfying object," the "wishful state" activates or evokes the satisfaction + percept memory. Without the key neurones idea, there is nothing to make ready the pain + percept memory, which suggests that the hostile object is necessarily relatively delayed developmentally, rather than taking temporal precedence.

With some rather broad allowances for what may or may not be going on in the mind of the infant, it seems to me that in these ideas from the

"Project" one can see the beginnings of a theory of the ontogenetic development of personal attitudes, of what might be called an "attitudinal object concept."

Freud's early ideas concerning objects were formulated within the theoretical framework of the distribution of energy in the nervous system. "Objects" cannot possibly play a primary role in a theoretical scheme of that kind. The hypotheses concerning objects are necessitated by the theoretical scheme itself, as adjuncts, but there is no suggestion of any necessary relation to observational data. The mother and child figures that appear from time to time are best understood as personifications of the ideas. The "key neurones" are perhaps the purest expression of the direction in which the theory tends. Freud's clinical orientation during this period continued along the line of the traumas he and Breuer had proposed, embodied in what is usually referred to as the "seduction theory."

During the next several years (1897–1900) Freud discovered the Oedipus complex, and, to some degree, infantile sexuality in general, and also recognized the extent and significance of unconscious mental processes. This had the effect of overthrowing the seduction theory, though the repudiation was not published until 1906.

Other people – objects, the external world – were especially significant in the causation of neurosis via seductions. Falsification of that theory, combined with the transition from neurophysiological to psychological theorizing, afforded by recognition of unconscious processes of mentation, then had the effect of focusing attention even more on mental processes as opposed to actual events. Freud's ideas on the psychology of the wish also necessarily gained importance. The next major development in theory was the construction of a mental apparatus, to be followed by a statement of the forces that drove the apparatus. Although neither of these steps requires a primary emphasis on "object," there are nevertheless provisions to be made for a role for other people in the functioning of the apparatus, just as there were in the neurophysiological apparatus of the "Project."

The hypothetical mental apparatus, the "topographic model of the mind" (1900, pp. 509–622), was explicitly intended to be homologous with the underlying neural apparatus (the reflex arc model, p. 538). Concepts that had originated in a neurophysiologic framework were now transposed to a psychological one. Freud proposed that excitation drives the mental apparatus as well, mental excitation with somatic sources, which makes different demands upon the mind depending on the source. Motivation was explained by the interaction of the energy (excitation) with certain characteristics of the apparatus. Wishes were now seen as the psychical manifestations of this outcome, evident in somewhat different forms in the different topographical systems (see Compton, 1981).

Within this framework, objects appear in an expanded and modified version of the "perceptual identity" theory cited earlier, now stated in psychological terms. As before, a component of the "experience of satisfaction" that relieves an internal stimulus is a particular perception.

> . . . the mnemic image of which remains associated thenceforward with the memory trace of the excitation produced by the need . . . [The] next time this need arises a psychical impulse will at once emerge which will seek to recathect the mnemic image of the perception and to re-evoke the perception itself...an impulse of this kind is what we call a wish . . . thus the aim of this first psychical activity was to produce a "perceptual identity"—a repetition of the perception which was linked with the satisfaction of the need [Freud, 1900, pp. 555–556].

> The primary process endeavors to bring about a discharge of excitation in order that, with the help of the amount of excitation thus accumulated, it may establish a small "perceptual identity." The secondary process, however, has abandoned this intention and taken on another in its place—the establishment of a thought identiy [p. 602].

What was designated as the hostile object in the "Project" is treated somewhat differently by Freud in the 1900 theory (pp. 600–601). The antithesis to the experience of satisfacton is called "the experience of external fright" or "a perceptual stimulus which is the source of painful excitation." Making the perception go away coincides with making the pain go away. Reappearance of the perception leads to "an inclination to drop the distressing mnemic image immediately, if anything happens to revive it, for the very reason that if its excitation were to overflow into perception it would provoke unpleasure (or, more precisely, would *begin* to provoke it)." The context of this discussion is Freud's setting forth the ideas of the primary and secondary processes.

Although the terms of discussion have changed from physiological to psychological, the comments about the physiological hypotheses still apply. The baby at the breast, engaged in an experience of satisfaction, is a theoretical construct, a dramatic personification of a set of highly abstract, theoretical ideas, centering now around psychic energy and its disposition. The two main bases of data for these hypotheses were the study of dreams and the study of neurotic patients through the technical procedures of the psychoanalytic method. Neither of these fields of observation provides any direct information about the experience of a nursing infant. It has only been in relatively recent years, beginning with the work of

Spitz (1965) and Peter Wolff (1966) on neonates and infants, that the systematic collection of data upon which theories concerning the infant's experience might be built was begun.

The purpose of these constructs in Freud's work at that point was to derive a workable model of a mental apparatus, one which could account for, or at least not exclude, the ontogenetic origin of mind — "this first psychical activity." The experience of satisfaction served the purpose. It should be noted again that the exteroceptive component of satisfaction is not essential, but rather incidental or artifactual, in the framework of the theory. It is only because of some characteristic of the mental apparatus, rather than of the need requiring satisfaction, that the memory of the associated percept becomes centrally important psychologically. Bowlby (1969) apparently based his unfair and inaccurate view of the psychoanalytic theory of socialization and human relationships on this or similar statements by Freud, saying that Freud's theory was that "...a liking to be with other members of the same species is a result of being fed by them (pp. 210–211)." Freud's theory was obviously different and already more complex in 1895.

The terms "satisfying object" and "hostile object" are not included in the 1900 discussion. From the perspective of the carefully phrased theory of chapter seven, the marked ambiguity of these terms becomes more apparent. Intentions to satisfy or to cause hurt to someone (subject) may well be present in someone else (object). "Hostile object," however, seems to apply equally to the actual person or to the percept or its mnemic image, and may mistakenly be read as implying some sort of mental activity on the part of the image. The other person and the mental image are subjected to confusion by the theoretical statement (rather than by the infant, which is another matter).

There is a further difficulty with these "objects." Subject and object, of whatever kind, are roles. They can exist only as a matter of choice or designation; they must be assigned. Such assignment requires a sentient observer, a viewpoint, and a field and method of observation, whether or not these elements are specified. In this universe of discourse, there are two categories of viewpoint: subjective and objective. The subjective viewpoint does not lead to observations or propositions, which are a part of science. However, an objective viewpoint, admits of two scientific possibilities, both important in psychology. The observer may, as it were, "remain outside" the subject organism, viewing the assigned subject and object within the observational field; or the observer may choose to view the field as if he were "inside" the subject, a choice that involves a fantasy on the part of the observer of "seeing" the object as the subject does. The terms satisfying object and hostile object condense not only the several types of object concept but also the pure objective and fantasy-objective viewpoints. (I have explored these steps more fully elsewhere [Compton, 1983].)

One further issue, which is of secondary importance in the development of Freud's theory at this point but becomes of consequence later on, also concerns the hostile object. A hostile object is one that is associated with an experience of unpleasure and which, when freshly perceived, provokes, or begins to provoke, unpleasure. But since unpleasure depends on an increase in excitation, some source must be found for the excitation, or the hostile object cannot be accounted for in this theoretical context.

By 1900 Freud had used the term object to refer to at least five different concepts, even though the significance of other people—"actual objects"—had decreased somewhat since his earlier theories. Object refers, first, to someone else, someone other than the assigned subject; it is the object of a subject, a generic usage, the *phenomenal object*. Next, object refers to the target for or releasor of a sexual trend, called at this point by Freud a sexual object, but defined more comprehensively in 1915 as a *drive object*. Third, a *percept* or perceptual object, is the object of a particular mental function, an extraorganismic element defined by that function. Freud called the form in which the percept is stored mentally a *mnemic image,* a memory object. Finally, in the ambiguous terms hostile object and satisfying object Freud presented what he later recognized (also in 1915) as an *attitudinal object* concept: loving and hating, he said, are attitudes of one person towards another and cannot be fully encompassed by drive terminology. "Attitude," which is clearly an attribute of the subject, does away with the ambiguity of "satisfying object."

Additional object concepts appeared in Freud's later work, but these five—phenomenal object, perceptual object, memory object, attitudinal object and drive object—deserve the designation of fundamental object concepts of psychonalysis. They emerged early in the development of Freud's work, relatively independent of sophisticated theoretical contexts; and they have persisted throughout the subsequent development of psychoanalytic theory, providing a basis for expanded and derivative object concepts.

So far as I have been able to discover no one had previously dissected the object concepts of psychoanalysis. Many authors seem to have assumed that there is only one object concept and that there is no need, therefore, for any definition of the term. The result of this oversight and inattention has been dispute, which is not fruitful in resolving or even clarifying differences.

SUMMARY

Freud retained his neurophysiological orientation when he began to attempt to explain hysterical phenomena. His basic organizational concept for theory formation was excitation of the nervous system. When such excitation arose from somatic sources, the nervous system had to produce certain specific actions to relieve the tension in the somatic source. Under some circumstances, either because of the nature of the source or the developmentally dictated helplessness of the organism, another organism was necessary to achieve the specific action. The hungry baby with the nursing mother and human sexual experience were chosen by Freud to exemplify this situation. In each case there was a subject in need of satisfaction that required someone else, an object, for its achievement. Use of the term object appears to have arisen from the descriptive necessity to distinguish a subject from others.

Two interrelated, overlapping, but nevertheless differentiable models began to evolve in Freud's work. One was an early form of instinctual drive theory that included feedback loop concepts, published only posthumously. In this model, seeking to explain sexual satisfaction and its disorders, the *sexual object* is both a source of excitation and a means to its relief.

The other model, personified in the baby at the breast, was transposed from neurological to psychological terminology. In this model, the object is only incidentally linked to the need–satisfaction by being a temporally associated percept, – a *perceptual object*. This perceptual object is distinguished from its mentally stored counterpart, the *mnemic image of the perception*. It is this memory, however, linking satisfaction and an object perception, which becomes psychologically central in future situations of need. What is wished for is a new perception that matches the mnemic image. At an experiential level, personal attitudes of at least a favorable and an unfavorable nature develop in relation to these memories of satisfaction and pain and their associated percepts.

In the course of development of these models, the term object acquired new meanings, determined by its position in the theoretical contexts. In neither model is the object necessarily a person. In fact, since the terms of discourse no longer involve a subject as a personality but rather certain mental functions, the objects of the drives or functions cannot either, within the theoretical contexts, conceptually be a personality.

it is, then, necessary to consider in Freud's work by 1900 the following object concepts: object of a subject; object of a sexual drive; object of the function of perception; object of the function of memory; and object of a personal attitude.

REFERENCES

Arlow, J. A. (1980), Object concept and object choice. *Psychoanal. Quart.,* 49: 109–133.

Bowlby, J. (1969), *Attachment.* New York: Basic Books, 1976.

Brenner, C. (1957), The nature and development of the concept of repression in Freud's writings. *The Psychoanalytic Study of the Child,* 12:19–46. New York: International Universities Press.

_____ (1973), *An Elementary Textbook of Psychoanalysis.* New York: Anchor Books, 1974.

Breuer, J., & Freud, S. (1895), Studies on hysteria. *Standard Edition,* 2. London: Hogarth Press, 1955.

Compton, A. (1972), A study of the psychoanalytic theory of anxiety. I. The development of Freud's theory of anxiety. *J. Amer. Psychoanal. Assn.,* 20:3–44.

_____ (1981), On the psychoanalytic theory of instinctual drives. I. The beginnings of Freud's drive theory. *Psychoanal. Quart.,* 50:190–218.

_____ (1983), The current status of the theory of instinctual drives. II. The relation of the drive concept to structures, regulatory principles and objects. *Psychoanal. Quart.,* 52:402–426.

Dorpat, T. L. (1976), Structural conflict and object relations conflict. *J. Amer. Psychoanal. Assn.,* 24:855–874.

Freud, S. (1888), Hysteria. *Standard Edition,* 1:39–59. London: Hogarth Press, 1966.

_____ (1892a), Notes on Charcot's "Tuesday Lectures." *Standard Edition,* 1:131–143. London: Hogarth Press, 1966.

_____ (1892b), Sketches for the "Preliminary Communication" of 1893. *Standard Edition,* 1:147–154. London: Hogarth press, 1966.

_____ (1893), Some points for a comparative study of organic and hysterical motor paralyses. *Standard Edition,* 1:160–172. London: Hogarth Press, 1966.

_____ (1894a), The neuro-psychoses of defence. *Standard Edition,* 3:45–61. London: Hogarth Press, 1962.

_____ (1894b), Extracts from the Fliess papers: Draft E. How anxiety originates. *Standard Edition,* 1:189–195. London: Hogarth Press, 1966.

_____ (1895a), On the grounds for detaching a particular syndrome for neurasthenia under the description "anxiety neurosis." *Standard Edition,* 3:90–115. London: Hogarth Press, 1962.

_____ (1895b), A reply to criticisms on my paper on anxiety neurosis. *Standard Edition,* 3:123–139. London: Hogarth Press, 1962.

_____ (1895c), Extracts form the Flies papers: Draft G. Melancholia. *Standard Edition,* 1:200–206. London: Hogarth Press, 1966.

_____ (1895d), *Project for a scientific psychology. Standard Edition,* 1:295–397. London: Hogarth Press, 1966.

_____ (1896), Heredity and the etiology of the neuroses. *Standard Edition,* 3:143–156. London: Hogarth Press, 1962.

_____ (1900), *The interpretation of dreams. Standard Edition,* 4 & 5. London: Hogarth Press, 1953.

_____ (1906), My views on the part played by sexuality in the etiology of the neuroses. *Standard Edition,* 7:271–279. London: Hogarth Press, 1953.

_____ (1915), Instincts and their vicissitudes. *Standard Edition,* 14:166–204. London: Hogarth press, 1957.

López-Piñero, J. M. (1983), *Historical Origins of the Concept of Neurosis.* Cambridge: Cambridge University Press.

Spitz, R. A. (1965) *The First Year of Life.* New York: International Universities Press.

Stewart, W. A. (1967), *Psychoanalysis: The First Ten Years.* New York: Norton.

Wolff, P. H. (1966), The causes, controls and organization of behavior in the neonate. *Psychological Issues,* Monog. 17. New York: International Universities Press.

A Note on the Nature and the Developmental Origins of Affect

The meaning of the noun *affect* and its theoretical implications vary widely. For psychoanalytic purposes, one must try to arrive at a working definition through a grasp of Freud's usage of the term and its further clarification by psychologists and psychoanalytic theoreticians. In *A Glossary of Psychoanalytic Terms and Concepts* (Moore and Fine, 1968) affects are described comprehensively, but in a way that leaves room for considerable clarification. The description includes:

> Subjectively experienced feeling states, usually perceived as pleasurable or unpleasurable in relation to the gratification or frustraton of instinctual drives, to realistic achievements, and to the fulfillment of ideals. There are physiologic components usually expressed through somatic manifestations . . . A psychic component is regularly present and may exist with little or no physiological manifestation, as in the case of feelings of happiness or sadness . . . Since affects are subjective experiences, they must be within conscious awareness and do not occur unconsciously in the same sense that other psychic phenomena do . . . [p. 18].

Among the issues glossed over is disagreement about the relation to affects of sensations and of feelings of pleasure and unpleasure. There is disagreement also about the extent of ego development necessary for the infant or child to become capable of experiencing affect. There is even a problem, recently introduced into psychoanalytic literature from neonatal research, concerning the meaning of "affective expression" in neonates, that is, whether any subjective experiencing can be attributed to that term. Within psychoanalytic theory itself there is disagreement among Freudian theoreticians about the extent to which affect can be en-

191

compassed within metapsychology, with some tending to exclude all organic and biological considerations and others emphasizing the experiential element as it relates to such actualities as pain, need, and gratification.

Before I attempt a brief historical account of Freud's own use of the term *affect* and trace a few key interpretations or deliberate modifications of Freud's usage by his intellectual heirs, a source of potential confusion requires discussion. Among psychoanalysts who are dissatisfied with Freudian theory in part or totally, some, seeking what they believe to be more verifiable and hence allegedly more scientific bases for new theory formation, have uncritically embraced the experimental findings of researchers in psychophysiology. Among this group, a few seem to have embraced as well the theoretical assumptions derived from that research. Examples are given later. As I understand those analysts, they believe that the infant's mental development can be explained without the need for any assumptions as to whether or not the infant is experiencing feelings or other subjective phenomena. Affect is regarded as a form of behavior, precisely measurable and understandable in terms of its significance as an aspect of communication with the mother. What is being communicated, however, (contempt and disgust are among the "affective behaviors" alleged to have been identified at birth or shortly after) is not assumed to exist as an aspect of the infant's awareness.

The purpose of drawing attention at the outset to an anti-Freudian trend is to avoid confusing it with an increasing emhasis by analysts well within the Freudian tradition upon evidence of early affect. A necessary corollary of that emphasis is a modification of Freud's view of the pleasure principle. Freud himself drew attention, in the "Outline" (1940), to the importance of arriving at an answer to the question of how the pleasure principle could ever become overcome; thus the modification to be presented is consistent with a Freudian approach, in sharp contrast to the revisionist trends mentioned. It is as important to differentiate a Freudian view of early affect from current efforts to circumnavigate the study of human feelings as it is to distingjish it from Kleinian theory.

As the editors of the *Standard Edition* noted in Volume 1 (p. xxiii), Freud's use of the words *Affekt, Empfindung,* and *Gefühl* (variously translated as *affect, feeling,* and *sensation*) was flexible. They also observed that the signification of these terms is in any case uncertain. A survey of Freud's use of the term affect discloses that flexibility is indeed noteworthy. One fairly consistent element is his linking of affect—"charge of affect"—with feeling and idea (1915, p. 152; 1925, p. 230; 1937, p. 258).

In Chapter XXV of his *Introductory Lectures,* however, in the context of a discussion of anxiety, Freud (1917) hinted at the depth and direction of the root of his concept of affect. (He explicitly indicated that he was not identifying affect with anxiety, however.) First, he described affect in a "dynamic sense": "It is in any case something highly composite. An affect includes in the first place particular motor innervations or discharges and secondly certain feelings; the latter are of two kinds – perceptions of the motor actions that have occurred and the direct feelings of pleasure and unpleasure which, as we say, give the affect its keynote" (p. 395). In pursuing the theory he added, "The core which holds the combination we have described together is the repetition of some particular significant experience" (p. 396). Freud's further explanation identified affects as "precipitates" of very early experiences, "placed in the prehistory not of the individual, but of the species" (p. ibid). He likened the construction of an affective state to that of a hysterical attack, emphasizing the difference of his psychoanalytic conception from customary psychological explanations – the James-Lange theory. An illuminating footnote was provided by the editors (p. 327). They suggested a possible basis for Freud's view of affect in Darwin's explanation in 1872 of affects as relics of action that originally had had a meaning. They noted that Freud had quoted Darwin about this in 1895 (p. 181) and repeated the argument in 1926.

Freud's concept of affect differed from the common psychological view of that time. The distinction, I believe, is in the exclusivity, for psychoanalytic theory, of the intrapsychic processes, clearly involving some degree of psychic structure, as distinct from reflex reactions and from mere awareness of somatic responses. Freud's view of the biological genesis of affect might well have been illuminated by the editors if they had drawn attention to Walter B. Cannon's classic volume *The Wisdom of the Body* (1932). Cannon's work underscored the survival value of the "motor innervations or discharge" to which Freud had alluded and narrowed the range of these from the scope of Darwin's opus. These bodily behaviors and their, according to Freud, phylogenetic psychological precipitates dealt exclusively with threats to individual survival and the response to these. *Pleasurable* affects received no attention in these considerations.

Jacobson (1953) discussed affects in the context of a review of Freud's writings. Freud said little about affects other than anxiety, she wrote, but he came to regard them all as adaptive reactions to traumata imposed by reality, with anxiety representing merely a special case. She noted Freud's emphasis on the ego as the site of initiation of affective experience and observed: "The questions of the sources from which the ego draws energy for the development of anxiety appeared to have lost significance," once the ego came to be regarded as a system endowed with psychic energy of its own (p. 42). One statement is remarkably prescient with respect to early ego activity: "As the greatest accomplishment of the ego with respect to the affects, we usually regard the transition from affective to functional motor activity, insofar as it leads to a general taming of the affects for the purpose of adequate ego functioning" (pp. 60–61).

Jacobson repeated Freud's often stated opinion that a "charge of affect" is separate from and can be detached from an "idea." That assumption is a philosophical abstraction rather than an established fact of human psychic life. Nor is it established that feelings, sensation, and emotions are entirely devoid of idea, in its most basic and primitive meaning or sense. Lewin (1965) noted that use of the word "afffect" antedated St. Augustine and that its early usage reflected confusion in distinguishing among perception, knowledge, feeling, and action. He observed: "If there were no concept of the independent observing cognitive self, we should have no corresponding concept of the independent feeling or the independent action" (p. 25). Lewin was clearly in agreement with Onians in denying the existence of pure thought, and he quoted William James to the effect that life involves constant motion and cannot be understood by concepts that arrest motion and immobilize the bits of life so conceptualized in a "logical herbarium" (p. 25). He observed that affect charge "goes back to cathartic days in analytic history . . . an evident vestige of faculty psychology in which an atomic affect representation is separable from a cognitive one" (p. 27). The practical need to assume a separate charge of affect was to account for "the empirical findings of repression, displacement and isolation, where the emotional representation has a fate different from the ideational one" (p. 36). Thus Lewin accounted for the persistence of a bit of Freudian theory, the awkwardness of which he had already anticipated: "Much that Freud formulated originally in terms of emotions has been shifted and rephrased into instinct theory, but pieces of affect theory have not been well absorbed and persist as isolated fragments" (p. 23). With a subsequent shift in emphasis to "ego theory," "object relations theory," and "self theory," these isolated fragments continue to persist.

Greenacre (1980), in brief, penetrating historical review, has suggested cogent reasons for the continuing emphasis on Freud's purely metapsychological works by some theoreticians. While acknowledging that these works form the basis for our psychoanalytic theory, she pointed out that that emphasis nonetheless deflected attention from some of Freud's early theoretical views, which he reaffirmed in his late essays. She drew attention to Freud's reassertion of the role of early trauma and screen memories (which always involve affect) in relation to reconstruction. Her observations bear upon the problems arising from insistence on a purity of metapsychological explanations distinct from and exclusive of experiential elements.

Schur's (1972) insistence on the necessity of separating metapsychology from experience led him into difficulties. First, he achieved a degree of theoretical consistency at the expense of having to criticize and reject some of Freud's basic opinions pertaining to the link between the pleasure principle and experiential elements (p. 324). Neither the pleasure principle nor the unpleasure principle can ever be fully detached from the experiences according to which these principles are named, and Freud never deviated from assuming an essential conectedness. Furthermore, Schur finally identified pleasure and unpleasure as affects and wrote: "The affects pleasure and unpleasure — like all affects — are complex ego responses having many genetically determined hierarchical layers, and dependent on the state of all three psychic structures and their relationship to the environment" (p. 322). This left in question what comprised the infant's psyche in earlier years. His insistence on identifying affects with the fully formed ego is part of the trend noted by Greenacre (1980), which left an enormous and currently flourishing field closed to Freudians but open to experimental psychologists and neurophysiologists.

Loewald (1971) has also criticized certain of Freud's theoretical views involving the biological, physical connections with intrapsychic elements. He included in his criticism Hartmann's hypothesis of "primary autonomy of the ego, primary ego apparatuses, and the like (p. 100)." According to Loewald, the energy postulated by Hartmann is "non-psychic, i.e., non-motivational." Also, he stated, "Personal motivation is the fundamental hypothesis of psychoanalysis" (p. 99), and "it cannot be stressed enough that such organizations [of "psychic fields"] is most vitally co-determined by the fact of the far higher complexity and organization of psychic energy obtaining in the — for the observer — surrounding or environmental psychic systems" (pp. 100, 101). This seems to be perilously close to a mystical solution to problems involving human interaction and communication. "Personal motivation" divorced from biology is the essence of poltergeists and of kindly spirits. The organs of perception, for example, were viewed by Loewald as unimportant to the psychoanalyst. That left unexplained the influence on the psyche of deprivation, or provison, of such biological necessities as food, water, and warmth. He ignored the influence of these aspects of mothering on the developing psychic structure of the infant. Rather, he viewed the mother and infant as sharing a "psychic field." Nowhere in Freud can one find either the assumption of fusion of the metapsychological entities of separate individuals (e.g., mother and infant), or the existence of psychic structure devoid of connections with the real world. Freud's opinions in this regard should still be entirely acceptable both to the nonanalytic, organically oriented theoretician and to Freudians. Freud recognized that communication between infant and mother involving coenesthetic perceptions (e.g., of biological rhythms) arise even before differentiation of the ego from the id and persist throughout life as id activities. The relevance to early affect and its communication is illuminated in Weil's (1976) beautiful description of the mutual influences of infant and mother on each other.

I referred earlier to Greenacre's pertinent comments in her essay in 1980. In 1979 she had stated, about analysands' nonverbal expressions of tension: "Frequently these are understood as part of a transference reaction or of some concurrent problem and conflict. This is true, but from experience I have found that patients who have had undue disturbances early show such reactions more plentifully and more sharply than others. . . . The body participates in the analytic situation to an unusual degree. . . ." Such patients, she wrote, have symptoms suggestive of oedipal conflicts, castration fears, and penis envy. "They are however oriented toward narcissistic aims, with a weakness in object-relatedness" (pp. 139, 140). Here again the contrasting views of the relation of biology to affect are clear cut. There have been many objections, of course, to focus on early trauma as a causative factor in neurotic suffering. Arlow (1981) and Stein (1981) have been particularly emphatic and clear about the dangers that attend interpretations based on trauma rather than on intrapsychic conflict. In no way, however, do these caveats suggest that early trauma does not occur, nor that when it does, it fails to leave any clinical aftermath. Kafka (1971) noted in cases of his own and in others selected from the literature a frequent correlation between early trauma and associations during analysis revealing the sensation of being a container filled with evil and disgusting contents.

Most analysts have followed, at least implicitly, either Schur's (1972, p. 10) or Brenner's definition of affect. Brenner's definition was made explicit in a theory of affects published in 1974. he has held to that definition and included it in a chapter of his 1982 book, in which he wrote of affect theory:

> It is a theory based on psychoanalytic data. It asserts that affects are complex mental phenomena which can best be understood in developmental terms . . . . At an early stage of psychic development memories and other ideas become associated with the sensations of pleasure and unpleasure connected with drive derivatives. The resulting complex of sensations and

ideas is an affect. . . . Ideas and sensations together constitute an affect as a
psychological phenomenon [p. 41].

Brenner's definition might seem at first glance to differ from Schur's
principally in that Brenner did not include pleasure and unpleasure
among affects but instead identified them as arising earlier, being simple
and not further reducible, and contributing to all affects. He has not distinguished his view of affect on that basis, however, but on his conclusion
that ideas are always a part of affects. Brenner emphasized that Schur,
among others including Novey and Lewin, had related ideas to feelings
but had not regarded them as an indispensible component of affect.

Brenner's meaning, in his reference to "an early stage of psychic development," relates to his views on the mental life of infants. He had already
been considering the issue much earlier. A statement he first published in
1953 was cited in the 1974 essay: "Anxiety is an emotion (affect) which
the anticipation of danger evokes in the ego. It is not present as such from
birth or very early infancy. In such very early periods the infant is aware
only of pleasure or unpleasure as far as emotions are concerned" (p. 534).
The parenthetic equating of affect with emotion at the beginning of the
quotation is unclear. At its conclusion, pleasure and unpleasure are la-
beled as emotions and are distinguished from affect. These nuances of
definition are of considerable interest because, later, Basch (1976) en-
deavored to separate *emotion* from *affect*; he considered emotion to be
more complex and a later acquisition than affect (p. 770). Valenstein
(1973) regarded the psychoanalytic concept of unpleasure as *encompassing* a specific affect (*pain*) (p. 366). Kernberg (1982) has asserted that
affect (also "affective behavior" and "inborn affective patterns") are present from birth (pp. 906, 911). Obviously, assumptions about affect in
earliest infancy are beyond demonstrable proof by the psychoanalytic or
any other method. Brenner's theory of affect as based on psychoanalytic
data offers an alternative to dependence on idiosyncratic definitions, particularly because he recognized that affect can best be understood in developmental terms. He cited two clinical vignettes in his 1974 essay (p.
546 f.). In the first, a patient's symptom "of 'isolation' or 'repression' of affect" was traced to an early experience (age not specified) when the patient's sister was born. The child felt unwanted and unloved when his
mother turned her affection to his sister, and he was afraid to express his
rage, because his mother punished him when he had an angry outburst
by putting him in a dark closet. He feared his jealousy "because to be jealous of his sister meant wanting to be a girl himself, which meant wanting
to be castrated, . . ." Here we have some of the "ideas" Dr. Brenner uncovered as illustrations of the *idea* as a component of powerful early af-

fects. The child was already sufficiently far along in development to have quite sophisticated ideas. In a second vignette, a conflict was traced back to the birth of a sibling when the patient was two-and-a half years old had also felt displaced by his sister and consequently was angry and jealous. It is not clear from his reconstruction whether Dr. Brenner believed that the child experienced affect or only feelings at that age. The account reported an event at age six that had proved to be of decisive importance in determining this analysand's adult reaction to being angry for any reason. These vignettes, which illustrated the distinction between conscious and unconscious affects, probably indicate the ultimate limits to which Dr. Brenner feels psychoanalytic technique can elicit memories that can be accepted as credible, that is, valid and not the result of telescoping, fantasy, or unconsciously determined retrospective falsification. This view, shared by Abend, Porder, and Willick (1983) stands in interesting contrast to that of Greenacre (1979, 1980).

Sandler and Sandler (1978) discussed the evidence for and importance of early infantile experiences of pleasure and unpleasure in the context of object relations as follows:

> . . . We could postulate that the first important distinction *recognized* by the child in the world of his experience is the difference between . . . the experiences of pleasure and satisfaction on the one hand, and those of unpleasure and pain on the other . . . These initial differentiated responses to the two major classes of experience, the two primary "objects" of the child are, in the beginning, biologically based.

Although it is not obviously necessary to label experiences as "objects," doing so enabled the Sandlers to make a vivid and valid distinction: The "objects" referred to here are constellations of subjective experience in which "self" and "non-self" have not yet been differentiated. These "primary affective objects" are relatively chaotic masses of pleasureable feelings and sensations on the one hand and unpleasureable ones on the other. This is not at all the same as the "good" and "bad" breast of Mrs. Klein. Moreover, we would consider that the child's psychological experience of his own very complicated biologically-based involuntary reactions (to promotings from inside and outside) are only gradually organized into anything at all psychically coherent—a view very different from the Kleinian view of extremely early unconscious fantasy. [pp. 292–3]

I wish to add to the distinction they make, because a more sweeping criticism of the Kleinian viewpoint asserts that Kleinians tend to replace the crucial issue of psychic conflict by explanations based on nonconflictual vicissitudes of infantile fantasy. Freudian psychoanalytic therapy concerns primarily the resolution of interstructural conflicts. Freudian theory, on the other hand, considers subjective experiences, including affects, prior to the development of structures sufficiently complex to permit intersystemic conflict.

At issue is the question of the initial arousal of the earliest id and ego components as psychic functions — implying a degree of primitive structure — at the dawn of the psyche, in contrast to the concept of an original mother–infant unit and independent of the concept of prepsychological "affective behavioral" reflexes. I believe that there is persuasive evidence of ego activity by the end of the third month. This is based on objectively verified observations of the infant's pleasurable interest, anticipation, and eagerness for repetition after its discovery of its own effectiveness.[1]

Vivid evidence of these capabilities is to be found in an experiment performed by Papousek and cited by Broucek (1979), in which infants of three to four months purposefully and repeatedly caused something to happen and showed signs of joyful interest when their anticipations were fulfilled. I must leave elaboration both of the example and of my understanding of it for a separate essay (on "function pleasure"). There I postulate a moment of transition, which occurs usually in the third month, during a period of alertness and without any indication of biological need. The infant's joy in discovering that it has the ability to make something happen — to be the Prime Mover — is postulated to be a departure from primary (absolute) narcissism and from regressive efforts to reattain that state. After that departure, what is evident is a narcissistic exuberance directed outward, to the kinesthetic and visual real world, the *actual* "outside." From the moment of transition, when the infant discovers that it can cause a response (in nonexperimental situations, by the mother), psychic structure formation and infant–mother "dialogue" commence the developmental surge. There is no need, in this account, to assume an initial mother–infant unity or symbiotic phase — only to recognize the extent of the intimate interrelationship between the mother and the infant (undifferentiated or differentiated). My explanation differs from that advanced by the Sandlers (1978) in that the infant's first "objects" exist in the actual world. Some experimenters (e.g., Newson, 1975, as cited by the Sandlers) and Tomkins, (1962–1963) identify early behavioral manifestations and acknowledge that these do not imply "that the human infant is some-

---

[1] I realize that the objection can be raised that even birds or fish exhibit changes in activity suggestive of interest, under certain circumstances, but I must leave the ultimate decision about when a human can correctly infer psychic activity in another organism — human or animal or in a nonliving complex system — for consideration elsewhere.

how possessed of the 'knowledge' that seen objects are tangible" (p. 293). Obviously, there comes a point at which the infant first acquires a datum of that knowledge; I believe the Papousek experiment demonstrates that point.

Mahler and McDevitt (1982) noted their agreement with early developmental psychologists that "activity is the most important trigger of the developing sense of self" (p. 835). They did not consider the infant's manifestations of pleasure in that context, however, nor did they suggest a psychoanalytic explanation for the dramatic change that accompanies the infant's discovery of its ability to make things happen.

In contrast to conventional Freudian views are the following. Basch (1976) has offered a reexamination of the concept of affect. His approach was innovative: he turned to facial expressions of infants as the forerunners of the extremely important paraverbal and preverbal means of communication, relating this to Darwin's classic investigation of facial expression as a means of communication among men and animals. Important in Basch's approach was his evidence that expressions of emotion on the human face are not learned by imitation and have neurological determinants in subcortical structures. Basch placed great emphasis on the work of Tomkins (1962, 1963) who believed that he could identify by observation "affective behavior," which seems to refer to presensate reflexes that lead to the development of later psychological experiences. In Tomkin's view, accepted by Basch, precursors to such affects as contempt-disgust can be identified by affective behavior such as "sneer: upper lip lifted" and "shame-humiliation: eyes cast down, head down" (p. 761). The first of these is alleged to be present from birth; the latter to require learning (the age is not specified except as observable in infancy). Four other affects are alleged to be observable at birth: surprise-startle, interest-excitement, enjoyment-joy, and distress-anguish.

No one can dispute that there is a variety of facial expressions in infancy. Postulating a manifestation of disgust, or contempt, at birth is another matter. Labelling it as affective behavior anterior to ego development does not obviate the objection. To assume that affective behavior communicates contempt, for example, which has had no possibility of having been experienced by the communicating infant raises questions as to the meaning of subjective experience to the experimenters. Basch's (1976) acceptance of Tomkins's (1962–1963) opinions is not easy to evaluate. At times he seemed to regard the alleged affective behavior as neurophysiological rather than psychological. For instance, in discussing at some length the infant's smile as communication at a distance—"getting her [the mother] to smile in return and thus extend her protection"—Basch stated that "the smile itself appears as early as three to four weeks while the recognition response to another's face does not occur until about three months. This suggests that the first smile is not one of recognition . . ." (p. 765). The precise dating of the first smile is not a key issue here. What is at issue is the contamination of a psychoanalytic theory of affect by communications theory, to which Basch is led, quite logically, from Tomkins's work. For Basch, the infant seems to be an automation that secondarily develops a psyche as a result of "messages" that bring about "whatever takes place within and to him." These "messages" are alleged to play an important part in determining the "eventual sense of confidence and 'basic trust' in his transaction with the environment"[2] (p. 766). "Patterns laid down in the first two years of presymbolic life" (p. 767) seem to refer to the infant's inborn and applied "programming," which in some obscure manner leads to psychic life. For that reason, I believe, Basch described *emotion* as a relatively late acquisition. He wrote:

> It is premature to attribute an emotional life, in the strict sense of the word, to infants, inasmuch as they have developed neither a symbolic concept of self nor the capacity for symbolic operation, which makes reflection possible. Yet no doubt infants behave *as if* they were happy, sad, excited, distressed, etc. [p. 768].

Gaensbauer, in 1982, provided a very thoughtful discussion of the issues raised by the findings of research. He approached the very difficult question of what early affect means from a standpoint that seems to contrast with that of the Sandlers, whose work is included in his review. Their assumptions suggested to him, within the context of object relations, that the infant's experiencing begins with pleasure and unpleasure, which, however nebulously, involve the already present *ego*, as Freud had concluded. What develops into adult affects (which Basch seems to have chosen to call emotions) originates, acording to the Sandlers, in these earliest experiencings and reflects increasing complexity of ego capabilities and accumulated (memory of) experience and knowledge. Gaensbauer assumed that ego — "the ego," with its panoply of subtle and complex affects — can be spoken of only after its consolidation, at around age two, from a variety of precursors. His own view is that neurophysiological precursors of the affects can be recognized extremely early, from (already systematized) ratings of reflex or reflex like behavioral responses to specific stimuli. These behavioral responses contribute to what will later,

---

[2]Eissler (1971), pointing out the psychological absurdity of imputing to the infant the ability to *hope* (postulated by Erikson), noted (p. 503) an early psychoanalytic derision, by Bernfeld, in a humorous description of a prayerful neonate.

with consolidation of the ego, come to be experienced as affects. Gaens-bauer is apparently undecided as to what the infant is experiencing from birth to two years, but his essay makes clear that he regards this as existing in the psychic rather than the reflex realm, despite his belief that the ego does not "consolidate" for two years. In his view, the diversity of behavioral responses, which in a case presentation he demonstrated to be appropriate to the actual situation, speaks "for the existence of a number of 'primary' emotions." These "would be presumed to have qualitatively distinct neuroanatomical and neurophysiological programs underlying each different affect" (p. 30). He finds this more reasonable than the view of others, including Schur and Brenner.

Gaensbauer (1982) presented a fascinating case history of an infant first seen at age three months, 25 days when, while hospitalized for a skull fracture and broken arm, she was referred for a psychosocial evaluation. There had been a previous hospitalization, at age two weeks, for an arm fracture, alleged by the parents to have resulted when her father had grabbed the infant's arm as she was falling off the bed. The caseworkers were impressed with the warmth and appropriate concern of both parents, and no further investigation was carried out. Even after the second hospitalization and the discovery of physical abuse by her father during brief episodes of rage, Jenny seemed to be doing quite well developmentally and emotionally. She was described as a "loveable baby — happy, cute and highly sociable." It was determined that the father alone had been responsible for the abusive incidents, and he was denied further access to his daughter while criminal charges were pressed. All the evidence Dr. Gaensbauer presented indicated that during the psychosocial evaluation, Jenny's behavior with her parents appeared to be normal. Jenny was nevertheless separated from both parents, which necessitated abrupt weaning, and sent to a foster home.

Three weeks after Jenny was placed in the first foster home she was seen for a "first playroom laboratory visit." Her behavior was "completely consistent with a diagnosis of depression." Investigation revealed that the foster mother was indifferent to Jenny and was negligent. A developmental psychologist skilled in rating facial expression "utilized the Maximally Discriminative Facial Movement Coding System of Izard (1979)." Analysis of the videotape revealed facial behavior called "sadness, fearfulness, anger, joy (smiling), and interest/curiosity. The expressions themselves were often transient, lasting no more than one or two seconds," interspersed in a session in which "the predominant facial expression was that of a subdued or serious face, which was somewhat difficult to interpret." Most remarkable is that, having shown no dread of her father prior to the disruption of the family, Jenny now reacted very negatively to Dr.

Gaensbauer's effort to approach her, whereas she did not so react to the effort of female strangers on the same occasion.

Jenny was transferred to a second foster home, and two weeks later she was again brought to the laboratory for observation. At that time there was "no evidence of sadness or depression in her behavior or demeanor" (p. 45). She smiled frequently in response to the foster mother's attention and showed no evidence of distress when Dr. Gaensbauer approached. In the facial expression analysis "no facial expressions of sadness were noted." Fear expressions were infrequent.

Gaensbauer stressed "the important role of affect in early development. The most striking findings involved the presence of facial expressions of discreet emotion in an infant at less than four months old" (p. 51). Gaensbauer mentioned that "a number of recent observations suggest that this transition from physiology to psychology commences at birth," (p. 53).

I have included the considerable data pertaining to Jenny and Professor Gaensbauer's description because two radically different views are encompassed in his essay. In his introduction to "issues in affect theory," Gaensbauer stated the following about "primary emotions": "Theorists emphasizing the phylogenetic basis of affective expression include Novey (1959), Engel (1962), Basch (1976), and Emde (1980). All these writers have hypothesized a number of "primary" emotions universal in the human species and present from the earliest weeks and months of life" (p. 30). It is, however, far from clear that those theorists intended, or were necessarily interested in equating "affective behavior" or "primary emotions" with the psychic life of the infant exhibiting the behavior they chose to call by psychological terms. Both Izard (1979) and Tomkins (1962–1963) included as affective expressions disgust and contempt at or shortly after birth; it is obvious that what is being described cannot reflect the experiencing of affect as generally understood by psychoanalysts.

As an alternative point of view to that of the existence of "primary" emotions, Gaensbauer stated:

> On the other hand, Blau (1955), Schur (1969), and Brenner (1974) see affective experience as centering around a pleasure unpleasure dimension, with further differentiation depending on ego development and the particular ideation associated with the internal states of pleasure and or unpleasure. Given the highly variable ideational possibilities, these authors tend to emphasize the unique highly individualized nature of affective experience [p. 30].

Gaensbauer turned to the area of his own bias, namely that the evidence of "emotions" is universal in the human species and identifiable with high reliability.

Although he offered interesting observations pertaining to the relation, for example, of affect and instinctual drive, the one point that is of special relevance to the current presentation is that all the facial expressions evaluated, like Jenny's overall behavior, reflected a very limited range of affective expressions. Many analysts would readily attribute that range of affects to an infant, namely, unpleasure (anger, sadnes, fear) and pleasure (surprise, interest, joy). At no point did Gaensbauer have to concern himself with such alleged "primary" emotions as disgust, contempt, and shame. His sensitive clinical description of Jenny at three and four months may or may not be rendered scientifically more credible by virtue of the skilled application of Izard's coding system. Such questions as whether or not Jenny had a "self," or an ego, seem entirely a matter of conjecture as well as definition. Did she "know" that she was depressed, frightened, angry? Can one assert with authority what degree of complexity of psychic structure exists at three or four months? Is there any reason for rejecting the Freudian view that (in however primitive and chaotic a state, and however undifferentiated from the id) an ego is functional from the beginning? I suggest that Jenny experienced affect, in a Freudian sense, and that when considered in relation to Papousek's findings, her behavior indicated that a sufficiently coherent ego exists at three to four months to justify the assertion that the child is experiencing affect. Out of a multitude of experimental observations, which are consistent with my view, I find the primary basis for this assertion in observations demonstrating with regularity the infant's capacity to act purposefully, with evidence of joyful feelings, (which suggest the existence of "idea," however vague), and the infant's capability to anticipate that the purposeful activity will lead to those feelings.

SUMMARY AND CONCLUSIONS

The Freudian view of affect has changed with time. With elaboration of the structural point of view, the ego has come to be viewed as a complex organization taking several years to consolidate. The ego has always been recognized as the component within which affect is experienced, and gradually, as emphasized in Schur's approach, the experience of affect came to be totally dependent on that complex organization, precluding consideration of the experience of affect in infancy. Furthermore, the (un)pleasure principle, according to which all psychic activity has the aim of reducing tension, overlooked the infant's pleasure potential in the narcissistic gratification of eliciting responses in the actual world. Finally, limiting psychoanalytic theory to the data recoverable from phases of childhood following the acquisition of language has diverted the attention of Freudians from the possibility and the significance of early affect, that is, affect recognizable by the time the infant is four months of age. Sandler and Sandler (1978) are among the few Freudians who have acknowledged the presence of early affect without emphasis on an initial mother–infant unity. The concept of mother–infant unity has the disadvantage of providing a means of recognizing infantile affect only as aspect of a symbiotic or quasimystical experience, thereby deflecting attention from the infant's unique, biologically based, and independent early ego. Acknowledging early ego as a functional entity furthers Freud's view of psychic life. It offers an alternative to, and perhaps an ultimate common ground with, research into neonatal psychology and neurophysiology in extending the theoretical explanation of the human mind.

REFERENCES

Abend, S., Porder, M., & Willick, M. (1983), *Borderline Patients: Psychoanalytic Perspectives.* New York: International Universities Press.

Arlow, J. A. (1981), Theories of pathogenesis. *Psychoanal Quart.,* 50:488–514.

Basch, M. (1976), The concept of affect: A re-examination. *J. Amer. Psychoanal. Assn.,* 24:759–777.

Brenner, C. (1974), On the nature and development of affects: a unified theory. *Psychoanal. Quart.,* 43:532–556.

_____ (1982), *The Mind in Conflict.* New York: International Universities Press.

Broucek, F. (1979), Efficacy of infancy: a review of some experimental studies and their possible implications for clinical theory. *Internat. J. Psycho-Anal.,* 60:311–316.

Cannon, W. B. (1932), *The Wisdom of the Body.* New York: Norton.

Darwin, C. (1872), *The Expression of the Emotions in Man and Animals.* 2nd ed. London: West, 1899.

Eissler, K. R. (1971), *Discourse on Hamlet and HAMLET.* New York: International Universities Press.

Freud, S. (1895), On the grounds for detaching a particular syndrome from neurasthetnia under the description "Anxiety neurosis." *Standard Edition,* 3:87–139. London: Hogarth Press, 1962.

_____ (1915), Repression. *Standard Edition,* 14:141–158.

_____ (1917). Introductory lectures in psychoanalysis. *Standard Edition,* 15 & 16, London: Hogarth Press, 1963.

_____ (1925), Negation. *Standard Edition,* 19:233–239. London: Hogarth Press, 1961.

_____ (1926), Inhibitions, symptoms, and anxiety. *Standard Edition,* 20:77–175. London: Hogarth Press, 1959.

_____ (1937), Constructions in analysis. *Standard Edition,* 23:255–269. London: Hogarth Press, 1964.

_____ (1940), An outline of psychoanalysis. *Standard Edition*, 23:139–208. London: Hogarth Press, 1964.

Gaensbauer, T. (1982), The differentiation of discrete affects. *The Psychoanalytic Study of the Child*, 37:29–66.

Greenacre, P. (1979), Reconstruction and the process of individuation. *The Psychoanalytic Study of the Child*, 34:121–144.

_____ (1980), A historical sketch of the use and disuse of reconstruction. *The Psychoanalytic Study of the Child*, 35:35–40.

Izard, C. E. (1979), *The Maximally Discriminative Facial Movement Coding System*. Instructional Resource Center, University of Delaware, Newark.

Jacobson, E. (1953), Affects and their pleasure-unpleasure qualities in relation to the psychic discharge process. In: *Drives, Affects, Behavior*, Vol. 1, ed. R. Loewenstein. New York: International Universities Press, pp. 38–66.

_____ (1964), *The Self and The Object World*. New York; International Universities Press.

Kafka, E. (1971), On the development of the experience of mental self, the bodily self, and self consciousness. *The Psychoanalytic Study of the Child*, 26:217–240.

Kernberg, O. (1982), Self, ego, affects and drives. *J. Amer. Psychoanal. Assn.*, 30:899–917.

Lewin, B. D. (1965), Reflections on affect. In: *Drives, Affects, Behavior*, Vol 1., ed. M. Schur. New York: International Universities Press, pp. 23–37.

Loewald, H. W. (1971). On motivation and instinct theory. *The Psychoanalytic Study of the Child*, 26:91–128.

Mahler, M. S. & McDevitt, J. B. (1982), Thoughts on the emergence of the sense of self, with particular emphasis on the body self. *J. Amer. Psychoanal. Assn.*, 30:827–848.

Moore, B. E. & Fine, B. D. ed. (1975). *A Glossary of Psychoanalytic Terms and Concepts*. 2nd ed. New York: American Psychoanalytic Association.

Sandler, J. & Sandler, A-M. (1978). Object relations and affects. *Internat. J. Psycho-Anal.*, 59:285–296.

Schur, M. ed. (1965). *Drives, Affects, Behavior*, Vol. 2, New York: International Universities Press.

_____ (1972). *Freud: Living and Dying*. New York: International Universities Press.

Stein, M. H. (1981), The unobjectionable part of the transference. *J. Amer. Psychoanal. Assn.*, 29:869–892.

Tomkins, S. S. (1962–1963), *Affect, Imagery, Consciousness*. Vol. I & II. New York: Springer.

Valenstein, A. (1973), On attachment to painful feelings and the negative therapeutic reaction. *The Psychoanalytic Study of the Child*, 28:365–392.

Weil, A. (1976), The first year: metapsychological inferences of infant observation. In: *The Process of Child Development*, ed. P. Neubauer. New York: Meridian.

PART THREE

The
Technique
of Psychoanalysis

There is no doubt that among the many contributions Charles Brenner has made to psychoanalysis, his writings and teachings about technique are outstanding. He has consistently and with great clarity advocated the unceasing, persistent application of classical psychoanalytic technique to the treatment of mental illness. The four papers in this section deal with various aspects of psychoanalytic technique.

Sander M. Abend reviews the concept of the psychoanalytic process, challenging the notion of easy definition. He thoroughly discusses the complexities and problems involved in its evaluation.

Harold Blum enters the realm of technique with an extensive discussion about countertransference, including its many definitions. Using clinical material, he shows how the current interest in a two-person analytic field of forces and the analyst as participant observer enhances our understanding of the therapeutic endeavor.

Paul Gray writes a carefully detailed paper on helping analysands observe intrapsychic activity. Illustrating his major points with a number of clinical examples, he shows how the interventions of the analyst can be crucial in the analytic process.

The concept of insight and its role in the therapeutic process is reviewed by Edward D. Joseph. He discusses the gradual emergence of insight during therapy and describes the factors that enable its development in both the patient and the analyst.

SANDER M. ABEND

Some Problems in the Evaluation of the Psychoanalytic Process

The term *psychoanalytic process* is frequently employed by psychoanalysts in their discussions of others' clinical work and occasionally in respect to their own as well. Although reference to psychoanalysis as a process goes back to Freud (1913), agreement on exactly what that term means has never been reached (Weinshel, 1984). The most general implication is that an analysis can be described as an unfolding of events that have an integral continuity of some sort and that move in a certain direction. E. Kris (1956) used it in just such a broad way: he meant by process merely that as an analysis progresses over the course of time, changes can be observed to be taking place in the analysand. But often when the term is used in evaluative situations, there appears to be a more specific implication that what constitutes a valid psychoanalytic process is both unique and specifiable and that its distinguishing features are easily recognizable.

It should follow, then, that an experienced and informed critic ought readily to be able to differentiate the true psychoanalytic process from those which characterize unsuccessful psychoanalyses, as well as from those of other psychotherapies. It is by no means uncommon during the course of clinical discussions for one analyst to suggest that a treatment conducted by another analyst, and considered by both the latter and his patient to have been a productive psychoanalysis, was in fact not a valid psychoanalytic process at all, but only a psychotherapy of some sort, though admittedly a helpful one. Given the absence of a rigorous definition of the psychoanalytic process, it seems that those who are called upon to make judgments are utilizing subjective criteria based upon their own convictions and drawn from their own clinical and educational experiences. While this may suffice in many circumstances, it is bound to fall short in those more difficult, questionable, or controversial situations where we would most like to have reliable and universally accepted standards to apply.

In Weinshel's (1984) scholarly and fascinating presentation, "Some Observations on the Psychoanalytic Process," which gave the initial impetus to my own interest in this topic, the historical basis of the concept of process in psychoanalysis is documented. He quotes at length from Freud's "On the Beginning of Treatment" (1913), and the passage in question bears repetition here. In speaking of the patient's desire to limit the scope of analytic inquiry, Freud says:

> The analyst . . . cannot determine beforehand what result he will effect. He *sets in motion a process* (ital. mine) that of the resolving of the existing repressions. He can supervise this process, further it, remove obstacles in its way, and he can undoubtedly vitiate most of it. But on the whole, once begun, it goes its own way and does not allow either the direction it takes or the order in which it picks up its points to be prescribed for it. [p. 130]

Weinshel is aware that this was a reflection of Freud's theory, at the time it was written, of the mechanism of therapeutic action of psychoanalysis, but he argues that with only minor evolutionary modifications the thrust of Freud's view remains applicable today. I will return to the specifics of Weinshel's position, but my point at present is to underline that the clinical observations that led Freud to characterize psychoanalysis as a process are indeed quite familiar ones, still encountered by present-day analysts of all persuasions. We generally acknowledge that the rate at which each analysis proceeds, the directions it takes, and how far it may go are by and large unpredictable; certainly they are not controllable by the analyst. Our ability to understand and communicate what we observe to our patients is only one variable; certain qualities within each patient, which still defy our explicatory powers, seem to be determinants that contribute to the course and outcome of the analysis in each case. I believe that these as yet mysterious factors that shape and limit analysands' capacities to remember, reveal, experience, comprehend, integrate, and ultimately utilize the data of which their analyses consist are both a challenge and a threat to analysts' sense of comprehension and mastery of our still young science. That which is outside the limits of understanding has always been ripe ground for magical explanations, in rational man as it is in the most primitive and superstitious. I think that the invocation of a quasi-mystical "process" concept in connection with the *terra incognita* of psychoanalysis is an example of that tendency. Perhaps that is one important reason why a theoretical term that enjoys rather broad currency has all the same remained so ill defined and unclear.

In this paper I try to demonstrate the diversity of approaches in employment of the concept of a psychoanalytic process, though for reasons that will become obvious, I cannot attempt to be comprehensive on that score. I will also point out the variety of situations in which the term is likely to be invoked in an evaluative sense. I hope that the difficulties inherent in its effective utilization will thereby be highlighted. It is not my intention to offer a clarified conception, but to help prepare the way for a more systematic effort to do so. Because the idea of a psychoanalytic process articulates with some of the most interesting and puzzling aspects of clinical theory—the mechanism of therapeutic action, the nature of resistances, working through, and the resolution of the transference, to name just a few—it remains a problem of compelling fascination. On the other hand, because of the limitations in its current usefulness, a consideration of its problematic aspects brings us up against a number of extremely important issues in everyday clinical practice, and I hope to indicate some of them in the course of my discussion.

I will begin by enumerating the problems of assessment in connection with which the concept of a psychoanalytic process is likely to arise. I do so because the frames of reference that give rise to the notion of process are so different that an organized critique of each in respect to problems of utility is impractical. Since I will therefore interweave my discussions of their limitations as I go along, I think an overview of the areas involved will be a useful point of departure and will make what I have in mind to do somewhat easier to follow.

There are three main headings under which problems in the assessment of the psychoanalytic process can be grouped, though some overlapping is inevitable. One concerns variations in what might be regarded as standard technique; a second is related to consequences of what Stone (1954) felicitously called the widening scope of psychoanalysis; and the third deals with clinical evaluations of proposed major alterations of theory and technique. In respect to the first area, my experience in postgraduate seminars on technique has given ample evidence of the frequency with which questions about the nature of the psychoanalytic process arise among colleagues, even when they share compatible theoretical orientations. Diffrent interpretations of what constitutes standard technique lead at times to lively discussions of their impact on the psychoanalytic process. Still more often, evaluation of technique and the psychoanalytic process arises as an educational issue. Supervision of candidates' efforts to learn to do analysis, measurement of student progression, and consideration of applicants for graduation and later certification are all situations in which the criteria of psychoanalytic process may be invoked by those charged with the responsibility to make judgments of the adequacy of others' work.

The second area of concern has arisen as a consequence of analysts' efforts to treat more troubled, and hence more difficult, patients psychoanalytically. Work with patients suffering from perversions or very severe character pathology, so-called borderlines, and the like frequently leads to questions about the nature of the psychoanalytic process. This is certainly the case when the practitioner employs intentional modifications of accepted technique; the question then arises whether the modifications result in a modified analysis or in something different from analysis. However, in clinical discussions similar questions may arise when there are long periods in treatment during which the analysand behaves far differently from the way ideally cooperative patients do in the analytic situation. This may be the case whether concurrent improvement in the patient's life circumstances and symptomatology is evident or not.

Finally, questions about the nature of the psychoanalytic process come up when certain colleagues espouse as advances in psychoanalysis major alterations of theory and technique that are greeted with skepticism by other analysts. A recent example is the advocacy of Self Psychology. Those analysts who have led in its elaboration maintain that this is a developmental step in the evolution of analytic technique, not a departure from it. Other colleagues dispute this claim, and many regard the practice of technique of analysis as described by the self psychologists as an abandonment of the fundamentals that characterize an analytic process as they understand its nature, despite the assertions of its practitioners.

Weinshel's (1984) approach to clarifying the concept of the psychoanalytic process hews most closely to Freud's original usage. He has attempted to adapt Freud's 1913 description of analysis as a process of resolving repressions to the subsequent developments in analytic theory. Weinshel said he thinks of psychoanalytic process more as:

> . . . the whole idea of a 'dynamic unconscious' and the work that needs to be carried out in order to deal with those forces which maintain the repressions, — all the mechanisms of defense and rsstance, not just the specific mechanism of repression. I will emphasize those external observables, the resistances, which from many sources become the obstacles to that work . . . [p. 67].

He makes it clear that his conception is of an interactive process between analyst and analysand, and something that takes place only within the patient. Impingements on their analytic task are reflected in what we call resistances: "That resistance together with its successful negotiation

by the analyst (most often by interpretation) is the clinical unit of the psychoanalytic process" (p. 69).

Weinshel (1984) also follows Freud's dictum that the transference can
become a significant resistance to analysis, but he does distinguisht he
two concepts to some degree:

> It is a futile question to argue which is most crucial to the analysis, the proc-
> ess or the transference; both are obviously vital. I see them as phenomena
> on somewhat different levels of conceptualization. The process-resistance
> is closely connected to the energic-biologic-quantitative postulates of our
> science; the transference and its vicissitudes become the principle (al-
> though not the only) vehicle by which we can observe, study and deal with
> the resistances [p. 72].

It can be seen that Weinshel has integrated the change in theory and
technique that shifted emphasis to the analysis of the ego, in particular its
defensive capacities, with Freud's original prestructural conceptualization. The psychoanalytic process, according to Weinshel, is characterized by the cyclic emergence and reduction of resistances to analysis, whatever form these may take and in whatever context they appear.
He contrasts this aspect of the analytic work, the repetitive, perhaps inconspicuous, unglamorous encounters with resistance patterns, with the
often more dramatic, highly satisfying moments of revelation, and the
synthesis and insight that presumably are made possible by it.

This appraoch concentrates on only one portion of the various activities constituting a psychoanalysis, albeit one all analysts acknowledge to
be of critical significance, and designates it as the "process" element of
psychoanalysis. Weinshel makes no suggestion that attention to the manifestations of resistance is unique to psychoanalysis, nor that it is the only
feature that distinguishes a true analysis from other therapies. Neither
does he attempt to suggest how this limited definition of the process concept can be applied to the problems of evaluation with which we are concerned, although it is clear, and I presume uncontroversial, that any therapy which did not address itself to the phenomena of resistance would
not deserve to be designated as psychoanalysis. Because of these limitations and because his circumscribed definition, despite its historical
roots, is not the one widely employed today, it does not in its present form
serve as a basis for resolving the practical questions to which we must pay
attention.

Greenacre (1968) noted that the emergence in the literature of the concept of a psychoanalytic process takes the form of scattered references in
a number of papers on theory, technique, and clinical findings. She did
not essay a systematic approach of her own, but she drew an analogy be-

tween the psychoanalytic process and the reinstatement of maturation, or, as she phrased it, a "recreative growth process" (p. 213). She observed that E. Kris (1956) had emphasized the freeing of countercathectic energies to participate in integrative reorganizations. However, as I have noted, Kris used the term process only in its more general sense, that is, to describe change over a period of time, and not in a more limited specified psychoanalytic sense.

Greenacre also observed that process and procedure are to some degree inextricable from one another. This helps to account for the variety of contexts in which the term is employed in the literature. A survey is therefore likely to be discouraging to one who seeks uniformity, because the term psychoanalytic process will be seen to be intimately linked with each worker's understanding of what constitutes the essential features of psychoanalysis from a philosophical, theoretical, and/or technical standpoint. These varied stances may or may not have elements in common, but they certainly incorporate competing, or at least different emphases, no one of which has gained universal acceptance among the larger community of psychoanalysts. At any rate, none as yet may be said to constitute *the* recognized standard for evaluating the psychoanalytic process in practical applications.

For instance, Weinshel (1984) cites with admiration Bernfeld's (1941) largely overlooked ideas, which emphasize psychoanalysis as a process of communication of secrets that is regularly interrupted by obstacles to their free revelation. These obstacles are equivalent to what Weinshel described more conventionally as resistances, and Bernfeld, like Weinshel, concentrated on the analyst's task in helping to overcome these recurrent obstacles to revelation. A comparable approach is embodied in A. Kris' (1982) work in which he elevates the phenomenon of free association to a place of central theoretical and technical significance. According to A. Kris, the analyst should be primarily a moderator and facilitator of the analysand's capacity to engage in free association.

Abrams (1980) focuses on the appearance of all four of what he regards as essential categories of resistance appearing in traditional analyses. These are characterological resistances, resistances to the transference, resistances to experiencing the infantile antecedents to the transference, and resistances to their resolution.

Gill (1982) employs the term analytic process only incidentally in his advocacy of a specific unique theoretical and technical stance. In contrast to Weinshel, he holds that all resistance has a specific transference meaning; and, believing that the transference is the sole locus for effective analytic interchange, he maintains that attention should constantly be directed to it. Gray (1973, 1982), working independently, also arrived at a similar viewpoint about the advisability of concentrating on the transference and on analysands' resistances to its elaboration, although he differs with Gill in other important respects.

Schafer's (1983) general description of the psychoanalytic process reflects his preference for a hermeneutic, as opposed to a positivist, natural science view of psychoanalysis and also incorporates some specific technical modifications he regards as useful, although the actual procedures involved in conducting analysis differ little if at all from those operations familiar to us in conventionally described analysis, if I read him correctly.

As can be seen, such generalized conceptual approaches do not pretend to provide yardsticks for evaluating whether a given treatment situation is to be regarded as a valid psychoanalysis or not except in the broadest terms. These examples are either too general in form to be used for more critical evaluations or are too idiosyncratic in one dimension or another to command the degree of acceptance a widely applicable standard must have.

If these efforts to formulate the psychoanalytic process do not serve as a pragmatic basis for its evaluation, what can be said about how evaluation has been practiced up to now? Most analysts who use the term psychoanalytic process do not subscribe to the unique and limited positions described above, but instead apparently rely on their own subjectively held views in formulating criteria. This is not to imply that there is no agreement among us. We can with relative ease construct a model of what occurs phenomenologically during a "good" analysis with a "good" patient that would evoke recognition from most practitioners. The following list of features, not meant to be definitive, would probably be a representative description: a more or less sustained effort to speak freely, audibly, and comprehensibly; a developing ability to reveal aspects of intimate life and thought, including fantasies; the willingness and ability to consider seriously the interventions of the analyst, even if they were initially unwelcome; the evolution of a commitment to understanding the meaning of one's mental functioning and behavior; a growing emotional investment in the analyst and in the analytic undertaking, which will be reflected in the increasing importance of and eventual expression of transference wishes and fantasies; and a progressive unfolding of new material in the forms of emerging memories and other mental contents. All these are familiar to every analyst as qualities of analyzable patients and of the productive analyses in which they engage.

An analogous catalogue of the behavior of analysts engaged in hypothetical "good" analyses would not be more difficult to create. However such descriptions would obviously be of little value in defining the more elusive qualities of the process, nor would they help us much with the more interesting questions of evaluation. These so-called good analyses comprise the minority, not the majority, of most analysts' caseloads, and this seems to hold true at all levels of experience from candidates to the most senior practitioners. We also know that even the "good" patients in "good" analyses may be more deceptive to evaluate properly than is sometimes thought, as Stein's paper on "The Unobjectionable Part of the Transference" (1981) so ably demonstrated.

What is more, successful analyses do take place with patients whose psychology precludes or at least limits their ability to act like the model analysand described above. I have in mind those patients with important conflicts concerning submission to authority, those with a powerful tendency towards enactment, those hyperconcerned with self-control, and those who cling to a realistic assessment of the analyst and his role in order to suppress the experience of emotionally laden transference wishes and fantasies. All these are examples of common variants in the psychoanalytic spectrum of patients with whom productive analytic work takes place despite their inability at the outset, or perhaps even much later in treatment (if ever), to fit the image of the ideal analysand.

When analysts use the term psychoanalytic process in any of the clinical contexts I have mentioned, they must have in mind some model of psychoanalysis to which they compare the material they are judging. Most analysts are not devoted to one specific, limited theoretical position; therefore, a less rigorously considered stance towards conceptualizing the psychoanalytic process must be what they use. The elements of it most frequently mentioned in discussions in which I have participated are the following: (a) the importance, if not the exclusive role, of the transference; (b) the necessity for attention to the analysis of resistance, or defenses, however this may be expressed; (c) some consideration of the need for the analyst's dedication to self-observing or self-analytic activity, as essential to his proper participation in the two-person nature of the analytic process; and (d) agreement that the appropriate stance for the analyst to maintain should embody the two fundamental principles of (1) nonjudgmental neutrality towards the analysand's productions and (2) abstinence, although just how much of the latter and under what circumstances might be grounds for debate. Like the positions of the authors mentioned, these broadly stated propositions do not address the quantitative variations in patients' appearance and functioning during analysis that strain our judgment about the nature of the psychoanalytic process most severely. All analysts accept in principle that every analysand regularly fails to verbalize certain conscious thoughts and feelings as one form of disturbance of free association. Attention to the nature and meaning of this phenomenon is an essential part of the analytic work; indeed in some of the schemata described earlier it may be the major part of it. But what of the patients in whom this is a dominant and persistent aspect of their response to the analytic situation? At what point of frequency or duration does this self-editorial behavior lead to the judgment that analysis is no longer a viable undertaking? If it continues as a clinical problem while nevertheless an increasing capacity to reveal significant mental contents is in evidence, would some analysts persist in analyzing, even though other colleagues on hearing of such a case, would conclude that the enterprise does not constitute a valid psychoanalytic process? Will still other analysts decide that such a patient requires alterations in technique — increased confrontation, or support, or attention to developmental deficits, or other activities of a special kind on the part of the analyst? And would different analysts then disagree about the consequences of such alterations, as far as the psychoanalytic process is concerned? As long ago as 1961, an entire issue of the *Journal of the American Psychoanalytic Association* was devoted to the problem of the silent patient (vol. 9, no. 1). This familiar example of a technical problem that may tax our judgment of the analytic process demonstrates the limitations of generalized formulations, particularly those which rest heavily on descriptions of the patient's behavior, in assessing individual analyses of this kind of patient or of those with comparable trouble in the analytic situation.

Attempting to define the analytic process by concentrating on the activities of the analyst appears at first glance to be somewhat more straightforward. Brenner, in *Psychoanalytic Technique and Psychic Conflict* (1976) offers a clear perspective. His deceptively simple prescription is that the analyst should adopt an analytic attitude towards all of the analysand's verbal productions and behavior in the analytic situation, and then should analyze what is observed. The second part of this formula entails, first, the attempt to understand the data of observation according to the analyst's view of mental functioning, and then communicating this understanding to the patient, guided by the dictates of tact and timing and the patient's capacity to utilize what the analyst has to say.[1] This is a limiting prescription in that activities other than analyzing are deemed inappropriate to the analyst's proper role. This is not to suggest that an increase in the patient's self-knowledge is the only consequence of the analyst's communications to him. Each patient feels many other effects as well; praise, blame, encouragement, guidance, reward, education, control, and rejection are among the multitude of experienced impacts common in each

---

[1] For a full exposition of Brenner's ideas of what constitues an analytic attitude, the tasks of the analyst and the method of interpreting, see Brenner (1976) chapters 1 and 2, pp. 8–58.

analysis. (Brenner, 1976, p. 49). These and similar reactions are not the intended result of the analyst's activity but are the inevitable consequence of the patient's psychological predispositions, influenced by his unconsciously determined relationship to the analyst and the analysis. As such, they are – or should be – themselves subject to analysis. For an analyst intentionally to guide the patient's conduct of life, or to educate him (except in the sense of helping him learn about his own psychology) or to praise, console, criticize, or otherwise control the patient is, according to Brenner, a departure from the analyst's proper domain.

Agreement in principle with this formulation is surely widespread among analysts. Some colleagues might, however, argue that less typical cases do require different handling. More explicit support, aid in testing reality, prohibition of dangerous activities, or intervention in critical family situations may be deemed necessary by some analysts, particularly in work with sicker patients. Even if this is not the case, differences exist even among analysts of quite similar general views, in interpretation of just how far the principles of analytic functioning described by Brenner should be carried. The technical handling of the analyst's cancellation of appointments because of illness or personal needs is an example. Differences of opinion about the advisability of explaining to patients, as opposed to maintaining a strictly analytic stance towards the patient's responses, are common. (see Dewald, 1982, and Abend, 1982, for a fuller discussion).

Although such differences about the application of technique may be regarded as slight variants, with only minimal impact on the analytic process in most cases, a far more important source of potential disagreement about the analyst's activity rests in the different ways analysts understand their patients' mental functioning from the observations made in the analytic situation. Competing theories among us lead to different interpretations of the data obtained in the consulting room and consequently to substantively different kinds of communication to the patient. Schafer (1983) addressed this problem most convincingly (pp. 39–43). Finally, it should be added that departures from the analyst's own analytic ideal are as much an everyday occurrence with experienced analysts as they are with beginners. The analyst's personality and fluctuating mental state contribute to minor, and sometimes not so minor, unintended distortions of his neutrality and of his application of the principle of abstinence. These may collectively be regarded as lapses of technique, whether or not one also chooses to call all such events manifestations of countertransference.

In short, in spite of what might seem self-evident and uncontroversial about any description of the proper behavior of the analyst, there are significant variations among us in how analyses are conducted. Questions about the influence of those differences on the nature of the psychoanalytic process frequently do come up, and the answers given depend very much on how each analyst regards the particular variations present in any given situation. Let us imagine a case presentation in which certain material is understood as indicative of a self-object transference and handled accordingly. Analysts who share the presenter's convictions about the validity of a self-psychological approach will evaluate the material from one standpoint, whereas those who do not will take a sharply different stance. They might, for instance, think of the patient's productions as illustrating a narcissistic resistance that was improperly understood and consequently mishandled, with serious results as far as the analytic process is concerned. One could just as easily construct this example in reverse order, and the corollary difference of opinion about the analyst's work would arise. It should be noted that the analysts who might disagree so categorically with one another would nevertheless each assert that they have scrupulously followed the principles of analytic conduct. Their critics would vigorously contend that because the other's understanding of mental functioning was faulty, analytic technique was incorrect and the analytic process distorted.

In this example, where competing theories of mental functioning are involved, even if one grants the possibility that all other aspects of analytic conduct on the part of both patient and analyst are in place, the single factor of how the material is understood is crucial to the evaluation of the psychoanalytic process. If the observer's understanding of the material differs substantially from that of the presenter, he may at best conclude that a faulty analytic process was involved, at worst that it was not an analytic process at all, but merely a psychotherapeutic one instead. This distinction, however graciously phrased, has decidedly pejorative intent. Often the judgment is diplomatically modulated in discussions with those who espouse the differing views, but baldly stated to like-minded colleagues.

Evaluation of the psychoanalytic process based on the way clinical material is understood is characteristic of, but not confined to, situations where competing theroies of mental functioning are involved. The history of psychoanalysis is full of examples, from the controversies that split the psychoanalytic community such as those initiated by Adler, Jung, Horney, and Thompson, to those which in spite of intense advocacy by opposing participants were somehow contained as ongoing debates within the existing psychoanalytic organization. Kleinian theory and the ideas of Alexander, of Rado, and now of Kohut and his followers are instances where the latter course has prevailed.

Less explicitly delineated differences in theoretical convictions also lead to alternative ways of understanding clinical data, which may in turn affect the resulting psychoanalytic process. In the analysis of more disturbed patients, in comparison with that of the typical neurotic analysand, it matters whether or not one thinks that substantively different conflicts are crucial. It also makes a difference if the analyst believes that different mechanisms of symptom formation are at work, or that developmental deficits, in addition to intrapsychic conflicts, contribute to the clinical picture. These beliefs will influence how the patient's productions are understood and interpreted. What one analyst hears as expressive of fragmentation, annihilation anxiety, fears of dissolution, of splitting or of ego deficit, another sees as defensively distorted derivatives, as manifest content of other unconscious sources of anxiety, as ego functions altered by the impact of conflict. Their views of the analytic task will vary accordingly, and their judgment of the analytic process resulting from alternative understandings will reflect these differences. To illustrate, analysts who absolutely agree on the centrality of transference and resistance may nevertheless not agree that certain clinical material reflecting faulty reality testing by the patient should be approached as expressive of transference fantasies, or of resistance, if they believe it reflects a developmental deficit. Theoretical differences of this order are likely to exist even among members of the same institute faculty and consequently affect classroom teaching, supervision, and the conduct of training analyses. Controversy about evaluating candidates' understanding of the psychoanalytic process may at times reflect such differences within the faculty.

Questions of whether the observing analyst agrees with the understanding of clinical material demonstrated by a student or colleague arise in a host of collaborative situations. These stem from idiosyncratic or personal differences in sensitivity to the material and, if they seem to be of great significance in a given case, may lead the critical analyst to conclude that a proper analytic process has not taken place. This judgment is much more likely to supervene if the presenting analyst describes behaving in some fashion that is inconsistent with the listener's own standards of acceptable technique. This is not the case with minor differences such as may arise about answering questions, making referrals upon request, dealing with absences or cancellations, and the like. However, if a presenter describes giving an ultimatum to an analysand to desist from some behavior, alcohol or other drug abuse for example, as a condition for remaining in analysis, debates about the effect of such an ultimatum on the psychoanalytic process are likely to spring up. It will not satisfy questioners' doubts that the analyst claims to have reached the conclusion that no viable analysis was possible if the drug abuse persisted, nor that he adds that he paid careful attention to his patient's reaction to the stricture. A critical analyst will conclude that the analytic process was at the least skewed, if not invalidated altogether, by the analyst's non-analytic behavior.

Issues of this sort seem to come up most frequently when major resistances persist despite attempts to modify them by interpretation. By major resistances I mean those types of symptomatic behavior which so handicap the activities of analysis as to appear to constitute insuperable obstacles to the work; silence, extreme lateness or frequent absences, drug usage of various kinds, and lying or deliberate concealment of important data are varieties of this problem. Such clinical situations lead some analysts to consider adopting modifications of technique; others somehow find themselves behaving in ways which depart from their own views of optimal technique, such as making implicit or explicit confrontations that may in effect constitute subtle threats to abandon the analysis unless change occurs. In either case other analysts considering reports of cases like these will question the nature of the resultant analytic process if the reporting analyst's behavior has wandered too far from the observer's criteria for appropriate analytic activity.

Naturally, more pronounced departures from the consensually accepted norm, such as sharply altering the frequency or duration of sessions or covert interference in the management of patients' lives, will undoubtedly lead most other analysts to conclude that the analytic process as they understand it has been invalidated thereby. Similarly, flagrant directive, educational, or exploitive interactions with patients would produce the same judgment, but that point need not be belabored.

I would like to take up in more depth those problems which surface when patients' behavior varies significantly from the model of the "good" analysand and the analyst continues to behave consistently in an analytically neutral and appropriate manner. Let us assume for the purpose of pursuing this question that we all agree on what is meant by the analyst's practicing of acceptable technique, that the patient maintains a firm conscious commitment to the analysis, and that the problematic behavior does not fall into the previously described category of major resistances that all but preclude productive analysis. Patients in the category I now have in mind whom I have treated or heard discussed by colleagues include some who never, or almot never, recall or report dreams; who regularly miss a session or two when difficult material surfaces, or when strong and disturbing reactions to interventions occur; who appear so to disregard the meaning of words that they can say anything that occurs to them, but without believing it for a moment, or who contradict themselves regularly without discomfort; who have difficulty curtailing their constant symptomatic enactments, and who may in addition fail to see the value and necessity of examining these behaviors analytically; who utilize the analytic hour primarily to recount the events and issues of their current lives, punctuated by only the briefest dips into the past or their transference reactions; who persist in a more-or-less controlled and structured, if not edited, version of their thoughts and feelings; and who quickly absorb the self-observing function and utilize it to try unconsciously to keep the analyst a passive observer of their self-analyzing conduct.

These characterizations merely indicate a prominent, easily recognizable clinical feature of these difficult cases, which of course will have many other interrelated dimensions of their psychopathology and of their responses to the analytic situation. I assume further that these problematic behaviors will have been the subject of regular, sustained analytic attention and thus that much of what has determined the phenomena in question will have become clarified in the course of their analyses. Nevertheless, these powerful resistances often may continue in evidence, perhaps for years, while the analytic endeavor goes on. Some able and experienced colleagues might argue that better technique would have addressed these complex resistances more successfully; others would agree that the behaviors in question were deeply entrenched aspects of the individuals' pathology, which could not have been pursued more vigorously without running the risk of distorting the analytic process through covert nonanalytic pressure, or perhaps of destroying it altogether.

If such patients show gradual changes in their mental functioning in the analytic situation, such as improving ability to acknowledge previously intolerably threatening mental contents, and if they also reveal evidence of better functioning in their lives outside analysis, their analysts are likely to persist in working with them analytically. Are these cases examples of what might be called a limited analytic gain, or are they examples of therapeutic benefits that result from something other than a true psychoanalytic process? All analysts profess to recognize that the achievements of successful analysis are not absolute; that even such familiar shibboleths as the resolution of the transference neurosis in the best of cases refer to relative degrees of change; and that perfectibility, as Weinshel (1984) called it, is a myth that analysts as well as analysands must guard against. In the more difficult cases like those I have just described, troublesome questions about the identifying characteristics of a true psychoanalytic process are quite likely to arise and thus highlight the potential inadequacy of our criteria, or at any rate the subjectivity with which they are employed. It is of more than passing interest that precisely such problem cases are the ones which participants in seminars and study groups on technique, if an atmosphere of mutual trust exists, most wish to present to one another.

Two other related, interesting, and relatively neglected problems to which difficult or atypical analytic presentations like these give rise are addressed in this concluding section of this paper. The first arises when one attributes the clinical improvement in certain cases to factors other than a true psychoanalytic process. How, then, do we as analysts formulate what led to the improvement, that is, the presumed psychotherapeutic, but not psychoanalytic effect? The second problem comes up when difficult, atypical cases whom one has attempted to analyze do not show signs of improvement in or out of the analytic situation. What are the criteria experienced analysts use to arrive at the judgment that a true analytic process is impossible to achieve and the effort should be abandoned?

In respect to the first problem, if therapeutic gains are attributed to the analytic situation but not to successful analytic work, we often speak of transference cures. This term is not employed here in the sense that Freud intended it in the papers on technique (1913). He meant by it something quite different, that is, an immediate disappearance of symptoms under the initial influence of the relationship to the analyst. He added that the problems would soon reappear in the context of the transference, where they would have to be worked through definitively; the transference "cure" he described was ephemeral and deceptive.

Our use of the term transference cure means something else altogether. We mean that a powerful beneficial impact on the patient's psychological functioning comes about as a result of the unconscious significance of the relationship to the analyst in the mind of the patient. We cannot go further here without noting that the theory of the method of therapeutic action, of working through, and of structural change to which a given analyst subscribes will play a role in whatever explanation is offered for how such a transference cure may work. Brenner's (1982) formulation that analysis leads to alterations in crucial compromise formations, which then promote more satisfactory psychological functioning, can be extended, as Boesky (1983) demonstrated, to account for other kinds of therapeutic change as well. Boesky cited intentional psychotherapeutic manipulation of the transference and spontaneous cures as examples of this application of Brenner's conceptualization. Our formulation of transference cures can be addressed in this way as well. We could then say that for some patients, the unconscious meaning of being in analysis and of the relationship to the analyst produces meaningful alterations in certain compromise formations involved in their disturbed functioning, which in turn leads to clinical improvement. The presumption is that it is the significance of the relationship alone that is beneficial, and not an understanding of its meaning, nor changes in mental abilities derived from analytic work on the vicissitudes of the relationship.

The case of attributing benefit to a transference cure is most persuasive when an outside observer believes that a critical transference issue was never correctly understood by the analyst and that hence it persisted unanalyzed. This would constitute a failure of analytic technique and is different from the situations I have in mind. Let us assume that the analyst has correctly identified the unconscious meanings of the analytic relationship and interpreted them ably to the analysand. This is of course exactly what we mean by analyzing the transference, *the* essential feature of all successful analyses. What is it that takes place when this analytic activity goes on and patients show clinical improvement, yet some persistence of their atypical behavior in analysis leads other analysts, or even the treating analyst, to conclude that there is not a true analytic process? How do we determine that a patient's desire for analysis, and his functioning as an analysand, is undertaken or maintained primarily to obtain an unconsciously gratifying relationship, rather than to gain an understanding of it and of himself (even though the patient remains unaware of this imbalance)? Every workable analysis also comprises this dichotomy of aim, as Freud recognized, and the negotiation of their incongruencies is an essential feature of the analysis of the transference.

Either the persistence of unusual resistance patterns completely hides from the analyst's view important aspects of the transference, which can thus never be adequately addressed, or we are forced to a less than fully satisfactory, though possibly correct, quantitative explanation. It seems that in the latter case we ought to extend our notion of relative analyzability rather than speak of transference cures in an invalid psychoanalytic process. It would help us if we could spell out more clearly just what features lead analysts to decide that a given case represents a transference cure of this kind, rather than a limited, though beneficial analysis. The more marginal the case, the more difficult the judgment; and in my opinion, this also points to the continuing elusiveness of the goal of identifying and defining the nature of the resistance to analytic change, a problem which has puzzled analysts since Freud's day and which he addressed in "Analysis Terminable and Interminable" (1937).

Transference cure is not the only way to account for symptomatic changes that take place in an analytic setting as a result of nonanalytic factors. There are also ways of influencing analysands' behavior that fall under the rubric of suggestion, and those which result from identification. Although overt suggestion is unequivocally regarded as a departure from analytic technique, covert forms of conveying values and goals that may influence the patient to conform, or rebel, undoubtedly are a pitfall in analysis and may be hard to evaluate. Novey (1966) pointed out that the selection of material for analytic attention may tacitly indicte the analyst's superego valuations, and he cautioned analysts to be alert for that possibility. Leavy (1983) and Isay (1983) each independently suggested that the analyst who undertakes the analysis of homosexual patients with the view that this form of sexual preference is pathological thereby presents an analytic stance that may influence the patient's views and behavior; such influence is a nonanalytic form of pressure.

The problem of whether identification with aspects of the analyst is inevitable, and whether it is to be regarded as a useful aspect of successful analysis (Sterba, 1934) or a contaminant of it, is equally difficult to sort out. I will not pursue it here as it is a familiar issue in our clinical theory. I would merely underline my view that the controversial aspects of inadvertant suggestion and identifications as change-inducing factors reinforce the difficulty of establishing absolute criteria by which the validity of an analytic process can be judged.

This brings me to the final problem I wish to address: the decision to terminate the analysis of a patient who apparently wishes to continue. To speak of relative analyzability is not to suggest that the effort is worthwhile in all cases. Our evaluations of prospective cases and our recommendations for their treatment are based on our predictions of whether an analysis promises benefits to the individual concerned commensurate with the effort. Whether because we wrongly predict they are analyzable or because we decide to try analysis despite reservations about the outcome, certain cases unfold in ways that cause us to reevaluate the effectiveness of the analysis. It is well known that particularly in work with sicker patients, doubts and discouragement arise in the minds of analysts, which should not lead to breaking off the analytic treatment. These doubts may be evoked by many factors: slow progress, periods of apparent stalemate in the transference, aspects of the patient's psychology unconsciously aimed to produce such feelings, the analyst's own ever present inner resistances to understanding certain aspects of his own as well as the patient's unconscious conflicts. We need patience to do analysis properly, and consultation with colleagues when doubts persist for longer than usual often helps to restore an appropriately hopeful analytic perspective.

But what of the situations where an analyst, however reluctantly or uncertainly, reaches the conclusion that further analytic effort is not worthwhile for himself and his patient? I know of no systematic study of the factors involved in those judgments. Analysts obviously rely on their own

clinical experience and perhaps on consultation with colleagues to resolve their doubts. Some of the factors cited by analysts I have asked
about this problem include: a loss of the sense of learning new things
about the patient (Reiser, 1983, personal communication); persistence of
qualities of mental functioning in a patient that are incompatible with productive analysis, such as the capacity to engage in fantasy (Abrams, 1983,
personal communication); repetitious handling of certain conflictual material in analysis in stereotypic, unchanging ways despite analytic attention to these patterns (Brenner, 1983, personal communication); and the
aforementioned one of concluding that the activity of analyzing has become a way of holding on to the analyst for the unconscious gratification
obtained from the relationship. No doubt reflection would bring to mind
other reasons for the decision to stop in other analysts; I mean here to be
illustrative rather than comprehensive.

It is obvious that all these criteria are in some measure subjective ones,
and certain of them may be said to be quantitative at that. Absent more
clearcut agreement among us, these considerations of the determination
of unanalyzability once more bespeak the difficulties of evaluating the
psychoanalytic process.

What can be said in summary of my comments on the nature of the analytic process and the problems of evaluating it in one's own and others'
work? First, that "process" is a widely used but nevertheless ill-defined
concept, even though its origin can be traced to Freud's early papers on
technique. Next, that when discussing the effects of variations in technique or the peculiarities of presentation in analysis that characterize patients with major resistances or other serious manifestations of severe pathology, on the effects on analytic treatment of modifications of clinical
theory put forth by colleagues from time to time, analysts may invoke the
term analytic process while describing their evaluations of the treatments
conducted by themselves and others. Such discussions imply that true
and valid psychoanalytic processes can be distinguished from therapeutic processes of a different sort, though not necessarily in a given instance
by the practitioner whose work is under discussion. The criteria by means
of which the distinction is to be drawn are not usually made explicit. The
term psychoanalytic process is employed by many different analysts in
contexts that reflect a significant variety of philosophical, theoretical and
technical precepts by which each believes analysis is best defined and
practiced. Generalized descriptions of psychoanalysis do not provide
precise standards by which the analytic process in debatable clinical situations can be objectively judged.

The evaluation of the psychoanalytic process seems to be inextricably connected with how analysts understand clinical material. Thus it is inevitably subjective and is affected by the individual sensitivities of each practitioner, as well as by his theoretical convictions. Attempts to define valid psychoanalytic processes by concentrating on the behavior of the analyst are only marginally, if at all, less subjective, since technique is inseparable from analysts' understanding of clinical material and from the theories they espouse.

Cases in which acceptable technique is practiced and clinical improvement noted may nevertheless be evaluated by others as not genuine psychoanalytic processes. Accounting for the therapeutic gains in such cases leads to interesting issues that are rarely addressed, such as clarifyng the nature of transference cure and the roles of suggestion and identification as mutative forces in treatment. These in turn lead to weighing the matter of relative analyzability and quantitative or relative versus absolute criteria for analysis, which have not as yet been rigorously and consistently clarified by our theoreticians. Such fascinating problems as the nature of resistances, the meaning of working through, and the meaning of resolution of the transference are involved. Finally, the clinical bases by which the analyst decides to abandon the effort to analyze a difficult patient remains a largely unexplored issue related to the same unsolved problems concerning the nature of the psychoanalytic process.

REFERENCES

Abend, S. M. (1982), Serious illness in the analyst: Countertransference considerations. *J. Amer. Psychoanal. Assn.*, 30:365–379.

Abrams, S. (1980), The Silent Process. Unpublished Manuscript.

Bernfeld, S. (1941), The facts of observation in psychoanalysis. *J. Psychol.*, 12:289–305.

Brenner, C. (1976), *Psychoanalytic Technique and Psychic Conflict.* New York: International Universities Press.

———— (1982), *The Mind in Conflict.* New York: International Universities Press.

Boesky, D. (1983, November), Discussion of Brenner's *The Mind in Conflict.* The New York Psychoanalytic Society.

Dewald, P. (1982), Serious illness in the analyst: Transference, countertransference, and reality responses. *J. Amer. Psychoanal. Assn.*, 30:347–363.

Freud, S. (1913), On beginning the treatment. *Standard Edition*, 12:123–144. London: Hogarth Press, 1958.

———— (1937), Analysis terminable and interminable. *Standard Edition*, 23:211–253. London: Hogarth Press, 1964.

Gill, M. M. (1982), *Analysis of Transference,* Vol. I. New York: International Universities Press.

Gray, P. (1973), Psychoanalytic technique and the ego's capacity for viewing intrapsychic activity. *J. Amer. Psychoanal. Assn.,* 21:474–494.

_____ (1982), "Developmental lag" in the evolution of technique for psycho-analysis of neurotic conflict. *J. Amer. Psychoanal. Assn.,* 30:621–655.

Greenacre, P. (1968), The psychoanalytic process, transference and acting out. *Internat. J. Psycho-Anal.,* 49:211–218.

Isay, R. (1983, December), On the analytic therapy of homosexual patients. Panel presentation at the midwinter meeting of the American Psychoanalytic Association.

Kris, A. (1982), *Free Association.* New Haven: Yale University Press.

Kris, E. (1956), On some vicissitudes of insight in psychoanalysis. *Internat. J. Psycho-Anal.,* 37:445–455.

Leavy, S. (1983, December), Male homosexuality: A reconsideration. Panel presentation at the midwinter meeting of the American Psychoanalytic Association.

Novey, S. (1966), The sense of reality and values of the analyst as a necessary factor in psychoanalysis. *Internat. J. Psycho-Anal.,* 47:492–501.

Schafer, R. (1983), *The Analytic Attitude.* New York: Basic Books.

Stein, M. (1981), The unobjectionable part of the transference. *J. Amer. Psychoanal. Assn.,* 19:869–892.

Sterba, R. (1934), The fate of the ego in analytic therapy. *Internat. J. Psycho-Anal.,* 15:117–126.

Stone, L. (1954), The widening scope of indications for psychoanalysis. *J. Amer. Psychol. Assn.,* 2:567–594.

Weinshel, E. (1984), Some observations on the psychoanalytic process. *Psychoanal. Quart.,* 53:63–92.

HAROLD P. BLUM

Countertransference: Concepts and Controversies[1]

Interest in the topic of countertransference occurs at an especially opportune time of parallel interest in the inner life of the analyst. I refer to the analyst at work in the psychoanalytic situation and to renewed interest in the analyzing instrument, the analyzing functions, the work ego, empathy, the formulation of interpretations. How does the analyst observe and infer, listen, learn, intervene? What is the analyst thinking and feeling during the analytic hour? What is his contribution to the analytic situation and process? There has been a noticable shift in recent years away from singular concentration on the intrapsychic processes of the patient and the patient's reponse to interpretation and other interventions to the thoughts, feelings, attitudes, and values of the analyst; the analyst's input and influence on the patient's associations; and the patient's overall adaptation to the analysis. Earlier psychoanalytic concerns about suggestion, education, manipulation of the patient, and, later, about the introduction of parameters have now focused on the personality of the analyst and the patient's reactions to it. The current interest in a two-person analytic field of forces and the analyst as participant-observer has many ramifications. The analyst is no longer a mythical mirror or completely objective observer. For some, who the analyst is becomes at least as important as what he does. In some quarters, attention to the real relationship and to the analyst's personality and influence has cast the transference of the patient in a new light. The analyst is not only seen as the classical object of

---

[1] Presented at the Regional Meeting of the New York Psychoanalytic Societies, Princeton, New Jersey, June 1984. Panelists: Drs. Jacob Arlow, Harold Blum, Charles Brenner, Martin Silverman.

transference but is so evocative and provocative of particular transference responses that the transference becomes more a response to the current situation than first and foremost a repetition of the infantile past. In a different direction, study of the analyst's own reactions and responses has intensified interest in that area of analyst reaction denoted by the term "countertransference." Countertransference is not an easily defined term, but it has classically dealt with impediments and interferences with the analyst's neutrality, empathy, and interpretations in the analytic process.

Freud introduced countertransference as a concept in 1910, when he had already formulated transference. Countertransference has also been relegated to lesser and later studies than have other aspects of the theory of psychoanalytic technique. It is not difficult to understand that beginning with Freud analysts would be reluctant to divulge their countertransference difficulties. I emphasize here the difficult aspects of countertransference in contrast to its beneficial uses, to which I shall return. It is difficult to do analysis, a very complex and intimate undertaking with many occupational hazards. Unlike other forms of medical and therapeutic endeavors, psychoanalysis involves much more than special knowledge, skill, and experience: It involves the personality of the analyst, his work ego and inner resources, his capacity for reversible regression and progressive reorganization and for maintaining neutrality and objectivity in the face of emotional storms. The analyst's exposure of his technique, of his technical difficulties or errors, is, in part, an exposure of his inner life, particularly of his own unresolved conflicts and problems. Attempts at open discussion of countertransference too often meet with an embarrassed silence. Both the analyst's discretion and his defenses account for the difficulty in obtaining clinical material illustrative of countertransference reactions. Anyone who has experienced and observed supervision knows the problems engendered by countertransference discussion. Yet it is from supervision that we can glean and discuss some outstanding examples of countertransference without presenting our own countertransferences, which may make us so uneasy. We may recognize the countertransference of colleagues in other situations such as reanalysis, training analysis, and the treatment of psychiatrists, not all of which are equally amenable to analytic neutrality, confidentiality, and comfort.

How the analyst handles the countertransference once it is recognized is another matter. The time-honored prescriptions have been to do more work in the training analysis (in the case of candidates); self-analysis; return to analysis (once recommended by Freud to be done every five years); and consultation. The difficulty with such conscious recommendations is that countertransference is not always fully recognized and once recognized, is not always fully accepted; and the response of the analyst to the awareness of the countertransference is highly variable. All the proposed solutions have their advantages and side effects. In the day-to-day work of psychoanalysis, we depend on self-analytic abilities to deal with countertransference issues. Analysts are vulnerable to all human frailties, to conflict and regression. Where self-analysis does not succeed in resolving countertransference, return to analysis or reanalysis may be indicated. The point I wish to stress here is that every analyst should have a capacity for self-analysis and that for the candidate, as distinguished from other patients, I would regard evidence of self-initiated progress in the analytic work and the manifestations of self-analytic initiatives as a requirement for termination. I myself do not expect the capacity for self-analysis of any group of patients except candidates; I think that, apart from analysts, most patients do not lead self-analytic lives. Moreover, our ordinary patients will not later be immersed in the analytic work that exposes them to stimulation, activation, and provocation of their own unconscious conflicts such as occurs in the daily life of the psychoanalyst.

The analytic countertransference may be defined as a counterreaction to the patient's transference, which is unconscious and indicative of the analyst's own unresolved intrapsychic conflicts. In defining the countertransference in essentially this form, Freud (1910) observed, "No psychoanalyst goes further than his own complexes and internal resistances permit; and we consequently require that he shall begin his activity with a self-analysis and continually carry it deeper while he is making his observations on his patients" (p. 145). There are many variations on the definition of the countertransference as counter to the particular patient's transference. A closely related concept involves the analyst's transferences, which are ready to attach themselves to a particular patient, his character or transferences, and are often activated by something within the patient that touches on the analyst's infantile unconscious conflicts. The analyst may have neurotic reactions to any aspect of the patient, not only to the transference.

Transference and countertransference are interwined transferential elements of the same analytic process, but it may be useful to distinguish, in theory at least, between the analyst's transferences to patients and his countertransferences to transferences. The distinction, which, seems and often is, impossible to make, may nevertheless be clinically useful, for instance, in an analyst's reaction to a pregnant patient because of her pregnancy. A transference reaction to the patient as a pregnant woman may not be identical to a countertransference reaction to her transference.

The term countertransference implicitly stresses what is evoked by the patient's transference, and in less precise definition, by the patient's psychopathology. The analyst may respond irrationally to a patient's presenting symptoms or to an aspect of the patient's history, for example, perverse tendencies. The patient's psychopathology is related to the analyst's countertransference but not necessarily to the analyst's use of the patient as a transference object. In this theoretical distinction, the analyst may also have a transference reaction to the patient at the point of referral before the analyst has a countertransference to the patient's analytic transference reactions.

The analyst's transferences may be displaced from other patients, as though the analyst were still consciously or unconsciously preoccupied with another patient. His own personal life may be associated with his vulnerability to countertransference reactions or the extension of his personal problems into his professional work. His own "agenda" may then interfere with the patient's free association, although the agenda is not necessarily directly evoked by the patient's psychopathology.

In analytic work, the analyst's countertransference and spontaneous transference to the patient tend to merge. Countertransference is based on the ubiquity of transference reactions (Brenner, 1982) and cannot be understood apart from the analytic transference. I do not believe, however, that the concept of countertransference can be usefully discarded as if it were just another species of transference. A circular process may occur, so that in the case of unanalyzed interfering countertransference reactions, the analyst has a countertransference to the patient's transference; and the patient, in turn, responds to the analyst's countertransference with the development of a so-called transference-countertransference, or unconscious transference-countertransference collusion. Some analytic stalemates, psychotherapy on the couch, and "wild analysis" suggest such bilateral neurotic enmeshment. The patient may, for example, masochistically adapt to persistent countertransference contempt. In extreme forms, the therapeutic relationship regresses to a pathological relationship and to a form of folie a deux.

Interestingly, many colleagues' reports of countertransference reactions suggest conscious awareness of the disturbance. The source of the disturbance in analytic function lies, at least temporarily, outside the analyst's awareness. The analyst may become aware of his countertransference in many ways, ranging from loss of attention and attunement, to symptoms, to inappropriate responses and interventions, parapraxes, fantasies, dreams, to violations of the framework with irregularities in the handling of time, schedule, and fees. The desire to help may be subverted by too much therapeutic zeal and rescue fantasies, or loss of therapeutic interest and concern, with boredom or subtle devaluation of the patient's efforts at mastery. Any aspect of the analytic relationship and analytic work may be compromised. It may be evident in silence or in speech with changes of pitch, pressure, syntax, and the like. Countertransference always involves some move by the analyst away from an analytic attitude and neutrality. Patients invariably have transference reactions to countertransference (Little, 1951; Gill, 1982) as well as to the analytic setting and the analyst's character, style, and interventions. It may be inferred that analogous reactions occur in life between any two people who have prolonged intimate contact, although the transferences of everyday experience are not analyzable.

It is certainly of importance whether countertransference occurs with a particular patient or with most or all patients; whether it is part of a general tendency or specific to a case with which the analyst finds himself in difficulty; whether it is acute or chronic; whether it is always present, like the transference; and whether it is symmetrical to the transference so that one might speak at times of the countertransference neurosis (Racker, 1968). To my mind, a countertransference neurosis would be such an extreme interference in the analytic work that analytic progress would be impossible. A. Reich (1960) wrote of permanent countertransference, which is doubtless related to the analyst's chronic neurotic symptoms and inhibitions and to character disorder. If the analyst is chronically angry with all his patients, is that angry analyst embroiled in countertransference? These reactions would not be counter to the transference as defined by Freud, but even here, close observation shows the nuances and variations on the theme with each case and how often the analyst's character disorder is interwoven with his transference and resistances toward his patients. The chronically angry analyst will be prone to acute and specific negative countertransference.

Before illustrating some of these problems of countertransference, I would like to indicate changes in the way some analysts define the term and utilize the concept. These analysts use a much broader concept of countertransference. In addition, some have a much more positive view of the contribution of countertransference to the patient's analysis, regarding it as useful, even indispensable. Sublimations of voyeurism and parental authority may enhance the analyst's professional gratifications in analytic work, but these aim-inhibited, sublimated countertransference contributions to analytic work are quite remote from the interference of countertransference seduction or dogmatic interpretation. (I doubt that countertransference is a prerequisite for analysis rather than an impediment and that, as A. Reich (1951) proposed, without it the necessary talent and interest are absent.)

Analysts who take the so-called totalistic, as opposed to the classical position (Kernberg, 1965), regard the countertransference as the total emotional reaction of the analyst to the patient. Going beyond conscious and unconscious reactions to the patient's transference, a reaction of the analyst that interferes with work with the patient may then be subsumed under countertransference. The boundaries between these different reactions may not always be easy to evaluate, but the totalistic reaction becomes quite diffuse and may confuse efforts to delineate the countertransference in terms of the analyst's narrower internal reactions to the patient's neurotic transferences and psychopathology. Definitions and concepts may be further complicated by confusing countertransference and diagnostic assessment, so that diagnosis and assessment of analyzability may depend to an unusual degree on countertransference reactions to the potential patient rather than on primary observation and evaluation.[1] There are, of course, countertransference reactions at the very inception of treatment, often seen with the student analyst and the low fee or clinic patient. Countertransference reactions to termination are common, for example, when the analyst also finds that old problems of separation and loss have resurfaced within himself.

The analyst's struggle to maintain neutrality appears related to controversies concerning the meaning of neutrality. For Freud (1914, p. 164), neutrality was maintained "through keeping the countertransference in check." Freud (1913) indicated that neutrality did not mean cold indifference or loss of spontaneity; he even recommended an attitude of "sympathetic understanding" (p. 140). Analysts have at times strayed from the neutrality recommended by Freud, and from contemporary "benevolent neutrality," in the direction of conveying positive interest and support. The anaclitic needs of the patient were to be met by a diatrophic attitude of the analyst (Gitelson, 1952); this, in turn, was to have a favorable effect in catalyzing the patient's capacity for development and for participation in the analytic process. In brief, a positive countertransference was advocated, and controversy immediately arose concerning whether the diatrophic attitude was really an abandonment of the analytic attitude and a substitution of preliminary supportive psychotherapy.

Two other controversies should be noted. The first concerns a point mentioned before—the beneficial use of countertransference to promote the analytic process. In this view, the countertransference first seen as a resistance becomes almost the carrying vehicle of the treatment, analogous to changing views of the role of transference in analysis (Tyson, 1984). While recognition of countertransference and overcoming the countertransference, as Freud recommended, is beneficial and often essential, it does not follow that unrecognized and unanalyzed countertransference is an asset rather than a liability in analytic work. The patient and his conflicts should not be confused with the analyst and his own conflicts. It does not follow, analytically or logically, that analysis of the patient can be accomplished by the analyst's self-analysis. If the analyst assumes that his reactions are identical to those of the patient or to those of significant objects in the patient's life, this is unanalyzed complementary and concordant identification, a form of counteridentification (Racker, 1968).

Following Racker, indirect countertransference has been described toward objects in the patient's life, for example, in relation to the parent in adult analysis (Jacobs, 1983) and in child analysis (Bernstein and Glenn, 1978). The analyst might identify with a patient's irrational blame and reproach of his mother for her purported inadequacies and pathogenic influence. The analyst's use of trial identification, a vital component of empathy, would be radically altered in the direction of persistent over-identification.

Fliess (1953) described both the analyst's transient trial identification and the analyst's more enduring identification with the patient. The analyst's uncontrolled regressive identification with the patient is a major dimension of countertransference—counteridentification. The patient and the analyst may have similar conflicts or complementary conflicts, or the analyst may unconsciously identify with a peripheral feature of the patient or situation that relates to his own conflicts (Arlow, 1985). Neither the process nor the products of such identification by the analyst, would be available for analytic scrutiny and judgment in the form of trial identification or empathy, in gaining analytic understanding of the patient (Beres & Arlow, 1974). Countertransference should not be confused with empathy. The analyst is not immune from subjectivity and countertransference, precisely because of his own unresolved unconscious conflicts. The analyst's own infantile conflicts and attitudes cannot be regarded as a replication of the patient's psychic reality. It is one thing for the patient to elicit and evoke countertransference reactions; it is quite another to assume that the patient places reactions inside the analyst and that the countertransference can be used to replace rather than to refine analytic empathy and understanding (Fliess, 1953; Blum, in press).

Heimann (1950) emphasized the value of the analyst's countertransference for comprehending the patient's transference; assuming the countertransference is correctly understood by the analyst, it became, for her, a major pathway in the formulation of interpretation. Little (1951) went a step further to propose that countertransference assumes even greater importance in the treatment of very disturbed and psychotic patients. Under these circumstances, the greater part of the analytic work would derive from countertransference data. Some analysts have proposed that the countertransference-transference relationships may recapitulate the infantile object relationships of the patient in a manner that is more complete and convincing than transference analysis alone. If the patient is seductive and the analyst responds with his own erotic fantasies, then this may indicate the repetition of the past object relations rather than transference considerations alone in the case of a patient with a history of primal scene exposure.

The patient's efforts to evoke, extract, or manipulate analytic response are part of the analytic transference relationship. For some analysts (Grinberg, 1962), the projection of omnipotent fantasy onto the analyst influences the analyst emotionally, and the patient attempts to control the analyst, who embodies the forbidden fantasy. This process has been called "projective identification," a complex term with imprecise, ambiguous meaning (Meissner, 1980). The analyst who is subject to the patient's communications and cueing may identify with what the patient attributes to him, thus conforming to the patient's fantasy expectations. This analytic reaction implies the analyst's passive submission to the patient's projective attribution. The analyst would feel and act out of character, ostensibly more because of the patient's conflicts more than because of his own neurotic reactions. (This is similar to Heimann's [1950] view of countertransference as a creation of the patient.)

Concepts of projective identification remain elusive. As an attempt to bridge the intrapsychic and the interpersonal, they call attention to introjective-projective processes in the transference-countertransference field, though other defense mechanisms are also important. If an object is moved to justify the subject's projection, as when a paranoid personality provokes the very hostility he expects from others, the behavioral communication and registrations inevitably involve a complexity that transcends projection and identification. Intrapsychic processes can only be inferred from their verbal and nonverbal behavioral derivatives.

Patients use highly variable strategies to induce and seduce the analytic response they expect or demand. Both analyst and patient may have shared fantasies (erotic, aggressive, narcissistic, etc.), which may derive from similar shared fantasies from childhood. Unanalyzed shared fantasies with some basis in childhood often underlie persistent countertransference difficulty (as in childhood seduction or other traumatic experiences).

In reviewing the problems of subjectivity, counteridentification, failure to reverse regression with a loss of boundaries between analyst and patient, and defensive countertransference distortion of the analytic data, I do not preclude the possible value of countertransference analysis for the clues it may provide for an enriched understanding of the patient. Countertransference analysis may secondarily convert a hindrance to a help,

adversity to advantage. If the patient does not meet our therapeutic expectations, if we are frustrated and disappointed with his or her progress,
if we feel irrationally critical of or angry at the patient, we are entitled to
ask what the patient is doing to provoke us, and how our silence or
speech, our interventions or failure to intervene appropriately are defending against or gratifying the patient's transference. We may find that
the countertransference does duplicate or mirror in some degree some of
the transferences of the patient, but this cannot be taken as an assumption
and can be understood only through reciprocal illumination of the transference and countertransference. The emergence of insight in the analytic situation is neither symmetrical nor synchronous in analyst and patient and depends on many observing, cognitive, and interpretive functions as well as affective responses. Without analysis the countertransference experience cannot reliably provide additional clues to the
transference conflicts in the ordering of the analytic process and tends to
favor the analyst's own conjectures and distortions over his objective observations of the patient (Blum, 1982).

I shall turn now to some clinical examples of countertransferenc, highlighting its distorting influence on the analytic process but allowing for the
potential usefulness of analyzed countertransference for both the analyst
and the patient. This potential was probably realized by the first analyst as
he surveyed transference-countertransference reactions in Anna O's
erotic feelings for her physician, Dr. Breuer, and Breuer's countertransference flight from the erotic transference (Breuer & Freud, 1895). In the
Irma Dream, Freud (1900) gives indications of his own countertransference toward his patient, his need to write the case up for his "supervisor" Breuer, and his particular efforts to deal with his guilt toward patients.
Despite the lack of an initial categorization or designation of the concept,
countertransference has been a significant issue in the inception and evolution of psychoanalytic thought. To repeat, there are countertransferences in every psychoanalytic treatment, since the analyst has both
transference reactions and realistic appraisals of the patient. Some
countertransference reactions can be extremely subtle, and others are
quite gross, for example, where the analyst falls asleep, calls the patient
by the wrong name, forgets the appointment, or can't wait for a particular
patient session that "makes his day," etc.

The transference repetition and abreaction of traumatic experience
may elicit intense countertransference reactions, as in cases of child
abuse or criminal assault. The pain, traumatic anxiety, grief, and guilt experienced by Holocaust victims do not fail to touch the inner life of the
analyst or therapist. The analyst may, in silent collusion with the patient,
avoid the issues altogether, engage in shared fantasies of rescue and re-

venge, focus on Holocaust experiences to the exclusion of other important material. Identification with the victim and the aggressor in the countertransference, taking on the patient's guilt and the guilt of those who hurt or failed to help the patient, are among many salient problems the analyst is likely to confront. "Horror stories" that were realities and realities that were nightmares may lead the analyst to overprotect the patient or himself and depart from an analytic attitude in working with the patient.

Analysts are aware of the countertransference potential in cases of massive trauma and that the countertransference may be one of the limiting factors in working with such patients. Many borderline patients have been severely traumatized and, reciprocally, many therapists have been severely tested if not traumatized in work with severely disturbed and regressed patients. Analysts treating patients with suicidal tendencies or with malicious behavior toward others, including the analyst, may all too readily find themselves enmeshed in transference-countertransference binds as well as in difficult treatment decisions. The introduction of parameters may be therapeutically indicated or unconsciously dictated by transference and countertransference reacations. Very ill patients with stormy, tormenting transferences stir up countertransference responses that are often easily recognized though initially unconscious. Analytic incapacity to confront chaos and primitive affects may transcend specific countertransference (Kernberg, 1965).

These rather dramatic instances of countertransference represent the visible part of the countertransference spectrum. As a universal response, countertransference can always be found, however, in a minimal, subtle, signal form. Major countertransference is not limited to the severely disturbed patient and represents the unconscious, unresolved conflicts of the analyst. If borderline and psychotic patients have stimulated interest in countertransference, it is an interest that has periodically surfaced in relation to all types of patients, whether hystierical and seductive or narcissistic and omnipotent.

The following clinical material has general application and is not restricted to seriously disturbed patients and therapists. Reciprocal and circular transference-countertransference influence is illustrated. The examples I present are not limited to candidates in supervision or the serious errors or oversights and misunderstandings of other analysts, but are graphic illustrations of ubiquitous problems that are only more likely to occur with the analytically inexperienced candidate who has yet to complete his own analytic training and often his own personal analysis. Moreover, analytic errors are not only or always due to countertransference.

The first example concerns a sadomasochistic patient who was frequently late, demanding, and complaining in the analysis. She tended to frustrate, annoy, and provoke her analyst. There was no sign that he liked working with this difficult patient, and it seemed as though he girded himself for a struggle and was disappointed with the failure of his interpretations to have any effect on the patient's complaints or her tendencies to act out masochistically. (Some analysts may unconsciously instigate, encourage, or enjoy the patient's acting out tendencies, unwittingly contributing to complications, if not impasse, in the analytic process.) Twice the analyst locked the patient out of the office, forgetting to unlock the waiting room door. One of these occasions was on the patient's birthday. In the next session, the patient spoke about an insolent waiter who kept her waiting "unconscionably" long and who provided terrible service. The patient vowed never to return to the restaurant, but she did return to the analytic session. She did not refer directly to the lockout and was afraid of the intensity of her disappointment and rage, which seemed to be outside awareness. She could not discuss her thoughts of quitting or her fears of being thrown out by the analyst. The lockout was also a message that she interpreted as "get lost," an act of neglect and rejection.

Another patient might have reacted with overt outrage, might have been openly critical of the analyst, or might even have been gleeful over the analyst's egregious error. In this situation, the masochistic patient elicited a sadomasochistic countertransference. Her final quitting of treatment was overdetermined by her transference conflicts and by the influence of the analyst's countertransference. But it is entirely possible that the patient's departure from treatment included a determinant of acting out of the countertransference fantasy of the analyst, like a child who acts out the unconscious fantasies of the parents. I previously described this (Blum, 1982) as a malignant cycle of unresolved transference-countertransference, distinguishing between the countertransference as an analytic reality to which the patient was reacting and the spontaneous, irrational, unconscious fantasies of the patient about the analyst.

This brings me to a point emphasized by Little (1951) and since then by many others. The countertransference always has an impact on the analytic process when the analyst's reaction is more than an internal signal. The patient was persistently reacting to the analyst's chronic countertransference, not simply to the episodic lockouts. The analyst tended to be sleepy during her sessions and was, in a sense, emotionally detached. She felt tuned out. Her masochism was gratified by the passive-aggressive withdrawal of her analyst. A correct interpretation of the patient's masochistic transference fantasies would have to take into account the grain of truth of mistreatment and victimization within the fantasy and that the fantasy was anchored to a reality in the analytic situation. Some dimension of the mistreatment was not transference distortion but a correct perception of a rejecting analytic attitude of "lockout" to which the patient masochistically adapted. Here, interpretation and resolution of the countertransference would have been indispensable to a fuller understanding of the patient's tenacious masochistic transference and to the establishment of a progressive analytic process. The countertransference was a reciprocal, rather than a mirror reflection, of the patient's transference, and the neurotic conflicts of analyst and patient stem from the individual pasts of both and were not created de novo in the analytic situation. It may be presumed that the patient's masochistic tendencies were not expressed, exploited, or gratified in the same form in other situations. The patient's fantasy memories of victimized rejection had a reality as well as a transference meaning.

Countertransference is often related both to the specific features of the patient's transference and to the analyst's character pathology. A very dependent and demanding patient with oedipal jealousy of the analyst, and also expressing her possessiveness of the preoedipal mother, had a pattern of preweekend anxiety and anger. She resented the weekened separation and would entreat the analyst for extra time and attention; the patient would speak with tension and some agitation or would withdraw into silence. The analyst would attempt to pacify her demands and complaints by talking more during the Friday session, and defended his behavior as being therapeutically indicated. It turned out that if the patient did not respond to the analyst's intervention, he too would tend to withdraw into silence. The alternation of speech and silence during the Friday hours was influenced not only by the proximity of the weekend but by the reciprocal response of both parties, including their nonverbal, psychological contact or distance. The peculiar adaptation or subversion of the analytic process was further complicated by the supervisory relationship. The analyst might be much more talkative, ready to interpret after the supervisory session. Conversely, a disappointing supervisory session might result in silent detachment from the patient. The supervisor could be appeased or defied in the analyst's response to the patient.

Here the analyst's own preoccupations persistently intruded and distracted the analytic process. The patient identified with the style of the analyst, who, in turn, demonstrated counteridentification with the patient and probably with the supervisor as well. The analyst's conflicts interfered with analysis and with learning about his own problems. Attempts to distinguish his problems from those of the patient were perceived partially as supervisory complaint and criticism. The analyst did not recognize the many references in the patient's fantasies to his controlling and critical attitudes and to his inconsistent closeness and distance. The patient felt she was being teased and had fantasies of seduction and abandonment, of sexual abuse and rejection by her father, of stimulation and withholding by big-breasted women representing her mother. The analyst had difficulty recognizing and self-interpreting the patient's transference reactions to the countertransference and the transference-countertransference bind in which he and the patient were enmeshed. His problems, activated by her provocation, were still sufficiently ego-syntonic that the critical observations of patient and supervisor were disregarded. The countertransference itself had many dimensions and exemplifies overdetermination and compromise formation (Brenner, 1985).

The analyst's own preferential listening and intervening and his preference for particular patient associations or behaviors are bound to influence free association and analytic comprehension. Analysis of the analyst's intrusion of his own injunctions and ideals, avoidances and preferences is essential for a grasp of the countertransference. Patients will also identify with the attitudes and defenses of former analysts and therapists. Such similar defense is not necessarily typical of divergent and diverse countertransference defences. The analyst may not only identify but also rely on the gamut of defenses. The patient may deny signs of the analyst's ill feelings or illness; the analyst may isolate feelings and only later discover repressed fantasies about the patient. Identifications with each other's defenses may range from the silent pact to shared humor to projected antagonism toward each other or a third party. Projective and introjective processes may be more or less important and are not necessarily predominant in any countertransference.

However clamorous the countertransference may be, its interpretation to the patient is generally silent. I do not advocate reporting the analyst's inner life to the patient. Historically, the more positive attitude toward countertransference interpretation to the patient probably derives from papers by Winnicott and Little. In particular, Winnicott (1949) advocated the modulated expression of countertransference hate in work with psychopaths or psychotics because the patient might need to objectively experience evoked hatred and because the analyst might need to convey such controlled, clarified countertransference. Little (1951), however, generalized that the sources of analytic errors due to countertransference should be explained to the patient. The analyst would be then recognized as human, candid, and unafraid of his own conflicts.

To my mind, countertransference explanation too readily becomes exhibitionism and confession, which only further "contaminates" the transference. The countertransference contamination, or difficulty, is then magnified by the analyst's self-revelation, which is a real departure from analytic anonymity and neutrality. The patient is likely to be confused, se-duced, or intimidated and hurt by the intrusion of the analyst's self-analysis. This does not mean that the analyst should represent himself as omniscient or omnipotent, as having flawless technique, but rather that he should not burden the patient with his own problems, with his own self-observations, and self-analysis. We may acknowledge to the patient that an error occurred, that our anxiety and anger were correctly per-ceived by the patient, and so forth. It is important for both analyst and pa-tient to understand the effect of the analyst's problems on the trans-ference in the analytic process, to analyze rather than simply acknowl-edge or apologize.

We have recently had reports of some of the subtle and difficult transference-countertransference problems encountered when the ana-lyst becomes ill (Abend, 1982; Dewald, 1982) and many of the issues of whether and how much to tell the patient have applications to more gen-eral countertransference considerations. How much information is use-ful or detrimental for a particular patient? Finally, in self-analysis as in reanalysis, those areas insufficiently explored because of previous coun-tertransference may be particularly problematic. If the trouble with self-analysis is countertransference, the trouble may be one's own counter-transference and the area of countertransference experienced (and not analyzed) in previous formal analysis. Certain forms of countertrans-ference may be based on identification with the countertransference of the analyst's analyst, perpetuating particular areas of difficulty in the next generation of analysts.

REFERENCES

Abend, S. (1982), Serious illness in the analyst: countertransference consider-ations. J. Amer. Psychoanal. Assn., 30:365–380.
Arlow, J. (1985), Some technical problems of countertransference. Psychoanal. Quart., 54:164–174.
Beres, D., & Arlow, J. (1974), Fantasy and identification in empathy. Psychoanal. Quart., 43:26–50.
Bernstein, I. & Glenn, J. (1978), The child analyst's emotional reactions to his pa-tients. In: Child Analysis and Therapy, ed. J. Glenn. New York: Aronson, pp. 375–392.
Blum, H. (1982), The position and value of extratransference interpretation. J. Amer. Psychoanal. Assn., 31:587–618.
———— (in press). Countertransference and the theory of technique: Discussion. J. Amer. Psychoanal. Assn.

Brenner, C. (1982), *The Mind in Conflict.* New York: International Universities Press.

Breuer, J., & Freud, S. (1895). Studies on hysteria. *Standard Edition, 2.* London: Hogarth Press, 1955.

_____ (1985). Countertransference as compromise formation. *Psychoanal. Quart.,* 54:155–163.

Dewald, P. (1982), Serious illness in the analyst: Transference, countertransference, and reality responses. *J. Amer. Psychoanal. Assn.,* 30:347–364.

Fliess, R. (1953), Countertransference and counteridentification. *J. Amer. Psychoanal. Assn.,* 1:268–284.

Freud, S. (1900), The interpretation of dreams. *Standard Edition, 4 & 5.* London: Hogarth Press, 1953.

_____ (1910). The future prospects of psycho-analytic therapy. *Standard Edition,* 11:139–151. London: Hogarth Press, 1957.

_____ (1913), On beginning the treatment. *Standard Edition,* 12:121–144. London: Hogarth Press, 1958.

_____ (1914), Observations on transference love. *Standard Edition,* 12:157–168. London: Hogarth Press, 1958.

Gill, M. (1982), *Analysis of Transference.* Vol. 1. New York: International Universities Press.

Gitelson, M. (1952), The emotional position of the analyst in the psychoanalytic situation. *Internat. J. Psycho-Anal.,* 33:1–10.

Grinberg, L. (1962), On a specific aspect of countertransference due to the patient's projective identification. *Internat. J. Psycho-Anal.,* 43:436–440.

Heimann, P. (1950), On countertransference. *Internat. J. Psycho-Anal.,* 31:81–84.

Jacobs, T. (1983), The analyst and the patient's object world: notes on an aspect of countertransference. *J. Amer. Psychoanal. Assn.,* 31:619–642.

Kernberg, O. (1965), Notes on countertransference. *J. Amer. Psychoanal. Assn.,* 13:38–56.

Little, M. (1951), Countertransference and the patient's response to it. *Internat. J. Psycho-Anal.,* 32:32–40.

Meissner, W. (1980). A note on projective identification. *J. Amer. Psychoanal. Assn.,* 28:43–68.

Racker, H. (1968). *Transference and Countertransference.* New York: International Universities Press.

Reich, A. (1951), On countertransference. *Internat. J. Psycho-Anal.,* 32:25–31.

_____ (1960), Further remarks on countertransference. *Internat. J. Psycho-Anal.,* 41:389–395.

Tyson, R. (1984), Countertransference Panel, Chairperson's Introduction. *J. Amer. Psychoanal. Assn.,* publication pending.

Winnicott, D. (1949). Hate in the countertransference. *Internat. J. Psycho-Anal.,* 30:69–75.

PAUL GRAY

On Helping Analysands Observe Intrapsychic Activity

A major goal of the analytic process is to help the analysand gain full access to those habitual, unconscious, and outmoded ego activities that serve resistance. There is, however, a paucity of methodology available for achieving this goal. I have discussed elsewhere (Gray, 1982) some forms of counterresistance to this challenging task. An earlier article (Gray, 1973) dealt with particular ways in which analysts, by focusing their observing skills, can favorably influence their own access to the analysand's unconscious defense-against-drive processes. Here I explore specific techniques for helping the analysand make better use of those observing skills that are essential for systematic analysis of the resistances to free association, as well as valuable in the development of a self-analytic capacity.

The crux of the difficulty in making the unconscious ego conscious is that the elements the analyst wants to bring into awareness are not "driven" toward the analysand's awareness, as are the id derivatives. Even-hovering attention and skillful, id-resonating interpretations in a transferentially enhanced authoritative atmosphere are, by themselves, relatively ineffective in bringing into the patient's awareness the unconscious ego activities that carry out repetitive forms of defense as resistance. To observe the simple or intricate defenses at work against specific id impulse derivatives, the analysand requires a form of observation distinguishable from the "experiential observation" (Hatcher, 1973, p. 388) that serves free association (Eissler, 1963).

I am interested in methodology for drawing more fully on the relatively autonomous capacities of analysands to strengthen both their motivation for and their work in analyzing. Nowhere are these autonomous capacities more necessary than in learning how to observe and comprehend one's intrapsychic process. Out of a range of measures that, I believe, can help the patient make use of these capacities, I have selected only two areas for discussion. The first area is a primarily cognitive, educative endeavor, while the second deals with the analyst's skill in creating the best working opportunities for analysands to become familiar with their capacity for self-observation. I am aware that one cannot do full justice to the often overlapping, or even simultaneous application of, technical measures in practice.

STRENGTHENING ANALYSANDS' MOTIVATION FOR DEVELOPING A CAPACITY FOR INTRAPSYCHIC OBSERVATION

Although patients may possess the optimum motive for entering into psychoanalysis, namely, a wish for relief from some form of neurotic distress, it does not follow that they are at once motivated to undertake the observing tasks required during the analytic hour (Friedman, 1969; Kris, 1975; Hatcher, 1973). In this discussion, I consider two forms of self-observation: 1) that required for the task set by what we have traditionally called "the fundamental rule"; and 2) that which is necessary as the patient attempts to perceive in close retrospection the phenomena which occur as manifestations related to intrapsychic conflict—specifically, those conflicts and solutions mobilized by, and occurring during, the analytic situation. Gradually, the analysand's second observing task can occur during the process of the defense reaction itself (see final clinical example later).

To teach analysands the first of these observing tasks, the analyst presents them with a relatively clear concept: that they must strive to set aside reasonable and moral judgment, permit a flow of inner spontaneity, and observe and put into words unreservedly "what comes to mind"—think out loud. This task of free association evokes resistance, which expresses itself by making difficult the comprehension of what is to be attempted. Sustaining that comprehension remains one of the extended efforts of the analysis. An added burden for analysands is learning that in order to undertake the second task, they must—at intervals determined by the analyst's interventions—attempt to enter into a rational observing alliance with the analyst. This reorienting from free-associative attention to an experience of what the mind produces, to an objective "intellectual contemplation" (Sterba, 1934) only sets the stage for a less familiar and usually unwelcome examination of *how* the mind works.

Regarding the second observing task, what Kris (1975) referred to as "the ability of the ego to . . . observe its own functions," (p. 267) typically is initiated by inviting the analysand to think back about a just completed mental activity that the analyst has reconstructed. Turning attention toward something just spoken or momentarily felt — something that "occurred" in the immediate past, but is now preconscious (yet close enough to the surface to be retrieved) — is not easy for the analysand. It takes practice just to learn that one can do that sort of thing.

Clearly, this complex second observing task we ask the patient to undertake requires, as in the case of free association, a good measure of motivation. Traditionally, motivation for the work of analyzing — sometimes distinguishable from the wish to "be analyzed" — relies heavily on response to or compliance with transferentially endowed authority; that is, it stems from a fear of punishment or a need to express devotion and gain love. This use of aspects of the positive transference (Freud, 1917; Nunberg, 1937; Fenichel, 1941; Gill, 1982; Gray, 1982) is a form of suggestion that is still widely used to overcome resistance. It is usually more accepted in practice than acknowledged in theory. Many analyzable patients have a capacity and a tendency to cling to this particular motivational source. Analysts who depend on it usually assume it will be relinquished near the end of the analysis. This is not necessarily the case. In my experience, a patient can also (and to greater advantage) derive motivation throughout the analysis from progressively acquiring a reality-based rationale for proceeding in a particular way toward a real gain (as differentiated from a fantasied gain) and, in addition, from learning through repeated observation that this particular way gradually accomplishes what it sets out to do, as the ego gains nondefensive strengths. In practice, there is always a mixture of rational and irrational motivating factors. My interest lies in identifying technical ways of reducing the irrational, that is, the use of suggestion, and increasing the rational use of autonomous learning as early in the analysis as the patient's characteristics permit.

Having so far dealt largely in principles, I shall now move closer to practice. In building a rational motivation in analysands for undertaking the tasks of observation, I want to provide them with a working concept of how those difficulties that made analysis the treatment of choice are manifestations of involuntary solutions to certain unconscious conflicts — conflicts that, in the beginning, neither the patient nor the analyst are able to identify, let alone resolve. The extent to which this working concept can be used varies with the analysand's available rational attention and his usable intelligence, and requires a sensitive and empathetic assessment by the analyst to determine how much the patient is able to digest at any one time. At some point, I would hope to convey to the analysand that the particular reasons why these conflicts have been kept out of the patient's awareness have been operating, in one way or another, since early in his life, when he was not yet old or strong enough to be able to work them out consciously. Once the patient understands in this general way the psychological nature of the difficulties, the analyst can usually describe how the analytic situation contributes to a resolution of the problem by the way it is conducted in order to gain access to those obscured conflicts. In my orienting comments about the functioning and aims of the analytic situation, I speak of the *two* kinds of self-observing that will become essential. In this paper, I give less attention to describing the task required in free association, there being not much I can add to what analysts already know and have long practiced. I do include the following observations though. Where appropriate, I explain the difference between free association in analysis and free communication, to which the patient may have become accustomed during some previous therapy. Sooner or later, I also convey the information that the patient can potentially and actively participate in influencing the degree of freedom with which things come to mind — that is, in the "flow" into consciousness — and that we are aiming for an increasingly greater spontaneity in this regard. (In analytic language, which I would not use with analysands, I try to acquaint them with their capability for bringing about a *degree* of facilitation of regression in the service of free association, by a voluntary, intentional use of the ego's capacity for this.) Further, I make clear that I am talking about an effort *toward* free association, since interferences regularly take place while we are working to carry out this task. I point out that it is precisely the study of these interferences and the obstacles to putting the observations into words that provides us with greater access to what is now out of reach and which contributes to the patient's problems; and that the *nature of the obstacles* to free association will be intimately connected with the *nature of the problems* or conflicts that brought the patient to treatment.

This motivating orientation helps some patients — especially where the form of a previous psychotherapy contrasts sharply with analysis — to understand basically why the analyst does not need to spend "equal time" interpreting the patient's contemporary life outside the analytic situation in order to be therapeutically helpful; the essential conflicts and issues will reveal themselves *in the analytic situation* as the work continues to give access to inner spontaneity. (This does not mean "transference only" and does not in any way mean ignoring the full range of thoughts, feelings, and impulses *referring* to the analysand's contemporary life.) Again, these guiding conceptualizations are parcelled out in accordance with the analysand's capacity to comprehend them. How soon and how much will vary from patient to patient; with some, they can be offered during the initial interview. Again, the intention is to provide, as early as possible, a rational basis for the motivation to develop the ability for self-observation, rather than to depend on an irrational basis of working for the analyst, a motivation that sacrifices a fuller development of autonomous faculties.

Having provided a basis for rational understanding of the point of the analytic process, the analyst is in a better position to bolster patients' motivation further as he gives them repeated opportunity throughout the analytic process to become familiar with their autonomous "tools" (Loewenstein, 1982, p. 214) of observation. Quite apart from arousing resistance, the effort to observe what spontaneously comes into one's awareness often encounters the inherent difficulty of an unfamiliar task. However, self-observation of the process of the mind's intrapsychic activity at its encounter with and defensive solution to conflict — conflict not ordinarily in the scope of attention — makes an even stranger demand (Freud, 1933) on the autonomous ego apparatus. Therefore, it is important to provide patients with clearly documented examples of their resisting minds at work. With repeated experiences, patients gradually learn that they can bring these activities more and more under conscious management. All of this contributes to a greater sense of what is involved in undertaking a freer inner spontaneity. It also lends positive motivation to the search for the meanings, present and past, of those involuntary defensive responses.

I anticipate that my description of this approach may stimulate the objection, "Doesn't this contribute to intellectualization?" My reply is: Any communication by the analyst, or contemplation of a task by the analysand, can be turned into intellectualization if that is a significant defense of the analysand. This would be equally true if one discussed "the fundamental rule" with the analysand, or, at some other time, how to approach a dream usefully. Certainly it is intellectual but so is any intervention at the point where the analysand can rationally comprehend it. I would argue that the intellect used as a defense is to be analyzed, not avoided through manipulation by not making demands on the analysand's intelligence. It is what the patient does with the information communicated that is important. Thus, any defensive intellectualization the patient may engage in should itself become a subject for the same technique described before. My thesis is that a technical orientation which encourages the analyst to describe the characteristics of the things that are observable, and which also provides rational, constructive *reasons for doing so*, can potentially arouse analysands to be willing to use their perceptual equipment more fully. To paraphrase Friedman (1976), by gradually familiarizing analysands with the characteristics of those identifiable processes within their verbalized thinking that are responses to conflict, the properties of otherwise unconscious ego activities become "objectified" and hence more accessible for repeated observation.

Some analysands can shift quite readily from observing what is in their awareness (for purposes of free association) to the rational observing focus of the analyst's comments. Other analysands experience difficulty at different points in the process of this shift. Patients whose participation is handicapped in this area may have general inhibitions against a rational alliance with the analyst, or there may be specific autonomous functions that are compromised. For them, the analyst may have to turn the analytic attention away from the study primarily of what the analysand has been saying to take up an examination of the very functions, the "tools," which the patient is neglecting, keeping the analysis from being, as Hartmann regarded it, a *shared* "scientific investigation" (Loewenstein, 1982, p. 220).

The more clearly we analysts can conceptualize for ourselves the detail of the analytic work of observing we may wish to have patients undertake, the greater the likelihood that we can facilitate their learning to do so. Let us look closer at the autonomous ego functions analysands need in order to observe the conflict-motivated defensive activities of their egos.[1] As analysands are interrupted by the sound of the analyst's voice, they must draw back from the more spontaneous and less rational mode and must now take up objective capacities. In this new and more rational alliance (Gutheil & Havens, 1979), they may sequentially undertake the following: (1) rationally attend to what the analyst is saying; (2) recognize that the interpretive intervention implies an invitation to turn objective attention back over the reconstructed or recounted sequence of material

---

[1] I am virtually equating manifestations of *resistance* with those manifestations of *defense* that are stimulated by the task of free association. I believe that such a theoretical perspective, though not exhaustive, is practical in comprehending and observing resistance during the analytic process. Except for the examples I give in the clinical illustrations, I shall not further elaborate varieties of defensive solutions to conflict. I am in agreement with Brenner that "the ego can use defensively whatever lies at hand that is useful for that purpose" (Brenner, 1982, p. 75). Defenses are not limited to "special mechanisms." For comprehensive views about defense and/or resistance manifestations see earlier contributons — Freud (1926), A. Freud (1936), Gero (1951), and Loewenstein (1982); see also Gill (1963), Schafer (1968, 1973), and Stone (1973). For more recent contributions see Abend (1981), Brenner (1976, 1982), Rangell (1983), and Wallerstein (1983).

the analyst has offered as evidence of a conflict the patient encountered during the attempted spontaneity and to which the patient's mind automatically responded with a protective, defensive solution; (3) comprehend that the motivation for the conflict solution was due in part (and this part will be explored) to the fact that while the analysand was revealing thoughts and feelings to the other person in the room, some fantasied risk of doing so arose; (4) analyze that irrational risk (a bit more each time) and through understanding it gradually reduce the automatic need for the patient to inhibit, by the specific means indentified, those particular elements that had shortly before come into conflict; and (5) return attention to the essential task of permitting a more spontaneous access to the inner self, in particular, allowing greater freedom to let emerge those conflicted elements, the inhibition of which had just been explored.

I wish to comment briefly on the first and fourth of the aforementioned stages. In regard to (1) "rationally attend to what the analyst is saying," precisely at this point, as suggested earlier, certain pathological problems may limit, transiently or indefinitely, any success in engaging the analysands' observing attention to their intrapsychic activity. For example, some of the persons Kohut (1971) designated as having narcissistic personality disorders hear the analyst give attention to an aspect of what they have been saying that goes beyond what they manifestly wished to communciate, and they become traumatized. This narcissistic wound handicaps the patient's observing capacity immediately, and any specific attention to the ego's activities becomes impossible. Understandably, Kohut (personal communication) indicated that he used free association with such patients less and less frequently. Others so limited are patients Sterba designated as having "a permanently unified ego" (Sterba, 1934, p. 120) and whom he regarded as incapable of achieving an observing "dissociation" or "split" (Freud, 1933, p. 58). Obviously, clinical and theoretical observations concerning limitatons in applying this technical approach, which stresses collaborative development of the analysand's observation of manifestations of mental activity during conflict solutions within the analytic hour, deserve extended attention. I plan to do this in a subsequent paper. I shall add here only the impression that patients who are severely passive generally present more difficulty in enlisting an observing alliance of the kind being described. This can also be true for a long time with people who have an excessive need to distance themselves from any form of close cooperative experience.

In regard to (4) "the analysis of the irrational risk," it is in the area of analyzing the inhibiting irrational fear that I see a primary application of genetic interest; this is in the service of analyzing the resistance against identifiable trends, ideas, memories, affects, impulses, *whether or not they pertain to the analyst.* It is here that I see the value in reconstructing, where possible, the conditions of originally perceived danger (A. Freud, 1936) that forced the analysand at an earlier time to abandon the freedom or capacity to be aware of and/or to reveal his desires, impulses, wishes, appetites, and to turn to defensive, automatic, immature but adaptively available means to resolve the intimidating conflicts — all of which resulted in inhibiting the now dreaded impulses by removing them from consciousness. I am aware that these remarks about genetics and reconstruction may not be central to enhancing the analysand's motivation for intrapsychic observations. I include them because I do not wish their absence to stimulate questions that may deflect attention from the difficult subject of self-observation of ego activities.

In summary, in this first section I have described ways of enhancing analysands' motivation for realizing and developing their skills for observation of certain crucial intrapsychic activities as they are brought into play during the analytic process. In the context of an available rational alliance, the analyst provides a basic, essentially ego-syntonic rationale or direction, emphasizing analysis of resistance against identifiable instinctualized mental activities. This primarily educational provision is followed up during the course of the analysis by interpretive interventions that give the analysand — from earliest opportunities — repeated observing experience of those ego activities that occur in the face of specific intrapsychic conflict phenomena. The objective is, of course, to make possible, through insight and experience, the gradual exchange of previously automatic, unconscious defensive activities, which were acquired adaptively during immaturity, for voluntary, more mature forms of control and a more realistic perception of the patient's internal and external environment.

I do not underestimate the predilection of some patients for utilizing, through suggestibility, less stable acquisitions, such as incorporative identification of the analyst's aims, rather than permitting themselves to learn and to use those concepts more and more autonomously. I am aware that what the patient learns about these things in the beginning of the analysis may be subjected to all the distortions that transference resistance can impose, in the same way that patients can neurotically modify all the other information they learn from the analyst, be it the appointment times, the dates of the analyst's vacations, the fee arrangements, or the carefully spelled out versions of "the fundamental rule." It is my experience, however, that without such a conceptual foundation, the patient's task of making conscious in an increasingly stable way the capacity to observe the ego's functions becomes more difficult. Typically, analysands gain in motivation when they understand what observing equipment they possess and how and for what purpose to use it. Let us leave the issue of motivation now and turn to the second area, that of trying to enhance the *effectiveness* of the analysand's observing experiences.

COOPERATING WITH ANALYSANDS' SELF-OBSERVING ACTIVITIES

The effectiveness with which patients can use their capacity for observing ego activities depends primarily on the nature of the burden the analyst's interventions place on them. The context in which such cooperative effort takes place surrounds those manifestations of intrapsychic conflict which occur during the analytic hour, "inside" the analytic situation. Although I feel that there are advantages to working in this context whenever possible (Gray, 1973), I am not suggesting doing so exclusively (Gray, 1984); I am trying here to describe more clearly how to do it.

Obviously, a discussion of where and in what way the analyst decides to focus analytic attention must deal primarily with choice of a surface. I say "a" surface, rather than "the" surface because, although there is wide agreement on analyzing "from the surface," surface means different things to different analysts. I regard as an optimum surface for interpretive interventions a selection of those elements in the material that may successfully illustrate for analysands that when they were speaking, they encountered a conflict over something being revealed, which caused them involuntarily and unknowingly to react in identifiably defensive ways. By "successfully illustrate" I mean to succeed in directing analysands' attention to things they can grasp in spite of never ceasing resistance. The interpretive task is to estimate sensitively the patient's ability to comprehend, in order to make a formulation that is not too superficial, yet does not stimulate more reactive defense (Fenichel, 1941).

To the extent that analysts are able to use an optimum surface, they will provide analysands with the best chance to use their self-observing equipment. So far, this rather simple expression of aims and general process fails to disclose a variety of obstacles that can make the task complex and challenging. Let us examine some of the most prominent difficulties.

Analysands are not familiar with the nature of the activities in which the mind-at-surface quietly engages while they are speaking. Indeed, they are barely even aware of the existence of these activities. For instance, the natural orientation of their thinking is restricted to regarding the things they say as references solely to what they have been talking about. Patients must learn that they can yield this natural stance as they gain familiarity with another function of their mind, a function that consists of their living out a piece of mental behavior while they are speaking, and must also learn how and why they are doing so. The educational help described earlier will assist significantly with this, but experiencing and practicing these skills is obviously essential. Part of the manifestation characterized by "there is a resistance to uncovering of resistances" (Freud, 1937, p. 239) often results from the analyst's failure to provide the analysand with the best opportunity to perceive the resistance.

Examples

During the early hours of an analysis, an analyst told a female patient, in very clear and appropriately spoken terms, that something the patient had just expressed had interrupted and replaced an uncomfortable preceding thought. The analysand, quiet for a few seconds, then responded in a serious and thoughtfully unprovoking tone, "What is it that I am supposed to do with that?" The analyst dealt with this by replying, also in a thoughtful tone, that the patient wished the analyst to do the thinking for her. Although there eventually would be times in the analysis for such an interpretation, it was not helpful at this point; for, in fact, the patient did *not* know how to try to make use of what the analyst had said. In a subsequent hour, following similar remarks by her analyst, the analysand, now more cautious, did manage to say that she "really" did not know what to do with his observation. This time, the analyst was able to say that by his comments he was trying to provide an opportunity for her to notice that in attempting to be spontaneous and candid in expressing her thoughts and feelings, she had reached a specific place that became difficult — there was some conflict — and suddenly she had turned to another line of thought, as if she had taken refuge in it. He added that if in retrospect she could confirm this, then she might be free, by "going back" to that difficult place, to try to understand with the analyst's help what sort of "risk" had inhibited her. If she could do this, she might not have to avoid such conflicted thoughts or feelings. Within the bounds of what her resistance permitted, she was subsequently able to begin the task of gradually bringing into her awareness how currently unnecessary were her ego's unconscious, reflexive, defensive activities.

Not wanting to distract us from looking at the method, I have deliberately left out of my account the particular content of the material that the analysand had found too risky to become more aware of and to put into words. Let us now look at some examples with more "content." In passing, we can note that the term content may apply equally well either to the defense or to the drive derivatives defended against (Loewenstein,

1982). Hence, a polarization of defense analysis with content analysis really only obfuscates an area already difficult to spell out.

There are countless examples in which the analysand arrives at critical or aggressive thoughts toward someone else and suddenly replaces them with self-criticism. This can be demonstrated easily to a patient. I have listened to a case report in which the analysand began to learn from the analyst how to observe his intrapsychic behavior. He grasped with such vividness his way of suddenly turning on himself in order to protect various objects that he said it was "like making a U turn." The analyst usefully adopted this simile to designate for the patient the progressively more subtle and complex versions of the "U turn" that continued to occur.

In another example, an analysand was able to follow the analyst's illustrations of turning on herself as a solution to conflict over some derivative of aggression. She was now increasing her capacity to study additional details of how this defense was being carried out. The analyst had recognized these details much earlier, but because of resistance and *because of their complexity,* to include them in the surface then being examined would have put too much of a burden on the analysand's observing apparatus. Now the patient could go beyond the observation that she was afraid to criticize the analyst and would escape by picking on herself. She found it possible to comprehend, where it could be demonstrated, that she carried this out by instantly *identifying with the victim* (Orgel, 1974) or potential victim of her feared aggression and, in increasingly elaborate detail, masochistically brought upon herself all of the cruel impulses she was *afraid to feel toward someone else.* She now began to understand very clearly the phenomenon of stopping her active observing and reacting toward another by becoming some part of that person. Needless to say, this learned capacity for observing *identification* as it took place within the analysis became valuable far beyond the specific form it took in the activity of turning on herself.

It can be instructive to the analyst to notice the specific ways that an interpretive intervention may *fail* to help the analysand's observing capacity and to see where the resistance has defeated the attempt.

Near the end of an hour, a woman permitted a new, less guarded level of recall and reexperiencing of resentment against a brother, a brother on whom she fondly depended but who had chronically traumatized her as a youngster. She recounted an episode during which she had observed an inappropriate, "crazy" behavior of her sibling. With this material, an edge of bitter resentment emerged. Although her memory had reached a new degree of vividness, she finally interrupted the flow with a form of defense — in essence, a reaction-formation, consisting of breaking off the description of the sibling's provocative behavior and moving quickly to recall instead the sibling's sad remorse subsequent to his behavior. This latter recollection was accompanied by a feeling of sympathy, rather than the previous growing resentment, and did not provide the analyst with any further disclosure of the bizarre, perverse cruelty of the sibling. The analyst then intervened to point out how the sympathetic feeling she was experiencing *now* – although also a part of her relationship with her brother – had come to mind in this instance and in a familiar way, interrupting her recall of the behavior she had described as "crazy." He pointed out further that the resentful feelings had vanished. The analyst drew her attention to the implied risk associated with the presence of the listening analyst, had she continued to pursue the original train of thought, imagery, and feeling.

Often, after such an interpretive intervention, the analysand would be able to return to the uncomfortable point of the defensive interruption and there to recognize the sense of discomfort or conflict, to "take it on," to explore that sense of danger to a greater extent, and to make possible the analysis of more detailed increments of the inhibiting fantasy which set off the defense. For her, one important fantasy connected with the danger was that if she continued angrily and vengefully to recall and expose more of her sibling's behavior, the analyst would cease to listen analytically and, instead, would feel shocked and disgusted and would behave in a specifically punitive manner. Also, with exploration she often recognized something more about the dangerously conflicted conditions that had prevailed early in life, when she became a distraught, emotionally traumatized witness, provoked among other things to angry, vengeful impulses toward her brother – impulses she so feared revealing that she was compelled to forget them. In this instance, she managed her forgetting by means of a complex form of reaction-formation, which, as a character trait, was now being repeated in the form of resistance.

During this particular hour, however, her resistance was especially heightened because of an approaching, longer than usual weekend interruption, and she regressively gave up some of her previously gained observing ability. Instead of exploring what had occurred during the hour, she continued to insist that her brother had "in fact" not "meant" to behave so badly and should have been better treated by those about, including the patient, and that further there was nothing more that had happened. "That was all."

In view of the heightened resistance of this analysand, the analyst could have made a less burdensome, more useful choice of surface by selecting and speaking only about her need to stop exposing the observed details of the sibling's egregious and bizarre behavior she had always kept in protective secrecy. Alternatively, he might have spoken only about her need to stop aggressive feelings that were mobilized in relation to the traumatizing events she was recalling and describing. In other words, it would have been more useful if the analyst had referred to one defended derivative at a time, rather than to two. Eventually in the analysis it was demonstrated that additional drive derivatives were being defended against, but then, as now, I was trying to refer only to those conflicted derivatives that could be usefully demonstrated for her observing ego.

I shall include one more consideration for improving the analysand's observing capacity. We depend not only on the attitude we convey in our manner of speaking and the sequence of references — that is, "defense before drive" — but also on our *choice of words*. Analysts hardly need reminding of the value of thoughtfully worded interventions. There are, however, some useful ways of conceptualizing aspects of this part of technique, if we wish to study the detail of reaching the analysand's observing functions. When we choose our words most wisely, we lessen the burden on analysands' rational listening, comprehension, and observation in three ways. First, we respect their ego by choosing language that does not strain their fund of knowledge; second, we choose so that we do not stimulate their conflicted instinctual drives; and third, we try not to attract their superegos into substituting a judgmental attitude for an objective one. Since a satisfying discussion of this area would be lengthy, I shall settle for brief examples of each of the three categories, in the hope of stimulating further thought on the subject.

First for the ego area: if the analyst uses a word that for the patient has a lifetime of meaning different from the one intended by the analyst, a sort of mini culture-shock may result. A common example is the analyst's use of the word "feel" or "feeling" to refer to an *unconscious* instinctual derivative. It may take the form: "I believe that you are feeling angry with me for being late (or going away, etc.)." I have in mind occasions when the analysand is in fact not "feeling" any such thing. It may be quite true and important that the analysand is at that point defending against reacting to a disappointment, but that is different from feeling something. An analyst's "suggestion" may temporarily melt the resistance and a feeling may *then* occur; on the other hand, such wording of the intervention may lend itself to the resistance and the analysand can quite accurately say that there is no such feeling. The word "feeling" is so ingrained as a reference to something of which one is aware that to use it otherwise does not provide a very good chance for the analysand to join the analyst in observing a useful surface. It would be easier to join the inquiry if, for example, the word were put in a familiar context by approaching from the side of the defense. For instance, one might ask what does it mean, in the face of a potentially clearly disappointing event, that the patient is *not* feeling disappointment in the analyst? It might be even better if the analyst can describe the *way* in which the chance of such a feeling is being involuntarily avoided.

Second, for the instinctual stimulation area: here words that are sometimes characterized as "seductive" apply. These are words that effect a transient "melting" of the resistance and add an impetus to the drive. An example would be if the analyst, referring to an intimate object of the analysand, uses the first name, or even pet name, of that person in a "familiar" way, thereby creating a momentary alliance based on the fleeting illusion of a shared familiarity with the mentioned figure. The analyst might avoid the seductive illusion by disclaiming any such shared familiarity, for example, by using the words "your wife" or "your husband," "your friend Harry," "your companion Jane." This would preserve the analysand's autonomous task with the effort required to think objectively in that context. Thus, patients' independent responsibility for their object relationships would remain more clearly in their own hands.

Third, for the superego attracting area: here, words are used that although quite accurate for the occasion in their dictionary definition, have become, over the years of parlor-analytic use or even legitimate therapeutic manipulation, rather pejorative in meaning. Such words instantly invite the superego into the scheme of things, and objective observing gives way to a moral judgment. Sometimes this superego invasion is so insidious that the analysand's appearance of seeking insight masks an inhibiting resistance-supporting "mental health morality" (Hartmann, 1960). Examples here include references that characterize analysands as regarding themselves "special" or "entitled." At some point, it is appropriate to bring these attitudes into consciousness, but the analyst can refer to them without muddling rational attention by using words that arouse the superego.

Finally, we come to some "working" examples. The effectiveness with which analysands can come to use their observing equipment — provided they have been allowed to practice — can be very impressive, even when it involves very quick, subtle defensive activity.

A man who had been overstimulated by his mother, and especially by his father, was giving to clinging to his thoughts, feelings, longings for particular women in his life, in order to keep away from the dangers connected with positive feelings for his analyst. At one point, when working through some of these fears, he recalled the day he had first telephoned me. He said, "When I heard you saying 'yes, I can see you . . . will next week be all right . . . or is it more urgent?,' I was so moved that tears came to my eyes." At this point, some emotion came into his voice; there was a very short pause and he continued: "It was a time when I was still living with R (a woman with whom he had been very close) . . . it was in the country . . . but I was so depressed, and something about your willingness to see me . . ." (the emotion had left his voice by the time of this last remark). At that point I drew his attention to what had just taken place. I pointed out that what he had just spoken last was said rather differently — with less feeling — than he had permitted himself when he first began to recall and think about me. I showed him further that he had apparently run into difficulty with those feelings about me and that his familiar solution was to reach — ever so briefly, but it was there — for thoughts about a gratifying woman. He was able to attend to this, to think back briefly and review for himself what he had inadvertently done. He could now sense that he had stopped himself from being moved emotionally toward stronger feelings for me. He could take advantage of the evidence that he was afraid of these feelings. With some conviction, he said, "If I don't do that, I will want to be with you all of the time . . . I *won't* become that dependent."

In another example, a woman who in many ways used her masochism to shield herself from the dangers of revealing or asserting her phallically associated aggression spoke at one point of an individual who had repeatedly disappointed her: "That man . . . (angrily) I'm pissed off at him . . . (very slight pause) he is always dumping on me." Although she was still upset, but because she had acquired the capability of being closely observant upon intervention, the analyst interrupted her before she could go on, and reconstructed what took place. He pointed out her need — by thinking of the man "dumping" on her — to turn partly on herself what she had actively permitted toward another just an instant before when she said, "that man — I'm pissed off at him." She was thoughtful for a moment and then recalled a recent exchange with a woman friend. In the memory, the patient is saying of another man: "I said 'I'm pissed at him' . . .and then, with a viciousness that surprised me, I said, 'What I want to say to him is FUCK OFF!' "

I cite this example, of course, to show that because of practice in using her own observing equipment effectively the analysand is capable, when shown, of seeing how she could switch virtually in mid-sentence — in the immediacy of process — from an aggressive stance to a masochistic position. For our purpose, it is beside the point that she was also defending, by displacement, against transference impulses toward her analyst, or that through the process of gaining insight into the nature of her resistance and permitting a clearer version of her aggression, she needed to bring another woman into the picture momentarily (her mother always tolerated anger toward men and toward her father in particular). It is also beside the point that she had not yet spoken of the still live fantasied danger of expressing aggression toward men in front of me. We can observe all this in the example, and in practice the analysis would deal with it in due time. I elaborate these elements in an attempt to attenuate an easy diversion from our focus on the elusive area of observation of the ego's activities during neurotic solution to conflict. In this often less familiar and for some less interesting area of technique, one must sometimes compete with the listener's attention drifting toward other fascinating aspects of the clinical material not being addressed.

Finally, here is one more brief clinical example of what I mean by the analysand's eventual ability for a more autonomous self-observation. A woman who, through repeated shared observations, had learned about a particular defensive solution to her fear of her aggressive phallic impulses, said the following: "Yesterday, my mother spent twenty minutes on the phone carping about my father, she always . . . (pause) . . . but I did the same thing today on the phone with my sister, so who am I to . . .(stops here) . . . (slowly) . . . I can *see* what I am doing . . . (pause) I start to protect her again by taking it out on myself . . . what I want to say . . . my mother behaves like a bitch."

Here we can see where multiple skills of more or less simultaneously observing id contributions, conflict, and ego solutions all come together for a moment of conscious self-analysis.

Almost fifty years ago, Sterba's classic observations (1934) regarding the *fate* of the ego as one of *therapeutic dissociation* provided analysts with a valuable concept of how the observing ego plays an important role during the analytic process. I believe we can move beyond the implications of the word *fate* by thinking of the changes in the self-observing ego as more than a kind of inevitable byproduct of the analysis. Systematic attention to self-observation, when clinically appropriate, can become a more explicit aim of analysis of the neuroses. It should become an integral part of analysis of the ego's manifestations of resistance through its forms of unconscious, defensive activities in the face of analytically mobilized conflict. Whenever this is successfully carried out, I believe we have secured "the best possible psychological conditions for the functions of the ego" which, as Freud said (1937, p. 250) is "the business of the analysis."

REFERENCES

Abend, S. (1981), Psychic conflict and the concept of defense. *Psychoanal. Quart.*, 50:67–76.

Brenner, C. (1976), Defense analysis. In: *Psychoanalytic Technique and Psychic Conflict.* New York: International Universities Press, pp. 59–78.

_____ (1982), Defense. In: *The Mind in Conflict*. New York: International Universities Press, pp. 72–92.

Eissler, K. (1963, October 4), Unpublished minutes of the Scientific Faculty Meeting of the New York Psychoanalytic Institute.

Fenichel, O. (1941), *Problems of Psychoanalytic Technique*. New York: Psychoanalytic Quarterly.

Freud, A. (1936), The ego and the mechanisms of defense. *Writings*, 2. New York: International Universities Press, 1966.

Freud, S. (1917), General theory of the neurosis. *Standard Edition*, 16. London: Hogarth Press, 1963.

_____ (1926), Inhibitions, symptoms and anxiety. *Standard Edition*, 20:87–172. London: Hogarth Press, 1959.

_____ (1933), New introductory lectures on psycho-analysis, *Standard Edition*, 22:5–182. London: Hogarth Press, 1964.

_____ (1937), Analysis terminable and interminable. *Standard Edition*, 23:216–253. London: Hogarth Press, 1964.

Friedman, L. (1969), The therapeutic alliance. *Internat. J. Psycho-Anal.*, 50:139–153.

_____ (1976), Cognitive and therapeutic tasks of a theory of the mind. *Internat. Rev. Psycho-Anal.*, 3:259–275.

Gero, G. (1951), The concept of defense. *Psychoanal. Quart.*, 20:565–578.

Gill, M. (1963), *Topography and Systems in Psychoanalytic Theory*. Psychological *Issues*, 10. New York: International Universities Press.

_____ (1982), *Analysis of Transference. Vol. I. Theory of Technique*. Psychological *Issues*, 53. New York: International Universities Press.

Gray, P. (1973), Psychoanalytic technique and the ego's capacity for viewing intrapsychic conflict. *J. Amer. Psychoanal. Assn.*, 21:474–494.

_____ (1984), The value of extra-transference interpretation. (Panel reporter E. Halpert) *J. Amer. Psychoanal. Assn.*, 32:137–146.

_____ (1982), "Developmental lag" in the evolution of technique for psychoanalysis of neurotic conflict. *J. Amer. Psychoanal. Assn.*, 30:621–655.

Gutheil, T., & Havens, L. (1979), The therapeutic alliance: Contemporary meanings and confusions. *Internat. Rev. Psycho-Anal.*, 6:467–481.

Hartmann, H. (1960), *Psychoanalysis and Moral Values*. New York: International Universities Press.

Hatcher, R. (1973), Insight and self-observation. *J. Amer. Psychoanal. Assn.*, 21:377–398.

Kohut, H. (1971), *The Analysis of the Self*. New York: International Universities Press.

Kris, E. (1975), Some vicissitudes of insight. *Selected Papers of Ernst Kris*. New Haven: Yale University Press.

Loewenstein, R. (1982), Ego autonomy and psychoanalytic technique. In: *Practice and Precept in Psychoanalytic Technique: Selected Papers of Rudolph Lowenstein*. New Haven: Yale University Press.

Nunberg, H. (1937), Theory of the therapeutic results of psychoanalysis. In: *Practice and Theory of Psychoanalysis*, Vol. 1. New York: International Universities Press. 1948, pp. 165–173.

Orgel, S. (1974), Fusion with the victim and suicide. *Internat. J. Psycho-Anal.,* 55:531–538.

Rangell, L. (1983), Defense and resistance in psychoanalysis and life: In: *Defense and Resistance: Historical Perspectives and Current Concepts; J. Amer. Psychoanal. Assn. Supplement.,* 31:147–174.

Schafer, R. (1968), The mechanisms of defense. *Internat. J. Psycho-Anal.,* 49:49–62.

_____ (1973), The idea of resistance. In: *A New Language for Psychoanalysis.* New Haven: Yale University Press, 1976, pp. 212–263.

Sterba, R. (1934), The fate of the ego in analytic theory. *Internat. J. Psycho-Anal.,* 15:117–126.

Stone, L. (1973), On resistance to the psychoanalytic process. *Psychoanal. Contemp. Sci.,* 2:42–73.

Wallerstein, R. (1983), Defenses, defense mechanisms, and the structure of the mind. In: *Defense and Resistance: Historical Perspectives and Current Concepts: J. Amer. Psychoanal. Assn. Supplement.,* 31:201–225.

EDWARD D. JOSEPH

Psychoanalytic Concepts of Insight

The term insight is an old one in the psychiatric literature. As Zilboorg (1952) stated, it seems to have come from nowhere, but became imbedded in the psychiatric terminology very early. It is defined as related to the patient's awareness of being mentally ill. In this sense it persists even today in descriptive psychiatry; the standard mental status examination includes an evaluation of the patient's insight utilizing as a criterion whether the symptomatology and psychopathology include an awareness of being marked as sick or not normal. It does not imply understanding of the nature of the illness. For the most part, when Freud used the term insight in his writings, he was referring to its psychiatric definition.

On the other hand, interestingly enough, in his early case histories in the "Studies on Hysteria" (1895), he wrote of the details of his case histories and of learning from them. He would speak of gathering an increasing insight into their illness. He was using the term insight as the dictionary defines it as "the capacity to discern the true nature of a situation; a penetrating or elucidating glimpse." It was Freud, then, who was gaining the insight and discerning the true nature of the situation, an elucidating glimpse, of which his patients only got fragments.

In any psychoanalytic situation there are, of course, two individuals involved. The analysand is seeking a therapeutic benefit from the psychoanalytic procedure, and the analyst is seeking, among other goals, to help

Presented as the Brill Lecture to the New York Psychoanalytic Society, November 28, 1984. Also presented in modified versions to the Cleveland Psychoanalytic Society, the Baltimore-Washington Psychoanalytic Society and the Miami Psychoanalytic Society.

the patient achieve the sought after benefit through an understanding of the nature of the internal conflicts involved. Implicit is the idea that the analyst will gain some understanding (insight, as it were) of the nature of those difficulties and will help the analysand to achieve sufficient and necessary clarification to gain from the procedure. The analyst's goals are most often directed toward the patient's achieving this understanding, and only gradually does the analysand come to accept this goal as the means for gaining the desired objective. Thus, both will work toward a goal of understanding (insight) the inner depth of at least one mind, the analysand's. Often the analyst will gain that understanding and penetration before the analysand does, and hence is able, via interventions, interpretations, and other technical measures, to aid the analysand to begin to achieve greater degrees of awareness (insight) of his or her own mental content. Thus achievement of insight, while possible for one person to do, is usually a collaborative effort, often with the analyst providing the impetus and guidance through his techniques to the analysand. In what follows, I consider insight formation first from the perspective of patient, then from that of the analyst.

INSIGHT: THE ANALYSAND

During the entire period when the topographical theory held sway, the psychoanalytic theory of neurosogenesis considered that symptom formation resulted from conflict between conscious and unconscious mental content. In the early years, Freud thought that making the patient aware of the nature of that unconscious mental content would suffice to clarify the situation, achieve a therapeutic gain and benefit, and remove the symptoms.

Without saying so, he felt, on the basis of his theory of the cause of the symptom formation, that giving or achieving conscious awareness (what is now called insight) by the patient, after the analyst himself understood the situation, would have a therapeutic benefit. With experience it was learned that the patient did not cooperate willingly with this undertaking. This led to the discovery of resistance, to the necessity of working out the causes of the resistance, and to further explorations of the workings of the mental apparatus. A multitude of new findings and new techniques followed, all designed ultimately to "make the unconscous conscious." The theory of symptom formation that lay behind these technical devices utilized the same theoretical formations as the causation of neurosis and was designed to achieve conscious awareness of the warded off unconscious mental content. The desired therapeutic effect would then eventuate through the achievement of what would now be called insight. Implicit in this concept is that what is called insight is a conscious process and requires the participation of the system consciousness if a therapeutic effect is to occur.

With the changed theoretical model offered by the structural theory, conflict was assumed to be between the three great systems of the mind, and the therapeutic achievement could be considered in a vein similar to that which previously had been applied to the topographical model. "Where Id was, let Ego be" could be substituted for "make the unconscious conscious." However, increasing knowledge again demonstrated that many of the conflicts occurred not just between systems but also within the systems. In spite of that, the achievement of a deeper understanding of the nature of unconscious mental content continued to be sought as a goal and served as a sign post of a satisfactorily proceeding analysis. To the extent that patients "knew" the nature of their unconscious "Id" wishes or Ego operations, the more likely they were, according to the theory, to achieve good therapeutic results.

Zilboorg (1952) pointed out that insight in psychoanalytic terms carried with it the implication of a deeper understanding of oneself than was implied by the psychiatric implication of the term. In 1954, Edward Bibring described two main varieties of psychoanalytic insight—insight through clarification and insight through interpretation. He said that the principle of clarification "aims at the detachment of the ego through more differentiated self awareness and subsequently at better control through a more realistic, 'knowledge' of himself and the environment" while "interpretation aims at those changes of ego, and indirectly of other functional systems of the *level of consciousness* with the result that the causal determinants of the various disorders are modified or removed" (p. 760) (italics added). It was, according to Bibring, interpretation leading to insight that was the principal therapeutic device and modality making for the therapeutic change. Interpretation was the mutative factor producing insight and ultimately therapeutic gain. Bibring, however, does not specify anything about the nature of insight other than stating that it lifts unconscious conflicts to the level of consciousness. He does point out that insight is achieved through interpretations, which lead to changes in the ego and in other functional systems of the personality and consequently permit the lifting of whatever is keeping unconscious conflicts from consciousness. The nature of these changes were not specified.

Two years later, Kris (1956), in an elegant paper, articulated in much greater detail the nature of the changes required in order for insight to be achieved. He also described various aspects of the nature of insight and its utilization within the psychoanalytic situation, and discussed its fate and relationship to the therapeutic outcome. Kris pointed out that the patient's acquisition of insight is an experience that progresses in the course of the psychoanalysis often from a flat, two-dimensional intellectual state of mind to a "real, concrete, three dimensional" experience. Cognitive elements merge with a particular kind of assurance and, depending on the nature of the insightful situation, with recent or more archaic modes of experiences.

Kris distinguished between the misuse of insight by the patient and the beneficial uses of insight. Insight may be used by the patient for purposes of defense or infantile gratification; as Kris particularly pointed out, it may decline into an intellectualization, as a pseudoinsight. Here the insight is used in the service of both id and ego gratifications and serves neurotic needs, becoming a symptom possibly in and of itself. On the other hand, insight may advance the analysis by overcoming barriers of defensiveness and resistance; and, through a partial increase in the self-observing function, it may stimulate inquiry and curiosity and facilitate introspection. The latter functions widen insight, leading to further changes in defense, memory, integration, and other ego functions, which in turn lead to possible alteration of patient's symptoms and/or character structure. Thus, insight is part of a *process,* the culmination of an analytic process involving dynamic changes. And "without other dynamic changes insight would not come about; but without insight and the ego's achievement which leads to insight, therapy itself remains limited and does not retain the character of psychoanalysis" (Kris, 1956, p. 170). Principal among these dynamic changes and the ego's achievements, Kris described the activities of the ego's integrative function, which proceeds silently and in ways unknown both to the patient and to the analyst.

Kris (1956) emphasized the analytic work, the undoing of defenses, the working through process, the reliving through the transference neurosis, the recall of memories and the reconstruction of both past and present life events and fantasies, all of which are grist for the operation of the integrative function. This involvement in the psychoanalytic process in its myriad details allow for altering of existing structures and symptoms, thereby leading to new insights as an integral part of the process. Once an insight is achieved, the process starts over again. The insights gained may be lost at a given time, Kris observed, but often as the analytic process continues, there is some continuity from one insight experience to the other. By the end of an analysis, he stated, there are many patients whose insight continues; they retain "a lasting awareness of their own problems, a high degree of ability to view themselves" (p. 270). On the other hand, in another group of patients who also have good therapeutic effect from the analytic work, the insight gained seems lost, as, for that matter, does a memory of the course of the analysis. Thus, "it seems that insight in some individuals remains only a transient experience, one to be obliterated again in the course of life by one of the defenses they are wont to use" (p. 270). But this does not in any way seem to correlate with the therapeutic effectiveness of their analysis nor with greater proneness to future disorder.

What emerges from Kris's discussion is that insight is not a phenomenon that is achieved at a given instant in an analysis and once attained is held onto forever. Rather, it is part of an ongoing process, the culmination of an analytic process thta might be said to proceed in ever widening circles from the beginning of an analysis onward. The insights from an early phase of an analysis are different from those from later stages. The insights from the beginning often are of a dynamic nature that refers to more current and immediate dynamic conflicts (clarifications, as Bibring (1954) would put it). As the analysis progresses, more and more data from earlier periods of life, from more unconscious levels, are brought into play and included in the insightful process (interpretations, in Bibring's terms). What may be integrated at a given moment may remain intact and conscious to the patient; or it may be obliterated and have to be "rediscovered" at future times in the context of other material.

A 42-year-old woman whose previous analysis had been interrupted some years before, when her marriage was breaking up and she was facing divorce, returned because her second marriage was encountering difficulties. During the first treatment period, her life situation was complicated by problems with her children, her mother's illness, and the difficulties with her husband. Much of the analytic work however had centered on her adolescent years and her reaction to the death of her father when she was 14, the family's coping with the consequences, and her apparent denial of any deep sense of loss. She maintained that since father had been out of the house so much, he played little part in her life and it was her much older brothers who were the significant males for her. Certainly, her first husband had often been compared unfavorably with her older brothers.

Soon after she resumed treatment, the patient and her new husband went away for a long weekend to a resort area with friends. In the session following that weekend, she spoke of her dissatisfaction with her husband because of his behavior with their friends and with acquaintances they had met. Her friends were important to her because they praised work she had done, much to her surprise, since she felt that her own work was not of much consequence. She was pleased by their comments and was especially sensitive to her husband's behavior toward them. She felt he had made a fool of himself and made her look bad before her friends and acquaintances. This led her to speak of other times and other situations in which she felt he had acted in a similarly foolish manner, appearing ridiculous in the eyes of other people, and certainly in her eyes. She would then add that perhaps he felt uncertain of himself with strangers. She, though, wished that he would keep quiet rather than speak foolishly. Even her previous husband had more social grace than this and could be counted on to make a good impression in a social situation. Perhaps she had been too hasty in terminating the previous marriage or in entering this one. Perhaps she hadn't realized how well off she had been.

After a relatively short pause, with a changed tone of voice with much greater intensity and sharpness, she suddenly exclaimed, "It's all the consequence of my father's death!" She went on to say everything bad that had happened had been since then. She continued that, being the youngest and the only girl, she had been his favorite of the three children. She recalled the fond looks he used to direct toward her, sitting on his lap as a little girl, the walks together to the ice cream parlor on weekends when he was not working, his leaving her allowance in her room before he left for work, and other ways in which he indicated his interest, attention and care for her. As she related these *new memories* in the treatment situation, memories neither recalled nor described when she first had been seen in analysis, tears were streaming down her face. My only comment at the end of the session was to say, "You didn't know when you were well off," picking up what seemed to be the connecting thought between the present-day circumstances and the memories of the past.

I shall not pursue this clinical example further, but rather address the insight that the patient produced seemingly unexpectedly and out of the blue. It is of interest because much of the preparatory work for this particular insightful statement and recollection had been done some years before, in the first period of her analysis. Since then a combination of life circumstances, change of situation, and new relationships with echoes into the past had occurred and been integrated into both current and past life, as well as fantasy events.

The unifying, perhaps integrating thought, really revolved around her awareness that she did not know when she was well off until it was too late. Although the phrase came out in conjunction with her first marriage, it led through the work done in earlier years to the trauma of her father's death, with its impact on her and her development. Although Freud (1926) states that the barriers of repression may occasionally be broken through spontaneously, it seldom happens. Therefore, one can assume that it was a combination of the work of some years before, together with the special circumstances coming together at that particular moment, that led to the insightful statement made by the patient.

Lest it be thought that insight production came about purely through intellectual or cognitive processing, which might have been the implication particularly of Bibring's statements about interpretations leading to insight and a possible misreading of Kris, Valenstein (1962), specifically articulated that insight is more than an intellectual or cognitive process. He pointed out the important contribution of the affective component and the need for the affective and cognitive components to be integrated for true insight to be obtained. He stated, "In psychoanalysis, the element of emotion, as it bears upon a proportionate and properly tuned integrated degree of emotional reliving, would seem to be of fundamental significance to the final development of insight" (p. 322). Thus, for him the mutative or dynamic insight combined "both affective, conative and intellectual components."

More recently, with widening psychoanalytic knowledge and changing technique, new considerations concerning insight have entered the literature. Work by Meyerson (1965) differentiated types of insight and some of the genetic interaction between child and parents that foster a potential for psychoanalytic insight. Hatcher (1973) emphasized particularly the ego function of self-observation as a major component, while Neubauer (1979), speaking of both child and adult analyses, gave particular attention to the part played by "the ego's synthetic, organizing, or integrating function." Blum (1979, 1981), Abrams (1981), Shengold (1981), and others have emphasized varying aspects of the insight process in more current terms. All concur, however, that insight is the penetrating or elucidating glimpse into unconscious processes made conscious and is the *sine qua non* of the psychoanalytic process.

Insight, in the sense of knowing oneself, has, of course, varying levels of understanding and comprehension. In a psychoanalytic sense, it refers to much more than an awareness of the existence of both problems and unconscious conflicts. In the course of the successful analysis, it includes ultimately the achievement of some idea of the nature of these unconscious conflicts. It is through the work of analysis, with its techniques of uncovering, analysis of defensive maneuvers, working through, reliving through the transference neurosis and manifestations and empathic communications, that unconscious content can be made conscious. Since much that is unconscious has never been conscious in any stage of development, the inferences and interpretations of analysis often supply linkages that make sense and connect various manifestations, providing more reasonable form to the mental products than they most likely possess. Often, therefore, what is communicated to a patient, or what a patient puts together as the result of the analytic process leading to insight, is something that has never been fully conscious before and becomes conscious only during the analytic process.

The patient's capacity to recognize an insight after achieving it and to react to it is a function of that part of the ego apparatus regarded as the self-observing function. In 1933, Freud wrote, "The Ego can take itself as an object, can treat itself like other objects, and observe itself, criticize itself and do Heaven knows what with itself. In this, one part of the ego is setting itself over against the rest" (p. 58). The capacity to observe oneself varies from individual to individual and is often used as one of the criteria for analyzability, as though this introspective quality will aid in the analytic process. It suggests that the capacity to view oneself, to take oneself as the object of observation, is something that certainly furthers the analytic process and may well do so by making the insight aspect of analysis easier to acquire, as Hatcher (1973) emphasized.

Outside the psychoanalytic situation people differ greatly in their introspective qualities. For many, the capacity to observe oneself is present even if they are not really conscious of it. Playwrights, poets, novelists and other artists display this capacity in their creations, even if in their personal life they show no traces of it. However, it is not only the gifted who are able to develop self-observing ability in the course of an analysis. Patients are often able to do so as part of the relationship with the analyst. Although the term has been criticized in the literature, the concept of the working alliance, or therapeutic alliance, is a useful one and describes a partial identification with the analyst and the analytic function of the analyst in examining the thoughts, emotions, and productions of a patient. It is a partial joining with the analyst in the analytic work.

A 30-year-old man, whose analysis had been stormy and whose recent sessions had been filled with long silences, drowsiness on the couch, lateness to sessions, delay in paying his bill, had begun to question whether analysis was worth continuing. He was aware of the difficulties he was having in expressing himself and felt that the gain was not worth the trouble he was encountering. He wondered if he should stop, pointing out that his life was neither so bad nor so difficult that he could not get along without analysis. At the end of one such session, in accordance with wishes he had expressed some time earlier, I told him of my holiday plans and of the proposed schedule for the fall. The next session he was on time, spoke freely and easily, telling many of the thoughts he had hinted at during previous sessions, giving the details of events he had said were too difficult to discuss. As this session went on, he suddenly broke in, saying, "Isn't it strange? For several weeks I've been telling you that I've been thinking of ending the analysis. Yet, here I am talking as though everything is fine, and I have no difficulty in speaking out. I cannot help but wonder if your mention of your vacation has in some way had an effect on me that this has happened?" I could only concur with him and say that he had taken the words out of my mouth.

His insight was, I believe, accurate and certainly based on the ability to observe himself as he was freely associating on the couch. This was in marked contrast to his earlier behavior. Not only could he observe the change in his behavior, but he could make a connection between that change and the altered event—the information about my vacation and hours scheduled for afterward—that might play a part. This was an instance of the observing function and the therapeutic alliance at work producing an insight that would further the course of the analysis by opening up the reaction to an impending separation. His observation and phrasing was couched in the best of analyst terms and could have come from either side of the analytic couch.

The ability to develop insight is certainly not inborn; its developmental sequence has recently been subject to consideration. Capability for insight in children seems not to be present in the very early years but rather to require a level of maturation and development past the stage of object constancy and well into mid-childhood. (Anna Freud, 1979, 1981; Kennedy, 1979; Neubauer, 1979). Thus, well-established defensive structures, well-developed cognitive and affective structuring, and a relative degree of self-and object-constancy are all required. The integrative and synthetic functions, to the extent that these have developmental aspects, also need a degree of maturation. All of this, together with a certain capacity for self observation suggest that the potential for insight is a relatively late developmental phenomenon. It has only recently begun to be studied by child analysts and much more work needs to be done in this regard.

INSIGHT: THE ANALYST

Obviously, the analytic situation is a dyad, and the analyst is involved in the process of insight formation and production. The usual view in the early literature assumed that the analyst's role was to provide a variety of interpretations that supplied the necessary links enabling the patient to achieve a state of insightfulness. For the analyst to do this, he must already have achieved an understanding, a knowing, of the meaning of the associations being presented. Therefore, the psychoanalytic literature on technique repeatedly advised the analyst to pay close attention to the patient's associations, but to allow his "freely hovering attention" to come into play so that his own unconscious processes would react to what was coming from the patient. Implicitly, the analyst was expected to achieve a state of insight – to understand what the patient was producing – in order to translate it back to the patient. He was expected to achieve this state through a combination of his theoretical knowledge and his understanding of the latent meaning of patient's associations, as well as their manifest form as processed through his own mental apparatus resonating in tune with the patient. The more he understood the patient, the more effective he could be psychoanalytically and ultimately therapeutically.

There was, at times, the implication that the analyst was, in effect, a mirror reflecting back what the patient had presented to him; but it became clear that this analogy was an imperfect one. Gradually, the concept of countertransference arose, and it was recognized that analyst might have difficulties of his own, which would interfere with his ability to listen to, be empathic with, understand, and hence translate and transmit to the patient. As is well known, out of the experiences arising from such situations came the recommendation that the analyst himself be analyzed so that his own inner problems would not interfere with his achieving an understanding, of gaining an insight into the analysand. This recommendation ultimately became one of the basic tenets of psychoanalytic education.

It also came to be recognized that the process of gaining understanding into the workings of the mind of another person was not a purely neutral procedure. Ella Sharpe (1947), Greenson (1967), and Tahka (1984) have written about this. Sharp described the pleasure of the analyst in comprehending through listening, looking, exploring, imagining – pleasure that makes for the optimal efficiency of the analyst. She emphasized that the analyst's curiosity must be free from conflict, guilt, and anxiety for him to sustain the lively interest and concern for the goings on in his patients. More particularly, though, she, and later Greenson, spoke of some of the problems that might interfere with this process – conflicts of a scoptophilic or sadistic nature or conflicts derived from oral or anal levels of development. Sharpe spoke of tracing such strivings to understand another human being in as intimate a way as insight implies as a return to a symbiotic fusion with the mother or to hostile destructive impulses toward the mother's insides; or, the desire to obtain insight may become a substitute for the sexual curiosity of the oedipal phase, for the frustrated sexuality of that period of life. In effect, both she and Greenson speak of the possibility that this insight-gathering activity of the analyst may become linked with anxiety or guilt, producing fantasies on the part of the

analyst that would interfere with his ability to function in a neutral, therapeutic manner. To the extent that he is well analyzed, or, more particularly is able to carry on a self analysis, he can and should be able to
deal with these situations as they arise. That is the real purpose of the
training analysis — to enable the analyst to carry on a self-analytic process,
since such conflicts can be revived in the course of one's work or other life
situations. It is not their revival, but rather the ability to deal with them,
that marks the well-analyzed person who has had a good analysis as part
of his training.

Having said this, the analyst must also be able to recognize which of his
various reactions come not from himself or his own past, but rather are in
response to the patient and the patient's productions in the form of what is
now called projective identification. For the changing nature of the patient population and more particularly with the deepening understanding
and widening scope of defensive procedures, it can now be seen that not
every reaction on the analyst's side of the couch is necessarily countertransferential, but may be part of an empathic response to a patient
and the patient's communication. It may in fact be as communicative as
anything else the patient is presenting. As such it belongs in the analysis as
one of the many associations leading to insight production.

The analyst brings to his role in the analysis not only himself but his
whole body of knowledge and experience, with all the changes that have
occurred in that body of knowledge and experience over the years.
Kohut (1979), for example, stated that his second analysis of Mr. Z. was
successful because of new theoretical "insight into the psychology of the
self" (p. 4). Compared with colleagues of an earlier day, the analyst of today has a much larger theoretical knowledge, which has been influenced
by studies of development, of the nature of borderline states, of earlier
phases of life. He knows much more about later stages of life such as latency, adolescence, youth, and adulthood. All of this additional knowledge helps shape his awareness and responsiveness to the patient's associations. In addition, in his empathic, freely hovering attention to these
associations, he, more than the analyst of the past, knows which of his reactions may be in response to the paient rather than countertransferential, in the older sense of that term. He still seeks to gain insight into the
workings of the patient's mind and to be able to interpret that understanding to the patient for the patient's benefit. Often, however, the analyst's
elucidation far outstrips the elements he is able to utilize at any given
time. Most analysts have had the experience of listening to the analytic
material and of seeing many implications and gaining much understanding of a patient at a given moment, much of which cannot be used at that
moment and only some of which can be focused on in any given session.

In the first example I presented, I focused on the bridging thought between present and past, rather than on the content and the many implications of that content in the session.

In psychoanalysis, much that may be understood by the analyst during the early sessions will in all probability be disclosed in the course of the analysis with the unfolding analytic process, progressing eventually to insight. Ideally, the earlier insights will come through the linking of contemporary material with superficially unconscious links, often by the transference, through to older, archaic unconscious fantasies and memories, with the establishment of connections that were not made before and often with the gaining of insight into fantasies that had never been conscious before.

In contrast to those of the analytic process, the insights of psychotherapy are most often those of the therapist. Given his psychoanalytic background and experience, he often percieves much and understands many of the patient's communications. Those that are shared with the patient are often of a superficial nature, not combining both current and archaic components. Nor is there the same working through of defenses and of transferences as in a complete psychoanalysis.

By virtue of his training, knowledge, experience, the psychoanalyst is in many psychiatric situations, able to understand the significance of the productions of other individuals, whether they be psychotic patients, neurotic, elderly or geriatric patients, character disorders. Often the circumstances of a consultation or even a social situation do not call for the utilization therapeutically of the elucidation that the analyst has at a given moment; but in a consultation, such elucidation may guide the recommendations that he might make. Pollock (1981) described the understanding and insights that he was able to achieve with several geriatric patients in the setting of a home for the aged that allowed for therapeutic handling of difficult situations by the staff.

The analyst must be careful, however, not to misuse the insight that he gains from patients and not to use it in the service of furthering some of his own needs, particularly when these may be of a sadistic nature (Bird, 1957). Of course, the transmission of the analyst's insight in these situations often is the transmission of an intellectualized insight, devoid of the affective component that makes of the insight process a living experience for the patient. For some patients, however, even this may have a therapeutic effect.

Many years ago, long before the concept of borderline became popular, I saw in consultation a patient who had a multitude of symptoms—

conversions, phobias, compulsions, obsessive thoughts, together with bursts of generalized anxiety. In tracing out the situations in which these various manifestations occurred and wishing to say something to him, as time was running out before arranging another session, I commented that whatever else his myriad symptoms indicated, it seemed to me that whenever he got angry, he seemed to have an increase in his generalized anxiety. When I next saw him a week or so later, he was beaming and stated that that had been the most illuminating and insightful statement he had ever heard. He had been applying it to himself and found that he was doing so much better. I had to ask what he was referring to, and he told me that whenever he began to feel anxious after seeing me, he stopped to ask himself what he was angry about. Since he could always find something, he immediately understood why he was anxious and would begin to feel better. He then added that he was going to use that insight. I felt that this insightful statement, whatever its transference implications, provided a degree of ego control that was beneficial to him; I thought it was better to leave well enough alone. Today, now that I understand borderline states somewhat better, I might perhaps have achieved the same result after much more work.

GENERAL DISCUSSION

In regard to insight and its relation to cure, Wallerstein (1965) observed that we make "a tacit assumption that the two develop together and in appropriate correspondence to each other—that is, that the achievement of analytic insights in the process of making the unconscious conscious is the constant and the necessary and the (implicitly) sufficient concomitant of the achievement of the outcome goals, to be able to love and to work..." (p. 763). It is this assumption and this correspondence that I wish to examine at this point.

As regards the assumption, Freud was a great believer in the power of reason as well as a great seeker of the truth. Valenstein (1981) quotes the psychoanalyst-historian Peter Gay:

> The most conspicuous trait in Freud's charcter, indispensible to his capacity for generating insights and his patience in developing them into a general psychology is his uncompromising commitment to truth. It was so powerful, he found it so natural, he rarely troubled to justify, let alone analyze it. If it is impossible to elucidate completely, its principal strands—curiosity, single mindedness, and intellectual courage—are manifest. Freud, above all, wanted to know . . . [p. 308].

Freud believed at that early point in his career that making known the truth of the cause of the symptoms would provide a convincing explanation and would have a "curative effect."

Freud never gave up his search for the truth and asserted in his later paper (1937) that "The analytic relationship is based on a love of truth..." (p. 248). He continued to feel that, regardless of the implications of his many new findings and new theoretical formulations, reason would triumph over illogic and internal conflict based upon fantasy, illogic (primary process type of thinking), instinctual forces, etc. Yet with all this, his belief was that as these could be made conscious through working through resistances, defenses, and the like, reason and intellect would take over and be curative. He stated it most succinctly in his 1927 monograph: "We may insist as often as we like that man's intellect is powerless in comparison with his instinctual life and we may be right in this. Nevertheless, there is something peculiar about this weakness. The voice of the intellect is a soft one, but it does not rest until it has gained a hearing. Finally, after a countless succession of rebuffs, it succeeds" (p. 53).

Thus for Freud part of the therapeutic benefit of insight was achieved through the discovery of the truth and of bringing, through the achievement of insight as an experience, to the attention of reason, to the attention of the intellect, the warded off unconscious mental content. Once the truth was known, it would triumph, a thought that has an almost philosophic or slight mystical quality about it. Anna Freud, in her lecture to the New York Psychoanalytic Society (1968), pointed out how the changing intellectual atmosphere has played down the role of reason in the life of people, making them less interested in psychoanalysis and its approach and therefore less amenable to its form of treatment. Regardless of the change in intellectual climate in contemporary society, psychoanalysis — with its search for the truth through the gaining of insight and understanding of the workings of another person's mind and making the other person aware in an experiential manner, as well as furthering the rationality of its approach — has remained the most reasonable of therapies.

It is not only the voice of the intellect leading to insight that has a therapeutic or curative effect. Six years after the previous statement, Freud wrote (1933) the definition of the analytic goal: ". . . to strengthen the ego . . . to widen its field of perception and enlarge its organization... where Id was, there shall Ego be" (p. 80). This well-known aphorism concerning the widening of the area of insightful ego activity implies a great deal and involves the whole analytic process. The psychoanalytic process now involves working through defensive maneuvers in conflictual situations of an unconscious nature; uncovering or recovering fantasies and memories that are no longer available; and dealing with aspects of developmental arrest that have to do with relationships with objects and with the self, with narcissistic elements that may obscure both object and self aspects as well as perceptions. Superego elements may well enter into the process, and certainly affective components of both a libidinal and aggressive nature and even of a depressive nature may occur. All of these take place within the setting of the analytic situation and of the transference-countertransference interaction, which includes the empathic comprehension of the analyst as an integral part of the interplay. The insight process, then, allows for new connections and reconnections, which may never have existed or may have been severed, and allows the silent integrative processes of the ego to operate so that a new understanding into "causes, meanings, and connections" (Blum, 1979) come into being. New integrations can take place, again often silently, so that the process is repeated as the analysis progresses.

It appears then that the therapeutic gains ascribed to the achievement of insight, to the understanding or elucidation process, are instead the result of the intensive and extensive psychoanalytic work done in the course of psychoanalysis and involve the many factors that enter into the psychoanalytic process itself. Whatever the nature of the psychoanalytic process, the subject of much study and much uncertainty, it does seem to include the ability to observe oneself as one component necessary for the achievement of insight.

In other words, with the acquisition of levels of insight, new levels of integration, ego mastery, and control are established in relation to a range of conflicts that previously gave rise to symptomatic behaviors. These conflicts come under more active ego mastery or at least there is a diminution of the symptomatic manifestations. We often learn in passing from patients of the disappearence of previously existing symptoms, although they have not been directly worked upon but rather have disappeared as a result of analytic work on more basic conflicts. One such patient whose fear of aggression had been the prime focus of his treatment recently reported, to his surprise, that during a recent flight he was halfway across the country before he realized that he was not afraid of flying, as he had been for a number of years. His fear of flying had not been directly analyzed, but rather his fear of retaliation for his many destructive fantasies had been worked on quite extensively. It was possible in this instance to establish the relationship between the two and gain an insight into the meaning of his fear of flying as a retaliatory concern for his "soaring too high."

An interesting phenomenon that still remains to be studied concerns those analyses that seem to be successful from a therapeutic point of view but in which the patient appears to gain relatively little insight into the nature of his conflicts. Similarly, there are other analyses in which much insight appears to be gained but with relatively little therapeutic benefit being achieved. This is not the same as the phenomenon in which insights successfully achieved in the course of an analysis are lost, or in which patients forget the analysis itself after they complete treatment, even though they continue to derive therapeutic benefit from it. Patients appear to deal in their usual defensive manner with the insights achieved as they deal with other memories and either retain some memory, have a few screening insights that serve for the totality of their memories of the whole experience, or lose the totality of the experience as they lose the totality of their memory. This seems to depend on their defensive style.

The relationship between achieving insight into and understanding of oneself and subsequent action following that understanding is a puzzling one. Rangell (1979) has pointed out that an insight that might be expected to lead to action very often does not. He discusses some of the factors that may produce such a stalemate. The issue remains to be clarified, since there is often a gap between the understanding during an analysis and its translation into a change in behavior or activity.

These and other questions point to an opportunity for both clinical research and controlled, systematic studies into the nature of the insight process and its role in the therapeutic outcome of psychoanalysis and its derivative therapies. Systematic studies are only just beginning to be done, partly because there has been a bias against such work and partly because of the difficulties implicit in doing it. Nonetheless, they are necessary studies for some of the questions raised in this paper and many others that could be raised (Wallerstein, 1983).

A final conjecture to conclude this paper. Since the initial work in psychoanalysis the concept of insight has always included the conscious awareness of some unconscious mental activity — conflict, fantasy, memory, and so forth. We are accustomed to utilizing the conscious derivatives for deducing the underlying unconscious content, but in the insight process we actually proceed, through the myriad aspects of the psychoanalytic process, in the direction opposite to achieving consciousness of the unconscious content. Insight always involves this conscious quality. Since the therapeutic effect of insight is assumed to be due not only to the alteration of underlying structures involved in the various processes that lead to the conscious insight, but also to the actual consciousness of insight itself, there seems to be an assumption that somehow consciousness makes possible therapeutic benefit. Yet we know so little of the nature of consciousness and most of our explanations are offered in terms of psychic energies that we must admit an ignorance of consciousness. Freud had various formulations for consciousness, but he never wrote the theoretical paper on consciousness that he intended. Consciousness is associated with speech and language, which are tremendously important human manifestations. In a paper on the Concept of Mental Representation, Beres and I (1970), discussing the concept of consciousness, raised the question, "Is there in man a continuous cortical activity similar to the continuous activity of the sub-cortical reticular and limbic system — the former capable of evoking imagery, thought and fantasy, the latter capable of evoking affective states and arousal? We do not know and we must leave this and other questions for future studying" (p. 8). The question is still unanswered, but it may well be that this is one of the connecting links between psychoanalytic psychology and the neurobiologies burgeoning in so many laboratories about the country. These can be no doubt that there are connecting links between findings at a psychological level and the laboratory findings at a neurobiological level. Recent writers (e.g., Reiser, 1984) have been suggesting this more and more.

ACKNOWLEDGMENTS

The author wishes to acknowledge the stimulation of the Westchester Psychoanalytic Society Study group, Drs. R. Gilder, I. Harrison, S. Lituchey, L. Rockwell and E. Rowntree.

REFERENCES

Abrams, S. (1981), Insight — The Teirisian gift. *The Psychoanalytic Study of the Child*, 36:250–269.

American Heritage Dictionary (1969), ed. William Morris. New York: American Heritage & Houghton, Mifflin.

Beres, D. & Joseph, E. (1970), The concept of mental representation. *Internat. J. Psycho-Anal.*, 51:1–9.

Bibring, E. (1954), Psychoanalysis and the dynamic psychotherapies. *J. Amer. Psychoanal. Assn.*, 2:745–770.

Bird, B. (1957), The curse of insight. *Bull. Phila. Assn. Psychoanal.* 7:101–104.

Blum, H. (1979), Curative and creative aspects of insight. *J. Amer. Psychoanal. Assn.*, 27 (Suppl.):41–69.

———— (1981), The forbidden quest and the analytic ideal: The superego and insight. *Psychoanal. Quart.*, 50:535–556.

Freud, A. (1968), Difficulties in the path of psychoanalysis: A confrontation of past with present viewpoints. In: *The Writings of Anna Freud*, Vol. VII, New York: International Universities Press, pp. 124–156, 1971.

———— (1979), The role of insight in psychoanalysis and psychotherapy. *J. Amer. Psychoanal. Assn.*, 27 (Suppl.):3–7.

_____ (1981), Insight: Its presence and absence as a factor in normal development. *The Psychoanalytic Study of the Child,* 36:241–250.

Freud, S. (1895), Studies in hysteria. *Standard Edition,* 2. London: Hogarth Press, 1955.

_____ (1926), Inhibitions, symptoms and anxiety. *Standard Edition,* 20:77–175. London: Hogarth Press, 1959.

_____ (1927), The future of an illusion. *Standard Edition,* 21:5–58. London: Hogarth Press, 1961.

_____ (1933), New introductory lectures on psycho-analysis. *Standard Edition,* 22:3–182. London: Hogarth Press, 1964.

_____ (1937), Analysis terminable and interminable. *Standard Edition,* 23:209–254. London: Hogarth Press, 1964.

Greenson, R. (1967), *The technique and practice of psychoanalysis.* New York: International Universities Press, pp. 380–400.

Hatcher, R. (1973), Insight and self-observation. *J. Amer. Psychoanal. Assn.,* 21:377–398.

Kennedy, H. (1979), The role of insight in child analysis. *J. Amer. Psychoanal. Assn.,* 27 (Suppl.)9–28.

Kohut, H. (1979), The two analyses of Mr. Z. *Internat. J. Psycho-Anal.,* 60:3–27.

Kris, E. (1956), Some vicissitudes of insight in psychoanalysis. In: *Selected Papers.* New Haven: Yale University Press, pp. 252–271, 1975.

Neubauer, P. (1979), The role of insight in psychoanalysis. *J. Amer. Psychoanal. Assn.,* 27 (Suppl.):29–40.

Meyerson, P. (1965), Modes of insight. *J. Amer. Psychoanal. Assn.,* 13:147–156.

Pollock, G. (1981), Reminisences and insight. *The Psychoanalytic Study of the Child,* 36:279–288.

Rangell, L. (1979), Contemporary Issues in the theory of therapy. *J. Amer. Psychoanal. Assn.,* 27 (Suppl.):81–112.

Reiser, M. (1984), *Mind, Brain, Body.* New York: Basic Books.

Sharpe, E. (1947), The Psychoanalyst. In: *Collected Papers on Psychoanalysis.* London: Hogarth Press, 1950.

Shengold, L. (1981), Insight as metaphor. *The Psychoanalytic Study of the Child,* 36:289–305.

Tahka, V. (1984), Dealing with Object Loss. *Scand. Psychoanal. Rev.,* 7:13–35.

Valenstein, A. (1962), The psychoanalytic situation: Affects, emotional reliving and insight in the psychoanalytic process. *Internat. J. Psycho-Anal.,* 43:315–324.

_____ (1981), Insight as an embedded concept. *The Psychoanalytic Study of the Child,* 36:307–316.

Wallerstein, R. (1965), The goals of psychoanalysis, *J. Amer. Psychoanal. Assn.,* 13:748–770.

_____ (1983), Some thoughts about insight and psychoanalysis. *Israel J. Psych.,* 20:33–44.

Zilboorg, G. (1952), The emotional problem and the therapeutic role of insight. *Psychoanal. Quart.,* 21:1–24.

PART FOUR

The Clinical Practice of Psychoanalysis

In *Psychoanalytic Technique and Psychic Conflict,* Charles Brenner writes of the importance of "the awareness of the nature of the analytic task as a whole — the task of understanding as fully as possible the nature and origins of each patient's conflicts." In this section, four experienced analysts demonstrate with detailed discussions of clinical material the effort to fulfill that task.

Lester H. Friedman takes up the issue of transference resistance and reconstruction in the analysis of a latency girl. He shows how the persistent focus on a powerful resistance in his young patient led to a reconstruction of an earlier period that had a profound impact on her. The working through of the conflicts revealed was crucial to the success of the treatment.

Theodore Jacobs, reporting on a number of clinical cases, also discusses the relationship between transference and reconstruction. He details convincingly how attention to and analysis of the relationships that exist between the multiple and shifting transferences that emerge in the course of every psychoanalytic treatment can lead to important and valuable reconstructions.

Yale Kramer writes that a detailed case report about termination is a rarity in the psychoanalytic literature. Correcting this omission, he offers detailed clinical material dealing with the ending of his patient's analysis. He concludes that the essence of the termination phase is the recognition and partial renunciation of the patient's most important infantile wishes.

Edward M. Weinshel reports on three women who each experienced significant perceptual distortions during analysis. With careful attention to the details of each patient's history and transference manifestations in the analytic situation, he demonstrates the role of the superego in the perceptual distortions and reality testing.

LESTER H. FRIEDMAN

Silence as Transference Resistance: Reconstruction in a Latency Girl

I n this paper I present a clinical example from the analysis of a latency girl in which her transference resistance of being silent and shutting me out by reading is a way of remembering the past. I describe this reconstruction during her analysis and its effect on the subsequent course of her analysis. A discussion of this clinical material and its relationship to the literature on transference, resistance, reconstruction, and silence follows.

REVIEW OF THE LITERATURE

Freud first called attention to transference as a feature of the psychoanalytic situation in the epilogue to "A Fragment of the Analysis of a Case of Hysteria" (1905, pp. 116–120). He noted that when a repressed sexual wish or impulse of childhood is aroused during analysis, the patient, instead of remembering what he had felt at that time and to whom the feeling was directed, applies it to the analyst as a current wish.

Freud, (1912) wrote, "If someone's need for love is not entirely satisfied by reality, he is bound to approach every new person whom he meets with libidinal anticipatory ideas; and it is highly probable that both portions of his libido, the portion that is capable of becoming conscious as well as the unconscious one, have a share in forming that attitude" (p. 100). Thus, Freud spelled out his view of transference and specified a

283

view of transference enounced by Brenner (1982), namely, that transference occurs with every new person.

Freud noted that transference emerges as the most powerful resistance to treatment:

> When analysis comes upon the libido withdrawn into its hiding place, a struggle is bound to break out; all the forces which have caused the libido to regress will rise up as "resistances" against the work of analysis, in order to conserve the new state of things [1912, p. 102].

> The unconscious impulses do not want to be remembered in the way the treatment desires them to be, but endeavor to reproduce themselves in accordance with the timelessness of the unconscious and its capacity for hallucination. Just as happens in dreams, the patient regards the products of the awakening of his unconscious impulses as contemporaneous and real; he seeks to put his passions into action without taking any account of the real situation [1912, p. 108].

Freud then stated that the struggle between doctor and patient over understanding versus seeking to act is played out in the transference. Freud noted that the greater the resistance, the more extensively will acting out replace remembering.

> If the patient starts his treatment under the auspices of a mild and unpronounced positive transference, it makes it possible at first for him to unearth his memories just as he would under hypnosis, and during this time his pathological symptoms themselves are quiescent. But if, as the analysis proceeds, the transference becomes hostile or unduly intense and therefore in need of repression, remembering at once gives way to acting out. From then onwards the resistances determine the sequence of the material which is to be repeated [1914, p. 151].

Noticing or naming the resistance is not enough:

> One must allow the patient time to become more conversant with this resistance with which he has now become acquainted, to work it through, to overcome it, by continuing in defiance of it, the analytic work according to the fundamental rule of analysis. Only when the resistance is at its height can the analyst, working in common with his patient, discover the repressed instinctual impulses which are feeding the resistance [1914, p. 155].

Freud noted that the working-through of the resistances effects the greatest changes in the patient.

Fenichel (1945) wrote, "Analysis succeeds in showing that a special defensive attitude was forced on the individual directly by a particular historical situation"; further, "In analysis the phenomenon of 'defense transference' makes its appearance; that is, not only warded-off instinctual

demands of the past but defensive attitudes as well are repeated in the relationship of the immediate present" (p. 524). Anna Freud wrote, "It may
happen in extreme cases that the instinctual impulse itself never enters
into the transference at all but only the specific defenses adopted by the
ego against some positive or negative attitude of the 'libido' " (1937, p.
20). She also stated that the patient does not feel the defense transference
to be a foreign body. "The form in which they [these phenomena] emerge
in his consciousness is ego-syntonic."

Brenner (1982) wrote that it is useless and misleading to ask whether a
transference manifestation is gratifying, defensive, or self-punitive, that is,
whether it derives from id, ego, or superego. He explained that a transference manifestation is a compromise among all three, noting that at a particular time one or another component may be more readily identified than others: "Wishes for gratification, anxiety, depressive affect, defense, and superego derivatives, all originating in early childhood, play
major roles in every object relation of later childhood and adult life" (p.
194).

Freud (1937) wrote, "The work of analysis aims at inducing the patient
to give up the repressions (using the word in the widest sense) belonging
to his early development." He continued, "With this purpose in view he
must be brought to recollect certain experiences and the affective impulses called up by them which he has for the time being forgotten." Later
Freud added, "The relation of transference, which becomes established
towards the analyst, is particularly calculated to favor the return of these
emotional connections." The analyst's task, as Freud saw it, is to construct
what has been forgotten from the traces left behind. The analyst "draws
his inferences from the fragments of memories, from the associations and
from the behaviour of the subject of the analysis" (p. 259).

Kennedy (1971) noted that Freud "introduced the notion that the analyst's reconstructions of aspects of the patient's forgotten past facilitate the
recovery of childhood memories" (p. 32). Ideally, "the interpretation of a
transference resistance will be followed by a freeing of material." Some
reconstructions, though not followed by the recovery of confirmatory
memories, do have a positive effect on the course of the analysis.

The genetic reconstructive approach is concerned with the analyst's reconstruction of the patient's past, on the basis of the analytic material
brought by the patient. The developmental approach may lean more
heavily on external sources for evidence of what went on in the child-
parent relationship. Kennedy noted that in child analysis we constantly
move from the developmental approach to the genetic reconstructive
and vice versa. A crucial question is the extent to which we permit external information, often biased, to prompt the formulation of a reconstructive interpretation, without its always being adequately substantiated by

the analytic material brought by the child. Kennedy suggests that we may occasionally focus too much on the genetic, reconstructive approach in our thinking.

"The questions we really have to examine are when and why we reconstruct such early experiences for the patient and how they become meaningful for him," Kennedy (1971) writes. She quotes Kris: "The analyst watches a reorganization of forces in the patient's behavior and guides this reorganization by his interpretations....In the course of this process the past emerges into the present, and a readiness, a 'need' for reconstructive interpretation may be noticed" (p. 58f.). Kennedy (p. 396) comments that Freud referred to this progressive aspect of the analytic process when he wrote (1937, p. 260f.), "The analyst finishes a piece of construction and communicates to the subject of the analysis so that it may work upon him; he then constructs a further piece out of the fresh material pouring in upon him, deals with it in the same way and proceeds in this alternating fashion until the end." She quotes Freud as saying that in "constructions" one lays before the patient a whole piece of his forgotten past. "The interpretation of the transference aims at showing the child why he tends to function in a particular manner at the moment, and not at the reconstruction of the past" (Kennedy, 1971, p. 400).

SILENCE AS A RESISTANCE

Calogeras (1966) wrote that the principal focus from 1914 to 1930 was on silence as a manifestation of resistance against anal-erotic wishes. During that period silence was viewed as simultaneously a defense and an instinctual wish. A broadening of the understanding of silence included a basic defense against oedipal impulses in some obsessional neuroses (Fenichel as cited in Calogeras, 1966, p. 538).

Writing during the period from 1930 to 1945, Fliess understood silence as the equivalent of the closure of a particular sphincter (oral, urethral, and anal). One technical recommendation from this period for coping with silence was introduced by Sterba in 1934. He demonstrated how a "strong, positive, libidinal transference" (Calogeras, 1966, p. 554) can act as the primary resistance "motivating" silence. The interpretation of the early signs of the transference eventually resulted in a dissolution of the silence and the forward movement of the analysis.

Silence, broadly conceived, takes on the "manifold aspects of an ego psychological dimension of personality" (Calogeras, 1966, p. 539). Zeligs characterized silence in 1960–1961 as a multidetermined ego attitude used in the service of resistance and wrote that silence may be a sign of ego regression or ego mastery (Calogeras, 1966, p. 539). Silence can be an identification with the silent object. Silence has been viewed as serving the structural hypothesis of mental function, that is, silence may represent intersystemic (id-ego or superego-ego) or intrasystemic conflicts (Arlow and Zeligs as cited in Calogeras, 1966, p. 540). Weinberger described those aspects of silence in patients who have suffered a developmental trauma in the form of a "loss of status" occurring between 18 months and the third year of life in relationship to the mother (Calogeras, 1966). According to Calogeras, Weinberger emphasizes that the particular closeness of the relationship, but not the mother herself, is lost; a triad of silence occurs consisting of silence, masochism, and depression. Freud's early references to silence were as resistance to transference thoughts regarding the analyst. Conceptions of silence culminated in "the current analytic view of silence as a multi-faceted psychic state serving many mental processes and systems of the mind (i.e., in the service of ego processes, as a function of transference and countertransference manifestations, and in relation to technique) with many degrees of depth" (Calogeras, 1966, p. 544).

Arlow (1961) wrote, "Silence during analytic treatment is essentially an ego disturbance of longer or shorter duration" (p. 48). He stressed the importance of observing whether the silence serves primarily the function of defense or primarily the function of discharge. Silence in the service of discharge is not related exclusively to gratification of id impulses:

> Failure, suffering, and provocation in the analytic situation may serve the self-punitive demands of the superego, and transference repetition may represent a persistent need to expiate guilt by using silence as a provocation of punishment [p. 52].

> Particular attention must be given to the total configuration of the silence in the transference, i.e., whether a specific pattern or significant event is being reproduced. In such instances, a silence may represent a classic expression of transference, a communication concerning experience in which silence was an esential component of the event. An interpretation which can correlate such a silence with a specific relationship or to some precise event in the individual's past is usually most effective [p. 54].

CASE PRESENTATION

Historical Background

Jane began analysis at age seven. A precociously bright girl, she was the third of four children, the only daughter of upper-middle-class parents. Her mother, a concerned and interested parent, sought help when Jane's distress interfered with her comfortable participation in their family life or when friends visited. At those times Jane often isolated herself. She wanted to be a boy; was moody, irritable, and hypochondriacal; felt she was stupid; feared dying in quicksand; disliked being alone at bedtime; and had had tantrums eight or nine months before. She was fearful and inhibited with other children. Her father was very sensitive to Jane's needs. Jane fought with her mother and was clinging with her father, who treated her with maternal tenderness. He neatly itemized Jane's difficulties in an obsessional manner. She read voraciously and did very well in a coed private school. She was close to her 14-month-older brother, Robert, and maternal with a two-year-younger brother, Edward. She was less involved with her four-year-older brother, Tom.

During infancy, Jane was easily satisfied, seldom cried, and "watched" while her mother was absorbed with taking care of Robert, who was a very active and demanding child. Jane's mother felt that boys were more important than girls. At the age of two, following Edward's birth, Jane experienced a relative loss of her mother, who had a severe depression of a year's duration and was very tired for 2 years. Jane began to wet again and ate poorly for the next two years. At age two and a half she became moody, whiny, and procrastinating. At times she was rude, which served the purpose of getting attention. Although she later wanted to be a boy and preferred wearing slacks, she was willing to dress like a girl and played with dolls, but did not especially like them. At age three and a half she was afraid of the other children in nursery school and was often hit, especially by one girl. She told her mother that she fantasied hitting this girl back. At age four, when tantrums began, she would sulk, slam doors, and have black moods. In the following year, Robert and Edward underwent tonsillectomies. Robert also had a herniorraphy. Her father was distressed when his two younger sons had serious illnesses. The analytic material demonstrated that these surgical procedures markedly increased Jane's castration anxiety, which had been prominent earlier because throughout these childhood years Jane was sexually stimulated by being bathed with Robert and Edward and by observing her parents naked. In the latter part of her fifth year, her drawings underwent a relatively abrupt change; her colorful drawings of flowers suddenly became somber and angry looking and displayed teeth. At five and a half, when she was in a combined kindergarten-first-grade class, she advanced from reading only a few words to reading at third-grade level; she tested higher than any other child in the group and was skipped a year. She preferred playing with boys, but also enjoyed playing with her mother's makeup. She now slept with a large stuffed animal, although she had not previously been fond of stuffed animals. For two or three months prior to beginning analysis, she would not allow her father to be physically affectionate with her.

COURSE OF HER ANALYSIS WITH THE APPEARANCE OF HER TRANSFERENCE RESISTANCE

Jane was a cute, small, feminine girl with short blonde hair and blue eyes. She readily displayed an impish smile. She was an unusually gifted patient, who brought rich material to her analysis. She first expressed her penis envy and castration fantasies; she dated her wanting to be a boy to Edward's birth. Soon, her hurt and fury from the time of Edward's birth was revived. In puppet play she expressed her feelings from age two years, when her brother was born, her mother became depressed, and she felt she had lost her mother. After this, she reported her primal scene experiences. She gradually elaborated her oedipal fantasies of a sado-masochistic nature and expressed her sexual excitement as she elaborated these fantasies. Eventually, her sexual excitement and her anxiety about it led to her elucidating both the precursor of a beating fantasy and beating fantasies. Jane's mother's current depression, which had intensified Jane's ambivalence about the female role, led to an intensification of Jane's need to defend against her excited and frightened view of the female role. Jane was stubborn and opposed wearing dresses to defend against this threat. She gradually spelled out her masturbatory fantasy that the girl is injured in her sexual activity with the male. Her excitement was increased in the face of any separation; she either fantasied or dramatized being knocked out or injured. As the excitement mounted, crucial oedipal conflicts were dramatically played out with much intensity at home and with increasing clarity in the transference. The analytic data involving her play with a rubber figure suggested that her becoming aware of sexual differences linked up with her primal scene experiences and propelled her into the oedipal conflict.

During a session 18 months after beginning her analysis, Jane felt "cold," looked sad, and sat in my chair in order to cope with her feelings about the approaching six-and-a-half-week summer interruption. She expressed an increased hunger, liked her hour "more and more," and noted all the places she can sleep in the office. She wanted to smoke my pipe and take on vacation a book she made in her hour. When she left, she took something with her and looked back longingly. Six and a half weeks later, she had the doorman ring me immediately before her first hour after our interruption to see if I was present (this was not her custom). She entered with a serious look, smiled impishly as she sat in my chair, showed me an injured thumb, and told me she had had an upper respiratory infection most of the month. She readily acknowledged that she had been unhappy and would have liked to have seen me. At her second hour after resuming, she sat in my chair pretending to doze and said, "I had a rotten summer."

Twenty-one months after beginning analysis and about one month after resuming, she began to spend a large part or all of the analytic hour reading, shutting me out. This phenomenon occurred when she was still under the impact of her summer interruption, had expressed a wish to be a male, and told of reading about a beating, torture, and execution of a man and about a bloody scene. When I said that we could talk further about her shutting me out by reading, she said with determination, "No, I won't." This occurred when she was tearfully anticipating an injured fingernail coming off. I interpreted her transference resistance of shutting me out by reading. A reconstruction was now made that, here with me, she was repeating her feeling of being shut out when very young and was showing me how it felt by doing that with me. She responded with silence and continued reading. She said, "A boy was born in a concentration camp and ran away when he was 12," adding that it was an exciting book. In her next hour, there was an increased libidinal quality and a kind of sparkle in her manner as she silently played games. Her mother reported that Jane had had a rigid, controlling nursemaid for six months between age two and three years. She began to sit in my recliner many hours and read to shut me out. She said that she liked sitting in my chair because it was "warmer." Her oedipal wishes appeared in the transference; when she felt disappointed, she expressed her fury by saying, "I'll be dead in a few days." When she missed me while away, I interpreted her sadness and anger; she said, "I nearly put my eyes out" (she had fallen into a bush). Prior to a three-week Christmas vacation (she was to be away), she asked me to promise to be here every summer.

Jane's transference resistance of silently reading was an attempt to defend against her positive oedipal libidinal longings, which frightened her because of her underlying fantasy of intercourse as sadomasochistic. Her reading also defended against her penis envy, her wish to be a boy, and her fantasy that she was a boy who had lost his genitals (which defended against the threat she experienced as a girl). I understood how Jane's controlling and stubborn behavior was also a response to her mother's unpredictability (Jane's mother had given me just a week's notice of the parents' one-week vacation).

Gradually a fantasy of being injured emerged as she came to her hours with various injuries to her extremities, usually to a leg. In September, after a ten-and-a-half week interruption, she beamed on seeing me and then matter of factly took my seat. Although communicative, she also read to shut me out.

During the next several weeks, she indirectly expressed her sadness and anger over the summer interruption. She told of playing a game in which a mean sister beats babies and throws them off the porch. A crocodile pulled the nose of an elephant, and that's how it got its trunk. I said, "It's appealing: if you want to make part of the body larger, you just pull on it." "It sure is," she replied, as she pointed to her genitals, and added, "That way I could just pull on it and have a penis." I said, "That's appealing because of not liking...." She interrupted and said, "Yeah, I know, having a hole." At the beginning of her next hour she joked about stealing my chair. She disliked wearing a dress and accepted my noting her disliking being a girl and wanting a penis. She continued to sit in my chair and made a slip saying, "I don't mind not being a girl." She liked the idea of being an "orphan boy" — she could be free that way. She told of her private games at age five. The theme of a boy getting lost emerged. She associated to her getting lost in a department store at age five to six and yelling for her mother. Something like that happened quite a few times. After her play with balls and phallic play with my ruler, I interpreted that she wanted to be an actor because she feels she was a boy with a penis and balls. She responded by saying, "Boy, you have some imagination — what makes you think that?" Soon, she sat in my chair and read to ward off her masculine longings and the regressive derivatives of suffering and being an orphan. She was ashamed of her anger at her parents and her wish to get rid of them.

THE SPECIFIC RECONSTRUCTION AND WORKING THROUGH HER TRANSFERENCE RESISTANCE

Thirty-four months after she began her analysis, Jane again sat in my chair, felt "cold," and told me that she felt sad when her mother was ill. She rubbed my cigar ashes on her, calling it perfume; put my phone wire on her finger, saying it's a ring; and then played with my paper clips, making numbers six, five, four, three, and finally two. I made a reconstruction that she felt sad, as she had at age two when Edward was born and her mother was sad and unavailable to her. I made the reconstruction at this time for several reasons: she said that she felt "cold" and sad when her mother was ill and less available; in her play with my paper clips in which she made the numbers six, five, four, three, and two, she linked up the sadness with age two. Jane had now verbally expressed a current sadness when she experienced a relative loss of her mother. The analytic data fit so clearly with the developmental information her mother had provided initially about her severe depression of a year's duration at the time of Edward's birth. Also, after about a year's time of being periodically shut out, I was able to spell out that she had wanted me to experience what it felt like for her when her mother became depressed. When she mildly denied this, I interpreted her shame; she turned to reading her Tarzan book in my recliner. She came late to her next hour and wanted to read because she disliked the silence. I said that she disliked the silence now because it reminded her of the silence she felt as a very young child when she wanted her mother to be there or when her mother was there and did not feel well — and there was a silence and she felt scared and sad. "I don't remember that."

I explained that she remembers by having the feeling with me now of not liking the silence. She looked at my lamp and asked why there was a "crack" (under the lights). I commented that she asked because she did not like "cracks." She spoke of her dog having a "crack" now (before she had called it a hole when referring to her dog being bitten by another dog). I remarked that she did not like being a girl and having a "hole" between her legs. She tried to disown this. I told her she did not like saying there was anything about her parents she did not like. She looked sad, cried, did not want me to see her crying, and put a book in front of her face. She verbally confirmed my interpretation of her not liking to be critical of her parents and then told of being afraid of muggers on the street, that one would stick a knife in her. She said she cried both because she liked Edward better than Robert and because she liked her housekeeper, Mary, better than her parents. In her next hour she again wanted to read to get rid of the silence, and, after losing a game, she eventually wanted to break my window with a ball (a ball represented a penis) and expressed the wish to mark up my ceiling in her play. She returned to sitting in my chair and expressed, in a derivative way, a wish to have a baby (her housekeeper had a spontaneous abortion) and asked if I knew French like her father. Jane was happier and more communicative. She expressed feeling exposed by my reconstruction and also felt excited. She recited a poem:

> I remember I remember the house where I was born
> The bathroom at the end of the hall
> Where 19 raced each morn
> My 13 brothers hated me
> My sisters didn't like me
> My mother never called me down to eat
> She didn't know my name.

She first expressed a wish to get a penis by swallowing my stick and then indicated it would be bloody to lose a penis – while she covered her genital area with both hands. She would get a penis by "having a doctor stitch it." "Like a tooth comes out, you put it back." "Somebody stole it from me," she said with anger. "It came off when I took off my tights and fell apart when my tights were put in the wash."

I said that she thought all this because she felt being a girl is being injured, damaged. She first denied this and then said, "I never thought all this 'til you brought it up." I acknowledged her sense of guilt. She came to her next hour with a "hurt ankle" and expressed a wish to be an old man in her play. When her pipe came off a stick, she associated to the guards' heads, which the queen cut off in a dream and which she had previously associated with a bowel movement she had had with blood in it in my bathroom.

After her Thanksgiving break, she balanced plastic acrobats, felt dizzy from somersaults, feared dying from bumping her head in her hour, expressed anger at me "for being away" (she was the one who had gone away). I told her that this was connected with her mother's "being away" when Edward was born. And at this time she anticipated her parents being away for five days. She associated from her somersaults to "acrobats, monkeys going from branch to branch in trees in the jungle." She fantasied being a boy with a jewel box who would inherit the throne.

Reading during her hour no longer played a prominent part in her analysis after the reconstruction and working through of this behavior as a transference resistance.

DISCUSSION OF CLINICAL DATA

Jane's transference resistance, silently reading, had begun largely as a way of expressing her feeling of being abandoned by me in the face of her heightened libidinal longings for me after a summer interruption of six and a half weeks. I believe that Jane chose to read rather than just being silent because it was an earlier adaptive response to the acute castration reaction she had experienced at the time of her brothers' tonsillectomies and herniorraphy (her analysis later confirmed that she had experienced her brothers' tonsillectomes as an upwardly displaced castration). Recall that her drawings became somber and angry looking with teeth in the latter part of her fifth year. It was soon after this, in a combined kindergarten-first-grade class, that she made a marked advance in her ability to read, going from reading just a few words to reading at third-grade level. As noted, she was also shutting out feelings and fantasies about her wish to be a male, thoughts about a beating, torture, and a bloody scene, when she anticipated losing a nail from a previously injured finger. An interpretation of this transference resistance in more general terms was followed initially by a heightening of the resistance. An awakening of memories occurred (Freud, 1914). She told me about a boy who suffered in a concentration camp and ran away. In Jane's analysis, her oedipal wishes, their disappointment, and her self-directed aggressive wishes as a revenge on me then emerged. Further interpretation of her sadness and anger led to a symbolic expression of her guilt over her underlying feminine sexual wishes. She read to be in control, to shut out her defensive wish to be a boy with a penis and her displaced castrating wishes in the transference (she had joked about snipping off my nose).

After the following summer interruption, her sadness appeared. Then her penis envy appeared with increased intensity, as well as her dislike of being a girl. Eventually I interpreted her fantasy that she had lost male genitals. Her transference resistance, reading in my chair, appeared to ward off her masculine strivings and the regressive expression of suffering and being an orphan.

Another factor that gave an important impetus to her wish to be a boy was her mother's preference for her brothers. Her brothers' operations and illnesses, as well as her mother's preoccupation with Robert (who was demanding), while Jane "watched," all played a role in Jane's desire to be a boy (and thereby receive the love and affection she witnessed her brothers receiving).

Thirteen months after the appearance of her transference resistance, reading in my chair, I reconstructed how her current sadness was a reliving of the way she felt at age two, when Edward was born and her mother became depressed. The working through of this transference resistance as a reliving of the past—doing to me what had been done to her—occurred during the next several hours. She wanted to read to avoid experiencing the silence and the associated fright and sadness she had felt at age two years and for the next year or two, when her mother was depressed. Her dislike of a "crack" was associated with her dislike of the silence that resulted from her mother's depression. As noted earlier, this crucial genetic reconstruction led to her reviving her fear of penetration, first via displacement; she feared a mugger's sticking a knife in her. To cope with her anxiety about her feminine wishes, she identified with the aggressor and turned passive into active, wanting to break my window with a ball (a symbolic penis). After expressing part of her oedipal wishes and defensively her sadness and penis envy, she expressed in a beginning way that she damaged herself by masturbating (Friedman, 1985). In the face of these conflicts, there was an increased threat of loss, which was displaced onto me in the transference (at a time when she anticipated her parents' being away for five days). Her balancing toy acrobats, feeling dizzy, and doing somersaults (turning passive into active) were all a response in part to the disequilibrium she experienced with the "loss" in the transference of me as mother when she felt threatened as a female by her sexual wishes (Friedman, 1979). Her response at this time was to fantasy being male and female, that is, a boy with a jewel box who would inherit the throne. She was happier and more communicative. The more specific reconstruction of her transference resistance enabled Jane both to work through this early sadness more fully (she expressed the sadness in her poem) and to experience more fully and work through her wishes to regain the penis she had fantasied losing. Her associations became richer, and there was a deepening of her associations. A new richness was manifested by her bringing in dreams and daydreams. The working through of this transference resistance critically facilitated the flow of her analysis.

FURTHER DISCUSSION OF CLINICAL DATA

When the transference became more intense, remembering gave way to action, although the action was in the analytic sessions. Jane defended herself against remembering and discussing her infantile conflicts with her mother (who became depressed for a year at the time of her younger brother's birth) by her behavior in the transference. She relived the infantile conflicts. She sat in my chair and read a different book daily, sometimes for two to three sessions at a time, shutting me out. Then, after two or three sessions of mostly silence, she gave rich material, just as she had previously during her analysis. One could say that a special defensive attitude was forced on her by the severity of her mother's depression after the birth of her brother. During this period of her analysis a specific defense seems to have been adopted by the ego against a positive attitude of the libido and the disappointment of these longings. She shut me out with her silence, just as we can reconstruct that her mother shut her out as a result of her depression. The form in which these phenomena emerged in consciousness was ego-syntonic. After about a year of her behaving toward me in the way I have described, I interpreted the transference resistance. I have the impression that my interpretation of the transference resistance would not have had the same significance or mutative effect on Jane if this transference resistance had not gone on for a considerable period. A "need" for reconstructive interpretation was noticed. In this instance the construction put before the patient a piece of her forgotten past. Interpreting the transference resistance in Jane's analysis is in the tradition of paying attention to the ego's unconscious defensive operations. When the resistance was at its height, we were able to discover the repressed instinctual impulses feeding the resistance.

Brenner (1982) enriched our understanding of conflict when he stated that the components of conflict include drive derivatives, anxiety and depressive affect, defense, and various manifestations of superego functioning, all originating in early childhood. It is clear that in Jane's case these components of conflict are present in the transference. Drive derivatives are evident with her expressing both a paternal and a maternal transference. She is anxious about her feminine sexual wishes, especially about penetration, though this did not emerge fully until much later in her analysis. Depressive affect is evident. Her silently reading serves to defend against her drive derivatives. She reports masochistic fantasies and a beating fantasy; although only fleetingly referred to in the material presented in this paper, it is central in her analysis (Friedman, 1985). Brenner noted that it is misleading to ask whether a transference manifestation is gratifying, defensive, or self-punitive, that is, whether it derives from id, ego, or superego; it is derived from all three. Jane's transference resistance of silently reading, when seen as an identification with her mother, expresses her love for her mother and at the same time expresses an aggressive, vengeful wish toward me as mother so that I would know what feeling shut out is like. I have already spoken of this transference behavior as a defense. There is a suffering and a sense of guilt, which are gratified in maintaining a silence that temporarily prevents a further understanding and alleviation of her suffering in her life.

As Freud (1937) wrote, the analyst's task is to construct what has been forgotten from the traces left behind — from fragments of memories, from associations, and from the behavior of the patient. I was able to understand that Jane again felt "cold" when she felt sad and felt sad when she disliked her mother's being ill and unavailable 34 months after she began her analysis. Her mother's unavailability revived the feelings Jane had experienced for four years from age two and gave an impetus to her wanting a symbolic wedding ring (the loop of telephone cord) from me. As mentioned earlier, her play with my paper clips, from which she made the numbers six, five, four, three, and two, enabled me to understand more fully that the sad feelings over her mother's unavailability went back to age two years and occurred until age six. The previous general construction played a part in eventually enabling Jane to produce new memories in her play with my paper clips as well as verbally, which enabled me to complete and extend the construction.

In this instance I waited for the analysis to provide the data that enabled me to make a genetic reconstructive interpretation. The developmental information I had obtained from her mother served as a confirmation and enabled me to appreciate more readily what Jane was communicating in her analysis. The reconstructive interpretation was aimed at showing Jane why she functioned the way she did at that moment and what made her feel so sad then, and was not so much a reconstruction of the past for its own sake.

DISCUSSION OF THE RELATIONSHIP OF OEDIPAL AND PREOEDIPAL MATERIAL IN JANE'S ANALYSIS

Jane began her analysis by expressing her penis envy, feeling castrated, and dating her wish to be a boy to Edward's birth. She soon expressed in her play the feelings from age two years—Edward was born, her mother became depressed, and she felt she had lost her mother. After this, derivatives of her oedipal conflict appeared with thoughts about babies, the primal scene, and eventually (in the face of more oedipal fantasies) beating fantasies. Gradually, the masturbatory fantasy of the female being injured in sex with the male emerged. In the face of increased libidinal longing for me and the attendant disappointment at the time of the summer interruption, the transference resistance of silently reading appeared. It appeared when she had expressed a wish to be a male, had read about a beating, torture, and execution of a man, and anticipated losing a previously injured fingernail. At this point a more general reconstruction was made that she was repeating here with me her feeling of being shut out when very young. It was during the period after this that there was a further working through of her oedipal wishes in the transference and her guilt. Her penis envy appeared with increased clarity. After the more specific reconstruction of her transference resistance was made (13 months after it appeared) and after the working through of her preoedipal conflict with her mother and its associated sadness, she first revived her fear of penetration (via displacement). I want to emphasize that the analytic data show that she moves back and forth between oedipal and preoedipal conflicts. I suggest that where there is a preoedipal trauma, such as a year's relative loss of a mother at age two years, one will see such an oscillation between oedipal and preoedipal material. In this instance, the full appearance and interpretation in the transference of the early preoedipal relationship with her mother focused around age two years facilitated the unfolding of a rich analysis (Friedman, 1985) in which beating fantasies, vaginal contractions, and her fear of penetration appeared.

DISCUSSION OF JANE'S SILENCE AS AN ASPECT OF HER TRANSFERENCE RESISTANCE

Jane would be more like the patient referred bo by Sterba (Calogeras, 1966, p. 554). The disappointment of the strong positive libidinal transference motivated the silence. Jane's silence can be understood as a multidetermined ego attitude used in the service of resistance, as an ego resgression, and as a sign of ego mastery of her mother's silence when she was age two to six years. Jane's silence may also be viewed as serving the structural hypothesis of mental functioning and represent an inter-systemic conflict (id-ego and superego-ego); her silence may also serve as a restitution of an object loss via identification. Jane would fit into Weinberger's category of patients who have suffered a developmental trauma in the form of a "loss of status" occurring between 18 to 36 months in relationship to the mother. Weinberger's triad of silence, masochism, and depression fits for Jane as well. Jane's silence and transference repetition were a provocation that was an attempt to expiate her sense of guilt. Arlow (1961) emphasized the importance of observing the configuration of silence and ascertaining whether a significant event is being reproduced. He noted that interpretively correlating silence with a specific relationship or event in the individual's past is usually the most effective. Understanding that Jane's silently reading to herself, shutting me out, and warding off her own drive derivatives were a revival of and an expression in the transference of her relationship with her mother, who became "silent" as part of a postpartum depression when Jane was age two years and Edward was born, was crucial in reconstructing and working through this 13-month-long transference resistance.

REFERENCES

Arlow, J. A. (1961), Silence and the theory of technique. *J. Amer. Psychoanal. Assn.*, 9:44–55.

Brenner, C. (1982), *The Mind in Conflict.* New York: International Universities Press.

Calogeras, R. C. (1966), Silence as a technical parameter in psycho-analysis. *Internat. J. Psycho-Anal.*, 48:536–558.

Fenichel, O. (1945), *The Psychoanalytic Theory of Neurosis.* New York: W. W. Norton.

Freud, A. (1937), *The Ego and the Mechanisms of Defense.* London: Hogarth Press.

Freud, S. (1905), Fragment of an analysis of a case of hysteria. *Standard Edition*, 7:3–122. London: Hogarth Press, 1953.

_____ (1912), The dynamics of transference. *Standard Edition,* 12:97–108. London: Hogarth Press, 1958.

_____ (1914), Remembering, repeating and working through. *Standard Edition,* 12:145–156. London: Hogarth Press, 1958.

_____ (1937), Constructions in psycho-analysis. *Standard Edition,* 23:255–270. London: Hogarth Press, 1964.

Friedman, L. (1979), The oral drive, clinging, and equilibrium. *The Psychoanalytic Study of the Child,* 34:329–345.

_____ (1985), Beating fantasies in a latency girl, their role in female sexual development. *Psychoanal. Quart.,* 54:569–596.

Kennedy, H. (1971), Problems in reconstruction in child analysis. *The Psychoanalytic Study of the Child,* 26:386–402.

Weinberger, J. L. (1964), A triad of silence: Silence, masochism and depression. *Internat. J. Psycho-Anal.,* 45:304–309.

THEODORE J. JACOBS

Transference Relationships, the Relationships Between Transferences, and Reconstruction

In this paper I shall discuss an aspect of the phenomenon of transference that thus far has received little attention in the literature. I refer to the relationships that exist between the multiple and shifting transferences that emerge in the course of every psychoanalytic treatment and to the fact that in certain instances investigation of these relationships can yield valuable clues in the process of reconstruction.

That every analysis contains within it a panoply of transferences that interact and interweave in diverse and complex patterns has ben appreciated by a numbeer of observers. Blum (1971) has noted that clinical transference is overdetermined with regard to object representation and past experience. He has compared the coalescence of images and experiences in transference to "the manifest content of a dream deriving from contemporary day residues and memories and fantasies of childhood" (p. 49).

Greenacre (1959) has spoken of "a constant panoramic procession of transference pictures merging into each other or momentarily separating out with special clarity in a way which is frequently less constant than the symptoms and other manifestations of the neurosis itself" (p. 485). And she has suggested that analysts pay consistent attention to the special forms, variations, and movements within the transference relationship itself.

Stone (1967) regards the phenomenon of transference in analysis as being composed of two different elements: the primordial transference, which derives from the effort to master the earliest experiences of separation from the mother and whose aim is renewed contact with her; and the mature transference, which is displaced from the parent of early childhood and which "tends toward separation and individuation" (p. 25). These two elements of transference are in constant interaction with each other.

Bird (1972) regards transference as one of the functions of the ego, and, as such, transference may be counted on to possess many characteristics of such a function. "The ego's ways of reality testing, for instance, its responses to internal and external stimuli, its uses of defense mechanisms," he writes, "may all reveal much about the basic phenomenology of transference" (p. 299). He also suggests that much may be surmised about transference's functional vicissitudes by assuming that transference "suffers the same general developmental and neurotic deficiencies, distortions, limitations and fixations to which various other functions of the ego are susceptible" (p. 299).

Brenner (1983) agrees with Bird that the commonly held views of transference as a simple projection or repetition of the past do not do justice to the complexity of the psychological processes involved. He points out that every instance of transference contains not only elements of drive and defense but superego components as well. The resultant of multiple forces, transference, in his view, should always be regarded as a compromise formation.

Kohut (1971) has stressed the importance of selfobject transferences in disorders of narcissism. In analytic work with these patients he observed that such transferences, derived from the infantile period, when self and object were not yet clearly distinguished, tended to emerge earlier in treatment than those more familiar transference configurations whose essential feature is the displacement onto the analyst of object representations of childhood.

Although Kohut was the first to utilize the term selfobject transferences, the phenomena he described are familiar to all psychoanalysts. Decades of clinical experience have shown that not only patients with narcissistic disorders may develop transferences of this kind; patients of all types may, at various stages of treatment, develop transferences that contain not only a mixture of perception and memory, ego and superego, drive and defense, but aspects of self and object representation as well.

Although modern perspectives on transference in the clinical situation have emphasized its complexity and its multiple roots, the forms, manner, and sequences in which transferences develop in analytic treatment have been comparatively little explored. Of particular interest is how the various transference pictures relate to one another, how the relationships between them may convey forgotten pieces of history as well as be utilized currently for the purposes of defense and of working through of residual trauma, and how understanding these relationships may assist the analyst in his reconstructive efforts. It is these issues that I wish to illustrate here by means of several clinical examples.

Why in any given case transferences emerge in the way they do is a matter to which comparatively little attention has been paid. It is clear, however, that the factors that influence the form and manner of their appearance are many. Among them are the character and life situation of the patient and the particular conflicts that are psychologically active; the manner in which he experiences the analyst and the memories and fantasies, both conscious and unconscious, that these perceptions evoke; the state of the patient's resistances at any given time; the intensity with which extraanalytic transferences are currently experienced and the manner of their interaction with the transference proper; reality considerations concerning the analyst (his age, gender, appearance, and personal style, including the extent to which he may, in fact, resemble physically or in behavior an important figure from the past); the analyst's countertransferences and the particular techniques that he employs.

As a result of the influence of these and other factors, the sequences and timing with which the various transferences appear in a particular case may, and often do, follow a pattern that is quite different from that which characterized the development of the corresponding self and object representations in childhood. It can be demonstrated, however, that for comparatively brief periods in some cases and for rather extended times in others, the form and manner in which transferences emerge and the patterns that they evolve are related in quite specific ways to aspects of an individual's psychological history.

The following case examples illustrating these relationships focus primarily on those aspects of transference that relate to object representations, although, of course, in each example the transference paradigm that developed was highly complex, containing contributions from several aspects of the personality. If, in light of the foregoing discussion of transference as containing multiple and complex elements, my own descriptions of it seem naive (if not simplistic), I ask the reader to understand that to illustrate the thesis of this paper I must deliberately focus on one narrow aspect of the phenomenon, for to do otherwise would be to obscure the central issue.

Some years ago I undertook the analysis of a bright and capable young woman whose relationships to others were marred by attitudes of wariness and suspicion. Born to a family of aristocratic background, Miss L was raised in an environment in which social position was of overriding importance. Her mother was a forceful, energetic, and highly ambitious person, whose constant involvement in luncheons and charity balls made her almost a caricature of the society matron. Miss L's father, an inhibited, anxious and vain man, devoted himself to playing the role of attendant and social companion to his wife.

Early in treatment it became clear that some of Miss L's difficulties in relating to friends and colleagues were attributable to her regarding herself as an imposter. Convinced that if she allowed others to become close to her the essential falseness and disingenuousness of her character would be revealed, she avoided intimate relationships. The reasons for this belief were not at all clear. Far from being an unreliable person or a devious one, Miss L was, on the contrary, totally trustworthy.

Why it was that Miss L held a view of herself that was so patently false was a mystery to which there were few clues. So far as I knew, there was no one in the family who could be described as an imposter or as having behaved in a deceitful manner. Nor could I discover in Miss L's case an historical event that might have thrown light on the origin of her beliefs, unconscious fantasies that might have explained it, or pronounced guilt feelings, conscious or unconscious, that might have contributed in a significant way to such a distorted self-image. The closest I could come to an explanation of this problem centered on Miss L's masturbatory conflicts. For some years in adolescence these had been intense, and she blamed her frequent skin problems at that time on this evil habit. I had no doubt that this conflict played some role in Miss L's view of herself as devious and a sham, but I questioned whether, by itself, it could have had so enduring an effect as to account for the puzzling symptom at hand. For some time, though, I had to be content with this explanation, as it was the only one that I had.

From the outset of treatment it was my hope that some of the unconscious factors at the root of Miss L's symptoms would be revealed through the transference. In this expectation I was not disappointed, but because the clues to deciphering this puzzling clinical picture depended on understanding not only the individual transference pictures that emerged but the relationships between them, it took several years for my hope to be realized.

Initially, and for quite some time, the dominant transference centered on the mother. Miss L experienced me, as she did her mother, as an active, energetic, socially ambitious person whose burgeoning schedule allowed precious little time for her. She treasured the hours set aside for analysis and from early on appealed to me to increase them. In silent protest, and with resentment, she observed the comings and goings of other patients and fantasized my greater attention to them. She imagined me busy each night with some social engagement, and when an important charity function was to be held at the Plaza or the 21 Club, she took for granted that my wife and I were among the sponsors.

Convinced that I too regarded her as false and devious, Miss L initially did all that she could to show herself to be a reliable person and of good character. Always prompt for her hours, she regularly paid her bill as soon as it was rendered; and on the infrequent occasion when it was necessary for her to miss a session, she offered to pay me in advance.

This behavior reflected Miss L's tireless efforts as a youngster to be the daughter she imagined her mother wanted—a well-behaved, obedient, reliable child, who made a point of being aware of the needs of others. It reflected, too, her method of competing with the parade of friends, acquaintances, and committee people who sought her mother's attention. Less obvious in the early months of treatment, but increasingly so as time went on and the extent of Miss L's ambivalent feelings toward her mother became evident, was the defensive aspect of her behavior. Concealed behind it lay powerful feelings of resentment that in childhood she had not dared to reveal to her mother and that now, with equal tenacity, she concealed from me.

The initial transference constellation held center stage in the analysis for approximately three years. Then, abruptly, without a hint of what was coming, it underwent a change. Still Miss L sought to please me, but now she did so by deliberate efforts to play up to me as a man. Suddenly, she had kind words for my ties, my haircut, the quality of my voice. Shifting in so rapid a manner that at first I was bewildered by the transformation, the prevailing object representation in the transference was now centered on me as the father—a father whose devotion to his tailor was exceeded only by his attachment to his Porsche.

That a development of this kind had taken place was not by itself surprising. To the contrary, for several years the transference focus had been on the mother and significant work had been done on the working through of competitive feelings with her, progress toward beginning to deal in the transference with sexual feelings for me, and with the frightening oedipal feelings that lay behind them, seemed a natural development.

The reawakening of such feelings did play an important role in the change that occurred. There was, though, something more to this sudden shift in transference focus. Hidden in it was the reliving of a piece of Miss

L's forgotten history. Of crucial importance in her development, this experience, however, could not be clarified until the transference had taken still another turn.

Once again the change occurred rapidly. This time, though, the shift took place only a few months after the predominant transference had centered on me as the father. During its short life, that transference constellation had been a complicated one. While Miss L's need for me to respond to her as an attractive woman was strong, and her behavior, initially, was teasing and flirtatious, negative feelings toward her analyst soon became prominent. Surfacing at first in an oblique manner as a piece of mockery in a dream or as the innocently quoted remark of a critic of analysis, Miss L's hostility gradually became more palpable. Within a few months after this phase of the transference had set in, her attacks became sharper and more direct. When, at one point, she saw me getting into a taxi and imagined that I wished to avoid her, her angry accusations were followed by pronounced feelings of depression.

It was at this juncture that the second transference picture receded. It faded, it seemed, as quickly as it had come, replaced now by the reemergence of a transference in which Miss L related to me primarily as her mother. The second mother-dominated transference, however, was, in significant respects, different from the first.

No longer was Miss L the good, responsible child, forever seeking affection. Now she was contained and aloof. Still polite and outwardly respectful, she nonetheless maintained a kind of formality and distance that I had not seen before. And apparent for the first time were both the insular quality and the sense of wariness that in later childhood and adolescence had characterized her relations with others.

To me the shifts that had occurred in the predominant transference paradigms — and particularly the rapidity with which they came on — were as puzzling as they seemed important. I knew from prior experience that in certain individuals the particular form and manner in which transferences unfold constitute an unconscious living out of specific psychological experiences of childhood or adolescence; but in Miss L's case no material had yet surfaced to suggest that sudden or unexpected alterations in her life situation or in her self or object representations had, in fact, constituted an important aspect of her development.

In the hope that the patient herself might provide some clue to these puzzling developments, I drew her attention to the phenomena I have been discussing. Intrigued by the overview that she now had of this aspect of her analytic experience and as interested as I was in the idea that the particular way in which it unfolded might have some meaning, she was equally perplexed about what that meaning could be. It was then that

Miss L began to question her mother about her childhood; and it was the mother, ultimately, who clarified matters.

At first, however, she was reluctant to do so. She possessed certain information that could clear up the mystery, but she had serious misgivings about sharing it with her daughter. It concerned a long-held secret in the family that the mother did not want to unearth. Fortunately, however, she had recently entered therapy for feelings of depression, and she discussed her dilemma with her therapist. That he had helped clarify the situation was evident, for one afternoon, after returning from a session, she summoned her daughter to the library and revealed to her the nature of the secret. It was not, however, the first time that she had done so. This discussion had taken place once before, when the patient was slightly over three years old. How long Miss L had remembered the facts disclosed at that time is unclear, but it was apparent that for many years they had been banished from consciousness.

What her mother revealed was that Miss L's father was not her natural father but her stepfather. The parents had been divorced soon after Miss L's birth, following her father's desertion of his wife in her sixth month of pregnancy. For a short time thereafter he kept in touch with the family but gradually his contact diminished and he vanished from the scene. Miss L never knew him.

Within a year the mother remarried, and her new husband adopted Miss L. As far as she knew, this man was her father. The name of her natural father was never mentioned in the house; in fact, it was a condition laid down by her stepfather prior to marriage that this rule be strictly enforced.

In all likelihood Miss L would never have known the true circumstances of her birth but for the intervention of the family pediatrician. This doctor knew the full story and he prevailed on the mother to discuss the facts with her child lest in later life she discover the truth and suffer irreparable psychological damage.

Under this pressure the mother reluctantly told Miss L about her natural father. This was to be a secret between mother and daughter. The mother conveyed still another message: It was a secret to be forgotten. Except for an incident that occurred several months later, the matter was never mentioned again. On that occasion, Miss L and her mother were walking on the street when the mother spotted her former husband in a crowd. Spontaneously she pointed him out to the child, who strained to see him. But before she could get close enough to get a good look, he hailed a taxi cab and was gone. For some time this experience remained in memory. According to the mother, Miss L played it out repeatedly. Then, in time, it faded. It was revived in the analysis when, by chance, she once observed me getting into a cab. However, coming at a time when she consciously knew nothing of the family secret, its significance could be grasped neither by patient nor analyst.

In discussing with her daughter the long forgotten events of childhood, Miss L's mother recalled the child's reaction to being told the truth about her father. She had said nothing, remained subdued for several hours, and then, without a further word, resumed playing as before. For some time thereafter, however, the mother noticed a marked change in the girl. No longer did she seek out her mother for attention and affection. She turned instead to her stepfather and with all the seductive charm of a three year old, sought to win his favor.

The stepfather was an exceedingly controlled man, embarrassed by open displays of affection, and he did not encourage the child in such behavior. She took his reaction as a rejection. When, repeatedly, she could not obtain from him the response that she wanted, she gave up the effort. In the course of doing so, she displayed increasing anger at the stepfather, and when in an unhappy incident he severely disappointed her, she turned on him with an outburst of tearful rage.

For some weeks her stepfather had promised to take Miss L to a puppet show. When the appointed time came, however, he reneged. Claiming as an excuse urgent business matters, and with the child watching glumly from the doorway, he drove off to the office. This disappointment, combined with the feelings of rejection she had been experiencing, caused Miss L to turn away from the stepfather. Thereafter her interest in him seemed markedly diminished.

Once again Miss L turned to her mother as the primary parent, but now their relationship took on a different quality. No longer was she the good child, forever eager to please. She had become more distant, more wary. Her manner seemed to convey a fear of being hurt and disappointed.

Once this forgotten piece of Miss L's childhood surfaced and could be integrated with the rest of her history, the forms and transformations of the transference, at first so puzzling, were now comprehensible. Clearly the shifts and changes that occured constituted in large measure a reactivation and reliving of memories of a crucial phase in Miss L's development. Motivated by a need to repeat and to master the psychological traumas of that period and guided by the workings of the unconscious sense of time, she recreated in the analytic situation not only the content of particular childhood experiences, but their essential form as well.

Reproduced were not only aspects of the child's early relationship to the mother, the shift to the stepfather, and the shift back again, but elements of fantasy and memory that related to the natural father. Thus Miss L's behavior toward me as the frustrating stepfather contained not only the revival in memory of the disappointments she had experienced at his hands, including the specific memory of his failure to keep his promise about the puppet show and his driving off without her, but the earlier memory of the natural father disappearing into a taxi cab. This memory, which apparently was worked over and elaborated rather extensively following its occurrence, became fused with the later experience. Thus, Miss L's anger at her stepfather—and at me in the transference—concealed long repressed rage at her natural father for his abandonment of her. It was this covert anger that in later years contributed to her wariness, not only of her stepfather, but, unconsciously, of all men.

Clarified, too, by recovering the forgotten piece of childhood history was the meaning of Miss L's view of herself as an imposter. Learning that the person she had known as her father all of her life was, in fact, no blood relation and that her natural father had deserted her produced the idea that she too was not the person she thought she was. It was as though she were someone else. Moreover, Miss L's mother had deceived her and could no longer be trusted. She too was someone other than who she claimed to be. And Miss L developed the fantasy that if her mother was not an honest person, as her mother's child she must be equally untrustworthy. It was this unconscious identification with the mother as an imposter that played a significant role in Miss L's distorted view of herself. There was, in addition, another piece of reality that, in all probability, played a role in the development of Miss L's self-image. This was the fact that as a young child she had participated in a deception. Having learned the truth from her mother, she joined with her in concealing that knowledge from her stepfather. Although over the years this secret became thoroughly repressed and was lost to the conscious awareness, it surfaced in another way: as a significant contributor to Miss L's feeling that she was an imposter.

In another case, that of Mr. A, study of the emerging transferences was instrumental in gaining insight into a particular type of resistance that he utilized: the defensive use of one transference against another. It also fostered understanding of the way that Mr. A had utilized in childhood a shifting investment in object representations to defend against anxiety.

From the outset of this analysis a dominant transference note was struck. Before the first hour had come to an end it was clear in what role I would initially be cast: that of an omniscient mother. A strong-willed, articulate and self-assured woman, Mr. A's mother never lost for him the image he had of her as a child—that of a powerful, invasive and overbearing presence who was absolutely necessary for his survival.

It was not surprising, then, that early in treatment Mr. A experienced me as a controlling person, whose unspoken intent was to have him do my bidding and whose guidance he both needed and resented. For some months, this transference dominated the scene, with Mr. A alternately disputing my every word and behaving as though without my assistance there was little chance of his surviving from one hour to the next.

During this time, references to the father were infrequent and transference perceptions of me as a father figure were fleeting. On occasion Mr. A complained that I was indecisive and lacked assertion—traits that in his mind characterized his father—and once or twice reported a fantasy that I, like his father, was undoubtedly a milktoast of a husband who was thoroughly browbeaten by my wife. For the most part, however, the predominant transference centered on the reawakening of Mr. A's relationship with the mother of his early years. While this clearly was important in its own right, the extent to which the transference prevailed struck me as significant in terms of both current resistances to experiencing me as the father and historical factors in Mr. A's childhood. It was not, however, until additional transference configurations made their appearance that the overall picture became clear.

Mr. A had two brothers, one several years older, the other a few years younger. Little material concerning them surfaced in the early months of treatment. Initially they were, like the father, shadowy figures. In time, however, they came into view both as figures in reality and in the transference. The sibling transferences had a special quality. Each gained prominence at particular—and ultimately predictable—times in the analysis: when pronounced anxiety was stimulated in Mr. A by the emergence of threatening impulses connected with the predominant transference of the moment.

This unconscious maneuver, clearly used in the service of resistance, became most evident in relation to the older brother. I noticed on more than one occasion that in the course of responding to me as a parent, and when his feelings were running high, Mr. A would, in a sudden shift, begin to refer to me as though I were this brother. These were, to be sure, not the only times that he perceived me in this way. On other occasions, however, there was no sudden shift from one central transference configuration to another. The fact that such shifts did occur when the prevailing transference stimulated anxiety-provoking impulses in Mr. A, lent particular importance—and interest—to such occurrences.

It was not unusual for feelings of aggression to constitute a large component of Mr. A's reaction to me as the dominant and overbearing mother. While seldom absent when this transference was in the ascendency, the extent of these aggressive feelings varied within a considerable range. When they grew in intensity and Mr. A was in a fury at me for what he perceived to be my wish to control his every action, he would, after experiencing much anxiety, shift gears and begin to talk to me as though I were the older brother to whom he could complain about their mother. This defensive shift occurred at other times too. It took place not only in connection with Mr. A's threatening aggressive feelings toward his mother (where clearly it served an object sparing purpose), but also in response to his libidinal ones. Though hidden behind his rages at and denunciations of his mother, such reactions were not entirely absent. When they were stimulated by positive feelings in the transference and memories of incestuous wishes began to surface, it was predictable that a perception of me as the brother would soon make an appearance.

The sexual feelings stirred up in the transference, however, were not limited to maternal ones. Yearnings toward me as the father whose love Mr. A yearned for were also mobilized, and it was these, even more than the forbidden wishes toward the mother, that had to be defended against.

Mr. A's relationship with his father was more complex and in some respects richer than had first appeared. When he was a young child, he and his father were quite close. For the first two years of Mr. A's life, in fact, they were inseparable companions. Later on, largely because of repeated depressions, the father withdrew emotionally from the family and the mother became the dominant parent. Mr. A's focus shifted almost exclusively to his mother, not only because of the changed relationship that developed between them, but for defensive reasons as well. By concentrating so exclusively on his mother, he could avoid recognition not only of his competitiveness with his father and the guilty triumph he felt at feeling himself the center of his mother's universe, but of his frustrated longings for his father's love. And in his efforts to protect against these feelings he utilized his relationship both with his mother and with his older brother.

This brother, in fact, became a substitute for the father. In turning to him in this manner, Mr. A accomplished two important goals. He was able to obtain at least a facsimile of the loving response that he yearned for from his father and, by concentrating interest and attention on the brother, was able to screen out both the rage he felt toward his father and the longings for him, which because of their homosexual implications, were threatening.

Thus, in the transference that emerged in Mr. A's analysis, the representation of the older brother could, when needed, serve for him a defensive purpose analogous to that accomplished at times by their real relationship. But as was also true of that relationship, the brother transference be-

came caught up in conflict. And when that transference provoked sufficient anxiety, a shift to another transference configuration regularly took
place.

This transference had at its central figure the younger brother. It came
into focus whenever Mr. A, experiencing his analyst as the kindly and
supportive older brother, felt unusually close to me. This shift reflected a
movement from one brother to another that had occurred with some frequency during Mr. A's adolescent years. Like the defensive focus on the
older brother described earlier, its aim was to protect against anxiety. As
was the case with the father representation, this anxiety was generated by
Mr. A's wish for love from the older brother and for me in the transference. Unconsciously this brother and the father were equated, and the
patient's yearnings for affection from one extended to the other. In the
case of the older brother representation, however, the situation was complicated by the fact that during his latency years Mr. A had joined his
brother in several episodes of mutual masturbation. The wish to repeat
this exciting and frightening experience, which remained as a residue of
these episodes, broke through to consciousness in adolescence and was
reactivated in the analysis.

In life Mr. A had responded to this threat by a familiar expedient. Finding reasons to avoid his older brother, he focused instead on the younger
one. Since frightening sexual feelings played no part in Mr. A's relations
with him, the young brother represented an island of safety. Moreover,
he provided an ideal vehicle for the living out of Mr. A's need to identify
with his powerful mother. Thus Mr. A's relations with this brother were
characterized by the domineering and overbearing attitude to which he
himself had been subjected.

In the analysis the protective shift to a transference dominated by the
younger brother took a characteristic form. Feeling threatened by feelings of closeness to me, Mr. A would,, at first, seek to distance himself
through an attitude of aloofness and indifference. Then focusing on some
area of business about which he imagined I had little knowledge, such as
the Stock Market or real estate transactions, he proceeded to show up my
deficiencies. Then, as a sophisticated business man, he would proceed to
instruct me in the fundamentals of those fields. For several weeks behavior of this kind, with which he regularly harassed his younger brother,
characterized his relations with me. Then, when his anxiety had been reduced and sufficient distance obtained from the threatening feelings that
had aroused it, perceptions of me as the older brother would once more
find their way into the transference.

Thus, by following the shifts and changes in the transference pictures
that emerged in Mr. A's analysis, it was possible to uncover some of the

unconscious roots of the persistent difficulty that characterized his relationships, not only with friends and family, but with colleagues as well. Understanding the way that when feeling threatened, he defensively altered his perceptions of me threw light on the similar unconscious displacements that had taken place in the past and that were still active in his relationships with others. It provided insights that served as a first step in his efforts to improve these troubled relationships.

In his reconstructive efforts, the analyst sometimes finds it valuable to trace out the longitudinal aspects of object relationships and the way they have undergone change over years. Intimately connected with shifting self-representations and with unconscious fantasies that have contributed to symptom formation and to character development, the history of an analysand's changing perceptions of centrally important figures in his life is a rich field for analytic investigation. In this effort, the close study of the relationships that exist between transferences can prove a useful tool.

This was true of the analysis of Mr. R, a successful and energetic professional man in his mid-thirties. Unlike Miss L, whose neurosis took the form of imagining herself an impostor, Mr. R was in many respects truly a sham. Quite striking was the way his polished style, youthful good looks, and unusual ability to ingratiate himself with clients could conceal the fact that he was far from the expert in his field that his outward manner suggested.

Mr. R's need to play the role of the charlatan despite good intelligence and considerable talent, however, shared with Miss L's symptoms an unconscious dynamic. In each, identification with a parent who was perceived as dishonest was of central importance. In the case of Mr. R, however, this perception had a more substantial basis in reality.

A shrewd and ambitious entrepreneur given to marginal business practices, Mr. R's father had on one occasion in the patient's youth run afoul of the Law. An investigation follwed and, as a consequence, he lost his business and the family fell on hard days. Although his parents tried to conceal from him the true reason for the abrupt decline in their fortunes, Mr. R discovered the truth. That discovery, as well as subsequent developments to which he reacted strongly, had a profound effect on his attitudes toward both his father and his uncle, the father's younger brother, who was also involved in the business. The transformations that took place in the way Mr. R viewed both men — views that were a mix of perception and fantasy — were reflected in the analysis in changing transference pictures.

For Mr. R, his father had always been a hero. From the patient's earliest years he regarded this parent as a powerful and magnetic figure whom he wanted to emulate. The uncle, too, was much admired, although in a very different way. While the father was viewed as the stable force in the family—the Director-General—the uncle, was a bon vivant. His good looks, dazzling clothes, and adventurous spirit were attributes to be emulated. When trouble developed in the family, however, Mr. R's views of both men—and, as a consequence, of himself—underwent marked change.

In the initial months of the analysis, two transference pictures took center stage, one related to the father, the other to the uncle. There was constant shifting and interweaving between these dominant transferences so that at one point Mr. R would perceive me as the powerful father, at another as the dashing uncle. Not infrequently, mental images of the two men overlapped, as they often had in Mr. R's childhood, so that a view of me as solid and stable, charming and debonair, father and uncle, captured Mr. R's imagination. For some months he regarded me as all but flawless, the perfect analyst, who not only was reliable and perceptive, but also, he imagined, drove a Mercedes sports coupe.

I was perfect until Mr. R found out through the grapevine that I no longer held a certain academic position with which he had associated me. Then his view of me changed. Clearly he was disappointed, perceived me as a much diminished figure, and had to struggle to retain a positive image of me. To do this he developed the idea that I was a victim, that I had been forced to relinquish my rightful place, and that to keep the peace in my department I had allowed myself to be sacrificed. From an initial reaction of rage and disappointment, Mr. R's attitude gradually shifted to one of solicitude and concern. At the same time, that part of the transference which related to the uncle seemed to fade away. He was mentioned only infrequently now, and on the few occasions when some aspect of my person called forth memories of him, Mr. R's voice took on a sarcastic tone.

This state of affairs persisted until another change occurred in my life: I was forced to relocate my office. Mr. R responded to this move with much distress. In his mind it was a setback, a sign of my professional decline. Disapproving of both the new location and the space I had obtained, he viewed the change as a sign of my economic failure. Once again I became a disparaged figure, but now Mr. R viewed me with scarcely concealed contempt. To him I had become a loser, a pitiful figure whose efforts to maintain the image of a successful practitioner were now revealed for the charade that they were.

At the same time, positive feelings towards the uncle were revived. In fact, during this period the only positive transference notes that were struck in an otherwise persistent refrain of negative comments about his analyst related to those aspects of my personality that Mr. R saw as sharing something in common with his uncle. Of particular importance to him were qualities that, in his mind, marked me as an assimilated Jew. While I was criticized for my ineptitude as a businessman and for my inability to earn an adequate living, the fact that I did not speak with a Bronx accent and that in neither dress nor manner did I call attention to being Jewish merited praise. At one point, Mr. R was convinced that in my private life I made determined efforts to conceal my ethnic background.

The shifts that took place in the evolving transferences and in Mr. R's views of me as father and uncle represented the reactivation in treatment of object representations that were closely connected to historical events in his childhood and adolescence. And it was by means of them that certain centrally important memories and fantasies relating to these two most influential figures in his life—and to perceptions of himself—could be reconstructed.

Following his discovery of his father's troubles and the truth about the loss of his business, Mr. R was thrown into a turmoil. No longer could he believe in his father's strength, his judgment, his business acumen. The man whom he had adored, and to whom he had looked for years as a model, had turned out to be a cheat and a failure. Despite the irrefutable evidence that this was so, Mr. R found the idea impossible to believe and did all that he could to prove to himself that it was not true. As had occurred in the transference when he discovered certain unacceptable facts about me, Mr. R concocted an explanation of the events that cast his father in the role of a victim. It was other relatives in the business who were the true culprits, he believed. Were it not for their greed, the financial crisis that had precipitated the trouble would never have occurred. He convinced himself that it was his father's wish to avoid a bitter disruption in the family and his willingness to protect others at his own expense that led him to shoulder the blame.

As part of the process of protecting the father, devaluation of the uncle took place. He too was classified among the guilty. His expensive life style and the inflated salary he demanded to support it had, in Mr. R's mind, contributed to the problem. For some time thereafter Mr. R lost interest in his uncle, and when they met, he treated him, to the uncle's amazement, with a coolness not unmixed with sarcasm.

This attitude toward the uncle, however, did not persist for long. Although Mr. R had managed temporarily to salvage from the collapse of his world a positive image of the father, this view could not survive a second disappointment. Further disillusionment occurred when the father attempted to establish a new business. Without the requisite capital and unable to borrow money, he was forced to set up shop in the back room of a dilapidated warehouse. He did not reveal to his family either the location of his new venture or the fact that within a matter of months the business was on the verge of bankruptcy. When as the result of a relative's slip the truth came out and Mr. R went to see where his father worked, he was crushed. A final illusion was destroyed. As part of his personal rehabilitation of his father, Mr. R had pictured him dictating letters in the office that he had visited as a child – a dark paneled room complete with a large executive desk and a dictating machine. Now he found his father closeted in a dingy back room without a proper desk or secretary. The disparity between reality and fantasy was overwhelming. It confirmed Mr. R's worst fears about his father: that he was a loser and that the image of a dynamic, aggressive businessman he tried to project was nothing but a facade.

In desperation, and in an effort to fend off the feeling of depression that accompanied this realization, Mr. R turned once again to the uncle. Seeking a man in the family of whom he could be proud, he tried to recapture the old image of the uncle as a charismatic figure. Part of Mr. R's reason for this was that in contrast to his father, who never recovered from the blow he had suffered, the uncle had prospered. He became the star salesman of an industrial firm and with the money to indulge his expensive tastes lived a flamboyant lifestyle. He became the family success story.

Along the way, however, something else had happened to the uncle. He turned his back on his religion and acted the part of a Christian. At work he tried to give the impression that he had been a lifelong Episcopalian. When once again Mr. R came under the uncle's influence, the latter encouraged him to follow his lead and to shed outward signs of his Jewish identity. For a year, Mr. R sought to pass himself off as a Protestant, and when he entered a new school he registered as such. This was a year in his life that Mr. R had completely blotted from memory. It was only in the course of analysis that it was recovered.

The final shift in Mr. R's view of his father and uncle took place in late adolescence and was reflected in transference attitudes that appeared toward the end of the analysis. No longer was Mr. R enraged at me, nor did he condemn me for my failings as a businessman. Rather, he adopted toward me a tolerant and even indulgent attitude, an attitude that, after much inner turmoil, had evolved toward his father.

Transferences centered on me as the uncle no longer surfaced very often, but on the few occasions when they did, Mr. R responded with a kind of amused detachment that did not preclude positive feelings. In reality, the uncle more or less had disappeared from view during Mr. R's young adult years. When their paths met it was with a tolerant eye that he perceived the man who had played a role of such importance in his life.

In fact, although by the time he entered analysis Mr. R had developed perspectives on both father and uncle that were well attuned to reality, it was the residues of the unconscious identifications that had taken place many years earlier that were of the root of certain of his difficulties.

Already mentioned was Mr. R's need in his professional life to live out the role of the charlatan, a role that caused him innumerable difficulties and that on one or two occasions threatened him with total ruin. Clearly operative in the formation of this symptom was not only an identification with the father as criminal, but unconscious guilt of a high order. While these feelings of guilt related in large measure to the contempt Mr. R felt toward his father at the time of his decline, it also contained important oedipal roots that had been buried under the impact of the later experience.

As an adult Mr. R also displayed certain character traits that he did not find compatible with his conscious ideals. Among these were a penchant for expensive clothes and cars and for a more lavish lifestyle than he could afford. Even more troubling, however, was Mr. R's attitude toward himself as a Jew. He was ashamed of being Jewish and although he disliked himself for this quality, he often attempted, particularly when making a new business acquaintance, to conceal this fact. It was not until the uncle's anti-Semitism had come to light and Mr. R's unconscious identification with this attitude brought into the open that he was able, finally, to free himself from this tendency.

In Mr. R's case the emerging transference and the patterns that they formed contributed not only to the reconstruction of particular object representations but also to the understanding of the vicissitudes of certain self-representations. Closely linked to his perception of his father and uncle, Mr. R's self-concept fluctuated with the particular images that he had of these central figures. When in the transference he viewed me as the powerful, effective father, he too felt powerful and effective. When he experienced me as a failure, he was very much diminished; he too felt like a failure and he became depressed.

Similar transformations in Mr. R's self-regard occurred through the uncle transference, although to a lesser extent. When he saw me as the exciting, magnetic uncle, he identified with this image and his view of himself was temporarily inflated. When in his mind I took on some of the negative qualities of his uncle—superficiality, greed, and a disregard for the value of money—he experienced himself as similarly tarnished. Although, clearly, multiple factors, including the mobilization of sexual and aggressive wishes, superego responses and resistances that were active, contributed to Mr. R's view of himself at any given time in the analysis, a meaningful correlation between Mr. R's current self-representation and changes in the prevailing transference configurations could be consistently made. Thus it was through observing these shifting transferences and the relationships that existed between them that fantasies and memories relating to crucial experiences in Mr. R's development over a period of a decade or more could be recovered. These fantasy-memories involved shifting views not only of the men who had played so large a role in shaping his early years, but of himself as well.

DISCUSSION

In the foregoing examples, study of the shifting and changing transference pictures that emerged in the course of analysis, including the temporal and sequential relationships between transferences, could be meaningfully related to aspects of a patient's history. In each case the manner in which the transferences unfolded followed patterns laid down in childhood and at times reproduced rather closely the vicissitudes of particular object representations. Why in these cases repetition of the past — an unconscous process central to the creation of all transference phenomena — included significant aspects of form as well as of content remains a matter for further investigation. As discussed earlier, this is not always, or even usually, the case. In many analyses (including substantial periods of time in the ones cited here), the manner in which the transferences emerge bears no clear relationship to the unfolding of the original object representations. Why, then, is history repeated in specific ways in some cases and not in others? Although the definitive answer to this question must await further research, one idea suggests itself on the basis of the foregoing clinical material. In each case, trauma of a not inconsequential kind played a significant part in childhood. In the case of Miss L, it centered on the discovery of the truth about her father; for Mr. A, on a troubled relationship with a disturbed mother as well as on the early loss of the father through depression and the seduction in adolescence by the older brother; in Mr. R's case, knowledge of his father's illegitimate business activities, followed by his steady decline, had a profound affect on the boy's development.

Analytic experience has shown that when certain individuals experience trauma of this kind there develops a tendency for it to be repeated in life, as well as in the transference. It may be that for some individuals part of the reliving of the experience includes the repetition of the forms and sequences in which fantasies, memories and perceptions were laid down as well as their content. Included also would be temporal relationships that are unconsciously linked to these emotionally important experiences. Like anniversary reactions, memories of certain traumatic experiences seem to be linked to the unconscious sense of time as well as to registration of the sequential order in which they occurred. It is these formal qualities that, along with content, are not infrequently reproduced in the course of reliving such memories in analysis. When this occurs, the forms that the transferences take and the relationships between them will appear as integral parts of the process of repetition.

SUMMARY

This paper has focused on an aspect of the phenomena of transference that has so far been little explored: the relationship between the multiple transferences that emerge in the course of any analysis. In certain cases, the investigation and analysis of these relationships can prove a valuable tool in the process of reconstruction. To illustrate several ways in which the vicissitudes of the developing transferences can be meaningfully related to psychological developments in childhood and adolescence, three clinical examples have been given. In these cases close study of the forms and transformations of transference permitted the reconstruction of material that was central in the analysis of each: a forgotten piece of history, the defensive way in which object representations were utilized in childhood and adolescence, and the longitudinal history of certain developmentally important self and object representations. Finally, in an effort to account for some of the phenomena described in these cases a tentative theoretical explanation was offered for the connection that not infrequently exists between the form and manner in which transferences unfold in analysis and the specific ways in which traumatic experiences are registered in childhood.

REFERENCES

Bird, B. (1972), Notes on transference: Universal phenomenon and hardest part of analysis. *J. Amer Psychoanal. Assn.*, 20:267–301.

Blum, H. (1971), On the conception and development of the transference neurosis. *J. Amer. Psychoanal. Assn.*, 19:41–53.

Brenner, C. (1983), Transference and countertransference. In: *The Mind in Conflict*. New York: International Universities Press.

Greenacre, P. (1959), Certain technical problems in the transference relationship. *J. Amer Psychoanal. Assn.*, 7:484–502.

Kohut, H. (1971), *The Analysis of the Self.* New York: International Universities Press.

Stone, L. (1967), The psychoanalytic situation and transference: Postscript to an earlier communication. *J. Amer. Psychoanal. Assn.*, 15:3–55.

Aspects of Termination: Theory and Practice

O ne impressive characteristic of the literature on termination since 1927 is the extraordinary rarity of clinically detailed case reports. Others have noted this psychoanalytic reticence in the presentation of clinical data pertaining to the terminal phase.

> The reluctance of many among us to participate in such clinical self-exposure touches upon one of the most insteresting features of the termination experience—that during termination the multiple meanings of this laborious therapeutic interaction for both partners often becomes more explicit than during the analytic phases that preceded it . . . Questions [of] how satisfied they are with the results of their efforts, or how disappointed, move into the analytic focus, with impact on both participants. Such questions are frequently sources of discomfort, which for some analysts militates against sharing clinical data with colleagues and students [Firestein, 1982, p. 496–497].

> Many analysts became anxious when we asked for permission to study their cases . . . this anxiety reaction was so common that I called it "research anxiety." . . . Research anxiety might be caused by an analyst's uneasiness about whether he had made errors which he had overlooked, or whether he had gone far enough in the analysis of the patient's character, or whether there was a transference-countertransference impasse [Ticho, 1972, p. 319].

There is in fact only one clinical presentation of a terminal phase that deals with the issues of termination and provides sufficient clinical detail for the reader to understand what went on in the analysis—what the patient understood and what the analyst interpreted (Dewald, 1972b).[1] The

---

[1]Although there are several other studies that provide limited clinical descriptions from the termination phase, these tend to focus on narrow issues—the illustration of a specific clinical phenomenon or technique (Orens, 1955; Miller, 1965; Pfeffer, 1980; Wilson, 1968).

321

major monograph on the subject (Firestein, 1972) provides descriptions of the terminal phase of eight patients, and although it sought to remedy the absence of empirical data about the termination phase (and for this we should be grateful) the data suffer from what Ticho (1972) called "research anxiety." The descriptions, though they are both from the patient's and the analyst's point of view, are almost completey devoid of any psychoanalytic data. The reader has little understanding of the analytic work that was done before or during the termination phase, and no hint of the interpretations that the analyst made or the dynamic understanding that was imparted to the patient.

In contrast to this dearth of clinical material—psychoanalytic data—there has been a proliferation of the theoretical literature on the subject. Much of this focuses on two favorite issues: 1) What are the criteria for termination, and 2) Is the termination phase unique—different from the rest of analysis—and if so, what are its essential characteristics?

In the days of Marienbad we had simple notions to guide us through the analysis and the terminal phase: "Where Id was, there shall Ego be". Since then, although each new contributor has found past criteria for termination wanting, each is loathe to relinquish any. Thus the list grows with each new contribution. Rangell (1966) has the following list:

1. To make the unconscious conscious.
2. Where id was, there shall ego be.
3. Genital primacy.
4. Heterosexual potency.
5. Mature object relationships.
6. The achievement of optimum self-esteem.
7. The ability to love and work.
8. The ability to have mature friendships.
9. The ability to live up to the capacities of one's ego.
10. The achievement of structural change.
11. The achievement of optimal relationship to reality.
12. The achievement of the "best possible conditions for the functioning of the ego."

Others in the literature have contributed different lists, some shorter, some longer—each list well discussed and rationalized, each term on the list abstractly defined, and each definition differing slightly from other definitions of the same term. These terms, more or less devoid of clinical meaning and with a high degree of ambiguity, have become in a sense theoretical cliches—slogans—with about the same degree of validity that cliches in other spheres of life have—comforting from a distance but not very helpful when one gets down to specifics, and of little use to a working professional. It is understandable, then, that when Firestein (1982) surveyed a dozen senior analysts, each with more than thirty years' experience, with respect to this issue he found that "although in the literature criteria are often framed in the language of metapsychology, such language was not prominent at all in the responses of my interviewees". Analysts often write one way and practice another.

These two tendencies in the literature—the dearth of clinical data and the parallel proliferation of theoretical cliches—may well account for a new trend: a view of termination that veers from older psychoanalytic concepts and values toward revised goals and standards (Klein, 1950; Payne, 1950; Reich, 1950; Loewald, 1961, 1979; Miller, 1965; Zetzel, 1965; Balint, 1970; Ticho, 1972; DeBell, 1975).

The model of pathogenesis articulated by Freud and elaborated by the ego psychologists (A. Freud, 1946; Hartmann, Kris, and Loewenstein, 1946) and more recently by Arlow (1966), Brenner (1982), Rangell (1982), Dewald (1972a), and others, is based on a theory of conflict whose elements can be observed in behavioral and mental manifestations and understood as words and pictures, that is, fantasies, involving conflicting human urges and wishes derived from childhood passions. The theory goes on to state that when these elements of conflict are made known to the patient in an emotionally meaningful way, their power to evoke dysphoric affect is reduced, resulting in a change in patterns of feeling and of automatic behavior. The basic assumptions thus are that the elements of conflict must be discovered and communicated to the patient in an acceptable and convincing way. It is a therapy based on cognition: in order to be cured the patient must learn something about himself that he did not know before the treatment started—that he was the owner and author of a set of unacceptable wishes.

In contradistinction to this classical model, an alternative model of psychoanalysis has emerged over the past two or three decades, claiming the attention of analysts and residing in parallel with classical theory. Some analysts partake of both, mixing and matching as they see fit. This alternative model had its origin in several loosely related subtheories of object relations (Klein, 1950; Winnicott, 1965; Zetzel, 1965; Kohut, 1977, 1979; Balint, 1950). These theorists, and those who follow them, do not necessarily disavow classical concepts and techniques in their writing, and probably not even in their practice. But they do emphasize an array of concepts and techniques which at best gives their analytic work a different thrust and at worst makes it difficult, or impossible, for certain kinds of analytic achievements to take place. Although many other elements are subsumed in this view of psychoanalysis, I wish to emphasize several in particular because of their direct relevance to the issue of termination. First of all, emphasis is shifted away from cognition and in the direction of affect: knowing about oneself—especially one's unconscious wishes—is less important than being in touch with one's feelings and expressing them. Catharsis is thus emphasized, as distinct from exploration, discovery and insight. Empathy in the analyst is highly valued, perhaps even to the exclusion of other important analytic instrumentalities, and, by identification, self-empathy in the patient becomes an analytic goal.

In this newer psychoanalytic model, emotional relearning is another highly valued goal in treatment, and therefore emotional reeducation, or analytic role playing, becomes an important therapeutic modality. This notion occurs repeatedly in the history of psychoanalytic treatment. Lorand (1946), for example, stated that "through the analyst's benevolent attitude he (the patient) realizes that it is possible to be treated differently than he was in the past and he also loses his fear of the world" (p. 223). In the fifties, it was Alexander's Corrective Emotional Experience; today it is Kohut's Transmuting Internalization. Of course, the idea of curing through love began far back in the history of Western civilization. It has emerged in psychoanalysis, however, in the work of those analysts who tend to emphasize preoedipal trauma as a source of pathology. Here, the focus is on various kinds of narcissistic traumata rooted in the loss or deprivation of maternal love. The treatment is often conceived of as undoing or repairing bad mothering by the substitution of good mothering.

These characteristics—preoedipal orientation, emphasis on catharsis and emotional containment, role playing, emotional reeducation—are based on a theory of pathogenesis that is quite at variance with the theory of pathogenesis based on intrapsychic conflict. And from this certain techinical consequences flow, especially with respect to the terminal phase.

Since one of the main goals of this new trend in analysis is emotional reeducation, and since one of the instruments of the cure is identification with a loving, accepting analyst, the technical communication of conflict—unconscious fantasies and defenses—remains relatively unimportant; the analyst's words, his "interpretations," are relatively unimportant. What is important is his role playing—his benevolent attitude, his acceptance, his patience. And when the patient has had a sufficient dose of this, his—the patient's—self-acceptance and self-esteem improve, and consequently his object relations as well. When this happens, the analyst "intuits" that the time has come for the patient to end the analysis. In short, the criteria for termination tend to be oriented towards general improvements in mental functioning, especially around issues of self-esteem and object relations. The amount of improvement is unspecified and is left to the intuition of the analyst. It is easy to see that this leaves considerable room for individual variation among analysts as to what represents a terminable or completed case (Flemming and Benedek, 1966).

This new view of things is often justified on the grounds that the "earlier perfectionism" of classical or orthodox analysts demanded the impossible—a resolution of the transference neurosis. And recent evidence (Pfeffer, 1980; Robbins, 1975; Schlesinger, 1975) suggesting that even in well-conducted analyses various degrees of transference persist into the postanalytic phase has been used to support the assertion that since transference cannot be resolved therefore analysis is interminable.

In any case, followers of this model of psychoanalysis tend to disavow "rigid, perfectionistic goals" (Robbins, 1975; Schlesinger, 1975) and see analysis as more or less interminable. Indeed, some writers have disavowed all criteria for deciding on termination (Shentoub, 1955), and some have invented euphemisms for analytic incompleteness, such as "natural termination" (Goldberg, 1985).

In the absence of clinical data, and where there are no precise or agreed upon theoretical standards, it is difficult to resist the regressive pull toward analytic nihilism and technical compromise.

In addition to the vagueness of termination criteria, another important result of this model of analysis is the tendency to view the termination phase as essentially and primarily an experience of loss, separation, mourning, and grief (Balint, 1950; Klein, 1950; Payne, 1950; Reich, 1950; Loewald, 1961; Miller, 1965; Zetzel, 1965; Ticho, 1972; DeBell, 1975). In this kind of analysis, in which the analyst is encouraged to engage, to a certain extent, in role playing as the loving, tolerant, accepting, repairing parent, it is understandable that some writers would suggest that the analyst is "a real object" and that the patient must mourn the loss of such gratification when the analysis is terminated (DeBell, 1975). Since the emphasis is on preoedipal issues in which oral wishes and anxieties are paramount, this is carried into the terminal phase, where the main focus of analytic work is separation anxiety, grief, and various defenses against them. Indeed, some analysts suggest "weaning" as a technical device in this phase (Buxbaum, 1950; Glover, 1955).

In summary, then, a review of the literature suggests that in the absence of much good clinical data, a view of the terminal phase has developed as an outgrowth of a nonconflictual theoretical model of analysis that stresses preoedipal trauma, emotional repair or reeducation, role playing, and catharsis. These values contribute to a concept of termination in which feelings of loss, separation anxiety, mourning, and grief must predominate and become the central focus of interpretation, and in which the criteria for termination are ambiguous and highly variable.

In light of the above, I would like to present the report of an analysis that brings evidence to bear on some of the current conceptions and misconceptions that have appeared in the literature on termination. I hope to present the report of this rather long analysis (1600 hours) in sufficient detail to give the reader a vivid picture of the entire terminal phase (eight or nine months) — a picture clear enough to suggest what, at the end of the analysis, the patient had learned about herself and how she had changed from when she was first seen.

I present this case report not because I think it is a model of optimal technique. On the contrary, I present it as an average case. Though it was probably quite imperfect, I was pleased with the final result, as was the patient, and I know that now, five or six years later, the patient functions well, is happy, and continues to show signs of growth. I present the case in some detail to encourage others to follow suit.

I would like to remind the reader, too, that many of the interpretations made to the patient in the course of the analysis were repeated many, many times. The case as reported here does not reflect those repetitions. Aside from the tactical interpretations, which continued to vary throughout the analysis, the most important interpretations were made to the patient many times in different contexts. How many? Enough times — more than five and less than a hundred — that by the end of the analysis there was no question in my mind that the patient's understanding of her conflicts, especially the drive derivatives, had left an indelible impression on her.

I ask the reader's indulgence for the length of the report. It is often difficult to find an optimal length — one that is short enough not to tire the reader, yet sufficiently rich in clinical data to draw a fair picture of how the analyst conducted the analysis.

CASE ILLUSTRATION

Mrs. S presented herself as a sunny, attractive young woman in her early twenties who was slightly seductive and eager to please. She complained that she had been having abdominal pains with mild diarrhea for about a year.

Further history revealed that she had serious sexual inhibitions, was frigid most of the time, had little or no self-confidence, and wanted desperately to feel independent but in fact felt quite the opposite. She was confused about her future and about her current role in life; although she had literary interests and perhaps some talent, she had dropped out of college after the first semester and was completely unable to develop these gifts in an effective way.

When I first saw her, Mrs. S was newly married. Her husband was 25, a recently graduated attorney working in his father's law firm. It was clear that the patient's tension and gastrointenstinal symptomatology were in large measure a response to ambivalent feelings toward her husband and his family, all of whom seemed to her to be difficult and demanding people.

At the outset, the essential features of her early history were these. When the patient was 3½ years old she suffered a moderately serious accident and was rushed to the hospital. She remembered that her clothes were cut and torn from her and she was placed in an oxygen tent. She stayed in the hospital for a number of weeks and has vivid memories of being mistreated by impatient nurses, being x-rayed, and being given enemas.

She remembers a change in her personality after returning home. She became sullen, irritable, clinging, and distrustful of her mother and also suffered severely from bowel retention and constipation.

When she was six years old, she fell under the spell of a friend two or three years older than she, a strong-willed active girl named Marian, who drew her gradually into an overt sexual relationship that lasted two years. These experiences occurred frequently, especially during the spring and summer of each year. Marian would boss her around and insist that she perform various sexual activities—mostly sucking her breasts, playing with her genitals, and playing the active male role. She became Marian's slave, admiring her strength, wanting her love and always afraid of losing it. She also felt very guilty and miserable about this relationship and longed for some external rescue from the situation but naturally was afraid to tell her mother.

When she was in the second grade her mother became pregnant, and her sister, B, was born when she was eight. The remainder of her latency seemed unremarkable.

She did well in school until the sixth or seventh grade, when she became pubescent, was very self-conscious, and began to have learning difficulties. Despite her intelligence, she developed fears about examinations and almost failed math. In high school she showed talent in art and literature and adopted a bohemian role in her social life, which hid from herself her own social and sexual anxieties. She was shy with boys, and much of her energy during adolescence was taken up in an intense sublimated homosexual relationship.

Early Phase of the Analysis

The early phase of the analysis was what might be called the sunny period. It was practically love at first sight. Mrs. S presented herself as a bright, perceptive, imaginative young woman. She came to her analysis four days a week brighteyed, good humored, and smiling. She worked hard in every session, elaborating her history in an imaginative way that provided richness, texture, and connections with her present life. She was always accommodating, always on time, and despite the hardships of having to get up at an extremely early hour to travel from the suburbs to my office and then to work, she was uncomplaining and clearly devoted to the analysis. No analyst could have asked for a more appealing or pleasant patient. Here is a session from this early phase of the analysis.

The patient walked into the consulting room with a portfolio and indicated that there was a small watercolor inside. She told me that this was a gift from Suburbia. (She was dabbling in painting at the time.) She commented that the time was going so fast that it was frightening to her. Already married two years. Already her friends were graduating from college. The day before she had gone with her husband to look for an apartment. He was irritable and he took her to terrible places, "I felt I had no rights; I just had to be a good wife. In the past year I've started getting angrier and angrier. I dread going back [home] tonight. I haven't been able to work on my painting, and I resent it. If I had my own money to pay for the analysis, I would separate. I can't stand my life the way it is now. There's nothing to get up for in the morning except to help H [her husband]. There's nothing for myself. When I was 21, I got the $3000 [settlement held in trust for her from her accident]. I always thought I would use it for education, but H put it in investments. I resent that he is paying for the analysis. I feel that I owe him something. I feel sick about going home and packing. I used to care about the house but now I don't care about anything. I'm afraid to say anything to H. Why do I have to do what he tells me?"

It was clear from the above that she wanted me to be her ally and to give her permission or advice — to rescue her from her situation,. I did not respond to her question but instead asked her about the "gift" from Suburbia. "I'm afraid you won't accept it. It's a painting. It's yours if you want it. I'd like to paint something special. Painting is one of my best characteristics. When you like someone you want to give them something. I feel like I have taken so much. I have nothing else to offer. The men I feel attracted to are educated and I feel so inferior, it's the only thing I feel confident about. He has never appreciated what I want him to love about me — my sensitivity, my imagination, my intelligence."

The ambivalent dependence she felt toward her husband, as expressed in the first part of the hour and which had been defended against until then, became the model for her later transference relationship. At that particular moment, however, she was completely unaware of any negative feelings toward me.

As her seductive behavior and romantic fantasies came under scrutiny and analysis, they became considerably reduced in her analytic sessions. The unconscious hostility in her seductive behavior and fantasies emerged eventually in the form of a Circe fantasy, but at this time the seductiveness was interpreted defensively as a way of warding off feelings of helplessness and undesirability.

Now that the cat was out of the bag, she was no longer constrained to be the "good girl" in the analysis. She becamse less hostile toward her husband and more openly resentful toward me. The sunniness began to cloud over, and she became quite another person from the genial, accommodating young woman who had started the analysis.

Middle Phase of the Analysis

Although this phase constituted the major portion of the analysis, only a very small part of the clinical data can be presented in a report whose focus is the terminal phase. I hope this representative sample will be sufficient to demonstrate the connections—the continuity of themes—between this phase and the final one.

In the third year of the analysis, the patient becamse pregnant during my summer vacation and that autumn was in the first trimester of her pregnancy. She announced at the beginning of a session one day that she felt depressed and nauseous and that everything seemed too much for her—her schoolwork (she had gone back to college by then and was doing well), moving their apartment. She felt overwhelmed. Then she said she felt anxious at that moment. She had had a sense of dread in coming to her session. Everything had been fine and then suddenly she hit a brick wall. She said she didn't want to work that day, she didn't want to sweat, that a part of her didn't want to change—she wanted to be finished with the analysis. She wanted independence; she didn't want to be dependent on me. She couldn't seem to quite grasp that she was coming to analysis for herself, on her own. It always seemed to her that she was coming to please me. She resented that.

Then she expressed disappointment in her pregnancy. She had thought that she would feel better about herself if she were pregnant. But it wasn't so. She thought that she would feel more important and that other people would think her more important and treat her that way. But it wasn't so, even though it brought her and her husband closer. She was irritated with him, about his work (he was working very hard and very well at the time). She was jealous of it. She would have liked to interfere with it but she didn't. She felt neglected and left out. She wanted to have a fuss made over her. She was angry at not being taken seriously.

I felt that it was important to undo the transference displacement and interpret her reflected anger and disappointment. And so I told her that I thought her depression was due to disappointment not in her pregnancy but in me; that she felt I was like a brick wall and she was angry at me for not making more of a fuss over her and making her feel more important; but that she was afraid to become aware of angry feelings toward me and it was safer for her to be depressed and to feel overwhelmed. I told her also that it seemed as though she had expected her pregnancy to cure her feelings of being defective; that the pregnancy and my admiration of it were in the service of making her feel respectable (taken seriously) and complete (independent) – just as she had always wished her father to do.

During this phase of the analysis, in which there was considerable depression and anger that had to be identified and worked through, she complained bitterly to me that she wanted more than anything else to be "independent" and "to be taken seriously," especially by me. It had become clear by then that these intense and pervasive yearnings had to do primarily with denial of castration. That is, to be "independent" and "taken seriously" meant that one had phallic powers.

In the next hour Mrs. S continued the theme. She told me she was irritated that she had to come to the session and that she was constantly angry at me because I was cold, aloof, and never seemed to acknowledge her. She said it was true that she was afraid of getting angry at me. She said that anger had never been expressed at home; one was never able even to think angry thoughts. She said that she was afraid she would lose control if she really got angry, that I would lose interest in her completely and then she would be totally helpless. This also made her think of the fear she had had as a child in the hospital – that if she got angry the nurses and doctors would hurt or exterminate her. (She often talked of the hospital as though it had been an extermination camp.)

In the subsequent hour she told me that she felt she was beginning "to show" (referring to her pregnancy). She remarked that it was a beautiful cool autumn day. She told me that she had written a really good poem the day before, that it had come effortlessly "like eating an apple." She said that she had a dream that night. In the dream she had promised to take her sister somewhere. It was dusk and clear, and she was driving a very little toy car and they got into a thick fog and her sister got panicky, but she remained in control. She turned the car and suddenly realized that "there was nothing in front of me." She had stopped at the edge of a cliff and had almost been killed. But, she told herself, "almost isn't the same as really" and backed away from the cliff.

Her associations to the dream were as follows: the fog was the unknown and her fear of going ahead in the analysis. Although she retreated, she did not give up. She thought that both her sister's fear and her courage in the dream were aspects of herself; she was not going to let her intense fear overpower her. She knew that she had to take certain risks in the analysis.

To the toy car in the dream, she associated that she was completely in control of it. She would be very uneasy if she had a larger car. "It might take over, and I would lose control. I have to be easy on myself. I have to do it one step at a time, but it is better than not driving at all." (This was at a time in the analysis when she had allowed herself to learn how to drive and was struggling with her intense discomfort in the situation.)

To the dream element "there was nothing in front of me," she associated that she had stopped in the nick of time, at the brink, and that she hadn't after all gone flying off the cliff. (Her dreams were punctuated with images of soaring and flying.) This reminded her of another dream she had had sometime during the night. That dream was as follows. There was something going on in the dining room. She told her husband H that he should check it. She knew that there was a disembodied nose in the other room, and she heard her husband screaming.

She said she felt guilty in the dream about sending her husband—that he had gotten killed and somehow she was responsible for the whole thing. She laughed and said, "A nose makes a pretty good phallic symbol." She continued half jestingly that it could be a "castrated penis." Continuing in this joking vein, she said maybe she did this to H, or to me, just to get even because I had in some way failed her. She said it also made her think of cutting off her nose to spite her face. (Actually one of the day residues of the dream was a Woody Allen movie that she had seen the night before in which somebody wore a false nose.) She thought it had to do with her feeling recently that she wanted to make me feel impotent through her stubborness and recalcitrance. She had the thought in the dream that she would have to pay for what she had done to her husband and that frightened her even more.

Her associations to the weather were that it meant a "fresh start." She remembered that she would start school every autumn with great resolve, realizing that she had made a mess the previous year and knowing that it was her own fault. She resolved to be more organized and to work harder, start fresh and to transform herself.

I told her that her associations to her dream suggested that some part of her had the idea that if the analysis continued into the unknown, some frightening thing would happen to the men in her life—me or H—and therefore she'd better hold back. I suggested that being stubborn was perhaps the safest way of dealing with her disappointment.

The material of the several sessions just described, the dreams, the associations, I think illustrate well the interrelated picture of the patient's symptomatology, her transference neurosis, and her core conflicts.

Throughout the analysis in one way or another the derivatives of these conflicts emerged, sometimes with greater emphasis on her defensive structure, sometimes with greater emphasis on drive components, and sometimes with greater emphasis on self-punitive trends.

Perhaps the most persistent manifestation of her transference neurosis was the depressive symptomatology and the thoughts and fantasies connected with it. The patient's depressive symptoms emerged after more than two years of analysis, during which certain reaction formations and her seductiveness were analyzed. At the time of the sesison just described the patient was becoming increasingly aware of her feelings of incompetence, stupidity, ugliness, and worthlessness—all derivatives of her fantasy of having been castrated and permanently injured at the time of her accident. The patient's sullen, depressive, obstinate mood during the sessions were stimulated by her disappointment and anger at me for not reassuring her that her attempt at denial of castration, that is, her pregnancy, had worked. In other words, she wished me to treat her as though she were "important" and to take her "seriously" because of her new pregnancy. Unconsciously this was a sign that she had repaired or mended herself. If I had made a fuss over her as she wished, then she would have been able temporarily to deny her feelings of castration.

In these hours, derivatives of phallic envy emerged in the form of irritation with her husband and wishes to interrupt his work and her spiteful and obstinate feelings toward me. All of these represented castrating impulses warded off by passive-masochistic-depressive defenses. If she lost control of herself, got angry, she was flooded with self-punitive fantasies of being destroyed and exterminated.

The derivatives of her castration complex were expressed clearly in the dream of the false nose; she wished to deny her castrated state, make me impotent through spiteful behavior, and murder her husband. The dream of the toy car yet again suggested her anxiety about having "nothing in front of me," as well as the reassuring fantasy of rebirth and transformation each year as a more competent person.

During these three sessions, I interpreted the disappointed wishes and anger that had been suppressed, reflected, and displaced away from the transference; and interpretations linking her symptomatology—manifestations of impaired self-esteem—with fantasies of castration were made. Direct interpretations of sadistic wishes were deferred, since at the time of these sessions these impulses were heavily defended.

Much later in the analysis, in fact a week or two prior to the patient's first orgastic experience in intercourse, the following session occurred.

The patient told me that she was uneasy about coming to her session that day. She needed an hour or so to relax before she came. Then she said that she had found out that a friend—an older man, a professor whom she had always admired and had occasional sexual fantasies about, and whom she equated with me—was having an affair with one of his students, a young woman whom the patient held in very low esteem. She felt disturbed and sad about this discovery. She felt that the woman, M, in some way had gotten one up on her. M somehow had gotten control over her friend, T, the professor. She then had the thought of many women fighting with each other over merchandise in a store.

She said then that somehow becoming sexually uninhibited is like a balloon that has been held by ropes—if the ropes let go, things get out of control, the balloon will blow up, will fill with air like an erection. "I have the feeling that if I become sexually uninhibited, I'll be a man—or I'll become a man. It will be cause and effect simultaneously—what I want and what I am." I told her that I thought the reason she was anxious about coming that day was that some part of her had been stimulated by the news that her friend T was having an affair with M, that some part of her wanted to have an affair with me just as M was having one with T, and that she both wanted to be sexually uninhibited and was afraid because in her mind being sexually uninhibited meant a violent interaction between us during which she would blow up, like a pregnant woman. I told her that for her getting pregnant meant having a violent knockdown fight with a woman, and that when she was little she must have been very frightened of her wish to have a baby because it meant fighting with, perhaps even getting rid of, her mother.

The patient started the next hour by telling me that she had had a fantasy about Dr. G, her sister's psychiatrist. She had the fantasy that she met and seduced him. She felt jealous of her sister's flirtatious talk about Dr. G. Her sister sounded, she thought, as though she were becoming a nymphomaniac. Then she talked about her sister's anorexia, the reason for her sister's treatment.

Next she told me that she had been very anxious the night before because of the previous day's interpretation. She couldn't sleep and felt sexually restless. She was afraid that some catastrophe would occur; perhaps the baby would get sick or suffocate. She felt crowded in the bed and angry at the cat. She felt as though the cat were going to bite her. After a silence she said that she was really afraid of becoming a nymphomaniac, afraid that she would want to bring men down like Circe. She thought of a powerful, earthy, lusty woman—a Diana. Then she lapsed into silence, and when I asked her what she was thinking she said she had the fear that I would pounce on her. After a few minutes, she continued, saying she was afraid that her lusts would get the better of her, that she would break up homes or do physical violence or become a homicidal maniac; that if she really let herself go and unleashed her sexual feelings she would become monstrous with her genitals, she would be sexually insatiable or end up completely frustrated.

I told her that not only was she *afraid* she would become violent sexually but some part of her *wanted* to lose control and do some home breaking and commit violent sexual acts with Dr. G and with me too.

Later still in the analysis—in the period prior to the terminal phase—the following session occurred. She reported a dream of the previous night. She was in bed with H, her husband. Two young women in underwear came in and jumped into bed and on top of her husband. Then they turned to her and asked if she minded if they had sex with him. She was enraged.

Her associations led to a conversation in a poetry class after which a friend told Mrs. S of her sexual affairs. This reminded her of yet another dream she had had two nights before in which Dr. Z, her husband's former analyst, encouraged him, H, to have sex with prostitutes. They (that is, H and Dr. Z) caroused together under the analyst's supervision. Again, Mrs. S felt enraged. Then she suddenly burst out, "You can't trust men! They have their own little cult. It's all a crock of shit. They're always looking for the zipless fuck." She continued to rail at her husband as an inconsiderate, incompetent lover because she had not had an orgasm the night before. (This was at a time when she was still only irregularly orgastic in intercourse.) She wanted to tell him, shout at him, "You had an orgasm and I didn't. I'm starving. I need a plain old orgasm. Everybody feels that way, I feel that way. Men can do it. I want to encompass somebody! I want to fuck somebody! I want to possess a woman. I want to take it. I feel like this lately. I wish I had a cock to rub. It's crazy. Men don't have breasts, but I feel deprived."

Based on the patient's associations, I made the following interpretations in this and several subsequent hours. I told her that her wish to be sexually aggressive—that is, to be a nymphomaniac like the young girls in her dream—represented a wish to be like a man; that she wanted me to give her the right and the power to become like a sexually aggressive man, the way Dr. Z in her dream encouraged her husband to have sex and carouse. Further, she was disappointed and angry at me for not giving her the permission, approval, and transformation that would allow her to achieve that wish. I also told her that she had the fantasy that the only kind of genital that had the power to afford sexual satisfaction was a penis and that was one of the reasons that she felt so dependent on and angry at men.

The examples of the clinical data described were highly representative of this, the middle phase of the analysis. Indeed, as the evidence suggests, much of the analytic work consisted of increasingly clear explication and verbalization of her feelings of castration and demands that I transform her into a phallicly omnipotent being. This fantasy involved giving her a transforming orgasm in which she ended up with my penis and impregnated.

Naturally, one of the results of the mobilization and articulation of these fantasies was a considerable reduction in the patient's sexual inhibitions. This, together with an increasing ability for self-assertion and independence, constituted the major change in the patient's functioning during this phase of the analysis.

Termination — The Final Phase

The work of the termination phase lasted approximately eight or nine months and seemed naturally to divide itself into three subphases. The first subphase lasted for about three months. Although the work of that period was continuous with what had preceded it, it was also characterized by frequent, nonurgent references to termination; by a feeling on the part of both the patient and myself that important changes had occurred in her functioning and that the analysis was almost complete. One or two sessions from this period of the analysis will illustrate what I mean.

One day the patient came to her session excited about rewriting the plot of a novel she was writing. The pieces had fallen into place she said, and she went on to describe in some detail some of the plot changes in her book. Essentially she had given up its supernatural aspects.

Almost as an afterthought, she added that she felt she had been growing "by leaps and bounds" in the last month or two. She was no longer afraid of people, she was busy and involved all of the time, she didn't feel like an outcast anymore. She was even premenstrual that day and still felt good. "Unbelievable! Sometimes I think I'm going to be punished for feeling so good. As though someone were going to say, 'How dare you!' ".

She continued, saying there was only one aspect of her life now that she still had trouble with. She still felt inhibitied in her sexual life. Somehow she couldn't feel comfortable in taking the responsibility, in taking the initiative sexually. Everything was all right if H, her husband, was very assertive. "But if I want to make love, I tend to suppress those feelings."

A few days later her self-assertiveness again came into focus. She reported that she had had a dream the night before. "I was very hurt. I felt I could never forgive you in the dream. I felt, 'Oh, God, I'm not in the mood for this. I'll pay you $60 just to go away.' "

She reported that she and her husband had made love the night before and although she had been orgastic she had felt to some extent restrained. Then she turned to the dinner party that she had given that night. They had had a dealer over who praised their antique collection. "I'd love to be able to show you the collection," she told me. "It would delight me. I'm going to have a big party in the fall. If I weren't your patient, would you come?" she asked jokingly. "I can't accept that I'll never see you. You know so much about me. I've gotten very comfortable with you, and I hate to give it up. I want you to feel some grief. How could you let me walk out of your life? It's difficult not to wonder about you. I wish that you were a little in love with me. I like to think that you would be more open with me too. I like to think of our future relationship like X. I love him very much and his wife. I guess the dream means that I have a lot of mixed feelings about the analysis coming to an end. I feel disappointed and relieved. I think the dream also means that I'm afraid that you'll be angry with me if I give you trouble about resolving the transference. Maybe I'll be too demanding. I'd like to absorb you into my life. I want to get you to make some commitment."

The patient's associations suggested the following:

1. Her sexual inhibitions, to which she referred at the beginning of the hour, were connected to her wishes to "absorb" — her insatiable oral-sadistic wishes toward men, her husband, and me.

2. She wished to terminate the analysis prematurely to: (a) avoid the analysis of her oral-sadistic, castrating wishes; (b) avoid the analysis of her "love" for me, in order to preserve the fantasy of phallic fulfillment; (c) gratify her vengeful wish — born of disappointment — that I should not get what I wanted, just as she had not gotten what she wanted.

3. All of the foregoing had been warded off by reaction formation and denial — feelings of love, attachment, and denial of any serious interest in terminating the analysis.

My first interpretations were directed at clarifying her preconscious wishes to terminate. Hence, I told her that I thought she did indeed have mixed feelings about terminating the analysis, that she had been making allusions and hints about the termination but had never been able to say straight out what she wanted. I told her that I thought that this was another example of her fear of saying what she secretly wanted, of expressing her conflicted feelings.

A week or so later she did assert openly that she would like to terminate the analysis at the end of the summer. (This was at the beginning of

March.) I told her that I was mindful of her wish to complete the analysis, but that before we actually set a termination date it might be desirable to explore more fully her feelings about terminating. To this she readily agreed. The issue of termination was now out in the open, and the second subphase had begun.

It was clear from the material already that the issue of termination had been drawn into the patient's core complex and was being expressed in the ambivalent transference. In her dreams she wanted to be vengeful, and in her analytic hours she was full of passive longings to be loved.

The second subphase lasted about three and a half months when a specific date was set. The period was characterized by a recrudescence of all her old conflicts and their associated feelings, much more poignantly experienced and pitched at a much higher level; and, to be sure, focused on her relationship with me. I, and my (projected) insatiable demands on her, her unfulfilled wishes toward me, and her residual sexual inhibitions and their roots in her oral and anal sadistic fantasies were the focus of the work of this period. The following series of clinical excerpts will illustrate.

As we begin to talk about termination more openly, it became increasingly obvious to her and to me that she was deeply disappointed in the analysis for not having transformed her into a more assertive individual. Since she was so afraid of her own aggressivity, as I will demonstrate, she wanted me to confer aggressive power on her. The following session from this period illustrates this.

At the beginning of the hour she told me that she had managed to be sexually assertive the night before but felt embarrassed about it. After a silence, she said she didn't feel much like talking. Then she remembered a dream: "I felt more educated than I was. Someone was asking me for information, and I was surprised that I knew so much."

Her associations to the dream led in the following directions. "I was taken seriously and respected. It was a wish fulfillment. I was an expert. I was pleased by the question. It was an intelligent question, and I was excited about it." Her wish to be taken seriously and respected had already been understood from previous analysis to be a derivative of her wish for phallic reparation. She went on to say that although she realized she had no excuse now for not being successful, somehow she continued to feel unsuccessful. She was losing her youth and felt even less attractive than before. "I don't have anymore tricks up my sleeve [seductive manners and attitudes she had used in the past]. "I have nothing to lose, so I might as well be a bitch. Being irritable is the only alternative left, I guess." She went on to complain that she didn't have enough drive, that her friends were "branching out" and she wasn't, and that everybody was leaving her behind — in particular her husband H and her friend A.

The next hour this theme continued. She reiterated, as she had many times in the past, that she felt "without definition," without any "rootedness." This too was a derivative of her feeling of castration.

Soon her depressed mood became bitter and reproachful. She told me that she was still the same, that she would never change, and that the analysis would never change her in the time that we had remaining. This had the condensed quality of both a complaint and a threat. She went on to say that she was deeply disappointed in the analysis and didn't really know why she should go on. Could I promise her anything different? I was driving her crazy with my promises and expectations.

I told her that she was indeed very disappointed in me for not having transformed her into a more powerful, masculine individual, and that some part of her had always had the unconscious hope that the analysis would give her masculine drive. I told her that she felt hopeless, in part because she wanted to be given assertiveness and power, because she was still afraid of letting herself become assertive, because to her it meant some dangerous catrastophe. I said that her wish to terminate the analysis was her way of getting even with me for the disappointment, that she wanted to make me feel as frustrated and helpless and impotent as she felt. Just as some part of her had always wanted to frustrate and get even with her father for disappointing her.

Closely related to these castrating and vengeful wishes were oral-sadistic fantasies, which became another powerful theme during this phase. She accused me angrily many times of being insatiable – that I was never satisfied with her. This was a projection of her own insatiable wishes and had become incorporated into her masochistic transference with me acted out in the past with her son, her husband and her father. This provided yet another motivation for her periodic wish to terminate analysis prematurely, to "get away" from her enslavement to me.

Anality also became a predominant theme during this phase of the analysis, as is clear from the following material. In a session close to her menstrual period she arrived feeling cranky and childish. She was aware of consciously withholding thoughts and feelings from me. "You have to pay. I want to make you suffer. I always tried to get my father to give me some acceptance. Now you're going to have to pay for being so unresponsive. If necessary I'll ruin all of this." Then she expressed the anxiety that her genitals smelled bad and that if she allowed herself to be uninhibited sexually, her lover would find out that she smelled bad.

There was further elaboration of this cloacal fantasy during her next premenstrual period, which led to the interpretation of sadistic, cloacal-oral fantasies in which she would degrade and humiliate me and other men. She started the hour by complaining that she couldn't seem to get sexual feelings and loving feelings together; she was afraid that if she really let herself go I would think of her as a bitch. She was afraid that she might become aroused and make demands on me and it would end in her humiliation. She had always had the feeling that "if you really want a man and let him know, he'll get rid of you." Then she likened herself to Medusa. She felt that Medusa had been unjustly portrayed by the male culture. "She took revenge on men in order to stand up to them. You have to be horrible. I'm afraid of being demanding sexually. I'm always worried that I'm smelling bad down there." She added that "the vagina and the anus are too close for comfort."

In her next hour she was menstruating. She announced that a period was like a sickness, like a cancer. She felt as though she were hemorrhaging and said angrily, "I don't know any woman who has a healthy attitude about it," as though I was expecting her to be demure...and mature. I told her that she was afraid that I wouldn't like her if she didn't act demurely. "You don't understand what it's like. I'm at the mercy of my biology. I feel like a big sloppy mess. My vagina is an ugly mess. I feel like a baby and smell like a fish." She lapsed into a silence, then told me that she was consciously withholding her thoughts, that she wanted me to suffer a little. Since I was so unresponsive, now it was her turn, and I couldn't make her talk.

Two days later she told me the following dream. "People were crowded into a bathroom. There was a rabbi. He was naked. They were having a sex orgy inside. I was standing outside and I said to myself I was damned if I was going to take part. Then the door opened. 'What's going on?' I said. Then I gave him a lecture. 'You should be ashamed of yourself.' Then he said, 'I won't be as demanding of your group.' He was sweating a lot."

Her associations pursued the following lines. There were Nazi overtones. People were being humiliated. It was an insult to Judaism (her father is Jewish and she knew that I am Jewish.) It reminded her of the hospital. When she was little she always thought of it as a kind of concentration camp, especially the experience of the enema—she had experienced it as anal rape by the hospital nurses. I told her that because she felt humiliated as a little girl, and even today had thoughts of being humiliated—anally raped, for example—there was a part of her that wanted to humiliate me, just as when she was little she had thoughts of humiliating her father. I suggested that perhaps she wanted to lecture me, make me stand naked, perhaps even give me an enema or rape me anally.

Several days later she reiterated the anxiety that her genitals smelled bad and that if she ever allowed herself to be uninhibited in sexual intercourse, her lover would feel that she smelled bad. This reminded her that when she was a teenager she had the same anxiety. She remembered that even earlier, when she was seven or eight, she had worried about smelling bad.

These anxieties, derivatives of her cloacal fantasy, underlay her residual sexual inhibitions. She had always had conscious wishes for cunnilingus, but had supressed them and in eleven years of marriage she had never allowed herself to think about these wishes or to talk with her husband about them.

One day during this period she again expressed the feeling that cunnilingus was disgusting and horrifying to her—slimy, like a turned-over rock. She remembered that at the onset of puberty she began to think of her vagina as being ugly. She felt there was something rotten and degenerating about it. She remembered also that after her accident she was afraid that if she moved her bowels, she would lose her organs and bleed to death. This fear led to her chronic constipation at that time. She said that she was afraid if she became emotional she would lose herself and turn to liquid, and I would reject her. Soon she accused me of being afraid of women and afraid to look at her unflinchingly.

It was clear from the data of this phase of the analysis that one of the patient's most conflicted infantile wishes was to humiliate a man by forcing him to confront her "horrible, smelly cloaca," for both reassurance and revenge.

I told her in the session just described that there was a part of her that wanted a man to find her genitals smelly and horrible, wanted to humiliate him and that because she also felt very guilty and anxious about this, she was afraid of letting go in her sexual life. This interpretation was made to her a number of times in the ensuing weeks and resulted in a significant lessening in her sexual inhibitions, including her inhibitions in foreplay. It also made clear that one of the major resistances to termination was the emergence of this infantile wish—termination meant for her a violent mutual humiliation.

As the reader may have discerned, there were primal scene components in the "Rabbi Dream" described earlier. The interpretation of this material resulted in a final, important analytic achievement: the recollection of an infantile primal scene memeory-fantasy that explained an infantile neurosis and a component of her current sexual life.

Insects had appeared many times before in the patient's dreams. It was not clear, however, until the following material was understood, what the meaning of these recurrent symbolic references to insects were.

One day in spring she arrived at her session and told me that she thought that I was angry at her because she hadn't paid me. (A derivative of an anal sadomasochistic fantasy.) Then she talked about the new house she and her husband had recently moved into and the garden it had. She seemed to have a fixation about insects, she said. "I hate killing bugs. I seem constantly concerned with the insects in and around the house. Maybe it's because I have spring fever." She was aware of feeling sexy. Then she remembered a dream she had had the night before: "I had a job. There was a chemical factory far off in the distance. There was this great flat land, kind of like a parking lot. I was working late, and there were only two cars left in the parking lot. There was a man unlocking the other car. Suddenly there was the mating sound of insects and thousands and thousands of winged moths. My car wouldn't start, and I got panicky. I got into the man's car. The air was filled with creatures and sound. Then he leaps on me and we have intercourse."

Her associations to the dream were as follows. She talked about her fear of insects, her discomfort with them. She indicated that the man in the dream was definitely me. She had seen a movie the previous night, some kind of sci-fi movie with Sean Connery, who, she said, resembled me. She felt aroused after seeing the movie. She was aware of sexual arousal at the moment. "I think I would like you to rape me. I think I could be extremely physical with you."

She complained that her husband was not physical enough, he was too cultured, he was not like me. After all, I could sail and was very physical. (She had the fantasy that I was an expert sailor.) She added that she thought that the dream was more violent than she had described it being. Her next thought had to do with the Kafka story, "Metamorphosis." She thought of a man being transformed into an insect. She complained again that her husband was not forceful enough and that she was aware of feeling sexually aroused but very embarrassed by it. She felt sexually aggressive and sexually demanding, but was afraid that if she actually let herself go "it would become a real experience." I asked her what it meant to her that I would be forceful with her. "That you would somehow tame me. That you wouldn't let me get too violent." What did that mean? "I don't know, maybe strangle you with my legs. Or crush you like a bug."

In the next session she complained at first about her son F, who had some problem with his hip. He was always sick, she said. He had so many quirks. "I feel like he reflects me. I always have intense emotional reactions to the most trivial things." She went on to reproach herself for having negative feelings about him and then declared that she had been missing her husband all day and feeling sexually insatiable. She added that she felt bad about having been insulting to me lately. Then she remembered a dream she had had the night before. "I lived alone with H (her husband). There was a secret crack in the wall, and I watched him undress."

Her associations were again to her son F, who the day before had asked to see her vagina. Then she added, as though the idea came out of the blue, "I think I once saw my parents having intercourse." She yawned. I commented that she was acting as though she was bored. She replied that she thought that was why she was so terrified as a child of cockroaches and grasshoppers. She remembers having many nightmares about giant insects devouring her. This was around the time of her accident, while she was sleeping in her crib (which she did until she was three and a half).

"I don't know why, but through the bars of my crib they looked as though they were insects." She added that later, when she was older, her fear of insects changed to a fear of dinosaurs chasing her. I told her that here was one more component of her fear of letting herself go in her sexual life and in the analysis with me—that there was some part of her that was afraid of eating me up, and yet another part of her wanted to eat me up, devour me, that in her mind letting herself go meant some kind of violent orgy of biting and mutilation.

I had occasion to tell her in the subsequent days that if she couldn't beg me to gratify her wishes, if she couldn't please me into gratifying her wishes, if she couldn't manipulate me through her suffering to gratify her wishes, if she couldn't trick me, or threaten me, then finally she would take matters into her own hands (or, to be more accurate, mouth-vagina) and steal-rape-castrate me and satisfy herself.

Thus termination for her meant a violent oral and/or vaginal confrontation resulting in humiliation and castration. This was what she wanted, and this was what she was trying to ward off by her threats of premature termination.

Following this second stormy subphase, there was an interval of several weeks of relative calm, during which she again broached the subject of termination, this time not in a provocative and threatening way. I was mindful that during the previous six months I had been able to explore and analyze the oral and anal sadistic components of her castration complex—those linked to her residual sexual inhibitions—and since there was very little that I knew about her mental life that I hadn't told her, I felt that it might be timely to set a termination date. One was finally agreed on two months hence.

The content of the analysis during this third subphase was familiar and not markedly different from what had gone before. However, although the themes were the same, the emotional intensity had diminished significantly. The material had a less defensive quality, and moments of humor or playfulness occurred more frequently. A clinical example will illustrate her immediate response to the setting of the termination date.

She started the hour by saying that she had been a little anxious since we had set the date (a few days before). She had been thinking about getting pregnant (the theme of pregnancy began to emerge at this time and will be discussed in more detail below). She had a dream. "There was a very large old victorian white house in the country. There were animals around. I was Circe. There was a leopard whom I could control, and it could devour and kill people. I had to kill certain people because they found me out. After killing someone, I could cause them to decompose. There was a lot of voyeurism in the dream. But the best part was when I took a stick and pointed it to the sky and flew up into a tree. A huge very old tree. I was soaring through space. Then I became very small and could sit in the tree and see everything without being seen."

She laughed and told me that it had been a very evil and glorious dream. She said she was sure she knew who the someone was that was supposed to be devoured and decomposed, that I had finally found her out and now she had to get rid of me. She was sure she was the leopard in the dream too, because it was so beautiful and powerful. "A perfect combination," she laughed. She realized, of course, all of the phallic implications in the dream; the wish for onmiscience and omnipotence. "It's hard to give up an idea like that—to be a god or a goddess. Do you think I should settle?" What did she mean? "Oh, for just being a rich, charming, beautiful housewife."

As I suggested before, the new theme, which began to intertwine with the older ones, was pregnancy. References to pregnancy, fantasies of being pregnant, and wishes to be pregnant cropped up with increasing frequency over the next several weeks.

One day at the beginning of August she started the hour by saying that she and her husband had had a very gratifying sexual experience the night before. She explained that she had taken the initiative, "I was very aggressive. Maybe not what you would call aggressive, but what I would call aggressive. I was in control of myself. I could arouse him no matter how grumpy he was. His bad mood didn't affect me." She added that she had had the fantasy that she had conceived during the intercourse. She wanted to have another baby. I asked her to tell me more about this wish. She said that this time it would be a girl. And this time she would do it right. She had learned from her experience with her son, and she would be neither anxious nor ambivalent. She would be competent and independent. "I'm envious of other women. I want two children. I really have a craving for it." I told her that she wanted to create a perfect being and do what she felt I had not been able to do for her—transform her into a perfect man/woman. She said that was probably true but irrelevant. She added, "And maybe I want to taunt you with my being luscious. Drive you crazy."

On the day of her last session she had the following dream. "There was a big black book on the table, but it didn't belong to me. It was huge. I picked it up. When I opened it my name was in it. I couldn't understand how it had got there, because it wasn't my book. It fell out of my hands—on my foot. I don't think it hurt but I'm not sure." Her associations followed.

There was something very serious and heavy about the book. It was kind of religious or medical, she said. She pointed to a book on the bookshelf across from the couch, a large black compendium of psychiatry, and said that the book in the dream was like that but even bigger. It was a book, she said, that God might have, full of all kinds of wonderful knowledge. "I suppose it was yours and that you either gave it to me or I took it—to remember you by." She laughed and said that she knew what I was thinking, and she supposed sooner or later she would have it. Well, she added, she would have to buy one of her own.

I asked her about the foot. It was the right foot, she told me, the one she had broken when she was twelve. That reminded her that only a few minutes before she had broken her ankle she had "accidentally" barged in on her father as he was urinating. She was flustered and embarrassed. A few minutes later, while she was walking the dog, she fell and broke her ankle. I reminded her that, for her, looking was like taking, and she had had to punish herself.

I asked her about the religious quality of the book. She thought of the upcoming Jewish holidays, which would occur when she would no longer be in analysis. I wondered whether she did not want to be inscribed by me in the Book of Life, so that I would not forget her.

SUMMARY OF THE CASE AND THE ANALYTIC REASONS FOR IMPROVEMENT

The reader will recall that the patient's chief complaint at the beginning of treatment was primarily of intermittent abdominal pain accompanied by mild diarrhea of about a year's duration; she was also aware of some degree of tension of approximately the same duration. These symptoms coincided with the beginning of her marriage, which had taken place approximately a year prior to the beginning of treatment.

The initial complaints subsided rapidly after the onset of treatment, and the gastrointestinal symptoms never returned. It became clear, however, shortly after treatment began that the patient suffered from a moderately severe character disorder, the symptoms and characteristics of which emerged only gradually during the first two years of treatment.

The major features of the character disorder, as they eventually became clear, were these. She suffered from severely impaired self-esteem, associated with considerable social anxiety, which she struggled to control. (Her low self-esteem, which at first was associated with social anxiety, later in the analysis became the core content of moderately severe depressive bouts.) Naturally, she was unable to be assertive on her own behalf, and her relationships with people were characterized by a wish to please, an automatic attitude of compliance, and an inability to say "no." This was especially true of her relationship with men. Finally, she was completely frigid in sexual intercourse.

Less important but troublesome nonetheless, she had serious inhibitions about driving a car, advancing herself educationally, and pursuing certain literary ambitions.

By the end of the analysis, all these symptoms had been markedly reduced or were absent. She had only occasional premenstrual depression and felt generally adequate and able to deal with her life. She was appropriately self-assertive in her relationships in general and with her husband and child in particular. With her husband she felt a coequal in the marriage and was regularly orgastic. She had written a novel and submitted it for publication and on the whole led a busy, active, fulfilling life, with a sense of who she was, where she blonged, and what she liked. She had left behind her compliant, intimidated, and inhibited self.

The psychoanalytic data described here is not in any way special or unique. On the contrary, it is representative of practically all the patient's material. And it represents a sequence of increasingly specific fantasy discovery by both the patient and analyst.

The data of the entire analysis, as exemplified by the clinical examples in this report, support the clinical hypothesis that the patient's major symptomatology—her masochistic-depressive character disorder—revolved around her phallic oedipal conflicts. The analytic reasons for the improvement consisted of a gradual revelation and exploration of the patient's unconscious phallic-oedipal fantasies. What the patient discovered in her analysis was that she had had the idea that she had been castrated and anally raped in the course of her accident and hospitalization and that she had experienced this as a punishment for her rivalrous wishes toward her mother. These vengeful wishes were defended by reaction formations and religious ideas of supplication and were unconsciously expressed in her spiteful, stubborn symptom of constipation as a child, and later, in the analysis, in her feelings of spite and withholding behavior.

In addition to her ambivalent and vengeful feelings toward her mother, she harbored intensely envious and vengeful feelings toward the men in her life—her father, her husband, her analyst. She envied their phallic qualities—the force of their personality, their ambition, their aggressivity, their sexual prowess, their brilliance, their knowledge.

In the analysis she learned that she wanted these phallic attributes: that she wanted to be like a demigod and that her wish to be loved by a powerful man was an attempt to acquire these desirable characteristics in order to repair her feelings of castration.

She learned that this fantasy of having been castrated – her feelings of genital inferiority – was associated with feelings of depression, displaced onto various ego capacities, such as intelligence and learning, and displaced onto other bodily features, such as acne (she would panic and become depressed at the sign of a pimple) and body configuration (any softness or body fat, any deviation from a boyish figure resulted in feelings of depression).

She learned that her wish to be loved by a man and her masochistic attitude toward men was a substitute for more aggressive, sadistic wishes and fantasies toward men in the service of acquiring what she felt she had lost, and in the service of repairing her integrity and independence. And, as I indicated, she became aware of fantasies of phallic incorporation, both biting and sucking, orally and vaginally. She realized that these sadistic wishes were involved in her sexual inhibitions: to relax in intercourse would result in catastrophic damage to her husband's genitals. He would become angry and kill her.

She became aware of rivalrous feelings and jealousy toward other women and aware that wishes to become pregnant and desire for sexual pleasure and taking responsibility for her own sexual pleasure were fraught with guilt and anxiety – that this somehow meant replacement of or destruction of her mother.

The insights and discoveries just enumerated do not exhaust the array of understanding that the patient achieved in her analysis, but they do represent the most important insights. (Issues of sibling rivalry arose, for example, but these were relatively unimportant in contributing to her pathogenic conflicts.)

The gradual revelation of these infantile wishes and fantasies and their connection with her symptomatology resulted in a reduction of her guilt feelings and a reduction in her need for masochistic defensive reaction formations and self-punishment. This allowed her to have sexual and other pleasures and reduced the part that suffering played in her life in general.

DISCUSSION

It is clear from the clinical evidence reported here that the terminal phase was continuous with the early and middle phases of the analysis.

The patient's conflicts remained the same, and the clinical data – her associations in each hour of the analysis – centered on these conflicts. The terminal phase represented a continuation and culmination of the rest of the analysis and did not reveal qualitatively new issues or material or require any special techniques.

What was different about this phase of the analysis was the heightened struggle over her conflicts, the uncovering of prephallic (not preoedipal) components of those conflicts, and the increasing specificity of her unacceptable oral and anal sadistic wishes and fantasies. These had as yet been unanalyzed and remained at the root of her residual sexual inhibitions.

The analysis of this material occurred largely in the context of termination. One of the powerful resistances during this phase was the patient's persistent threat to quit the analysis prematurely. In fact, the unconscious meaning of termination for her was that it would become a violent sexual confrontation between us that would result in castration, humiliation, and impregnation – her oedipal wish. Her wish to quit was both a defense against the realization of the fantasy and a way of holding onto it and to her hopes for future transformation.

Several points about the case are worth noting. Separation anxiety and issues of loss did not play an important part in the termination process. Nor had they played an important part in earlier phases of the analysis. Reactions to vacations or weekend interruptions were mild and relatively infrequent, despite the trauma of her earlier hospitalization and separation from home and mother at the age of three and a half. It's not that there weren't associations during the terminal phase that spoke of loss and separation, nor was she devoid of feelings of sadness. All of these did occur, but they did not dominate the psychological picture, nor were they ever the chief issue in her mind.

It should be noted that the termination date was not set until *after* the critical point of the terminal phase, that is, after the analysis of the regressive components of her core conflicts. The final month or two of the analysis represented a period of "mopping up" after the major struggle and reinforcing the earlier work. It seemed to me at the time that *not* setting the date resulted in a technical advantage, enabling us to analyze her wish to terminate prematurely. Setting a date earlier might have resulted in considerable relief from anxiety and reassurance and allowed unresolved conflictual elements to remain repressed. We would have ended our relationship on a pseudoloving note, with her ambivalent dependent transference unanalyzed. This suggests that the technical maneuver of setting the date may or *may not* be conducive to achieving the essential goal of the termination phase, namely, recognition of the patient's infantile wishes and the need for their renunciation. This is discussed further later.

It is worth noting as well that although the analytic work was surely imperfect, it was not interminable. The patient left the analysis with a solid understanding of what her major conflicts were, and I had a sense that there was nothing I knew about her unconscious life that I hadn't told her many times. The patient has been living a normal, busy, contented life since then—no recurrence of symptomatology. (She keeps me informed with a newsy letter about herself and her family every year or two.)

The two most important questions that arise in the discussion of termination are invariably What are the criteria for termination? and, related to this issue, What are the goals of analysis? As I have suggested, much of the vast literature concerned with the discussion of these issues is meaningless because of the ambiguity of the terms and the absence of clinical data.

Based on the case reported here, other terminated cases, and the work of Dewald (1972a, b), Rangell (1982), Glover (1955), Arlow (1979; Arlow and Brenner, 1966), and Brenner (1976, 1977, 1982), I suggest that the goal of a well-conducted psychoanalysis is not the resolution of the transference neurosis, but the unambiguous clarification and indelible registration of the patient's core conflict—not its resolution, because resolution (whatever that may mean) is, I believe, beyond the capacity of the analyst. Whatever resolving powers exist, exist in the patient. THe psychoanalytic goal stated thus is essentially a *technical* goal, which is within the competence and power of the analyst. He can clarify for himself and interpret to the patient over and over again, so that it becomes unambiguously clear and indelible, what the patient's unacceptable wishes are, what his defenses against them are, and how they are connected with his symptomatology. The rest is up to the patient. In the case I have reported, the important news I had to tell the patient was that she had to inhibit herself and experience depression because she was in the grip of the unconscious fantasy that she suffered from genital inferiority that had resulted from her accident as part of a punishment for rivalrous feelings against her mother; that she had powerful wishes for genital reparation and transformation as well as violent and sadistic wishes of revenge; and that these were warded off by her passive, dependent, and masochistic defensive structure. The most perverse (i.e., pregenital) and aggressive components of these unconscious wishes were explicated during the termination phase.

This suggestts, at least in the case reported here, that the essence of the termination phase is neither the setting of a termination date nor the analysis of separation anxiety, but rather clarification of the specific perverse and aggressive components of the patient's core conflicts. The recognition and indelible registration of these gives rise to the further recognition that they are incapable of gratification and thus must be disappointed. The sense of disillusionment, rage, and some form of partial renunciation usually occurs during the terminal phase — in this case: "It's hard to give up an idea like that — to be a god or a goddess. Do you think I should settle...for just being a rich, charming, beautiful housewife?" This renunciation — acceptance of reality, if you wish — I suspect continues into the postanalytic phase. If the notion of mourning in connection with the termination phase has any meaning at all in a universal sense, that is, having to do with *all* terminating analyses (as distinct from those cases in which problems of separation are paramount), it is in the sense of mourning for one's lost infantile wishes — the renunciation and grief following the recognition that we can never have what we have always wanted.

With this in mind, I suggest that the essence of the termination phase is the recognition and partial renunciation of the patient's most important infantile wishes — in the case reported here, genital transformation with all its derivative implications; and the mode of achieving that is the accomplishment of the technical goal of unambiguous clarification and indelible interpretation.

The art–science of psychoanalysis is in no better position than any of the other therapeutic arts such as surgery or medicine. The healer can have only technical goals. He can only engage in the proper manipulation of the organ; nature must do the rest. The surgeon cannot heal the wound; he can only debride correctly. The analyst cannot "improve the patient's object relations"; he can only interpret correctly.

REFERENCES

Arlow, J. (1979), Some problems in current psychoanalytic thought. *World Biennial of Psychiatry and Psychotherapy*, Vol. 1, ed. S. Arieti. New York: Basic Books, pp. 34–54.

———— & Brenner, C. (1966), The psychoanalytic situation. In: *Psychoanalysis in the Americas*, ed. R. E. Litman. New York: International Universities Press.

Balint, M. (1950), On the termination of analysis. *Internat. J. Psycho-Anal.*, 31(3): 196–199.

Brenner, C. (1976). *Psychoanalytic Techniques and Psychic Conflict*. New York: International Universities Press.

———— (chairman) (1977), Psychic change in psychoanalysis. *Internat. J. Psycho-Anal.*, 25:669–678.

———— (1982), *The Mind in Conflict*. New York: Inernational Universities Press.

Buxbaum, E. (1950), Technique of terminating analysis. *Internat. J. Psycho-Anal.*, 31:184–190.

DeBell, D., Panel (1975), W. S. Robbins, reporter. Termination: Problems and techniques, *J. Amer. Psychoanal. Assn.*, 23:166–176.

Dewald, P. (1972a), The clinical assessment of structural change. *J. Amer. Psychoanal. Assn.*, 20:302–324.

_____ (1972c), *The Psychoanalytic Process*, New York: Basic Books.

Firestein, S. (1974), Termination of psychoanalysis of adults: A review of the literature. *J. Amer. Psychoanal. Assn.*, 22:873–894.

Firestein, S. (1978), *Termination in Psychoanalysis*. New York: International Universities Press.

_____ (1982), Termination of psychoanalysis: Theoretical, clinical, and pedagogic considerations. *Psychoanal. Inq.* 2(3): 473–497.

Fleming, J. & Benedek, T. (1966). *Psychoanalytic Supervision*. New York: Grune & Stratton, pp. 172–202.

Freud, A. (1946), *The Ego and the Mechanisms of Defense*. New York: International Universities Press.

Glover, E. (1955), The terminal phase. In: *The Technique of Psychoanalysis*. New York: International Universities Press, pp. 138–164.

Goldberg, A. & Marucs, D. (1985), "Natural termination": Some comments on ending analysis without setting a date. *Psychoanal. Quart.*, 54:46–65.

Hartmann, A., Kris, E., Lowenstein, R. (1946), Comments on the formaton of psychic structure. *The Psychoanalytic Study of the Child*, 2: 11–38.

Klein, M. (1950), On the criteria for the termination of a psycho-analysis. *J. Amer. Psychoanal. Assn.*, 31:78–80.

Kohut, H. (1977), The termination of the analysis of narcissistic personality disorders. In: *The Restoration of the Self*. New York: International Universities Press, pp. 1–62.

_____ (1979), The two analyses of Mr. Z. *J. Amer. Psychoanal. Assn.*, 60:3–27.

Loewald, H. (1961), Internalization, separation, mourning, and the superego. *Psychoanal. Quart.*, 30:483–504.

_____ (1979), Reflections on the psychoanalytic process and its therapeutic potential. *The Psychoanalytic Study of the Child*, 34:155–167.

Lorand, S. (1946), *Technique of Psychoanalytic Therapy*. New York: International Universities Press.

Miller, I. (1965), On the return of symptoms in the terminal phase of psychoanalysis. *Internat. J. Psycho-Anal.*, 46:487–501.

Orens, M. (1955), Setting a termination date—an impetus to analysis. *J. Amer. Psychoanal. Assn.*, 3:651–665.

Payne, S. (1950), Short communication on criteria for terminating analysis. *Internat. J. Psycho-Anal.*, 31:205.

Pfeffer, A. (1980), Memories of positive experiences in the resolution of conflicts: Illustrated in a case of hysteria. *J. Amer. Psychoanal. Assn.*, 28:309–329.

Rangell, L. (1966), An overview of the ending of analysis. In: *Psychoanalysis in the Americas*, ed. R. E. Litman. New York: International Universities Press.

_____ (1982), Some thoughts on termination. *Psychoanal. Inq.*, 2:367–392.

Reich, A. (1950), On the termination of analysis. In: *Psychoanalytic Contributions.* New York: International Universities Press, 1973, pp. 121–135.

Robbins, W. (1975), Termination: Problems and techniques. *J. Amer. Psychoanal. Assn.*, 23:166–176.

Schlessinger, N. (1975), The psychoanalytic process: Recurrent patterns of conflict and changes in ego functions. *J. Amer. Psychoanal. Assn.*, 23:761–782.

Shentoub, S. A. (1955), Contribution to: Comment terminer le traitement psychanalytique. *Rev. Fran. Psychanal.*, 19:529–532. In: *The Unconscious Today: Essays in Honor of Max Schur*, ed. M. Kanzer. New York: International Universities Press, pp. 288–338.

Ticho, E. (1972), Termination of psychoanalysis: Treatment goals, life goals. *Psychoanal. Quart.*, 41:315–333.

Wilson, C. (1968), Psychosomatic asthma and acting out. *Internat. J. Psycho-Anal.*, 49:330–333.

Winnicott, D. W. (1965), *The Maturational Processes and the Facilitating Environment.* New York: International Universities Press.

Zetzel, E. (1965), Depression and the incapacity to bear it. In: *Drives, Affects, Behavior*, vol. 2, ed. Max Schur. New York: International Universities Press, pp. 243–274.

EDWARD M. WEINSHEL

Perceptual Distortions During Analysis: Some Observations on the Role of the Superego in Reality Testing

I am reporting on segments of the analyses of three women in their mid or late twenties, all of whom had been in analytic treatment for at least three years. None were psychotic or "borderline," and none had manifested gross disturbances in their reality testing capacities. However, all three experienced a perceptual distortion that involved their seeing or being convinced that they would or might see the analyst's penis. Further, their subsequent associations indicated that they also suspected that their perceptions were erroneous. Nevertheless, they insisted that they had "decided" to maintain the distortion even if that decision meant that they were "crazy." In what follows, I focus on the analytic data connected with these events rather than presenting a comprehensive review of the patient's history or of the analysis as a whole.

Mrs. A walked into my office and stopped at the door for a second or two before proceeding to the couch. She seemed considerably agitated and promptly informed me that what first had caught her attention as she entered was a small Japanese print that hangs on the wall adjacent to the couch. She quickly added that she had noticed the picture many times before and that it had never made enough of an impression on her to warrant any comment. (In fact, it was a rather innocuous, muted, unobtrusive decoration). But on this day, looking at the picture, she was absolutely

353

convinced that a definite protuberance emerged from its surface. She was further convinced that the bulge was due to an erect penis that was covered by the print. At the same time, she realized that this could not be so; nevertheless, even after glancing again at the print while lying on the couch, she could not completely rid herself of the perception of the protuberance. Mrs. A went on to say that the whole thing was "crazy" and that she must have had an hallucination of some sort. Only later, in her associations, and in a manner that revealed a definite reluctance to share it with me, she mentioned another thought that had passed through her mind very rapidly and virtually in the same split-second as she had become aware of her perception of the bulge. That thought can best be summarized — although, obviously, it did not come to her so coherently — as, "If I recognize that protuberance as real, then I would be crazy, because I *know* that there is no such thing on that painting. But my 'decision' is still that there *is* such a protuberance."

The second vignette, concerning Mrs. B, occurred two years later, shortly after I had returned from the midwinter psychoanalytic meetings with a bad cold and a very stuffed head. Somewhere in the middle of the analytic hour, Mrs. B accused me of having fallen asleep. She was hurt and angry; she insisted that she could tell I was asleep because of my deep breathing. My falling asleep was evidence of my indifference, my being bored with and not caring for her — even as a patient. I had not been asleep, but she had been correct in her perception of the somewhat troubled breathing. As we were discussing her feelings and fantasies about this event, she suddenly broke off in the middle of a sentence and told me that it was not really true that she thought I had been asleep. She explained that at the moment that she had become aware of my labored and noisy breathing what had actually occurred to her — and again this was very brief and transient — was that I must be masturbating. For a moment at least, she was convinced that I was masturbating. She tried to dismiss this unwelcome idea, and then "I made up the business about your being asleep even though I knew you would think that it sounded crazy." She explained that she would prefer to be crazy than to face up to the possibility that I was masturbating. What was so threatening to her about that possibility was that she would have to turn around and look at me and my erect penis.

The incident with my third patient, Mrs. C, took place about a year later. Mrs. C was my first afternoon appointment, and it was necessary for me to pass the waiting room, from which she could readily observe me. It had been a typical San Francisco day with intermittent showers, so I was carrying by black raincoat. Folded over my arm, it covered the area of my crotch. A few minutes later, when the patient was lying on the couch in the office, she began to muse that it was most interesting that I would have a *white* raincoat. She went on at considerable length about how strange it was for a *man* to wear a *white* raincoat. Wasn't this evidence of some kind of "problem"? However, after a spate of these somewhat forced associations, she acknowledged that she had not told me the whole story – even though, she insisted, that what she *had* told me was genuine and reflected what she had been thinking. The reader can surmise what it was that Mrs. C had omitted from her original version of what had gone through her mind as I passed her in the hallway. She had looked at my crotch and was for a moment convinced that she had seen my penis. She consciously repudiated the perception and the thought. These were replaced by the conviction that she had seen a white raincoat. She knew the perception was distorted but "preferred" that what she saw was a white coat. Even though Mrs. C did not articulate a preference for being "crazy" to an acknowledgment that she might see my penis, there was no question that this was implied.

Before I present additional clinical material about each of these patients in order to provide a clearer understanding of these phenomena, let me sketch a number of qualities and characteristics shared by all three patients:

1. All were neurotic, essentially hysterical characters, who demonstrated phobic symptoms, although only one (Mrs. C) offered a phobia as a presenting complaint.

2. None had exhibited gross or consistent difficulties in reality testing or had significant perceptual distortions. However, all three, in varying degree, had noted at times a striking and inexplicable lack of faith and confidence in their assessment of reality. This difficulty was especially conspicuous in situations when their own estimation and judgment of what they had perceived was in conflict with the assessment made by another person, particularly when that person was meaningful to them. In such circumstances, the patients tended to lose confidence, to question their own judgment, and, usually, to accept the judgment of the other person. What all three expressed in somewhat different terms was a vague feeling of remorse and of not having done the right thing. They felt, in effect, that in order to stay on good terms with the other person, they had temporarily relinquished their own confidence that they could perceive reality correctly.

3. All three patients manifested strong exhibitionistic and voyeuristic conflicts. These tendencies had undergone considerable inhibition, which was reflected in their character structures. Both Mrs. A (the Japanese print) and Mrs. C (the white raincoat) came to analysis as quiet,

mousey, almost achromatic persons. They were shy and withdrawn, and explained that it was important for them to be unnoticed and inconspicuous. They spoke in almost muted voices, and their clothes were inappropriately drab and unflattering. They did nothing to enhance an intrinsic and potentially marked attractiveness. They were scrupulous in avoiding their curiosity about me, especially my private life; and they found it very difficult to look at me at the beginning and the end of the analytic hour. A great deal of analytic work had focused on these conflicts, their attendant anxieties and depressive affects, and the resultant defenses and inhibitions; and, as the analysis progressed, definite changes occurred. Prior to the "perceptual distortion" episodes, both Mrs. A and Mrs. C had become more openly and comfortably curious, attractive, and outspoken.

Although Mrs. B (who accused me of falling asleep) was outwardly almost the obverse of the other two, her inner situation was quite similar. Until marriage in her late teens, she had behaved in a very quiet, "tight," and colorless manner. After her marriage, and especially after the birth of her daughter, Mrs. B became loud, seductive, almost a caricature of the "life of the party." In fact, one of the conscious reasons Mrs. B sought psychoanalysis was her discomfort at being such a "show off" despite her husband's undisguised disgust with the exhibitionistic behavior. She had become markedly overweight; but instead of grooming herself and wearing clothes that might minimize her heaviness, Mrs. B went out of her way to dress, talk, and act in a fashion that would make her and her defects the center of attention. At times, the overall effect bordered on the grotesque.

4. In all three cases, the episodes described were preceeded in the analyses by considerable work on the manifestations in the transference of the exhibitionistic/voyeuristic drive derivatives. It was not difficult to demonstrate fantasies (partly conscious from the beginning) of exposing themselves to the analyst and to have him find them sexually attractive. Also it was possible to deal with their fantasies of seducing the analyst into exposing and exhibiting himself.

5. These patients presented a number of other common experiences that appeared to be of significance in understanding the perceptual distortions. As so often happens in the course of analysis, additional information both clarifies and complicates our understanding of the patient and the analysis. The material in question deals with "ambiguous" incestuous activity in childhood. I say "ambiguous" because in spite of careful analytic work, it was never possible to determine with certainty whether or not actual physical interchange with the father had occurred. The patients could never be sure—and neither could the analyst—that what they were recalling was a real event, a distorted elaboration of an ambiguous event, or the product of a sexual fantasy. Within the analysis following the

perceptual distortion, all three recalled particular sexual traumas during the latency period and their recognition that their parents were somewhat corrupt in regard to reality testing and their consciences in general.

Mrs. A's concerns about ambiguous sexual contact with her father centered around a number of experiences between the ages of five and six. Her memories of close physical contact were vague in detail but strong in regard to the associated belief that her father's behavior may have exceeded the limits of paternal propriety. Beyond this, nothing more definite could be established. However, these suspicions and concerns were reinforced during adolescence, when she observed her father making clumsy advances towards her girl friends. She was aware of sexual feelings towards her father; she had always displayed a penchant for older men, and early in the analysis some of her acting out had involved affairs with considerably older men of prominence in the community. Also, around the age of five and six, there had been a number of instances of sex play with her brother four years older than she. She had strong memories of fascination and awe at the sight of his erect penis, and these memories had not been repressed.

In the period after the protuberance-on-the-Japanese-print event, Mrs. A recaptured the memory of an incident that had occurred when she was nine years old. One Sunday, after a strenuous (and apparently sexualized if not sexual) afternoon of play with her brother and some cousins, the patient was sent off with an older man, a close family friend, to get some refreshments. While enjoying an ice cream soda, she became panic stricken that this man (who as far as could be determined was behaving appropriately) might make some sexual advance and expose himself. Then she had the thought (and again this is in "translation"), "If I can act like my grandfather did, then everything will be all right." The panic subsided almost instantly, and the rest of the outing went off uneventfully.

Mrs. A's maternal grandfather, who had been an important figure in her life, had died not long before this event occurred. He had been warm, protective, and considerate toward his granddaughter (in many ways more than her mother), and there was nothing to indicate that he had in any way abused her sexually. In the last years of his life he had become psychotic, most likely as a result of advancing senility. She could not remember clearly all of the details of his disturbance; but it was clear to her that because of his mental illness, the grandfather was permitted special license and special privileges. She recalled that many aspects of his behavior, which ordinarily would have been considered peculiar and offensive to her family, were tolerated and accepted with, "Well, that grandpa and his mishagas." Even though Mrs. A did not have a precise idea of what "craziness" involved, she evidently associated it with the general concept of diminished personal responsibility and with the specific idea of diminished adherence to reality. As we reconstructed this episode, what emerged was the patient's notion that if *she* were crazy, then she would not have to look, not have to see – and whatever else happened, it would not be her fault. In that portion of the analytic work, Mrs. A volunteered the speculation that in the play that had preceded the outing with the older family friend there may have been some mutual exhibitionism among the various children and that her sexual excitement may have carried over into her thoughts about the older man later that day. It was my impression that she had feared the repetition of an earlier traumatic event associated with the perception of the male genitals, and that to avoid reexperiencing this trauma, she had adopted a new set of defensive patterns, one of which included being able to "decide" that she should be "crazy."

At various times in the analysis, Mrs. A complained about the consciences of both of her parents and of her husband. The mother lied to the father about money she had received from her parents and involved the patient in these deceptions. The mother would also insist that something the patient "knew" to be true was not true, or vice versa. My patient had a vague notion that her mother had been aware of the sex play between her brother and herself but that she preferred not to notice it. Mrs. A's father was repeatedly involved in obviously foolish business ventures that always failed, in part because he had siphoned off money for his equally foolish personal expenditures. I have already related the patient's concern over his behavior with her and even more with her adolescent girl friends. The patient's husband, though successful in business, achieved a certain notoriety for shady financial dealings and lied regularly to his wife about these matters. When confronted with his fabrications, he insisted that she had misperceived and misconstrued what he had said and done – even in the face of incontrovertible evidence to the contrary. Mrs. A, like the two other patients, did not have a good deal of faith in the integrity of either the reality testing capacity or the honesty of her parents, her husband, or herself. After the analysis, Mrs. A divorced her husband, primarily because of irreconcilable differences associated with these issues, to which she was no longer so vulnerable.

With Mrs. B, the "ambiguous incestuous sexual activity" was considerably less ambiguous. Her father was an alcoholic. When she was about five years old (and just before the father left the home; after the parental divorce) her father had "quite likely," while intoxicated, attempted to play with her genitals. This was an exceedingly traumatic event, which led to a several-month period of phobic disturbance and nightmares. Mrs. B was never sure whether her father had exposed himself during this episode or on other occasions; yet it always remained clear in her mind that her mother had known of her husband's behavior but had chosen not to do anything about it.

In the weeks after her perceptual distortion in the session, Mrs. B reintroduced memories that had appeared earlier in the analysis under quite different circumstances and without either the affective charge or the specific connections that characterized the current recounting of the material. A number of years after the divorce, the mother remarried. When Mrs. B was around eight or nine years old, the family was living in a flimsy, jerry-built house not far from the San Francisco airport. Her mother and stepfather carried on an active and rather noisy sexual life, which both excited and frightened the patient. She knew, even then, that the noises were reminiscent of comparable disturbances that had aroused and bothered her before her parents had been divorced. During the same period, the patient's sleep was also disturbed by the noise of the planes from the nearby airport, noises she later recognized had a definite sexual significance for her.

The particular episode that Mrs. B connected with the perceptual distortion in analysis (in reaction to my noisy breathing) occurred when she was nine years old and already having difficulty in her relationships both at home and at school. She recalled being awakened from her sleep by unusually loud sounds from the parents' nextdoor bedroom, especially by piercing and sexually explicit cries of encouragement from her mother. Not long before, the patient had tried to talk to her mother about these nocturnal disturbances and had, indirectly, asked her mother to tone down the activity. But the mother had flippantly and from the daughter's point of view rather callously dismissed the girl's concerns and entreaties. On the occasion in question, the patient became more and more excited and increasingly anxious; she feared (and wished) that she would be able to see what was going on, and she feared that she was going to lose her mind.

While this was taking place, the patient was simultaneously aware of the noises coming from the planes that were landing and taking off. The sounds were experienced as assaults. Then, in the midst of all this turmoil, Mrs. B had the thought that if she concentrated on the sounds of the airplanes and that if those sounds drove her crazy, then somehow she would be able to tolerate this seemingly overwhelming experience. This is precisely what happened for her, and the patient was able to go back to sleep. Furthermore, the remainder of the time that the patient and her family remained in this inadequate house, she invariably dealt with the discomfort over the sounds of sexual intercourse by invoking—almost as an incantation—the formula that she had created that night. Mrs. B's latency age solution featured, first, the selective perception and displacement of her perceptual activities from a more to a less emotionally charged stimulus and, second, the determination that she would be "crazy" on a more or less active and conscious rather than passive and unconscious level. Mrs. B had constructed a "new" set of defenses.

Her defensive configuration also involved an identification with a psychotic object, her mother, who as far as the patient was concerned tended to behave in a crazy and unrealistic fashion. Mrs. B's mother was a naive, superstitious, and gullible woman, who constantly and consistently lied to her daughter whenever it appeared easier to lie than to face the truth. She turned a deaf ear and a blind eye to the patient's pleas and concerns and was promiscuous in relationships with men and unfaithful in three marriages. She was careless in these and other ways in regard to the care of herself and of her household.

Mrs. B's father was an irresponsible alcoholic who abused both his wife and children physically and verbally. The patient's maternal grandmother and her first stepfather, however, seemed to have been responsible, solid individuals with whom she had relatively close relationships. Mrs. B was an excellent student and a talented writer, who was "adopted" by many of her teachers. These relationships, which were crucially important in her later development, probably permitted reasonably effective superego functioning in her adult life in spite of the impact of her parents' pathology.

Mrs. C, shortly after the black-white raincoat incident, recalled a traumatic episode from the age of eight. While she sat alone at a Saturday afternoon movie, an older man sat next to her and made sexual advances, including a surreptitious exposure of his penis. At first she sat there more or less paralyzed; eventually she was able to get up and change her seat. The man attempted to follow her; and, when the usher asked Mrs. C if the man was bothering her, she lied and said no. The reason for doing so, she remembered, was the feeling that if she accused him of sexual wrongdoings, there would be counteraccusations and she would end up the guilty one. (She expected, of course, that the same would take place in the analysis). She could not even imagine that the usher would believe her story. In fact, when the patient returned home and related the harrowing incident to her mother, the mother was unsympathetic, pooh-poohing the whole affair, and insinuating that her daughter had either made it up—or if it really happened, it must have been her fault. It is difficult to reconstruct the overall ego state in effect at that time; but, on the basis of comparable situations in the transference, the patient could not be entirely sure if she was lying, denying, or merely stating the facts as she had experienced them. And, even though Mrs. C explains that episode as if she were deliberately lying in order to protect herself, I am not convinced that the dynamics at that moment were so clear cut.

However, in the context of the movie memory, the patient related an experience from the age of six or seven. She awakened in the middle of the night ostensibly to go to the bathroom. Noticing some light coming from the living room, she walked into it and saw her mother together with her current boyfriend. Mrs. C then, as she recalled it, turned around, closed the door, and went into the kitchen to get a snack—she could not remember whether or not she ever went to the bathroom! In her associations to this event, she insisted that her mother and the boyfriend were not engaged in any sexual activity; at the same time, she realized that this was probably not correct and that she had peremptorily shut the whole thing out of her mind (her shutting the door behind her is probably a symbolic screen representation of the attempt to repress and deny her perception of sexual activity). When Mrs. C first told me about the memory, most impressive about it (and the focus of the work) was the way she glossed over, both in her perception of what had occurred and in her recounting of it, that part of the memory relating to seeing her mother in the living room. At the same time she overemphasized those portions of the memory having to do with going to the kitchen and enjoying a snack. It seems, therefore, that even at that early age, the patient utilized selective perception, with a hypercathexis of the relatively innocuous and regressive oral element as a means of diluting the potential impact of the more frightening sexual perception.

Mrs. C reported, as had Mrs. A and Mrs. B, disconcerting parental attitudes toward "moral" issues and an inappropriate lack of responsibility. Her mother was a childish, ineffective dreamer, who neglected her household and other caretaking chores whenever the prospect of more immediate pleasure was available. She made her daughter a precocious confidante and made no effort to protect her from noxious sexual stimuli and experiences. The mother was flamboyantly unrealistic in regard to her own talents and insisted that, even in middle age, she could still become a world famous ballerina. The father was a tyranical, unstable (and possibly paranoid) person, who would shower his children with overly expensive clothes and take them to exorbitantly priced restaurants. After the exotic meals, which he selected, he would rail at them for spending so much money. Although we could not be absolutely certain, it is likely that Mrs. C's father had been involved in some kind of sexual activity with her.

It is, of course, impossible to reconstruct precisely the dynamic factors that led to such behavior by the parents of these patients. What is of importance is that – whatever the actual source of pathology – these women understood a good part of their parents' behavior in terms of defects of conscience and reality testing.

When I presented this clinical material to various analytic societies, the diagnoses offered by the discussants ranged from overt psychosis to "a hoax" to neurosis to psychopathy. Different analysts will view and understand this material in somewhat different fashions. The focus here is on the perceptual distortions reported by my three patients. For the sake of brevity, I will discuss the material in a composite manner. Although the three cases are hardly identical, the issues involved are sufficiently similar to justify such a blending.

As for the perceptual distortions themselves, I am confident that the material presented by the patients was genuine. The patients experienced transiently and vividly what could best be described as illusion. That is, each reacted to a stimulus in the external world, but the perception of that stimulus was distorted by internal wishes and conflicts, anxiety and depressive affect, and the products of defensive operations. These reactions occurred during periods of intense transference involvement with considerable anxiety and evidence of both instinctual and ego regression. The patients were struggling with frustrated wishes to possess the analyst's penis (breast, baby). These frustrations and the underlying wishes were either conscious or close to consciousness and were related to thoughts and fantasies of getting the analyst to expose himself so that the penis could be incorporated visually or by way of intercourse. These fantasies involved both libidinal and aggressive drive derivatives, the content of which included the wish for her *own* penis; for taking the penis from the analyst-father; for taking the penis from the analyst-father for the mother; and for revenge.[1]

At the time that the perceptual distortion took place, the balance between the drives and the defenses had been altered sufficiently (resulting in increasing pressure from the drive derivatives and decreased effectiveness of the defensive structures opposing them) so that the heightened cathexis of the forbidden wishes could be attached to an external percept. It is not surprising, of course, that the external percept so cathected was intimately related to the person of the analyst (the picture on the wall of his office, the sound of his heavy breathing, his raincoat), a fact that facilitated the process of displacement. For the moment at least, the faithful testing of reality and the fidelity to the reality principle were abrogated;

---

[1] It is interesting to look back at Freud's (1910) pioneering contribution, "The Psycho-Analytic View of Psychogenic Disturbances of Vision."

the hitherto repressed or partially repressed forbidden wishes emerged in the distorted perception of the analyst's penis. We can view the product — here presented as a schematized version of a much more complex series of compromise formations — as a symptom providing transient and partial gratification for the patients.

Such a solution, however, cannot be tenable for a nonpsychotic person. These patients were not altogether convinced (in spite of some of their disclaimers) that they had really seen either a penis or its symbolic distortion. Neither were they convinced that they had *not* done so. The result was a mixture of doubt, confusion, and uncertainty connected to the memory of comparable ego states in the past, when they had been confronted with similar difficulties in dealing with a potentially threatening reality.

In addition, the patients *felt* vaguely that in acceding to the break with reality, they had done something wrong. This incipient feeling of guilt involved more than the recognition that the gratification of the underlying wishes was "bad"; there was also the realization that rejecting a realistic appraisal of reality was contrary to the precepts of their own conscience. In opposition to this set of superego demands were those introjects and identifications within the superego with certain elements of the behavior and superegos of their parents, who had been egregiously unconcerned about respect for reality and reality testing.

At this point in the analysis, the regressive process impinged on the superego as well as the ego. The integrity and stability of each had been further compromised. As a result, in addition to the various intersystemic conflicts, the patients were struggling with intrasystemic ego and superego conflicts. One of the compromises that emerged from those conflicts was the identification in action with the behavior of parental objects who flouted the demands of the recognition of reality and the acceptance of self-responsibility. Further, the patients "preferred" to surrender their superego in order to retain the tie to and/or the love and approval of those objects. This was reenacted in the transference with the analyst. Such behavior is reminiscent of Freud's statement in "An Outline of Psychoanalysis," "if the patient puts that analyst in the place of his father [or mother] he is also giving him the power which his super-ego exercises over his ego, since the parents were, as we know, the origin of his super-ego" (Freud, 1940, p. 175).

Particularly striking in these three incidents is the insistence of each of the patients that even though she "knew" she had distorted a piece of external reality, she would not unequivocally repudiate the distortion. Each "decided" that she preferred to appear "crazy" or "a liar" rather than surrender the compromise-distortion-symptom; and each made it abundantly clear that the reason for doing so was to avoid acknowledging the possibility of seeing my penis. That possibility evoked intense anxiety and was experienced as preliminary to a full-fledged trauma. Somewhat less intense were concerns about being punished for the misdemeanor (the forbidden looking) and mild depressive affect at the prospect of losing a loved object or the love of that object. It was not until later that it became evident that these reactions were repetitions of earlier traumatic experiences connected with seeing a penis or the wish or possibility of seeing one.

This complicated series of psychological events illustrates the multi-determined, interdigitating activities that occur in a situation of psychological conflict, the necessary participation of all three psychic agencies, and the resultant compromise formations (see Brenner, 1982, especially pp. 7, 75, 89, 91, 125, 136–7). There is no way that *all* the elements involved in these events could be teased out and understood. For instance, it is not clear to what extent these patients utilized denial or counterphobic mechanisms as defenses in their insistence that they preferred to lie or to be crazy rather than unequivocally renounce their distorted perception. Masochistic tendencies were conspicuous in all three women, particularly in regard to their superego functioning (Brenner, 1982, pp. 126–8). In the analytic work, material came up that had many parallels with lying (see Weinshel, 1979, where the close relationship between lying and the vicissitudes of the oedipal phase conflicts is examined), with fetishism (Freud, 1927, p. 155), with negation (Freud, 1925; Weinshel, 1977), with "screens" (Freud 1899, 1937; Fenichel, 1927, 1939; Greenson, 1958; Reider, 1953) and with "Gas-Lighting" (Calef and Weinshel, 1982). All of these topics touch in one way or another on the problems of reality, reality testing, and the superego; and all of them warrant considerably more inveistgation.

We cannot be satisfied with only the partial understanding of many aspects of these phenomena now available to us. It is particularly difficult to tease out of the analytic data what should be attributed to the superego and what to the ego. Often the task of translating the "sense" of superego activity into ordinary language seems awkward. There is an aura of mild confusion about this material; the responsibility is not mine alone. (See Greenacre, 1973, in regard to role of primal scene memories). My patients felt confused and readily acknowledged their confusion during these portions of the analysis; they were also *confusing.* Their own sense of reality and the sense of themselves vis-à-vis that reality were somewhat disturbed; and, sometimes, they complained that they felt they were not telling the truth, lying, or just a bit befuddled, even when they *knew* otherwise. Part of the "confusion," the feeling of uncertainty, that I experienced when listening to my patients reflects the nature of the superego, its development, and its somewhat unstable—if not capricious—relationship to the ego.

Stanley Goodman, in his opening remarks on the 1965 Panel, "The Current Status of the Theory of the Superego," explained that the urgent reason for a reevaluation of the superego was that there are still so many unanswered questions and still so many aspects of unclarity in regard to superego functioning. Part of the problem, reported Goodman, was that so many of our "relatively precise" theoretical formulations appear inadequate when we apply them "broadly to our clinical data." (Panel Report, 1965). Twenty years later, most of the same questions and problems remain unclarified.

Although it has not been a crucial or vigorously debated issue, there has never been a concensus about the role of the superego in the testing of reality, either inner or outer. Even after the publication of "The Ego and the Id" (Freud, 1923) where Freud seemed to have assigned the function of perception, especially the perception of the external world, to the ego, there were lingering doubts about the locus of the testing of reality, especially of internal reality (self-observation). Perhaps an extract from "The New Introductory Lectures," which contains a resume of the pertinent material, will give a hint of why some of this doubt persisted:

> We can best arrive at the characteristics of the actual ego insofar as it can be distinguished from the id and from the superego by examining its relation to the outermost superficial portion of the mental apparatus, which we describe as the system *Pcpt-Cs*. This system is turned towards the external world, it is the medium for the perceptions arising thence, and during its functioning the phenomenon of consciousness arises in it. It is the sense organ of the entire apparatus; moreover it is receptive not only to excitations from outside but also to those arising from the interior of the mind. We need scarcely look for a justification of the view that the ego is that portion of the id which was modified by the proximity and influence of the external world, which is adapted for the reception of stimuli, comparable to the cortical layer by which a small piece of living substance is surrounded. The relation to the external world has become the decisive factor for the ego; it has taken on the task of representing the external word to the id—fortunately for the id, which could not escape destruction if, in its blind efforts for the satisfaction of its instincts, it disregarded that supreme external power. In accomplishing this function, the ego *must* observe the external world, *must* lay down an accurate picture of it in the memory-traces of its perceptions, and by its exercise of the function of "reality-testing," *must* put aside whatever in this picture of the external world *is an addition derived from internal sources of excitation*. The ego controls the approaches to motility under the id's orders; but between a need and an action it has interposed a postponement in

the form of the activity of thought, during which it makes use of the mnemic residues of experience. In that way it has dethroned the pleasure principle which dominates the course of events in the id without any restriction and has replaced it by the reality principle, which promises more certainty and greater success [Freud, 1933, pp. 75–6, italics added].

I will not review the history of Freud's vacillations on this subject; excellent summaries can be found in the Panel Report (1965) and in Stein (1966). However, the foregoing extract from Freud raises two questions. The first has to do with the three italicized *musts* in regard to the ego's "accomplishing this function." It is possible, of course, that these imperatives are merely stylistic or linguistic coincidences, but we should also recall that the function of the superego is "to observe and to criticize, approve, disapprove, or punish the ego or the self as we would say today" (Loewenstein, 1966, p. 302). Later Loewenstein adds, "We call the superego that organization within the mental apparatus which becomes a systematic third independent variable in the intrapsychic conflicts, and which exercises control over drives and some essential tendencies and functions of the ego, e.g., individual self-interest and even self-preservation" (p. 302). Freud, discussing the various functions of the superego, speaks of its "keeping a watch over the actions and intentions of the ego and judging them, in exercising a censorship" (Freud, 1930, p. 136). A few years later, Freud (1933) argued that "it is more prudent to keep the agency [the superego] as something independent and to suppose that conscience is one of its functions and that self-observation, which is an essential *preliminary to the judging activity* of conscience is another of them" (p. 60, italics added).

Freud, in describing the activity of the ego-ideal and the shift from ego-ideal to super-ego, utilized imagery and metaphors having to do with watching and observing. As mentioned earlier, the observation was merely a preliminary step in evaluation (measuring the ego against the ego ideal), judgment, criticism, and punishment. Although evaluation and testing of external reality does not at first appear to be a "moral" issue derived from the conflicts of the oedipal phase, a closer examination indicates that it is more complex.

Not only does observation entail all the conflicts about looking and forbidden looking, curiosity, knowing (and not only in the Biblical sense), responsibility, truth ("*Face* the truth even if it hurts"), and so forth, but the very process of the renunciation — relinquishment of the oedipal object — depends on varying degrees of observing and accepting the facts of reality.

The superego, I suggest, does play a significant role in the testing of reality in the external world. That role is in partnership — albeit a junior partnership—with the ego. Among its functions is to keep watch over the actions and intentions of the ego, judge them, and exercise censorship over them—including the monitoring of the ego function of reality testing. Stein (1966) asks: "Does the superego, like an ideal policeman, ever prompt the ego in the direction of more adequate reality testing?", a question he answers in the affirmative (pp. 281, 288; see also Blum, 1981).

The second question suggested by the extract quoted earlier has to do with the other quintessential task of reality testing; the ego "must put aside whatever in this picture of the external world is an addition derived from internal sources of excitation," that is, the differentiation of outside from inside, object from subject, reality from fantasy. This junction has to do with more than the "musts." It deals with an equally important area of the superego's contribution to reality testing and the sphere of the most useful aspect of the ego-superego partnership vis-à-vis reality testing. Freud's caveat refers to the synergistic interdependence between self-observation and the observation of the external world.

There is a reasonable consensus among analysts who have studied self-observation that this function is the domain and responsibility primarily of the superego, with the ego playing a secondary role (e.g., Freud, 1933; Hartmann, 1956; Kris, 1956; Hartmann & Loewenstein, 1962; Gitelson, 1964; Jacobson, 1964; Loewenstein, 1966; Stein, 1966; Schafer, 1968; Calef & Weinshel, 1980; Blum, 1981). Stein's observation in the 1965 Panel Report is particularly enlightening. "The closer to the clinical level," he notes, "the more likely it is that self observation will be treated as a superego function and visa versa" (Panel Report, 1965, p. 180).

In his definitive 1966 essay, "Self Observation, Reality, and the Superego," Stein states: "Self observation is an essential element in the process of reality testing...self observation and self evaluation are inextricably linked, and are intimately involved with superego functions. Therefore, the superego functions play an essential, if indirect role, in reality testing and reality adaptation" (p. 275). The very nature of reality, however, argues Stein, is dependent on "that which is determined by the inspection of one's own mental processes" (p. 276), that is by self-observation and the superego. Quoting Hartmann, "In a broader sense, reality testing also refers to the ability to discern subjective and objective elements in our judgments on reality," (Hartmann, 1956, page 256), Stein concludes, "It is reasonable to assume that reality testing as applied to the outer world, and that which is directed toward one's own mental processes, are interdependent" (p. 276). Stein suggests that self-observation plays a ubiquitous role in reality testing and that "the latter would be subject to serious limitations or impairment *were there not a constant flow of stimuli from the inner world and were the capacity lacking to perceive and evaluate these inner stimuli"* (p. 276, italics added). For these reasons, Stein maintains that self observation "is a necessary, although not a sufficient or sole determining factor in the adequate evaluation of reality" (p. 276; see also Freud, 1936, for example, of the role of the superego interference with adequate reality perception).

It is true, of course, that the pressures from the outer world can disrupt the processes of self-observation and interrupt the proper perception and evaluation of the internal stimuli. Thus, there is an ongoing interdependence between those processes that regulate the functions of testing external and internal reality.

In addition to its crucial heritage from the id and the instinctual drives, so much of the superego and its contents come from the external world. The most important of these contributions are from the parental and other early significant objects. These objects not only become the basis for the pivotal superego identifications during the oedipal phase conflicts in the formation of the superego structures, but the content of some of those identifications may relate more specifically to the external world and reality testing. The parents of each of the patients described in this paper had a cavalier or grossly corrupt attitude toward the exigencies of reality and reality testing. Hartmann (1947) talks about the individual "who constantly emphasizes the matter-of-fact view of life he has, his realistic attitudes, and the high degree of rationality he has reached...." (p. 64). These individuals have a specific relation to reality in that "while parts of reality are emphasized, other parts, mainly of inner reality are scotomized." Hartmann (1956) describes people whose "values" about reality and reality testing are often passed on from generation to generation. The children of such parents will hear admonitions and/or exhortations like (and these are all familiar one with all sorts of variations) "You must face the facts," "You have to realize that we live in a cold, hard world," "Be a man and stand on your own two feet." These remarks are internalized to some degree and become a part of the superego's relationship vis-à-vis the external world. The impact may be to enhance the tendency towards more stringent reality testing; it may also, for a number of reasons, result in defiance of such admonitions and a reluctance to follow other parental precepts. The tremendous importance of the early objects to the child also entails dependence on the object's values, even including dependence on parents' atypical, idiosyncratic, and grossly distorted pictures of reality (pp. 255–6). Greenson's (1958, p. 259) epigrammatic "Parents who

deny create children who lie" could be said equally well in the reverse order (Parents who lie create children who deny) since the young child cannot differentiate with any accuracy between denial or overt lying. It is the
realistic importance of and dependence on the parents, and the fear of
losing the parental objects and/or the love and approval of those objects,
that intensifies the possibility of the child's incorporating those parental
"manipulations" of reality and reality testing.

In a similar, but (usually) less critical way, culture and society exert their
influence on the values that eventually become part of the overall superego structure, particularly, the contents of the structure. These influences
are important elements that account for the diversity of superego content;
and as Brenner (1982, pp. 137–8) warns, variations in superego functioning should not be mistaken for superego pathology.

The role of culture in the formation and maintenance of the superego,
particularly in establishing what may be called "the conditions for repression" is noted in Freud's (1917) rendition of Nestroy's "In the Basement
and on the First Floor," the Viennese version of England's TV series
"Upstairs-Downstairs." In this well-known portrayal of the consequences
of sex play between two "invented" six-year-old girls, the daughter of the
caretaker of the apartment house (in the basement) has already witnessed
adult sexual activity and had access to sexual knowledge. As a result, the
childhood play did not have any deleterious effect, and the girl grew up
free of sexual problems and neurosis. Her partner, the daughter of the
landlord (on the first floor), however, "came under the influence of education and accepted its demands." Therefore, while still a child (because
of the "tendency to conflict, arising from the development of the ego,
which rejects these libidinal impulses") she will feel that she had done
something wrong, will give up masturbation after considerable struggle,
turn away from adult sexual intercourse, prefer to remain sexually igno-
rant, and suffer from neurosis (Freud, 1917, pp. 352–4). In spite of its
somewhat Victorian, melodramatic tone, Freud's depiction of the impact
of the social-cultural milieu is a vivid one.

Hartmann (1956) dealt with these more general issues of the role of the
superego in the creation of the conditions for repression in his *Notes on
the Reality Principle*. He pointed out that with the advent of the superego,
the question of what is pleasurable and what is not becomes much more
complicated. He said, "The aspect of structure formation under scrutiny
now has changed also the conditions for pleasure gain; it has not only limited them but also newly defined what is and what is not pleasurable or
less pleasurable" (pp. 247–8).

The superego, like the other principal agencies of the mind, is not a fixed structure, certainly not with the "sharp frontiers" that might be inferred from the diagrams of the psychic apparatus. Freud warned that the divisions of the personality are essentially artificial ones and that

> after making the separation we must allow what we have separated to merge together once more....It is highly probable that the development of these divisions is subject to great variations in different individuals; it is possible that in the course of actual functioning they may change and go through a temporary phase of involution. Particularly in the case of what is phylogenetically the last and most delicate of these divisions – the differentiation between the ego and the superego – something of this sort seems to be true [1933, p. 79].

We see this blurring most conspicuously in regressive states and dissolution of the superego structures and functions, but the reverse is also true. Freud implies that with maturity of superego development, there may be an ongoing integration of the superego activities into the ego, especially when there occurs a gradual diminution of the "moral" elements of a particular superego function and pattern. (Comparable views are expressed by Arlow, 1982; Loewenstein, 1966; Loewald, 1959, and Stein, 1966). This blurring of ego-superego boundaries and the merging of the superego with the ego are, in part, reasons why, on the clinical level at least, it may be so difficult to ascertain whether a particular activity – including the testing of reality – is governed by the ego or the superego.

Two other aspects of superego development deserve comment. First, as the child becomes more active motorically and begins to explore the outer world, the child's behavior often evokes responses from the parents that are simultaneously frightened and angry. These responses occur in reaction to behavior that is potentially or actually self-destructive, or even life threatening: events like crossing the street alone, climbing up to high places, playing with matches, opening bottles containing dangerous substances – the list is long. For the child, a certain degree of uncertainty and confusion ensues, the distinction between what is related to self-preservation and what is related to something "evil" is neither altogether clear nor convincing. It takes a long time for the child to be able to distinguish moral conflicts from other conflicts; and, although with the gradual development of the superego this distinction becomes more evident, "we are never completely free of this equation of danger with 'evil' " (Loewenstein, 1966, p. 302). Similarly, the analyst will have problems in differentiating those functions which are closely dependent on the influence of the ego, those of the superego, and those which are the product of their collaboration.

Part of this "joint venture uncertainty" is reflected in the double meaning of certain words. For example, "good and bad," "right and wrong," "straight and crooked," "correct and incorrect" can have either a moral connotation or one that reflects the ego's adaptive functioning. "Judgment" can pertain to a particular assessment of reality, but the phrase "passing judgment" raises images of judges, juries, and punishment. Even the innocuous word "observation" carries with it not only the ordinary meaning of looking but also the morally tinged idea of "observing" the rules and the laws.

A second important role of the superego is the way in which we see and relate to the external world has to do with moods. This is especially true in regard to those moods in which the superego has exerted a significant influence, although to some extent the superego plays a part in all mood formation. Depression and mania are the most conspicuous examples, but a comparable distortion of reality to fit the mood can also be noted in paranoid and masochistic conditions. To see the world "through rose colored glasses" is more than a figure of speech. The outside world as viewed by a severely depressed patient and by one who is hypomanic is hardly the same world. The whole area of moods and their influence on relations with the external world is one that has not been pursued carefully by analysts (see Jacobson, 1957, and Weinshel, 1970).

The civilized person may not always be moral, but at least our so-called civilized world is one of morals, of rules, and of regulations and limitations; and in spite of all-too-frequent horrendous and egregious exceptions, human beings must maintain a certain minimal degree of morality in order to exist in that world. In that sense, a reasonable degree of effective superego functioning is essential for adaptation and survival. We know all too well, however, that the constancy and reliability of the superego and its various activities are considerably less than ideal. One of the outcomes of a reasonably successful psychoanalysis is the enhancement of the autonomy and the fidelity of those superergo functions, but we recognize that these changes are only relative. An additional vignette involving Mrs. A, the patient whose story began this essay, is illustrative.

Several years after the completion of what we both considered to be a gratifying analytic experience, Mrs. A sent a UNICEF Christmas card with a report on her current life and progress. After detailing a series of satisfying events and changes in her work and her personal life, she wrote:

...And I enjoy it, and my logical powers have sharpened – you would not recognize me, so different from the old fuzzy-headed, don't dare look-under-the-Japanese hanging me I used to be. In fact, I now look under everything, around, up, neath. And I question im- no one is a more – which in a way....I card – to show even advertise quite good taste – and when the 恭 賀 新 禧 **SEASON'S GREETINGS** **MEILLEURS VOEUX** **FELICES FIESTAS** **С НОВЫМ ГОДОМ** as well as down, be- look at every aginable, and wizard any- is kind of sad send you my you that I myself (in of course) occasion demands it, I can be self assertive like anything....I have thought several times of coming in to see you in spite of my super-positive tone – then changed my mind because a certain amount of sadness is existential....

The note was, of course, gratifying to me. I was, however, also intrigued: the image on the card was almost identical to the image of the Japanese print: The familiar UNICEF "logo" served as the "protuberance" that instigated the perceptual distortion described and discussed earlier.

Neither my explication of these cases nor my presentation of the role of the superego in reality testing is complete. Just as in analysis, much remains unclear and unfinished – and the power of the unconscious is undiminished!

REFERENCES

Arlow, J. (1982), Problems of the superego concept. *The Psychoanalytic Study of the Child,* 37:229–244.

Blum, H. (1981), The forbidden quest and the analytic ideal: The superego and insight. *Psychoanal. Quart.* 50:535–556.

Brenner, C. (1982), *The Mind in Conflict.* New York: International Universities Press.

Calef, V. & Weinshel, E. M. (1980), The analyst as the conscience of the analysis. *Internat. Rev. Psycho-Anal.,* 7:279–290.

———— ———— (1981), Some clinical consequences of introjection: Gaslighting. *Psychoanal. Quart.,* 50:44–66.

Fenichel, O. (1927), The economic function of screen memories. In: *Collected Papers,* First Series. New York: Norton, 1953, pp. 113–116.

———— (1939), The economics of pseudologia phantastica. In: *Collected Papers,* Second Series. New York: Norton, 1954, pp. 129–140.

Freud, S. (1899), Screen memories. *Standard Edition*, 3:301–322. London: Hogarth Press, 1962.

_____ (1910), The psycho-analytic view of psychogenic disturbance of vision. *Standard Edition*, 11:210–218. London: Hogarth Press, 1957.

_____ (1917), Introductory lectures on psycho-analysis. *Standard Edition*, 16:243–463. London: Hogarth Press, 1963.

_____ (1923), The ego and the id. *Standard Edition*, 19:3–66. London: Hogarth Press, 1961.

_____ (1925), Negation. *Standard Edition*, 19:234–239. London: Hogarth Press, 1961.

_____ (1927), Fetishism. *Standard Edition*, 21:149–157. London: Hogarth Press, 1961.

_____ (1930), Civilization and its discontents. *Standard Edition*, 21:59–145. London: Hogarth Press, 1961.

_____ (1933), New introductory lectures on psycho-analysis. *Standard Edition*, 22:3–182. London: Hogarth Press, 1964.

_____ (1936), A disturbance of memory on the Acropolis. *Standard Edition*, 22:239–248. London: Hogarth Press, 1964.

_____ (1937), Constructions in psycho-analysis. *Standard Edition*, 23:256–269. London: Hogarth Press, 1964.

_____ (1940), An outline of psycho-analysis. *Standard Edition*, 23:141–207. London: Hogarth Press, 1964.

Gitelson, M. (1964), On the present scientific and social position of psychoanalysis. *Internat. J. Psycho-Anal.*, 44:521–524.

Greenacre, P. (1973). The primal scene and the sense of reality. *Psychoanal. Quart.*, 42:10–41.

Greenson, R. (1958), On screen defenses, screen hunger, and screen identity. *J. Amer. Psychoanal. Assn.*, 6:242–262.

Hartmann, H. (1947), On rational and irrational action. In: *Essays in Ego Psychology*. New York: International Universities Press, 1964, pp. 19–36.

_____ (1956), Notes on the Reality Principle. In: *Essays in Ego Psychology*. New York: International Universities Press, 1964, pp. 241–267.

_____ & Loewenstein, R. (1962), Notes on the superego. *The Psychoanalytic Study of the Child*, 17:42–81.

Jacobson, E. (1957), On normal and pathological moods. *The Psychoanalytic Study of the Child*, 12:73–113.

_____ (1964), *The Self and the Object World*. New York: International Universities Press.

Kris, E. (1956), On some vicissitudes of insight in psychoanalysis. In: *The Selected Papers of Ernst Kris*. New Haven: Yale University Press, 1975, pp. 252–271.

Loewald, H. (1959), Internalization, separation, mourning, and the superego. In: *Papers on Psychoanalysis*. New Haven: Yale University Press, 1980, pp. 257–276.

Loewenstein, R. (1966), On the theory of the superego: A discussion. In: *Psychoanalysis: A General Psychology*, ed. R. M. Loewenstein et al. New York: International Universities Press, 1966, pp. 298–314.

Panel Report (1965), S. Goodman, Reporter. The current status of the theory of the superego. *J. Amer. Psychoanal. Assn.,* 13:172–180.

Reider, N. (1953), Reconstruction and screen function. *J. Amer. Psychoanal. Assn.,* 1:389–405.

Schafer, R. (1968), *Aspects of Internalization.* New York: International Universities Press.

Stein, M. (1966), Self-observation, reality, and the superego. In: *Psychoanalysis: A General Psychology,* ed. R. M. Loewenstein et al. New York: International Universities Press, pp. 275–297.

Weinshel, E. M. (1970), Some psychoanalytic considerations on moods. *Internat. J. Psycho-Anal.,* 51:313–320.

_____ (1977), I didn't mean it: Negation as a character trait. *The Psychoanalytic Study of the Child,* 32:387–420.

_____ (1979), Some observations on not telling the truth. *J. Amer. Psychoanal. Assn.,* 27:503–531.

PART FIVE

The
Teaching
of
Psychoanalysis

Charles Brenner has taught thousands of psychiatrists and psycho-analysts through his many articles and books. For those who are fortunate to have been taught by him firsthand in seminars, group discussions, lectures, and supervision, the experience is a memorable one. In this section, Martin Wangh writes about the teaching of psychoanalysis through the supervisory process. In a frank and open discussion, he draws on his long experience as a teacher to advocate a more collegial relationship between supervisor and supervisee. In such an atmosphere, he believes, both participants will learn and the patient will gain from their collaboration.

Some Notes on the "Supervisory" Process

Consultation about his patients with a more experienced colleague has long been an integral part in the training of the young psychoanalyst. Freud's self-education as an analyst began with his introspecting about the impact the behavior and verbalizations of his patients had on his own mind and emotions. Being helped through the process of self-observation and learning to use self-evaluation for effective and creative psychoanalytic work has become a central aim of consultation among psychoanalysts. From early on, these consultations have been called *Kontroll-analysen* in German-speaking countries and *supervisions* in English-speaking ones.

Over the years, Freud (1910, 1911, 1912a, 1912b, 1913a, 1913b, 1914, 1915, 1919, 1927) wrote a great number of papers in which he counseled the practitioner on the attitudes needed for psychoanalytic work. In them he also warned of the pitfalls of this work for the practitioner.

Ever since psychoanalysis organized itself as an international body, generations of teachers have increased their insight into the intrapsychic and interpersonal effects of these educative consultations. I will mention here, in chronological order, a few of the more significant, post-Freud contributions to our subject. Among them was Bibring's (1937) report on the deliberations of the "International Training Committee of the Four Countries." Another was DeBell's (1963) excellent survey of all that had been written on the subject up to that time. In the same year, Arlow's (1963) paper, "The Supervisory Situation," opened an interesting new perspective on the supervisee's adoption of the patient's defense. Two comprehensive books on the subject have been published since then: In *Psy-*

choanalytic Supervision, Joan Fleming and Therese Benedek (1966) researched the field with thoroughness, impartiality, and great clarity; and, more recently, under the editorship of Robert Wallerstein (1981), Becoming a Psychoanalyst detailed the result of long years of scrutiny by the Study Group on Supervision of the Committee on Psychoanalytic Education of the American Psychoanalytic Association.

DeBell (1963, p. 546) said that learning psychoanalysis through discussion of a patient's treatment with a more experienced colleague was to be considered an "apprentice system." The ultimate result of such a system should be that the erstwhile "apprentice" eventually becomes a "master" himself. Ideally, this master (whether a man or a woman) teaches the young psychoanalyst all that he knows about his art or science. His teachings may also include questions that have arisen in his own mind on various clinical or theoretical issues. All of this would be the master's gift to the apprentice.

We like to imagine that such open giving was what took place in the medieval guild-workshops. While the student-apprentice analogy may be an apt one for characterizing the consultative process in psychoanalytic training, certain major differences exist between the apprentice model of old and the present-day analytic student situation. A guild's apprentice, lacking skills and, presumably, preconceived notions, usually entered the master's shop at a very young age. This is not the case with the psychoanalytic candidate or the resident psychiatrist eager to learn about psychoanalytic psychotherapy. He comes to his consultant with previously acquired skills and is not innocent of theory. Also, he will not be introduced into his work by being given minor menial tasks while slowly being led, step by step, to acquire the master's skills. The novice psychoanalyst or psychotherapist bears from the start an awesome responsibility — the care of another human being, his patient. He usually finds himself secluded with his patient in some sparsely furnished cubicle — his office — and becomes anxious, merely by the isolation in his work.

Once, when I asked the residents in a psychiatric hospital whether they would not prefer to start their training by treating psychoneurotic patients in a clinic setting rather than by treating psychotics in a closed ward, I was astonished that almost unanimously they said no. Their reason was that in a ward they could work as members of a team with nurses, occupational therapists, junior and senior staff members with whom they could share the responsibility for their patients. Furthermore, they argued, a neurotic patient might be too much like themselves, and that would make them even more "anxious."

Anxiety often does not function as a mobilizer of effective action. Rather, it disturbs the ability for optimal therapeutic intervention. Therefore, the advice of a more experienced colleague becomes much sought after. These consultations have as their major focus, of course, the welfare of the patient.

By putting the *responsibility for a patient and the anxiety it evokes* as the primary motivation for the consultative interchange, I emphasize something that is fundamental for the pure psychoanalytic and the psychoanalytically oriented psychotherapeutic process. Any person who wants to become a psychotherapist or a psychoanalyst must *caringly* wish to fathom what is in another person's mind. But this is not enough; to understand another, he needs to know about his own fears, motivations, thoughts, and feelings. He must become his own guinea pig. Only when he has an "interest in himself as an object of scientific exploration," said Dr. Evelyne Kestemberg (1978), a French colleague, can he become an effective psychotherapist. Only when one is capable of empathy with oneself, with one's own feelings, present and past, can one have empathy with others. And empathy is a major tool in psychotherapy. Empathy implies that the other (it could even be an animal) is viewed as being like oneself, as a being with whom a relationship is possible.

It follows that without the capacity for what we call "object relations," one cannot become a psychoanalyst or psychotherapist. This is so for all the "students" or "residents" in any psychoanalytic institute or in any psychoanalytically oriented psychiatric or mental health facility, regardless of whether they are drawn from medicine, psychology, social work, or any other humanistic or scientific discipline. A merely intellectual wish to acquire knowledge about psychotherapy through the consultative interchange with an experienced colleague does not suffice. This wish must be accompanied by a willingness to explore, in an encompassing way, the vicissitudes of one's own soul — as Freud originally called the totality of the mind.

Up to this point I have spoken about a fundamental, characterological quality that must be present in the student, candidate, or resident if he truly is to acquire knowledge through the consultative process. Now let us talk about this process itself and the role of the consultant in it.

With the introduction of formal psychoanalytic training, the consultative process was called, as I have said, in the German-speaking countries *Kontrollanalyse*. English speakers either adopted this term as "control-analysis" or substituted for it the term "supervision." The latter has, since the establishment of regular Institutes of Psychoanalysis, been the more commonly used.

I have avoided — almost strenuously — the use of either of those terms, because both *Kontrollanalyse* and "supervision" imply that the "master," the "professor," the supervisor has magical powers; that he can control the interchange between the therapist and his patient; that he can over-see and, by specific work directives, guide this interpersonal interchange.

While the use of such terms as control analyst or supervisor enhances the image of the consultant as omnipotent and omniscient, it, by the same token, reinforces the consulter's view of himself as small and helpless. He is, in his own eyes, a disciple, a "discipulus," which literally translated means "learning boy" or "knave." (And a knave hopes eventually to be ele-vated, first to squire, then to baron, and so on up the ladder of aristocracy, which in a psychoanalytic institute is represented by the "training ana-lysts.") The implicit "infantilization" of the beginning psychoanalyst be-comes even clearer when we consider the Swedish term for supervision: "Handledning," or "leading by the hand."

Because the young psychotherapist or student-psychoanalyst who seeks consultation with his older, more experienced colleague is usually at the same time in some form of dynamic psychotherapy or analysis him-self; and because, inherently, during these curative procedures some re-gressive ideational and affective trends are mobilized; and because some spillover of these regressive stimulations in the form of actions outside the treatment room is apt to occur, an inclination toward a regressively based overestimation of the consultant's wisdom and power is frequently car-ried over from this treatment into the consultative setting. If we add to this that in an Institute the consultant is, on behalf of the Institute, the judge of the student's aptness and capability as a psychotherapist, the informa-tional interchange between consulter and consultant may easily become distorted. Lewin and Ross (1960) have called the dual role of the supervi-sor *syncretic* and see it as an insurmountable impediment during psycho-analytic training. Fleming and Benedek (1966) assume a more optimistic stance in regard to this dilemma. But in their scrutiny of the supervisor's approach, they do warn of three possibly noxious interferences affecting the creation of an optimal climate between consulter and consultant. First, the consultant may stress solely the instructional aspect of teaching. He may confine himself to giving information on the dynamics of the pa-tient or to giving prescriptions for the correction of mistakes made by the student. Second, the consultant may be so patient oriented that he feels himself to be the patient's analyst and may thus relegate the student to the role of middleman. Finally, the consultant may focus only on the student-analyst's or the psychotherapist's blind spots, or on his countertrans-ferences, and proceed to "analyze" these. Although in this way he seem-ingly maintains his identity as a therapist, he confuses therapeutic with teaching objectives (Fleming and Benedek, 1966, p. 3).

What, then, should be the optimal atmosphere of the consulter-consultant encounter? Ideally, it should be a peer relationship. This "group of two" is a task-oriented group with the common aim to be "students" of a subject. Here I understand the term "student" in its original meaning: To be a student is to be "eager" and "zealous" to reach understanding (*Century Dictionary,* 1914). Every analysis (and psychoanalytic psychotherapy) is a voyage of discovery into mostly unknown territory. As fingerprints are unique for each person, so are the constitution and balances within the personality. These are what both consuler and consultant will try to chart together. They will have to collaborate in this and in doing so will have to uncover all the obstacles that stand in the way. In their historical review, Fleming and Benedek (1966) write:

> As we trace the development of psychoanalytic education, it is interesting to note the informality which characterized the relationship between teacher and student. Dedication on the part of each to the task of learning the still embryonic body of psychoanalytic theory and technique probably accounts for much of this atmosphere which did not seem troubled by the syncretic dilemmas of today [p. 10].

By now we may have better maps, apply finer measurements, but these lead only to more refined questions; hence, the need for discovery remains. Each time the consultant succeeds in finding new elements that contribute to the formation of a symptom, or that pinpoint what has altered an existing balance in the patient's mind, he will want to share this new discovery with his younger colleague. They are then witnessing together the condensative, condensed, and ambiguous processes that emerge in the conscious mind from the unconscious.

Jacob Peyton, Jr. (1981) also believes strongly in the need to foster a peer relationship between consuler (candidate) and consultant (supervisor). He proposes a "supervisory pact," which ends in the following elegant and concise paragraph: "Let us both consider that we are on the frontier of psychoanalytic knowledge; we are both students. It is granted that I have had more experience, but an overemphasis on the student-teacher relationship will detract from a mutual exploratory attitude toward this unique 'experiment in nature,' your case" (p. 207).

Because he wants to foster an attitude of setting out on a shared exploratory expedition, the consultant will try to counterweigh the growing awe of him of which I have spoken (he will also be trying to prevent a counterreaction to it). He may, for instance, simply point out to the consuler that, unlike the counsel seeker, the consultant is, after all, not directly exposed to the patient's demands for immediate relief. Also, the consuler may, because of therapeutic eagerness frequently born of an omnipotent rescue fantasy (a likely base element in his professional choice), feel challenged to provide immediate relief. Not being able to provide it may make him anxious or depressed because he cannot satisfy this self ideal through immediate success. One may then want to say to the consulter that just by listening to a patient's complaints in the quiet calm of one's office, one may already be giving him an extraordinary gift, a gift he may never have experienced before: being fully heard out by anyone.

Elsewhere, I (1966) have spoken of the fact that the "psychoanalytic situation," in which the analyst sits behind the couch, behind his patient, offers the analyst great psychological "safety." How much safer is the consultant, who is physically completely removed from the patient! In this "safety"[1] zone, he can let his mind roam with greater freedom, not only over what he hears about the patient but also over how the material is presented by the consulter; at the same time, he can explore what these communications evoke in himself.

I mentioned earlier that there may be a counterreaction to the inclination to be awed by an older, experienced colleague. The "overestimation" may be displaced from the therapist's therapist or may stem from the transfer from an original object (Brenner, 1982). "Anxiety of being influenced," a theme about which literary critic Harold Bloom (1973) wrote very persuasively in regard to the burden of the young poet, may dominate the young therapist's relationship toward his consultant.

Fleming and Benedek (1966) caution the supervisor not to try to take over the patient's treatment; to do so may be extremely nefarious. The consultant may be perceived as a usurping rival. Unconsciously, any younger colleague worth his salt has such feelings of rivalry, but under these circumstances they become easily projected, and onto an apt object to boot. Any peer relationship is then severely impeded. The consultation scene is then one of combat, where to win or to submit is the main issue, and the wish for study and the welfare of the patient are neglected. The institutional conditions, by lending, promoting, or demoting power to the supervisor, may aggravate these flaws. Howard Shevrin (1981), in a chapter entitled "On Being the Analyst Supervised" in the book *Becoming a Psychoanalyst,* bitterly denounces such invasions of the consulter's autonomy.

I cannot stress enough the importance of an atmosphere of trust and reciprocal respect in the consultation process. Such a climate is just as necessary for consultation as it is for the psychotherapeutic process itself.

---

[1]Featherton (1978) has spoken of the institutional constraints that may cause the "training-analyst" or the "supervisor" anxiety and/or depression in his work with the analytic candidate. The supervisor, in turn, may be apprehensive about the judgment of the "Educational Committee" if his student-patient, his apprentice, does not seem to make sufficient progress.

True, both the patient and the consulter may come to the session with some trust-impeding prejudices. But anything that may give nourishment to these prejudments should be exposed to the light of day in mutual discussion.

In summary, the encounter between consulter and consultant should not be an "encounter" at all, but a meeting between peers. Its purpose is the shared study of a patient's life and therapy. A priori, both participants in this endeavor must have the capacity for object relationship and empathy. Their collaboration in the voyage of discovery of the complexities in another one's life must take place in an atmosphere of trust. Trust is particularly needed by the consulter, because inevitably, through his presentation of the treatment material, some self-revelation will occur. Hence, he needs to feel "safe" with his consultant.

Kubie (1958), in an article entitled "Research into the Process of Supervision," is highly skeptical of the *scientific* value of the supervisory process. "We pretend that the student's report . . . can provide a true and representative sample of that which has actually taken place in the analytic sessions. . . . The student who pleases us by the facility of his reports is usually less perceptive and less accurate than his more labored and more conscientious confrère, who stirs us to impatient criticism" (p. 227).

Acknowledging the emotional strain to which the student is exposed in the supervisory situation, Kubie thinks that we are asking the reporting psychotherapist to do the impossible.

> To record and recall both the patient's free association and his own, and simultaneously to record and recall the "how" of the patient's expressions, and also to evaluate these, while at the same time responding to the patient's free associations with his own associations . . . is asking him to be free and bound at the same moment . . . something which as analysts we know to be psychologically impossible . . . Indeed, what actually happens is . . . that the student recalls, and reproduces screened, biased, altered versions of that which happened in the analysis [p. 229.].

As a remedy for the discrepancies between reports of and the reality of psychoanalytic sessions, Kubie (p. 231) proposes that psychoanalytic hours be tape recorded and then listened to by the consultant and the student together during the supervisory hours. This, in Kubie's opinion, would give the student a chance for self-criticism and the supervisor a more accurate picture of how the psychoanalytic dialogue between patient and student actually evolved.

From both a practical and an epistemological, heuristic point of view, Kubie's observations and their proposed remedy are unrealistic. In part, they are based on a misunderstanding of how the consultation process takes place and what it must fundamentally aim at. To listen to the tape recordings (better still, TV tapes) of all psychoanalytic sessions and then to discuss what was heard demands so much time of both consulter and consultant that none but a very specialized and well-subsidized institution could pursue such a proposal. At best, one or two cases usable for group discussion recorded in this way could be funded by such an organization. Beyond the economic aspect, we must ask ourselves whether this sort of accuracy of recording and reporting of the words spoken during an analytic hour is in fact needed for therapist and consultant to reach understanding of what went on in a given psychoanalytic session. Must we hear "every association" of the patient and every association of the therapist to comprehend the flow of an analytic hour? Is this not too mechanistic, too language-bound a conception of the analytic process? As it is simply impossible to reproduce in one hour what has been heard, perceived, and responded to in the course of the usual four or five sessions of the weekly psychoanalytic work, we can expect the therapist's report to be only a condensation of them. The same holds true for reports on one or two psychotherapeutic sessions. Any condensation is inherently a product created by the therapist — it is his "creative production." Is this a matter to be lamented?

David Beres (1957) has likened the psychoanalytic treatment process to the artistic, creative act. In the psychoanalytic situation, the patient's communications — verbal, gestural, and pausal — are like the imagery (tonal, visual, or verbal) that emerges into an artist's consciousness. The difference in the analytic situation is that the creative execution lies in the analyst's response, in his clarifications or interpretations. True, the end result of this *action à deux* does not aim at achieving aesthetic delight but at understanding and insight. Insight may not always bring pure pleasure, but this may equally be true with a work of art. The student's report, being of necessity a product of his creative condensation, is in turn to be perceived and worked over by the consultant — not unlike the communication of the patient by the therapist. The consultant is challenged by the presentation in an overdetermined way: he pays attention to the report about the patient's productions, he listens to the therapist's responses to them, and he observes the manner of the reporting itself. Besides this, he has an ear toward his own simultaneous reactions. He then must weigh what he has become aware of. Is it pertinent to the task at hand, or is he intruding into it with his own self-concerns? Is there heuristic value in communicating what he is perceiving to his younger colleague at *this* moment? How much can his colleague, his co-student, absorb at this point in his psychoanalytic development? These are pedagogical questions. Is it, for instance, appropriate to refer to his own clinical experience, and should he, at that point, send the student to read pertinent literature? Will the first not be felt as exhibitionistic or boastful, and will the second enhance intellectualizing? And of major importance is the *when* and *how* inner obstacles to listening to and understanding the patient should be pointed out. Do these impediments spring merely from ignorance or from unrecognized countertransference? If one points out countertransferences, one must not fall prey to "wild analysis." How far does one go in tracing the source of unrecognized countertransferences, which may have led to scotomata or error?

The freest possible presentation of the clinical material, unbound by a previously thought-out text, will offer the optimal field for the consultant's scanning attention. Hence, he will not demand verbatim reports of sessions; he will even discourage any reading from written notes. I myself say to my younger colleagues: "Tell me what happened as you would tell it to a friend." As a matter of fact, since I lived near New York's Central Park, we often walked through the park during our consultation time. This peripatetic activity by itself diminishes tension and discourages reading from notes. There is an additional advantage in reporting freely. One of my students said, "It makes me think in terms of the continuous flow of the sessions; I don't think in terms of hour by hour, each hour separated from the others."

To sum up this section: As in any creative production, the presented material will radiate in a variety of directions. The consultant will listen to it in the open fashion he listens as a therapist. And, as in therapy, timing and manner of intervention are important in the consultative process. It stands to reason that the removal of obstacles to the understanding of the patient's communications will become a primary goal of the consultation. Toward this end, the beginner must learn what is meant by psychoanalytic process. He may have to unlearn the hitherto practiced technique of active intervention in and manipulation of the patient's situation. He must learn to listen with *seeming* passivity. He must learn to make conscious to himself what he has empathically perceived. He must learn to recognize and acknowledge his countertransference feelings; else, unrecognized, they will stand in the way of his empathic listening.

A psychoanalyst's empathy is a biphasic process (Beres and Arlow, 1974; Beres, 1966). Often, as Arlow illustrates (1963), the student behaves during his presentation of the material in the very same manner as his patient has behaved in the therapeutic session. The consultant must understand this as an identificatory, often nonverbal communication belonging to the material. For instance, the presenter may say, "Oh, I have forgotten the dream the patient told me," or this or that part of the session. If he is allowed to continue his report without pressure to remember then and there, the available material that follows will more often than not bring some understanding of the issue at hand. After this has taken place, very frequently the forgotten section is recalled. We can then recognize that the patient had been involved in a struggle against the revelation of some repressed item. The presenter, in such instances, took in what the patient communicated—his empathy was at work, but he failed to make this empathic percept conscious to himself; instead, he reenacted the patient's defensive maneuver.

Somewhat more problematic is the failure to become aware of one's countertransference. Acknowledged countertransference is a most important instrument—a guideline for the therapeutic intervention of the psychotherapist/analyst. Failing to recognize one's countertransference, particularly when this recurs frequently and in relation to similar items in the patient's communication, represents a major resistance in the therapist himself. It is absolutely necessary to bring such failures to his attention and to encourage him to search for the superficial or deeper sources in himself of this obstacle to the full perception of the patient's communication. If the problem is deeply grounded in the therapist's personal history, the consultant can only call the problem and its repeated appearance to the consulter's attention, and it will be up to him to seek analytic investigation of it. But often matters do not lie so deeply buried. They do not have to be investigated by going deeply into personal genetic sources. Often the obstacle is so common to all analysts, or so common for the situation of the therapist's age group, that it might be quite appropriate to point out the source at hand. Here are some instances: Particularly when it comes time for taking a vacation, short or long, the consulter cannot hear signals of the patient's separation anxiety or note his rage. It may well be that "separation" is a problem for the therapist himself, deeply rooted in his own past, but it may also be that he feels too anxious for financial reasons at this stage of his career to take that much time off. It may be sufficient to discuss the intrusion of these latter concerns at this moment in time. Or, in another instance, the consulter, whose own analysis is about to end, cannot hear that the patient is saying, "I think I am ready to end treatment."

Two other instances of countertransference in which the difficulties can be interpreted without the need to "intrude as analyst" into the student's deeper psychological life, where simple human understanding suffices, follow. In the first example, the student had to miss two appointments with his psychoanalytic psychotherapy patient. When the patient saw him again and talked of matters very important in his career, the student felt bored and then insisted that the patient should have raised questions about his, the therapist's, absence. On the face of it, he seemed justified; yet he seemed to have been off in his timing and his insistence, particularly because for the patient very vital, real issues were at stake. Also, to react with boredom was inappropriate. So I inquired into the reasons for the student therapist's absences. The first absence was due to an emergency in the hospital; the second resulted from the death of the student's grandfather. He spoke of how impressed he was by his own father's mourning. I asked how close he himself was to his grandfather and then gave him my condolences. To point out that he is avoiding awareness of his own mourning by displacement might be an analytic intrusion; but by giving my condolences, I imply that he is in mourning. I pointed out to him that his inability fo follow his patient and his insistence that the patient should have been concerned about his absence, accompanied by his boredom with what the patient was speaking about, was related to his own need for attention and consolation at a time of mourning.

Another example of a situation where some degree of personal intrusion by the consultant seems to me quite appropriate, after a trusting atmosphere has been established, is the following. While the student reported on her 38-year-old patient's concern about a tubal operation to help her become pregnant, she failed to pick up on the *urgency* of this wish. The issue was mentioned only in passing. The student herself is in her early 30s. She is still unmarried. I brought to her attention her de-emphasis of this matter. I wondered out loud whether being childless might not be of concern to herself. She burst out crying.

Both examples show that the consultant can remain well within the boundaries of plain human understanding when he points out some present countertransferential obstacles. He does not thereby become the analyst of his younger colleague and consequently a competitor with the colleague's analyst, who would presumably work toward linking the observed obstacles to the genetic and dynamic problems of the student. But at other times the advice of the consultant may indeed be: "You may wish to go back into treatment yourself in order to gain some insight into the material you constantly tend to overlook."

In a particular instance, the patient's sibling rivalry remained steadfastly unobserved. At first I thought the consulter had been an only child, and hence knowledge of sibling rivalry might be of less significance for her. When I learned that in fact she had several siblings, the more remarkable was the scotoma. A new analysis, with someone else (not her previous analyst), led to great progress in her work and life. In another instance, the consulter's discomfort with the patient seemed to lie in the indirect professional contact with the patient. But behind this issue lay the patient's

profound fear of the aggressive, castrative fantasies toward her male analyst and his surrogates. Here, too, further analysis of the consulter was
indicated.

Finally, I would like to mention a few separate technical methods, the
conscious use of which may speed psychotherapeutic understanding:

1. I encourage the younger colleague to make a conscious effort to
place himself mentally in the patient's childhood environment.

2. I emphasize that words must be heard with their affective tone, or
with attention to the lack of expectable affect. Pauses between words are
as important as the words themselves. "Tone and rhythm make the
music."

3. I stress the mental conversion of metaphors or dream descriptions
into visual imagery; this accelerates understanding. An image offers a *simultaneity* that the sequential, logical, verbal percept does not.

Of course, many more therapeutic issues than those mentioned here
come up in a prolonged contact between consulter and consultant. They
include matters of diagnosis or of development and cultural influence;
they may be about theoretical, psychoanalytic biases—the list is long.
What I have tried to discuss here are matters that, in my opinion, have not
been spoken of or not sufficiently stressed in other expositions on the subject; others just seemed to me worthwhile to rediscuss in my own way.

In summary, I have spoken of my misgivings about designating the
consulter-consultant relationship by the terms "Kontrollanalyse" or "supervision"; they reinforce "infantilization." Ideally, the consulting atmosphere is one of mutual trust and peership. A basic requirement for becoming a psychoanalytically oriented psychotherapist is the capability for
object relationship, combined with a willingness to look into one's own
motivations and their sources, as well as into the patient's mind. The psychoanalytically minded therapist must make conscious to himself the
empathic responses the patient's communications awaken in him. He
also must become conscious of his countertransference feelings, which
can be either guide or obstacle to understanding. Both empathy and
countertransference are exposed during the consultation. Impediments
to understanding the patient's communications may be mundane enough
to be discussed with the consulter. When deeply anchored problems intrude, their psychogenetic investigation must be left to self-analysis, or
the consulter must seek help for them through analytic treatment. Long
years of psychoanalytic teaching have shown that one's consultant
should not also be one's analyst. Finally I added in conclusion that the
conscious placing of oneself mentally into the patient's childhood constellation is especially useful; that, besides the words of the patient, tone,
pause, and gesture must be taken into account; and that visualizing meta-

phors and dreams facilitates understanding because picturing something has advantage of simultaneity over that of perceiving only sequentially. This may, according to the latest neurological findings, also mean that both cerebral hemispheres are called on to function for the benefit of psychotherapeutic understanding (Hoppe, 1975, 1977, 1978).

REFERENCES

Arlow, J. (1963), The supervisory situation. *J. Amer. Psychoanal. Assn.*, 11:576–594.

Beres, D. (1957), Communication in psychoanalysis and the creative process, a parallel. *J. Amer. Psychoanal. Assn.*, 5:408–423.

_____ (1968), The role of empathy in psychoanalysis. *J. Hillside Hosp.*, 4:362–369.

_____ & Arlow, J. (1974), Fantasy identification in empathy. *Psychoanal. Quart.*, 43:26–50.

Bibring, E. (1937), International training committee of the four countries. *Internat. J. Psycho-Anal.*, 18:364–372.

Bloom, H. (1973), *The Anxiety of Influence*. New York: Oxford University Press.

Brenner, C. (1982), *The Mind in Conflict*. New York: International Universities Press.

The Century Dictionary: Encyclopedic Lexicon of the English Language (1914). New York: Century.

DeBell, D. (1963), A critical digest of the literature on psychoanalytic supervision. *J. Amer. Psychoanal. Assn.*, 11:546–575.

Featherton, C. (1978), The institute in the training analysis setting. *Psychiat. J. Univ. Ottawa*, 3(2).

Fleming, J. & Benedek, T. (1966). *Psychoanalytic Supervision (A Method of Clinical Teaching)*. New York: Grune & Stratton.

Freud, S. (1910), "Wild" psycho-analysis. *Standard Edition*, 11:219–227. London: Hogarth Press, 1957.

_____ (1911), The handling of dream-interpretation in psycho-analysis. *Standard Edition*, 12:89–96. London: Hogarth Press, 1958.

_____ (1912a), The dynamics of transference. *Standard Edition*, 12:97–108. London: Hogarth Press, 1958.

_____ (1912b), Recommendations to physicians practising psycho-analysis. *Standard Edition*, 12:109–120. London: Hogarth Press, 1958.

_____ (1913a), On beginning treatment. *Standard Edition*, 12:121–144. London: Hogarth Press, 1958.

_____ (1913b), Observations and examples from analytic practise. *Standard Edition*, 13:191–198. London: Hogarth Press, 1953.

_____ (1914a), Remembering, repeating and working through. *Standard Edition*, 12:145–156. London: Hogarth Press, 1958.

_____ (1915), Observations on transference-love. *Standard Edition*, 12:157–168. London: Hogarth Press, 1958.

_____ (1919), Lines of advance in psycho-analytic therapy. *Standard Edition*, 17:159–168. London: Hogarth Press, 1955.

_____ (1927), Postscript to "The Question of Lay Analysis." *Standard Edition*, 20:251–258. London: Hogarth Press, 1959.

Hoppe, K. (1975), Die Trennung der Gehirnhälften. Ihre Bedeutung für die Psychoanalyse. *Psyche*, 29(10):919–940.

_____ (1977), Split brains and psychoanalysis. *Psychoanal. Quart.*, 2:220–244.

_____ (1978), Split brain and psychoanalytic findings and hypotheses. *J. Amer. Acad. Psychoanal.*, 6:193–213.

Kestemberg, E. (1978), As quoted by Shelley Orgel in his report on the 7th Precongress on Training. *Internat. J. Psycho-Anal.*, 4:511–515.

Kubie, L. (1958), Research into the process of supervision. *Psychoanal. Quart.*, 27:226–236.

Lewin, B. & Ross, H. (1960), *Psychoanalytic Education in the United States.* New York: W. W. Norton.

Peyton, J. (1981), The San Francisco project—the analyst at work. How the analyst works: Thoughts of a supervisor. In: *Becoming a Psychoanalyst: A Study of Psychoanalytic Supervision*, ed. R. Wallerstein. New York: International Universities Press.

Shevrin, H. (1981), On becoming the analyst supervised. In: *Becoming a Psychoanalyst: A Study of Psychoanalytic Supervision*, ed. R. Wallerstein. New York: International Universities Press.

Wallerstein, R. (ed.) (1981), *Becoming a Psychoanalyst: A Study of Psychoanalytic Supervision.* New York: International Universities Press.

Wangh, M. (1966), Original contributions from the first Pan-American Congress for Psychoanalysis. In: *Psychoanalysis in the Americas*, ed. R. E. Litman. New York: International Universities Press.

PART SIX

The
Application
of
Psychoanalysis

Charles Brenner has consistently maintained that compromise formation, arising out of conflict, is present in all of human thought and behavior, not only in neurotic symptoms, traits of character, or disturbed behavior. Therefore, the knowledge derived from the psychoanalytic method can be applied to an understanding of many areas of human endeavor. Leon Balter uses his knowledge of psychoanalytic thought to investigate the complex relationship between religion, the state, and the socialization of children. In a scholarly paper, he focuses on such topics as the function of groups, the role of the charismatic leader, and the nature of idealization.

LEON BALTER

Religion, the State and the Socialization of Children

This paper derives from a previous psychoanalytic investigation of groups led by charismatic leaders (Balter, 1985). That research inferred the group members' group-formative mental processes. Thus, correlations and connections could be made between the *social* and *psychological* levels of conceptualization by relating the various manifest collective phenomena of these groups and the mental processes of the individual members that compose them.[1] The study of charismatically led groups suggests that Religion and the State are highly specific and very specialized charismatically led group formations. Consequently, certain psychological phenomena associated with membership in these two great group formations and certain of their important social characteristics may be brought into close relation. Further, these two near universal human institutions span generations. Children are reared in their context. The psychology of the charismatically led group may then shed light on the socializing processes by which children become members of these institutions. For a discussion of the group psychology of Religion and the State, it is necessary first to review the previous study on the charismatically led group. As will be seen, the psychological theory of the charismatically led group is an elaboration and emendation of Freud's (1921) general theory of group formation.

---

[1] An analogous investigation by the present author (Balter, 1978) has also been made regarding leaderless groups.

THE PSYCHOLOGY OF THE CHARISMATICALLY LED
GROUP

The manifest social structure (morphology) of a charismatically led group is: a set of individuals characterized by their (1) cohesion, (2) uniformity, (3) collective subordination to another individual (the charismatic leader) who is considered by them to be extraordinary and exceptional in comparison to themselves, and (4) equality in their respective relationships to the leader. The members' subordination to the leader is closely correlated with their viewing him as extraordinary. Their cohesion bespeaks their need to be with or associated with one another in some way. Their uniformity consists in their sharing one or several characteristics that express their joint subordination to the leader. The equality they all have in their individual relations to the leader derives from their uniformity of subordination to him.

The psychoanalytic study of the charismatically led group (Balter, 1985) showed that the individual's membership in a charismatically led group corresponds to and is effected by psychological processes that, taken in all their functional significance, may be considered a circumscribed transformation of the superego. These processes have all the regulatory aspects of the superego. But the processes are rearranged and the regulatory aspects are altered to produce an essentially different psychological configuration: the psychological modular unit of a charismatically led group. This unit replaces autonomous superego regulation with integration into a charismatically led group. Put another way, this modular unit and its replicas automatically form a supra-individual entity: a charismatically led group. Two psychological processes make up this modular unit, this circumscribed transformaton of the superego. One pertains to the individual's relation to the charismatic leader, and the other to the individual's relation to the other group members.

The mental process pertaining to the leader is *idealization*. This process corresponds to the individual's viewing the leader as extraordinary and exceptional in comparison to himself. Idealization entails a circumscribed regression of superego functioning, whereby internal autonomous regulatory activity to some extent disappears and its place is taken by an object relation characterized by submissive (i.e. masochistic) orientations of the phallic-oedipal period.[2] The submissive masochistic rela-

---

[2]Presumably, the sphere of superego functioning that undergoes transformation derives developmentally from those masochistic elements of the infantile oedipus complex that become manifest in the member's relation to the charismatic leader. For idealization as a masochistic phenomenon, see: Freud, 1905, p. 150, p. 158 n 1; Freud, 1921, pp. 112–116; Reich, 1940; Greenacre, 1966.

tion to the extraordinary and exceptional individual makes the lender a moral arbiter for his follower and/or the incarnation of the follower's ideals. In either case, the leader assumes regulation (i.e., authority) over the follower. Having placed the leader in this emotional-instinctual position in his mental life, the follower may further make the leader his critical inspector and/or his arbiter of truth. In this manner, the regulatory superego functions of conscience, ideals, and self-observation and the ego function of reality testing[3] may be "externalized" onto the leader by his follower.[4]

The psychoanalytic study of the charismatically led group (Balter, 1985) also showed that the qualities of the leader that the individual member-follower deems extraordinary may be any whatsoever. Further, in order for the transformation in superego functioning to take place, the exceptional attribute(s) of the leader need not be admirable: the leader may just as well be frightening and awesome—or even a mixture of admirable and fearsome. For the study, this necessitated an extension of the term "idealization" to include attitudes in the follower of being fearful of and intimidated by the leader. Correspondingly the sociological term "charisma" had to be extended to include fearsome qualities in the leader.

Just as the superego is a cluster of compromise formations, of resolutions of conflicts (Brenner, 1982), so also the idealizing masochistic object relation to the leader is a resolution of conflict. However, in contrast to the superego, where the conflict resolutions are specifically of the phallic-oedipal period, the idealizing relation to the leader may resolve any sort of conflict.[5] This is, in fact, a special case of Brenner's (1959, p. 214) general formulation that there is no specificity to the kind of conflict resolved by a masochistic orientation.

Parenthetically, it should be noted that some degree of idealization takes place in all groups led by leaders. In this respect, the charismatically led group is not distinguished from all other group-types with leaders. However, in a future communication, the argument will be presented

---

[3]It will be remembered that Freud (1921) originally designated reality testing as a constituent function of the "ego ideal," the psychic agency he later was to call the superego. He was impressed that reality testing undergoes transformations in group phenomena and hypnosis in the same manner as do conscience and ideals.

[4]The oedipal nature of this process in the member often endows the charismatic leader with a sexual attractiveness and/or a threatening dangerousness he might not otherwise possess.

[5]The study (Balter, 1985) showed that idealization may resolve conflict between jealous hatred and fear of losing the hated (and loved) object, conflict between murderous wishes and fear of retaliation by the threatened object, conflict between sexual or aggressive wishes and guilt embodied in criticism by a moralistic individual, conflict between unruly impulses and strict moral standards.

that in all other group-types with leaders, the members identify themselves with the leader to some degree; and also that a reciprocal relation
obtains between the degree of idealization of the leader and the degree of
identification with him.[6] This formulation would then distinguish the
charismatically led group from all other groups with leaders in that there
is *no identification* with the leader and there is *only idealization* of him.
This is the psychological correlate of the group members' considering the
leader exceptional and extraordinary in comparison with themselves.

A conflict resolution entailing a submissive, masochistic relation with
an object perceived as admirable and/or frightening would not, by itself,
impel the individual to cohere with other individuals to form a group under the leadership of that object. However, just as the superego, once it is
formed to resolve oedipal conflict, may subsequently come into conflict
with any sort of motive (Freud, 1924; Brenner, 1982), so the conflict-
resolving, idealizing object relation with the charismatic leader may itself
come into conflict with any sort of motive. This is the psychological situation that motivates the idealing individual to become a member of a
charismatically led group. *The member is a potential disrupter of his own
idealizing conflict resolution.* To preserve the conflict-resolving object relation to the charismatic person, the individual needs to be associated
with others who are similarly submissive to that same exceptional person.
The individual identifies himself with those others, in their masochistic
submission. The individual's *partial identification with the other group
members* is the second group-formative mental process. The member's
identificatory tie to the other members sustains the idealizing conflict resolution he has established for his own idiosyncratic motives. It is this tie
that brings the disparate followers of the charismatic leader together to
form a group.

In the charismatically led group, therefore, a collective (identificatory)
conflict resolution bolsters a tenuous idiosyncratic (masochistic) conflict
resolution. Indeed, membership in a charismatically led group is itself an
indication of tendencies in the member that would disrupt his idealiza-

---

[6]The inverse relationship between *idealization of the leader* and *identification
with the leader* in groups with leaders would be a manifestation of the paradoxical
tension within the superego concerning the dual parental injunctions: "You *ought
to be* like this (like your father)" and "You *may not be* like this (like your father) —
that is, you may not do all that he does; some things are his prerogative" (Freud,
1923, p. 24; italics are Freud's).
Freud addressed identification with the leader at only one point in *Group Psychology and the Analysis of the Ego* (1921, p. 134). In that instance, he pointedly
excluded it as a group-formative mental process. It was Redl (1942) who established identification with the leader as a group-formative mental process.

tion of the leader. Even the desire to belong to a group of like minded adherents to an idealized person indicates the shakiness of the idealization.
Thus, in the strictest sense, the idealization of the leader is the basic *cause*
of the group's formation; but the partial identification of the members
with each other actually *effects* the group formation. Dissimilarity among
the members will endanger their individual idealizations and destroy the
group. The disruption of the idealization (through disillusionment with or
destruction of the leader) will destroy the group.

The social manifestation of the members' group formation is their
sharing one or several common submissive qualities that bespeak their
shared subordination to the same leader. The common submissive quality is the content of their mutual partial identification, and it is specific to
their group. Since each of the members is a potential disrupter of his own
submission to the leader, the content of the mutual partial identification
must embody the defense of reaction formation. Further, the study of the
charismatically led group (Balter, 1985) showed that the member is not
conscious of his own insubordinate attitudes toward the leader. Accordingly, repression is also embodied in the mutual partial identification of
the members. Thus, just as the superego fundamentally embodies the defenses repression and reaction formation against the oedipal wishes of incest and parenticide, so also the mutual partial identification of the members fundamentally embodies the same defenses against the motives to
disrupt the idealizing submission to the leader.

Indeed, just as the superego establishes the oedipal taboos as the core
of the individual's morality, so also the mutual partial identification of the
members establishes a group-specific taboo against insubordination to
the leader. This latter "morality" is not internal, idiosyncratic, and personal, but rather external, stereotyped, and social. This is because each
member needs the conformity of all the others' submission in order,
through partial identification, to bolster his own submission. Any deviation from submission by any other member will thus jeopardize the member's own idealizing conflict resolution. The members' respective relations with the leader must, therefore, be equal in quality and intensity.
For any more antagonistic relation with the leader will naturally be seen
as insubordinate; and any more affectionate relation with the leader will
also be seen as mitigating a subordinate relation to him. There will thus be
very strict conformist pressure among the members to adhere to their
shared mode of submissive expression. In fact, in contrast to leaderless
groups (Balter, 1978), charismatically led groups characteristically mobilize intense aggression against any members who deviate from the group-
specific uniformity of submission. The members themselves will express
that aggression, if the leader himself does not. This intense antidevia-

tionist aggression in the charismatically led group is the homologue of guilt and shame of the superego.

The psychoanalytic study of the charismatically led group (Balter, 1985) showed that the conditions of membership allow for a wide variety individual attitudes and motives. Membership does not depend on which superego function is externalized onto the leader; nor on which attribute of the leader the member deems exceptional and exraordinary; nor on just how the submissive content of mutual identification serves to resolve potentially disruptive intrapsychic conflict about the submissive idealization of the leader. Hence, much heterogeneity among the members may obtain, provided they all idealize the same leader and all share the same submissive characteristic(s) in regard to the leader.[7] Accordingly, charismatically led group formation may organize and mobilize very different kinds of people to act in concert. It is thus of particular utility in desperate and emergency situations.

The psychoanalytic study of the charismatically led group (Balter, 1985) also demonstrated the following properties of this group-type. A charismatically led group may be effected: (1) spontaneously by the members themselves to resolve intrapsychic conflict, (2) through conflict-provoking intimidation by the leader himself, or (3) by a complementary combination of the two. Charismatically led groups may have any sort of manifest pragmatic "group task." Also, the group-formative attributes of the leader and of the other members need not exist in actuality; the member's two conflict resolutions depend on his *belief* that the leader and the other members have the necessary qualities (exceptional and submissive, respectively). It is not even necessary that those persons actually exist — only that the member *believes* they do. Further, contrary to Freud's (1921) assertion, leader-member and member-member relations may be overtly instinctual without destruction of the group's cohesion. It is essential only that the *equality* of the members' respective submissive relationships to the leader be preserved. The leader must have overtly instinctual relations with all the members equally, and/or all the members must have overtly instinctual relations with each other as a shared submission to the charismatic leader.

Because the charismatically led group has no specificity regarding the types of conflict it resolves, it would have near universal appeal as a conflict-resolving device. One would expect it to appear naturally, spon-

---

[7]This is not the case in leaderless groups (Balter, 1978), where the conditions of membership necessitate a high degree of psychological homogeneity among the members. The motives for membership in that group-type are confined very narrowly to the sharing of guilt over very specific circumstances.

taneously, and to be prevalent in human social life. And, in fact, it does and is, in two particularly conspicuous forms: Religion and the State.

RELIGION AS A CHARISMATICALLY LED GROUP

Religion has all the properties of charismatically led groups. Religion differs from all other kinds of charismatically led groups in the nature of the charismatic leader, who is supernaturally omnipotent. Whether the leader is *beyond* Nature or *embodied* in natural phenomena, he is omnipotent in that realm. This quality makes the leader exceptional and extraordinary in comparison to his adherents (worshipers) and is the basis of their idealization. The existence of the leader may be either a concrete reality or a fantasy; but the leader's supernatural power is, by its very essence, in the fantasy life of the worshiper. The worshipers-followers see the supernatural leader as protecting them; but also as commanding them, imposing injunctions upon them. The leader is the externalized correlate of their conscience and/or the embodiment of their ideals. The leader's pronouncements are The Revealed Truth, and the followers experience the leader as being able to look into their hearts and minds. Hence, the leader usually takes over the superego function of self-observation and also the ego function of reality testing. The leader is thus in the emotional-instinctual position of the oedipal parent.[8]

In modern times, much has been made of Religion as being operative in nonreligious adaptive (e.g., political, economic) aspects of social life. However, *new* religions—not having had time to be integrated into general social life—have shown something else. Galanter, Rabkin, Rabkin and Deutsch (1979) reported a significant decrease in neurotic distress in individuals who joined a particular new religion: the Unification Church led by the charismatic Reverend Sun Myung Moon. The "relief effect" of Religion noted by Galanter (1978) may thus be explained by the relative ease with which the charismatically led group resolves a wide variety of conflicts. Religion accomplishes as its basic "task": relief from the pain of psychic conflict through the substitution of neurotic conflict resolution by a group-formative conflict resolution. Religion is probably the oldest "supportive" psychotherapeutic group formation in human existence.

---

[8]In fact, the broad assortment of gods and goddesses that have been conjured up through the ages are incarnations of the oedipal parents. They correspond to most, if not all, of the images that any particular child has of his or her unique oedipal parents (Freud, 1912-1913; Freud, 1927).

Freud (1921) was quite cognizant of the psychotherapeutic and psycho-prophylactic properties of Religion.

> . . . it appears that where a powerful impetus has been given to group formation neuroses may diminish and, at all events temporarily, disappear. Justifiable attempts have also been made to turn this antagonism between neuroses and group formation to therapeutic account. Even those who do not regret the disappearance of religious illusions from the civilized world of today will admit that so long as they were in force they offered those who were bound by them the most powerful protection against the danger of neurosis. Nor is it hard to discern that all the ties that bind people to mystico-religious or philosophico-religious sects and communities are expressions of crooked cures for all kinds of neuroses (p. 142).

Freud's triumphant dismissal of "religious illusions from the civilized world of today" was premature. Indeed, the psychologically palliative effects of Religion are so potent that it may never disappear.

The protective supernaturally omnipotent leader commands the worshipers. Being a fantasy, the supernatural omnipotence of the leader has no intrinsic concrete value to the worshiper. Rather, it supplies the requisite (regressively oedipal) charismatic authority by which the follower-worshiper resolves, through masochistic submission, multifarious, very common and very basic human conflicts — for instance, through obeying the last six of The Ten Commandments.

But the individual's masochistic submission to a supernaturally omnipotent leader does not by itself induce that individual to cohere with others to form a group. The typical collective activities of the religious group, however, give some insight into the motive for the group formation. The disparate religious followers come together to perform collective actions (rituals) and affirm collective beliefs (dogmas). *The rituals and dogmas always express collective submission to the leader.* Further, the members not only feel the inner compulsion to adhere to these collective rituals and affirm these collective beliefs, but also insist that their fellow members do so too. That is, the members identify with each other in their rituals and dogmas. Freud (1907) and Reik (1951) pointed out that these rituals and dogmas are the communal analogues of individual neurotic compulsions and obsessions, respectively. Like their symptomatic counterparts, they embody the defenses repression and reaction formation and thus resolve intraphysic conflict, which constantly threatens to recur. The collective submissive preoccupations of the worshipers with the leader shows that the conflict is always about *the member's tendency to overthrow the leader's conflict-resolving leadership.* The group formation — embodied in the collective submissive rituals and dogmas — may then be seen as supporting and maintaining the individualized submissive conflict resolution of the worshiper.[9]

Each member thus *consciously* experiences the collective conformity to these rituals and dogmas as an imperative; that conformity *unconsciously and defensively* wards off the possibility of renewed intrapsychic conflict and unpleasure. The defensive conformity is enforced by the threat of aggression against any deviant. Because the omnipotence of the leader is a fantasy, the members themselves police their uniformity with remarkable ferocity. Frequently, the antideviationist aggression reaches the intensity of murder. Violation of the supernatural leader's extraordinary status by the member's identification with him is prohibitied as a sacrilege.[10]

THE STATE AS A CHARISMATICALLY LED GROUP

The State—that is, political society—also has all the qualities of charismatically led groups. The term "state" is frequently, and confusingly, used to designate the leadership agency. Most appropriately, "state" refers to the charismatically led group; and the charismatic leader is called "government"—earlier, and more personally, "sovereign." Obviously, governmental leadership was originally personal, as religious leadership has remained. Only recently did it become corporate and relatively abstract. Even so, there is always a tendency to personalize government according to the most prominent person in it. In any case, the leader (or the leadership agency) is omnipotent—not in the sphere of Nature, as with Religion, but rather in the sphere of concrete, coercive force. While the religious leader has all-power over Nature, the State's leader has all-

---

[9]This formulation thus serves to supplement Freud's (1907) remarkable paper on the relation between idiosyncratic (neurotic) obsessive-compulsive phenomena and stereotyped (collective) religious phenomena. Although Freud's analogical discussion of religious practices came very close to that presented here, he did not explain the *collectivity* of religious phenomena. It is primarily this aspect of Religion that the present discussion seeks to explain.

[10]The Greeks called such an identification with the supernatural leader *hybris*. The Jews don't even have a word for it! The identification of the religious member with the supernatural leader *does* occur (to some very attenuated degree) in Christianity—through the injunction to imitate Christ. This modification of Christianity's essence as a charismatically led group had profound consequences throughout its turbulent development and clearly derives from Christ's *dual* nature—being both supernatural (immortal, extraordinarily *unlike* his followers) and also human (mortal, *like* his followers). Freud (1921) discussed this in his "Postscript" to *Group Psychology and the Analysis of the Ego.*

power over people. The idealization of government and its resulting authority are based on this concrete social omnipotence. The reality of that omnipotence is constantly tested; for when the members cease to perceive governmental power as an effective intimidation, the charisma and authority of government immediately dissolve, as do its group-cohering functions.

When government was strictly embodied in a single person, its oedipal nature was more easily seen. Kings and emperors were "fathers" of their people and countries. As government became more complex and differentiated, the personalized oedipal attitudes directed toward it have become less discernible.[11] In its parent-like material, coercive omnipotence, government imposes demands on the members of the State, directs and coordinates (over a greater or lesser sphere of their lives) their relations with each other and with others outside the State. The members of this sort of group, the citizens, have their group-specific submissive uniformities expressed in the State's laws. The equality of the citizens' respective relations to their government, through these laws, is the basis of the concept of *justice.* Conformity to these laws is enforced by the threat of aggression against any deviant. The most dire punishment, usually death, is characteristically reserved for the effort to destroy the group-formation itself—especially through the destruction of the leadership agency (treason). The omnipotence of government, being in the realm of concrete reality, enforces adherence to the laws. The government maintains its extraordinary status through a monopoly of coercive force (Weber, 1921). Accordingly, the members themselves are prohibited from the use of government-like policing and punitive aggression.[12] Govern-

---

[11]The *composition* of the government (of one, few, many, or all—or any combination of these), its mode of *selection* (heredity, election, conquest), its internal *organization* (executive, legislature, judiciary, military, police, and so forth and their mutual relations), as well as the *policies* it establishes, will all very much determine the emotional attitudes its followers direct toward it—or even whether societal cohesion occurs at all. While these factors are crucial in practical politics and are the subject matter of most political-scientific studies, they are nevertheless still variations on a more basic theme: the very existence and nature of political society as a collective entity. From this point of view, one may adopt in the present discussion an artificial blindness to the specific *kind* of government involved, as long as it establishes the social cohesion necessary for the existence of the State.

[12]Vigilantism, *vendetta,* private militias or armed forces, para-military organizations, and dueling are thus essentially antithetical to the State's group formation since they all qualify the government's charismatic (exceptional and extraordinary) position of omnipotence, of paramount coercive force. These institutions are adaptive only in the *absence* of the State.

ment, through the laws and their enforcement, assumes the position of moral arbiter in political society. Thus, not only the ideal function of the superego (referring to the ideal of being omnipotent) but also the super-ego function of conscience, is externalized onto the government. Through its investigative and surveillance agencies, government may take over the citizen's self-observing function. Governments also disseminate information (sometimes as propaganda) to their citizens, and so may also take over their ego function of reality testing—and frequently do.

The "group task" of the State is to provide protection for its members from material danger—from each other and from others outside the group. As Thomas Hobbes (1651) so cogently pointed out: without political society, everyone would suffer "continual feare, and danger of violent death." Natural inequality, random fortune, and the inherent aggressivity of human beings induce individuals to take advantage of each other—as may be seen clearly enough when the fabric of societal organization comes undone. Each person's freedom is a concrete danger to the freedom of all the others. The inherent intrapsychic conflict between the wish for one's own freedom and the fear of the freedom of others is obviated through the collective and equalizing subordination of all individuals under a concretely omnipotent government—aptly called by Hobbes in quasireligious terms "that Mortall God." Still, there is a sharp contrast to Religion. In the latter, the leader's omnipotence—being a fantasy—has no material impact upon the worshiper. It serves only to establish authority for subordinating conflict resolution. In the State, the concrete protective omnipotence of the leader is its essential and central attribute.

Within this societal group formation, each individual, in uniformity with all the others, submissively obeys the laws set down by the government—and so effects a reaction formation. For this keeps under repression the problematic impulses that would disrupt, for the citizen and others, the protective function of the government. The citizen does this through partial identification with other submissive citizens—confident that his fellow citizens similarly, in partial identification with him, inhibit their own aggression toward him. This is the mutual trust implicit in societal cohesion.

Mutual trust between people and the expectation of justice and equal protection diminish abruptly, and very frequently disappear altogether, outside the boundaries of the state to which they belong. Very elaborate, and fundamentally fragile, procedures evolve to obtain security for citizens of one state within the domain of other states. Usually this is done by reciprocal arrangements between two states, each guaranteeing the safety of the other's citizens in its domain. When an individual is not a member of *any* state, he is utterly vulnerable and subject to the wanton aggression of others. History— and contemporary events—show the catastrophes wrought upon individuals by depriving them of their status — and thus their protection — as citizens.

THE MENTALITIES OF RELIGION AND THE STATE

Religion and the State were extremely closely related until very recent human history. The charismatic leader in each has the same basis for charisma: protective omnipotence. In the earliest forms of social organization, the leadership claimed, and was accorded, omnipotence in both the concrete social and the natural realms. Because these two realms were the sources of greatest danger, it was logical to blur the two kinds of protective charisma.[13] Nevertheless, to the extent that the concrete social and natural realms *are* distinguished, so are the two kinds of charismatic leadership. This allows the psychological qualities of each kind of charismatically led group to be seen more clearly.

The Mentality of Religion

Some essential differences between Religion and the State derive from the fact that the protective omnipotence of the former's leader is a fantasy and that of the latter's leader, a necessary concrete reality. In Religion, there are no efforts to test the reality of the leader's omnipotence, because belief in the dogma of its existence establishes the psychological conditions that resolve conflict. In fact, efforts to test the reality of the leader's omnipotence are attacked by the members of a Religion with great vehemence, often violence. This is, after all, a general quality of charismatically led groups: the mobilization of intense aggression against deviation from the group's submissive uniformity. Along with the low valuation put on reality testing, faith is highly prized. This does not, however, depreciate any evidence which tends to *demonstrate* the leader's supernatural power. Indeed, the accounts of witnesses to that omnipotence are highly valued and often are incorporated into the Religion's dogma. This one-sided attitude toward the fantasy of the leader's omnipotence gives religious dogma the psychological qualities of a collective delusion.

Due to the exemption from reality testing, the conflict-resolving fantasies concerning the leader and his protective relation to his followers remain relatively constant — relatively unmodified by experience or by the

---

[13]Even into relatively modern times, the kings of England and France were accorded the supernatural power to cure scrofula ("the King's Evil") through their royal touch (Freud, 1912–13; Bloch, 1961).

exigencies of practical, adaptive, realistic concerns. Thus, religious belief and practice are always extremely stable. When scientific progress calls religious dogmas into question, there is great resistance to giving them up and accepting the scientific view. In the cases of the Copernican, Darwinian and Freudian scientific revolutions, Freud (1916-17) saw such resistance as due to humanity's inveterate narcissism. However, the present discussion points to the conflict-resolving function of Religion, which strongly tends to keep religious beliefs inviolate from scientific incursion.

This also points to the causes of religious *change*. The content of the fantasy of the leader's supernatural power and the cluster of the Religion's specific rituals and dogmas will undergo change only when there are very important *adaptive* problems in the members' mutual relations. But since those relations are integrally connected with the members' uniform (submissive and protected) relation to the leader, the dogma about the leader must also come into question. Hence, controversies over religious doctrine frequently mask truly crucial pragmatic issues in collective life, very often in the economic realm.[14] Nor should cynical motives be attributed to the religious disputants—as if they were duplicitously hiding baser motives in their controversies over religious ideology. If their conflict-resolving religious uniformities drastically interfere with material and concrete adaptation, those uniformities and even the particular protective relation to the leader may change. If not, new sorts of religious organization will arise, and some will eventually be selected for their conflict-resolving capacities in the changed environmental circumstances. Given the psychology of charismatically led groups, such a process of revision

---

[14]This may be seen in the correlation between the parallel breakdown of slavery and of paganism in the classical world and the parallel emergence of Christianity and of feudalism (Anderson, 1974), and between the parallel disruption of the Catholic Church and of feudalism in the Middle Ages and the parallel emergence of Protestantism and of capitalism (Weber, 1920; Tawney, 1926). The mutually influential relation between the prevailing Religion and the prevailing economic system must be profound, intimate, and very complex. Clearly, the socialization functions of Religion importantly affect the ontogenetic development of children so that they become adults who participate in common economic activity in a stereotyped manner. Historical explanations correlating changes in Religion and economy must then take into account not only the general laws of childhood psychological development but also the manner in which Religion enters into and determines the particular expression of those general developmental laws. Psychoananlysis has provided the most powerful theory of childhood psychological development. The present psychoanalytic study of Religion attempts to describe how Religion influences individual and social development—that is, socialization.

will be both emotionally painful and extremely aggressive. History has borne this out.

The Mentality of the State.

As already indicated, in the State, conflict resolution depends on the government's demonstrating its ability to protect the citizens from each other and from others. The members-citizens constantly test the reality of that ability. This orientation toward the leader and its qualities effects the nature of the mental life associated with membership in the State. It is attuned to current, immediate, practical, realistic concerns. Issues of means and ends, costs and benefits, advantage and disadvantage are more relevant in the State than in Religion. The contents of political concerns and activity are much more fluctuating and therefore more unstable. While the mental content in Religion corresponds closely to *unconscious* fantasy life, in that it is not modified by experience, mental content in the State corresponds more closely to *conscious* fantasy life. It shows the constraints of adaptation and problem solving much more forcefully. Religion, with its fundamental preoccupation with the leader's dominance over the natural world, is more concerned about Nature and scientific theories than is the State. Political interests revolve more around "what works" than around "what is." When the State loses its flexible responsiveness to fluctuating reality—as sometimes happens in modern totalitarian states—political life approximates the more static forms of Religion. One sees the belief in a transcendent (if not strictly supernatural) power that guides the destiny of the world and humanity, a greater emphasis on dogmatic ideological assertions and a greater participation in collective rituals.

The previous discussion points to the conditions of *change* in the State—that is, in the character of the charismatic leader (government), in the group-specific uniformities (expressed in laws), and/or in the group task (the modes of collective protection). To the degree that the State's social and material environment and/or the concrete relations between its members fluctuate any or all of those three aspects of this charismatically led group must change also. In contrast to Religion, the correlation between change in the State and change in material and social conditions is direct, obvious, and relatively simple. Since the State is a charismatically led group and therefore resolves intrapsychic conflict, changes in the organization of the State are attended by great emotional pain and often violent aggression, just as are changes in Religion.

These two groups, both founded on the charisma of protective omnipotence, tend to cooperate with one another. Relations evolve between them that enhance the survival of each. The State's leader has concerete power, which Religion's does not have. Religion has relative stability, which the State does not have. Accordingly, the two forms of social organization evolve symbiotic relations of many sorts, but all share the same basic mutuality: government will support the power of Religion's leader in the concrete world of people and things; and Religion will support the stability of the State by pronouncing the latter's organization as sacred (that is, affirmed and protected supernaturally).

THE RELIGIOUS AND POLITICAL SOCIALIZATION OF CHILDREN

The Availability of Religion and the State to Children

The two great charismatically led groups, Religion and the State — one devoted to psychic comfort, the other to physical survival — are extremely effective in their organizing capacities, as a result of their broad ability to resolve intrapsychic conflict and the central importance of their tasks. They thus tend to endure longer than most other groups — charismatically led or otherwise. *They usually endure long enough for children to be born to the members.*

These two great charismatically led groups may then be available for conflict resolution *by children.* Although the ability to identify with other members clearly antecedes the phallic-oedipal phase, the ability to form a masochistic oedipal object relation with the leader obviously can come into being only at that time of life. Further, contrary to Freud's (1923, 1924) notion that the infantile oedipus complex is normally "destroyed" with the formation of the superego and the onset of latency, it is generally recognized now that the infantile oedipus complex maintains a latent existence and manifests itself through numerous derivatives — not least of which is the superego itself (Brenner, 1982) — and makes possible the regressive recurrence of oedipal object relations (and thus conflicts about them). These facts suggest a hypothesis upon which the following discussion of the socialization of children is based: that beginning with the phallic-oedipal phase, children have the *emotional-instinctual* basis with which to resolve conflict through membership in Religion and the State; and that the child must also have the *cognitive* capacity (depending on ego development) to comprehend the omnipotent leader's nature and his protective-authoritative relation to the members. Both the psychosexual and the ego-developmental factors are the necessary and sufficient prerequisites for the child to become, psychologically, a member of a religion and/or of a state.

According to this hypothesis, the earliest age when charismatically led group formation takes place (appropriate to the members' cognitive ability) would be during the phallic-oedipal phase. And indeed Edith Buxbaum (1945) observed that group formation first takes place with any stability around the age of four and is charismatically led (typically by a teacher in a school setting). In the present study, it is important to note how the child's psychological membership in Religion and the State comes about during or after the phallic-oedipal period.

Resolution of Oedipal Conflict Through Religion

The oedipal child with his oedipal conflicts, or the postoedipal child with his regressively reactivated oedipal conflicts, derives psychic relief from conflict through membership *specifically in the Religion of his parents* – to the extent that he is able to comprehend the leader's omnipotent nature and protective relation to the members-followers. The child's rivalry conflicts concerning his parents will be resolved to some degree when the child and the parents become equal in common subordination to the same omnipotent, supernatural leader – a leader who protects and directs his followers equally. The child will feel protected from the feared aggression of his rivalrous parents and will feel them protected from his own magical aggression.[15] On the other hand, the child's oedipal desire to be like his parents, to have what they have, will also be gratified through his membership in their Religion. Membership in his parents' Religion will thus be a compromise formation resolving oedipal conflict.

Resolution of Oedipal Conflict Through the State

As stated earlier, the mentality of the State is much more influenced by reality testing, adaptation and pragmatic problem solving than is the mentality of Religion. Because of this, children tend to develop the capability for utilizing Religion for conflict resolution earlier than they do the state. Given this difference, analogous considerations nevertheless obtain concerning the child's psychological induction into membership in the parents' State. The defensive and oedipally gratifying equality, being jointly subordinate with one's parents to the same omnipotent temporal leadership agency, will be of positive value to the child.

---

[15]Children's prayers typically ask for protection – for themselves *and* for their parents.

But other attractions also accrue to the State for the child, owing to the great revolution in human social organization that took place when governmental power extended into the family and, in selected spheres, overrode parental authority there. The child's conflict-resolving membership in the State has since been based on political reality—insofar as the child is cognitively able to perceive that reality. Governmental intervention directly effects the concrete power relations among family members, as demonstrated, for example, in government's regulation of marriage. Parental union is no longer, in fantasy or in fact, the prerogative of the parents themselves. It must take place under governmental control, with governmental approval and subject to governmental prohibition. This cannot but emotionally impress the oedipal or postoedipal child with the government's power regarding himself and his parents. This impression is accentuated by the fact that governmental approval (legality) of his parents' marriage effects the child's own "legitimacy." The legitimacy often ensures not only the child's future position in the State as a protected citizen-member, but also that the child will, in the future, inherit his parents' estate, take his parents' place.[16] The child's psychological membership in this charismatically led group is thus a resolution of his own current or regressively revived oedipal conflicts. This membership is a compromise formation, for it reconciles the child to the union of his own parents, while guaranteeing the child their prerogatives in the future.

Governmental power invades the family in other areas also. Government legislates the welfare and education of its future adult citizens. This inevitably entails the curbing of the child's will, the imposition of immediate frustration upon his impulses. But frustration will become more palatable when the child can comprehend it as a submissive obligation of State membership, with equalizing frustration for the parents, whose retaliatory and punitive impulses (fantasized or real) he fears and whose gratification (fantasized or real) he hates. Further, the child—under the influence of the manifest or latent oedipus complex—imagines that his parents do not favor his aspirations to adult prerogatives. Accordingly, the child will accept the curbing of his own will as a group member by the charismatic government when he is sure that his future in the State, his material and political patrimony, is thus being prepared.[17]

---

[16]Psychoanalytic clinical practice amply demonstrates the (often intense) oedipal significance of patrimony in general and of concrete inheritance in particular. Recourse to the guarantees and arbitration of the omnipotent government is extremely frequent.

[17]The preceding shows the validity of the argument in *The Crito* where Plato stated that the citizen's abject obedience to the dictates of government and to its laws comes from the fact that the government regulated his parents' marriage, his welfare, and his education.

Membership and the Superego

The developmentally dominant or regressively revived infantile oedipal conflicts may be resolved either in individualized ways (most notably through superego formation) or in group-formative ways (most notably through membership in Religion, the State, or both). Superego formation establishes internal, individual, and idiosyncratic morality and ideals for the child — reflecting the uniqueness of his biological endowment, his personal past development, and the peculiarities of his parents and his familial constellation. The other form of oedipal conflict resolution studied here is characterized by its external, collective, and stereotypical morality and ideals — reflecting the two great charismatically led group formations to which children are introduced by virtue of their parents' affiliation with them. Religion and the State may resolve oedipal conflict in the child during the phallic-oedipal period (at the expense of subsequent superego formation) and after it (at the expense of established superego functioning). Thus, what might have become or been the idiosyncratically formed conscience and ideal function become instead the group-specific morality and ideals. *In the child, membership in Religion and the State is a substitute for superego functioning.*

This formulation provides the structural basis for distinguishing between *autonomous* moral and ideal systems (uniquely personal, uninfluenced in their origins by social conditions and producing no charismatically led group affiliation) and *socially determined* moral and ideal systems (employing the two group-formative mental processes of charismatically led groups, bespeaking charismatically led group affiliation).[18] This formulation also provides a structural basis to differentiate *moral* anxiety (fear of superego condemnation) from *social* anxiety (fear of social aggression visited upon deviation from a great charismatically led group). Finally, this formulation elaborates to some degree Freud's (1933) too sketchy description of cross-generational transmission of standards and values.

> . . . a child's superego is in fact constructed on the model not of its parents but of its parents' superego; the contents which fill it are the same and it becomes the vehicle of tradition and of all the time-resisting judgments of value which have propagated themselves in this manner from generation to generation. . . . Mankind never lives entirely in the present. The past, the tradition of the race and of the people, lives on in the ideologies of the superego, and yields only slowly to the influences of the present and to new changes. . . . (p. 67)

---

[18]See the remarks of Hartmann and Loewenstein (1962, pp. 167, 171, 177–178) in this regard.

This study explains "tradition" (the correspondence of one generation's values and standards with the previous generation's) not by the child's superego identification with his parents' superego, but rather by the child's membership in his parents' religion and state, as a *substitute* for superego functioning. Also, "the ideologies of the superego"—an idea that seems to mix the individual and social levels of conceptualization—may be replaced with "the ideologies of the parents' religion and state." Further, tradition's slow rate of change, noted here by Freud, is explained by the continuity of Religion and the State across generations and by the ease of childhood psychological membership in those institutions.

The foregoing discussion indicates in a general fashion how the child takes on membership in his parents' religion and/or state. That process does not occur through deliberate indoctrination by the parents or by any established institutions. Rather, membership in precisely *the parents'* great charismatically led groups is a mode of oedipal conflict resolution *sui generis.* It would occur within the child automatically whenever oedipal conflicts arose, in accordance with the child's own motives and devoid of parental guidance. Needless to say, any encouragement and educative ministrations by the child's parents or their institutional substitutes will only strengthen an affiliating process that originates and proceeds on the child's own, largely unconscious, initiative. This is not to undervalue the family as the crucible of the religious and societal socialization processes. Rather, this discussion elucidates the psychological group-formative processes by which that socialization is accomplished within the context of the family.

LIFE-LONG MEMBERSHIP IN RELIGION AND THE STATE

Permanent Membership

The discussion so far has dealt with how the child's membership in Religion and the State help to resolve his oedipal conflicts. But the utility of these groups for conflict resolution is not confined to oedipal conflicts. The groups continue to be present and available beyond childhood. Once membership has been established in childhood, possibly as early as the phallic-oedipal phase, these same groups may be used thereafter by the individual to resolve nonoedipal conflicts, developmental or not. The course of life presents a myriad of occasions when recourse to the justice and protection of governnment, or to the solace and hope of supernatural intervention, will resolve intrapsychic conflict. The special protected relation to the omnipotent charismatic leader, through membership in the group led by that leader, will entrench that group membership within the psychic functioning of the individual even more strongly as time goes on. The membership will be a constant participant in the member's psychic economy, a conflict-resolving fixture of his personality. The submissive characteristics peculiar to the group will become structured in the member's character. For this reason, lifelong membership in specific religions and states is associated with particular characterologic qualities of their members. Those characterologic qualities will channel as well as limit the direction of political, economic, and cultural activities on the collective, and on the individual, level.

Also, because multiple conflicts, developmental or not, are resolved through enduring membership in Religion and/or the State, the importance of that membership to the individual will far outweigh many other motives — gratifications, values, standards, defenses, and adaptations — which contradict that membership. Deference to those contradictory motives would disrupt the membership and so evoke again a whole series of developmental and other conflicts undergone and resolved by the member during the previous course of his life. This sort of membership will accordingly mobilize the member to great sacrifice, pain, and effort because the psychological consequences of its disruption would be so dire. Lifelong religious adherents and native-born citizens do go to extreme lengths to follow the injunctions of their leaders and the norms of their groups. Their submission is subjectively experienced as volitional when no other, or merely weak, motives contradict it; when strong contradictory motives do exist, the submission is consciously experienced as a "duty." In fact, the submission is neither volitional nor dutiful. It is, in the strictest clinical sense, *compulsive*. It is a form of behavior that maintains conflict resolutions such that if the behavior is not enacted, intense psychic pain will result.

Vicissitudes of Membership

Memberships in Religion and the State do not have to persist. They may become undone. If they do, then the conflicts resolved by them have ceased to exist (e.g., as in some adolescent conflicts); or, if the conflicts persist, they will have to be solved by other means, such as by individualized forms of conflict resolution (e.g., neurosis, changes in character traits) or by other group-formative modes. But group membership may also continue to perform its conflict-resolving function in the psychic economy and nevertheless become unconscious — that is, for whatever reason, it may undergo repression and become a *latent* fixture in mental functioning. This is analogous to latent character traits and to latent child-

hood object relations, both of which are structuralized conflict resolutions, stable compromise formations that contain the impulses, painful affects, and defenses of childhood. Both are unearthed only after extensive
psychoanalytic work. In an exactly analogous manner, childhood group
memberships in Religion and the State—each of which contains an
(idealizing) object relation *and* an ego "trait" (by mutual partial identification)—may become and remain unconscious and still perform their
conflict-resolving function. The result is unconscious group membership.

However, the persistence of childhood group membership in Religion
and the State may take a form somewhere between complete conscious
continuity from childhood and complete repression. Various aspects of
the membership may be repressed, while others remain conscious and
manifestly active. What is and what is not repressed are determined by
the adaptive and defensive needs, standards, values, and morals that develop subsequent to childhood. There may be a condescending, nostal-
gic, embarrassed, or even guilty memory of the childhood membership.
Its manifest remnants may be relegated to a relatively obscure and private
corner of the member's adult life. The presence of seemingly vestigial residues of membership is often rationalized in more or less inadequate
ways.

The intermediate adult forms of childhood membership in Religion are
various. There may be continuing belief in the leader's supernatural
omnipotence, but without any conscious compulsion to adhere to the rituals characteristic of the religious group. Or conscious belief in the
leader's omnipotence (even existence) may seem to be gone, but the soli-
darity with the religious group may continue—with or without a feeling of
obligation to share the group-specific rituals and dogmas. Or some of the
religious group's shared qualities may be consciously retained, and others
dropped. In these cases, it would be a mistake to take the manifest, conscious aspects of adult religious membership as all that remains of the
original childhood one. The membership is an organic whole, composed
of the two group-formative mental processes specific to charismatically
led groups. In any given instance, psychoanalytic investigation would, in
principle, be able to demonstrate the continued unconscious existence
of the other aspects of the original childhood membership. In fact,
Brenner (1983) wrote about this phenomenon from another vantage
point and showed this to be so. Regarding the persistence of religious orientations, he cited

> data obained from the analyses of atheistic patients living in societies which
> are not officially atheistic, but in which large segments of the populace are,
> in fact, atheists. [The conclusion] suggested by such data from this source as
> are available is that *religious beliefs tend to persist, though disavowed. Often*

enough the same thing, or something similar, is true for religious practices as well as for religious beliefs. For example, atheistic patients in modern society react to religious holidays as do those who professedly believe in their significance. They dream of babies at Christmastime and of infanticide and parricide at the time of Passover and Easter. They call on God to bless themselves and to curse others. They enjoy sacred music—a Bach cantata or a mass by Mozart, for instance—while professing disinterest in the words for which the music was written. Not infrequently they attend religious services which, at the same time, they sincerely maintain have no meaning for them whatsoever. In short, they seem to have adopted at least some of the religious beliefs and practices of the society in which they were born and raised, while consciously disavowing both belief and practice. In attempting to assess the significance of such data it must be kept in mind that they come in large part, if not entirely, from the analyses of *persons who were exposed to some kind of religious influence during their childhood or even to formal religious instruction* [p. 242; italics added].

Analogous phenomena obtain in the realm of membership in the State. Adulthood may bring a more skeptical, critical, or even cynical view of government, its wisdom or, ultimately, its omnipotence. Nevertheless, even with those attitudes being conscious and manifest, modern and sophisticated citizens may, under stress, adopt an attitude toward their government that has all the naiveté, gullibility and trust which characterize childhood membership in the State. That is, they view as axiomatic the government's charismatic omnipotence (it takes over the ideal function), its charismatic moral rectitude (it takes over the function of conscience), its charismatic surveillance (it takes over the function of self-observation), its charismatic wisdom and sincerity (it takes over the function of reality testing).

The foregoing was demonstrated in an unpublished study carried out by The Colloquium of Psychoanalysts and Social Scientists at The New York Psychoanalytic Institute (1977-1978). Several sets of randomly chosen adults were interviewed to ascertain their attitudes about nuclear war, nuclear armament, and nuclear disarmament. The subjects were well informed and mature. They shared the view that the United States government should have preeminent nuclear might (i.e., should be omnipotent) to protect them from foreign aggression, especially from the Soviet Union. They also believed that the government's current policy of escalation of nuclear weapons did *not* lead to such protection; that, in fact, given the Soviet Union's evident desire for nuclear parity, the government's policy made the potential for nuclear war even greater. This rather sophisticated view of the matter led to a conflict between their desire for their government to be protectively omnipotent and their desire to avoid nuclear war. The subjects tended to use three defense mechanisms to ward off anxiety about nuclear war: denial, dissociation, and avoidance. Of interest here is that the latter two defenses involved adopting a childlike view of the government, corresponding to childhood membership in the State.

> *Dissociation.* The conscious realization of the objective situation is met with a state of intellectual and/or cognitive confusion. Practical solutions in terms of governmental policy or personal and political activity seem without relevance, efficacy or reason. This mental process is bolstered by highly technical military and esoteric political information supplied to the public by governmental officials and agencies. Correspondingly, the government, whose efficacy to prevent war is acknowledged to be faulty, becomes the repository of war-preventing expertise. The anxiety allaying confusion allows the ceding of policy-making power to governmental agencies. *Avoidance.* The perception of objective danger is met by a withdrawal from engagement with it. The most frequent manifestation of this mental process is the assertion of powerlessness in face of the imminence of nuclear war. This mental process is bolstered by governmental disclosures to the public of very powerful weapons in domestic (and foreign) arsenals. Correspondingly, the government, whose escalating policy to prevent war is acknowledged to be faulty, becomes the fantasized repository of war-preventing might so long as it keeps escalating [New York Psychoanalytic Institute, 1977-1978].

Partially or completely repressed childhood memberships in Religion and the State bespeak a latent tendency to become a fanatically loyal and enthusiastic *adult* member of the childhood Religion or State. This occurs under critical circumstances that induce regression—for example, massive and acute psychic or physical trauma, economic or social catastrophe, drug-induced mental states, chronic material deprivation, or even developmental stress such as puberty or menopause. Such phenomena are common. The regressive activation of childhood charismatically led group memberships is a special case of a more general psychic tendency to regress to previously successful modes of ego mastery (Arlow and Brenner, 1964, p. 80).

SUMMARY AND CONCLUSIONS

Conceptualized psychologically, membership in a charismatically led group is a conflict resolving, circumscribed regression in the superego that entails a masochistic oedipal relation to the leader and a mutually identificatory relation with each of the other members. Religion and the State are not psychologically unique group formations. Rather, they share the same basic psychological properties—those of charismatically led groups in general. They are highly specialized charismatically led groups that are devoted, respectively, to psychic comfort and to physical survival. Their broad conflict-resolving appeal causes them to endure sufficiently long for their members to reproduce and raise offspring. Possibly as early as the phallic-oedipal phase, children avail themselves of these groups for conflict resolution. In so doing, they psychologically become group members and therefore perform the socialization process on their own initiative. Since Religion and the State continue to be available for conflict resolution during the remainder of life, membership in these groups becomes integrated into psychic functioning so importantly that members will sacrifice much, often their very lives, to preserve their membership and their group. This compulsive "reciprocal altruism" (see Trivers, 1971) among the members enhances the group's survival. Thus, the durability of these group formations makes possible the internal recruitment of children, which in turn further strengthens the groups' capacity to endure. For these reasons, Religion and the State are forms of social organization that dispose to individual and collective survival *on the group level* through the psychology of the charismatically led group.

This discussion indicates how human *biological* endowment (which organically determines the infantile oedipus complex and superego formation [Freud, 1905, 1924; Freeman, 1967]) finds expression in human *sociality* (Religion and the State) through the *psychological* mediation of charismatically led group formation.

REFERENCE

Anderson, P. (1974), *Passages from Antiquity to Feudalism*. London: Verso Editions.

Arlow, J. & Brenner, C. (1964), *Psychoanalytic Concepts and the Structural Theory*. New York: International Universities Press.

Balter, L. (1978), Leaderless groups. *Internat. Rev. Psycho-Anal.*, 5:331–350.

_____. (1985), The charismatically led group: The mental processes of its members. In: *The Psychoanalytic Study of Society*, ed. A Muensterberger, L. B. Boyer, & S. A. Grolnick. Hillsdale: NJ: The Analytic Press, 173–215.

Bloch, M. (1961), *The Royal Touch: Sacred monarchy and Scrofula in England and France* (trans. J. E. Anderson). London: Routledge & Kegan Paul, 1973.

Brenner, C. (1959), The masochistic character: Genesis and treatment. *J. Amer. Psychoanal. Assn.*, 7:197–226.

_____. (1982), The concept of the superego: A reformulation. *Psychoanal. Quart.*, 51:501–525.

_____ (1983), *The Mind in Conflict.* New York: International Universities Press.

Buxbaum, E. (1945), Transference and group formation in children and adolescents. *The Psychoanalytic Study of the Child,* 1:351–365.

Freeman, D. (1967), Totem and taboo: a reappraisal. *The Psychoanalytic Study of Society. Vol. 4,* ed. W. Muensterberger, L. B. Boyer, & S. A. Grolnick. New York: International Universities Press.

Freud, S. (1905), Three essays on the theory of sexuality. *Standard Edition,* 7:130–245. London: Hogarth Press, 1953.

Freud, S. (1907), Obsessive acts and religious practices. *Standard Edition,* 9:115–127. London: Hogarth Press, 1959.

Freud, S. (1912-13), Totem and taboo. *Standard Edition,* 13:1–164. London: Hogarth Press, 1953.

Freud, S. (1916-17), Introductory lectures on psychoanalysis. *Standard Edition,* 15 & 16. London: Hogarth Press, 1963.

Freud, S. (1921), Group psychology and the analysis of the ego. *Standard Edition,* 18:69–143. London: Hogarth Press.

Freud, S. (1923), The ego and the id. *Standard Edition,* 19:12–59. London: Hogarth Press, 1961.

Freud, S. (1924), The dissolution of the Oedipus complex. *Standard Edition,* 19:173–179, 1961.

Freud, S. (1927), The future of an illusion. *Standard Edition,* 21:3–56. London: Hogarth Press, 1961.

Freud, S. (1933), New introductory lectures on psycho-analysis. *Standard Edition,* 22:3–182. London: Hogarth Press, 1964.

Galanter, M. (1978), The "relief effect": A sociobiological model for neurotic distress and large-group therapy. *Amer. J. Psychiat., 135*:588–591.

_____ Rabkin, R., Rabkin, J., & Deutsch, L. (1979), The "Moonies": A psychological study of conversion and membership in a contemporary religious sect. *Amer. J. Psychiat.* 136:165–170.

Greenacre, P. (1966), Problems of overidealization of the analyst and of analysis: Their manifestations in the transference and countertransference relationship. *The Psychoanalytic Study of the Child* 27:360–400.

Hartmann, H. & Loewenstein, R. (1962), Notes on the superego. In: *Papers on Psychoanalytic Psychology,* ed. H. Hartmann, E. Kris, & R. Lowenstein. New York: International Universities Press, 1964.

Hobbes, T. (1651), *Leviathan.* London: Oxford University Press, 1909.

New York Psychoanalytic Institute (1977-1978), Project on attitudes toward nuclear war by the Colloquium of Psychoanalysts and Social Scientists (reported by Leon Balter, M.D.) Unpublished.

Redl, F. (1942), Group emotion and leadership. *Psychiatry,* 5:573–596.

Reich, A. (1940), A contribution to the psychoanalysis of extreme submissiveness in women. *Psychoanal. Quart.* 9:470–480.

Reik, T. (1951), *Dogma and Compulsion.* New York: International Universities Press.

Tawney, R. (1926), *Religion and the Rise of Capitalism.* New York: Harcourt, Brace.

Trivers, R. (1971), The evolution of reciprocal altruism. *Quart. Rev. Biol.,* 46: 36–57.

Weber, M. (1920), *The Protestant Ethic and the Spirit of Capitalism* (trans. T. Parsons). New York: Scribner's, 1952.

Weber, M. (1921), Politics as a vocation. In: *Max Weber: Essays in Sociology,* (ed. and trans.) H. H. Gerth & C. W. Mills. New York: Oxford University Press, 1958.

Author Index

Numbers in *italics* denote pages with bibliographic information.

Subject Index

(cont'd) Anxiety
in women, Horney on, 74-79
genital, 79
infantile, 99
infantile unpleasure and later, 12-13
moral vs. social, 410
operations of ego against, 98-99
over responsibility for patient, 378-79
research, 321, 322
separation, 99, 347, 348
shifting investment in object representations as defense against, 309-13
signal, 15
Apprentice system of teaching, 378
Armature of psychoanalytic theory and
method, 89-106
analytic attitude, 22, 91-95, 217
anxiety, operation of ego against, 98-99
conflict, focus on, 96-98
insight, 100-102
judging change against, 90-91
reconstruction, 100-101
therapeutic alliance, 22-24, 92-95, 101,
246-47
transference, 99-100, 101
Assessment of psychoanalytic process,
problems of, 211-12
Association, free, 23-24, 53, 95, 214, 246,
248
Attitude, analytic, 22, 91-95, 217
"Attitudinal object concept," 183, 186
Autonomy
ego, theories of, 131-32, 133
primary and secondary, 163

B

Becoming a Psychoanalyst (Wallerstein),
378
"Benevolent neutrality," 234
Biological perspective of Horney, 78-79
Biology, affect's relation to, 195-96
Bisexuality, Horney on, 77-78
Bodily sensations, representational value of,
120-21
Borderline cases, 97-98, 212, 238
Boston City Hospital, 30-32
Boston Psychopathic Hospital, 30

C

"Calamities" of childhood, 14-15
Castration complex, 99
Brenner on, 15
examples of, 288, 289, 293, 297, 326-46
in women, Horney on, 74-79
Catharsis, 52-53, 324
"Character and Anal Erotism" (Freud), 155
Character formation, Freud on, 155
"Charge of affect," 192, 194
Charismatically led group, 393-416
manifest social structure of, 394
membership in, 396-99
morality of, 397
properties of, 398
psychology of, 394-99
religion and state as, 399-404
life-long membership in, 411-15
mentalities of, 404-7
socialization of children and, 406n,
407-11
"Choice" conflicts, 96-98
Choice of analyst, 92
Cholin derivatives, electrical activities of
cerebral cortex and, 31
Christianity as charismatically led group,
401n
"Civilization and Its Discontents" (Freud),
158
Clarification, insight through, 265
"Classical" analyst, credo of, 1
Classical model of psychoanalysis, 323
Climate, supervisory, 380-83
Clinical examples
alternative ways of understanding, 219-21
of castration complex, 288, 289, 293,
297, 326-46
of complicated perception organized by
compromise formation, 136
of countertransference, 237-41, 386-88
of homophonic transformation, 115-18
of penis envy, 289-97
of transference relationships, 304-18
of ubiquity of compromise formation,
138-48
of understanding signs and symbols,
114-22
Clinical observation, relation of theoretical

Cs. system, 169
Culture
   devaluation of women in, 75-76
   Horney on, 75-76, 80, 82
   sublimation of instinct to higher, 154-56
Cure
   relation of insight to, 275
   transference, 223-24
"Current Status of the Theory of the
   Superego, The" (Goodman), 365

D

Death instinct, 8-9
Decision, agent of, 102
"Defense and Defense Mechanisms"
   (Brenner), 17
Defenses
   A. Freud on, 160
   balance between drives and, 362-63
   Brenner on, 15-18, 169, 171
   countertransference, 241
   idealization, 94, 394-97, 402
   importance of analyzing, 42
   "repertory of," 17-18
   transference, 284-85
   See also Perceptual distortions
Defensive conformity, 400-401. See also
   Charismatically led group
Defensive intellectualization, 249
Defensive style, insight and, 278
Deficits, treatment of, 97-98
Depression, 14-15, 43-45
"Depression, Anxiety and Affect Theory"
   (Brenner), 13
"Depressive Affect, Anxiety, and Psychic
   Conflict in the Phallic-Oedipal Phase"
   (Brenner), 14
Developmental reconstructive approach,
   285-86
"Dilemma" conflicts, 96-98
Discharge, silence in service of, 287
Distortions, perceptual. See Perceptual
   distortions
Dogma, 400-401, 404, 405
Dora case, 156
"Draft E. How Anxiety Originates" (Freud),
   180

Dream(s), 108-12
   as compromise formations, 20-21, 108-9
   formation in Freud's adaptation model,
      70
   interpretation, Brenner's reconsideration
      of, 20-21
   manifest content of, 108-9
   regression in, 112
   representation, 115-22, 123
   work, 108, 113, 123
"Dreams in Clinical Psychoanalytic
   Practice" (Brenner), 20
Drives
   Brenner on, 7-10
   distinction between drive derivatives and,
      169
   as exclusively psychological, 168-69
   expression and gratification, ego
      development and, 10
   in libido theory, 71
   mindless, 163-64
   perceptual distortion and balance
      between defenses and, 362-63
Dual drive theory, 160
Dual instinct theory, 156
Dual role of supervisor, 380, 383
Duty, experience of, 412

E

Economic system, religion and, 405-6
Education, psychoanalytic. See Supervisory
   process
Ego
   autonomy, 131-32, 133
   Brenner's use of term, 15
   consolidation of, 201-2
   defenses against id offered by, 15
   development, drive expression and
      gratification and, 10
   Freud on characteristics of actual, 365
   functions, 10, 17-18, 164
      integrative, 266
      reality principle and, 131, 133-34
      of reality testing, 367-68
      self-observation, 250-52, 270-71
      transference as, 302
   ideal, 156, 366, 395n

(cont'd) Sublimation
  internalization and, 167
  neutralization and, 162-65, 167
  psychic energy and, 156-58, 163-64, 165
  sexual gratification and, 165-66
  stability of, 165
  superego and, 163
  in terms of object relations theory, 166
  therapeutic task and, 161
Submission to leader, 394-98, 400, 402,
    403, 412
Successful analysis, lack of insight and,
    277-78
Suggestion, 224-25, 257
Superego
  Brenner on, 10-11, 169-70
  circumscribed transformation of, 394-95,
    397, 398
  confusion over, 264-65
  development, 368-71
    culture and, 369
    parents and significant objects and,
      363, 368-69
  distinction between moral and other
    conflicts, 370-71
  externalization onto government, 403
  Freud on functions of, 365-66
  as group of compromise formations, 42
  "ideologies" of, 411
  importance of analyzing, 42
  intrasystemic conflict with ego, 363
  introjection of analyst as good object in,
    56-57
  language of interpretive intervention
    attracting, 258
  membership in religion and State and,
    410-11
  reality testing, role in, 353-74
  repression, role in creation of conditions
    for, 369
  sublimation and, 163
Supervisory process, 377-89
  anxiety and, 378-79, 382
  apprenticeship, 378
  climate of, 380-83, 388
  countertransference, recognition of, 385,
    386-88
  empathy, conscious perception of, 385-86
  "infantilization," 380, 388
  primary goal in, 385

reporting on analytic sessions, 383-85
student, character of, 379
supervisor
  dual role of, 380, 383
  overestimation of, 380, 382
  safety of position, 382
supervisory pact, 381
technical methods, 388
"Supervisory Situation, The" (Arlow), 377
Surface, choice of, 253, 255-60
Symbol formation, 112-14
Symbolic interpretation, 56
Symbolism, universal, 122
Symbols in structural theory. See under
    Structural theory
Symptoms
  formation of, Freud's theory of, 264
  hysterical, Freud's first model of dynamics
    of, 51-55
  insight and diminution of, 277
  symbolic reference to, 114-22
Synonymy, 113, 119, 120-21

T

Taboo, group-specific, 397
Teaching, supervisory process in. See
    Supervisory process
Technical goal of analysis, 348, 349
Technical methods of supervision, 388
Technique, Brenner on, 18-25. See also
    Countertransference; Intrapsychic
    activity, helping analysands
observe; Insight; Psychoanalytic process,
    evaluating
Tension, nonverbal expressions of, 196
Termination, 321-51
  case illustration of, 326-46
    early phase of analysis, 327-29
    middle phase of analysis, 329-35
    rarity of, 321-22
    summary and reasons for improvement,
      344-46
    termination phase, 335-44
  countertransference reactions to, 234
  criteria for, 322-23, 325
  essence of, 348-49
  goal of analysis and, 348-49
  literature on, 321-23